T0326506

Classical Economics Today

ANTHEM OTHER CANON ECONOMICS

The **Anthem Other Canon Economics** series is a collaboration between Anthem Press and The Other Canon Foundation. The Other Canon—also described as "reality economics"—studies the economy as a real object rather than as the behavior of a model economy based on core axioms, assumptions and techniques. The series includes both classical and contemporary works in this tradition, spanning evolutionary, institutional and post-Keynesian economics, the history of economic thought and economic policy, economic sociology and technology governance, and works on the theory of uneven development and in the tradition of the German historical school.

Classical Economics Today

Essays in Honor of Alessandro Roncaglia

Edited by

Marcella Corsi, Jan Kregel and Carlo D'Ippoliti

ANTHEM PRESS

Anthem Press
An imprint of Wimbledon Publishing Company
www.anthempress.com

This edition first published in UK and USA 2018
by ANTHEM PRESS
75–76 Blackfriars Road, London SE1 8HA, UK
or PO Box 9779, London SW19 7ZG, UK
and
244 Madison Ave #116, New York, NY 10016, USA

British Library Cataloguing-in-Publication Data
A catalogue record for this book is available from the British Library.

ISBN-13: 978-1-78308-750-1 (Hbk)
ISBN-10: 1-78308-750-1 (Hbk)

This title is also available as an e-book.

CONTENTS

ILLUSTRATIONS

Figures

Tables

PREFACE

This collection of essays provides a tribute to Alessandro Roncaglia, one of the most important representatives of what has come to be a threatened species: the classical political economist.

His work has provided insight into the joint journey of economic theory with economic history and its application to economic policy related to both the past and the present problems of an evolving economy.

While economic history serves the classical economist as insight into the diverse theoretical development underpinning of economic policy debates, the focus is always on the objective of understanding the economy in which he/she lives and works. The classical economist is thus bound to think that economic theory is "historically conditioned" (Sylos Labini, 2005): as social systems evolve, the appropriate theory to represent a certain phenomenon must evolve too. Therefore, plurality in methods, including history of economic thought, must be a deliberate choice.

As Salvatore Biasco stresses in his contribution to this volume,

> At the base of a nonmainstream way of looking at the economy, from a descriptive and normative perspective, cannot be but social complexity, uncertainty and innovative dynamics. Through these lenses, the aggregate behaviour of the economy is studied as determined by constantly evolving endogenous events, which are fed by a number of driving forces: unstable and potentially explosive relationships; nondeterministic developments; a financial system closely interconnected to the real economy but also able to acquire an autonomous dimension; and a social dynamic that changes in parallel to the whole process and that at the same time affects it.

These contributions in honor of Roncaglia's work follow in this tradition, dealing with themes that have characterized his work or that represent expressions of his personality, his interests and method. Geoffrey Harcourt, Heinz Kurz, Nerio Naldi and Neri Salvadori all deal with one of Roncaglia's major contributions to classical economics, that is, the presentation, interpretation and extension of Piero Sraffa's work on the classical theory of prices. Marcella Corsi, Carlo D'Ippoliti, Peter Groenewegen, Cosimo Perrotta, Alfonso Sánchez and Gianni Vaggi all provide essays reflecting the great legacy of classical economists and the interpretation of their work, a permanent source of inspiration for Roncaglia. Jan Kregel, Michele Salvati and Mario Tonveronachi provide an integration of the work of the classics with the more modern contributions to this tradition in the work of John Maynard Keynes, Hyman Minsky and Josef Steindl, economists who also provided inspiration for Roncaglia's work on economic policy. Other contributions deal with topics of great relevance for Roncaglia (e.g., the oil market) while the macroeconomic picture of the impact of austerity measures given by Davide Antonioli and Paolo Pini is much in line with Roncaglia's view of economists not "as servants or as princes" but as citizens, socially and politically engaged, as any citizen should be (Roncaglia, 2017).

It is our hope that these essays will incite an interest in Alessandro Roncaglia's life work and a revival of interest in classical political economy.

Marcella Corsi, Jan Kregel and Carlo D'Ippoliti

References

Roncaglia, A. 2017. "The Economist as an Expert: A Prince, a Servant or a Citizen?" In *Experts on Trial: A Symposium.* New York: Institute for New Economic Thinking (INET). Available at: https://www.ineteconomics.org/research/research-papers/experts-on-trial-a-symposium.

Sylos Labini, P. 2005. "Storia e teoria economica: due casi degni di riflessione," *Rivista di Storia Economica* 21: 181–89.

ACKNOWLEDGMENTS

We are grateful to Elizabeth Dunn and Iolanda Sanfilippo for their editorial advice and support. A special thank is due to Agnese Marcigliano for her help in drafting the book cover. The usual disclaimers apply.

Chapter One

THE RECONSTRUCTION OF AN ALTERNATIVE ECONOMIC THOUGHT: SOME PREMISES

Salvatore Biasco

1. Introduction

Alessandro Roncaglia has given us fundamental reflections on the methodological and conceptual canons that should be the cornerstones of a realistic (and at the same time, stylized) vision of how the capitalist economy behaves.[1] Roncaglia has taught us that reconstructing the political economy on alternative methodological assumptions—in a direction opposite to the dominant neoclassical vision—involves an interpretation of history, and also of the present as history. Of course, not all of its branches or issues can be treated as a part of a comprehensive "model," as Roncaglia frequently states. Optics that do well in one field may not be as good in another; each branch also has its technical specificity. The reconstruction can take place even in separate pieces, and can involve retrieving and updating what, of precious developed writings, one finds scattered in the critical literature on economic and social sciences. But what is important is that the methodological and epistemological apparatus maintains a uniform inspiration as well as should remain the points of reference of the analytical approach.

In what follows I devote my attention to some basic points of setting an alternative vision, knowing that on so much Roncaglia and I agree in full, but that there are minor distinctions between us.

2. Complexity

In a nutshell, at the base of a nonmainstream way of looking at the economy, from a descriptive and normative perspective, cannot but be social complexity, uncertainty and innovative dynamics. Through these lenses, the aggregate behavior of the economy is studied as determined by constantly evolving endogenous events, which are fed by a number of driving forces: unstable and potentially explosive relationships; nondeterministic developments; a financial system closely interconnected to the real economy but also able to acquire an autonomous dimension; and a social dynamic that changes in parallel to the whole process and that at the same time affects it.

In complex systems, the whole is more than the sum of its parts. Although the representation of a society and an economy's aggregate behavior cannot ignore their components (not only individual actors but also collective and institutional ones), the interaction of these components results in an outcome that is not predictable from the parts themselves and not necessarily inferable from them. This is the opposite of the mainstream idea that the system can be observed from the standpoint of the representative agent.[2]

Despite this complexity, it is always possible to establish macroeconomic relationships of cause and effect in a rigorous academic framework or to draw a theoretical framework for state action. It would be a mistake to leave to mainstream economics the power of generalized abstraction. As economists deal with the inborn dynamism of the production and social system, the most appropriate abstraction for them is extracting—in the specific process under analysis—the causal chains relating to the dominant forces at work and conjecturing about the strength of forces and counterforces (and contingent circumstances) that determines which would prevail. This then entails the necessity of putting in a logical sequence (short) chains of cause-effect relationships that can capture the points of tension (or friction or imbalance) and reduce the analysis to a core of simplified propositions, which are compact and logically solid. Following general interdependencies (and seeking their equilibrium) only obfuscates the hierarchy of processes. Pretending to move relations mechanically (even to the ultimate consequences) leads to losing sight of the fact that the material that economists deal with is not constant, homogeneous, or stable, and cannot be reduced to parametric determinations.

The cause-effect sequences placed at the center of a representation of any single macroeconomic process can be nothing but abstractions drawn from the wide empirical knowledge of a reality that demands to be known and studied in detail (and that is the background of all single conjectures), without necessarily being a bare transposition of that reality. That empirical world, however, burst back onto the scene since the plausibility of a theory (and its lifeblood) rests on how many microeconomic phenomena that theory crosses, or manages to encompass within it or gives an account of, once confronted with a complex and differentiated society. This is the only test of a theory.[3] "The master-economist," writes Keynes, "must possess a rare combination of gift. He must contemplate the particular in terms of the general and touch abstract and concrete in the same flight of thought."[4] Therefore, a sensible alternative economic theory can only be based on the study of actual social interactions, markets, specific situations, and institutions and also rely on studies in the field, case studies, and even on significant anecdotal evidence. It cannot but be, in essence, inductive and empirically oriented (much like the dominant thought is axiomatic and deductive), even in the awareness that a work of synthesis and abstraction must follow from it. Such a work must be aimed at reconstructing the order of phenomena or their internal engine, taking into account that many microrelationships change in perspective at the aggregate level. It is unlikely that a deterministic configuration is the right frame for this synthesis.[5] Among the underlying forces considered in any specific theorizing, those relating to social structure and collective action, to institutions and distribution of income, to wealth and power are of key importance in the economic dynamics. Social identities forge economic choices. This means that the economy should be a tributary to sociology, political science, history, and law as well as the behavioral sciences (which do not support the hypothesis of full rationality and exclusive utilitarianism).

3. Instability

Let us now put aside issues of methodology.[6] Concerning matters of merit, however, a context dominated by instability requires a paradigm for instability, that is, the way in which it is generated endogenously. At its center there is the logic of capital accumulation and of finance. Within a methodological approach aimed at studying (as it should be done) processes under conditions of permanent disequilibrium and the irreversibility of real decisions, it would be easier to grasp that such processes, once begun, do not necessarily imply a point of arrival. This means that there is no attraction toward an indefinable equilibrium. Indeed, an initial imbalance more likely leads to further imbalances, even if of a different nature or size, and, in doing so, it induces institutional and behavioral changes along the path that the economy is following.[7] Instability is an endogenous feature of the economic system stemming from many factors: the internal chains of phenomena, the difficulties faced by operators in assessing the situation, uncertainty about the future, the variability of responses, and the internal logic of markets. When left to themselves, internal causal relationships can potentially lead to spiraling developments, and this is especially evident if one takes into account the strict links between macroeconomic facts and the financial structure, and vice versa (finance and the real economy do not live in two separate worlds). Accordingly, expectations cannot be firmly anchored to some point of convergence, and nothing can be inferred about the characteristics of the "long period."

4. State

Sometimes spirals either remain in the background as a potential outcome or end by themselves (with lasting consequences), but more often it is public action that manages them, either leaving them in a latent state (which erroneously may let the economy appear stable) or intervening to block them once they are already in action. If an anchor of the economy exists, it can only be found in a cooperative framework of rules of the game, organization of markets, and state monitoring.

In this context, the role of public decisions shares in the overall complexity. Public actions are not, differently from what is assumed by orthodox economics, either juxtaposed to a stable economy or destined by their own nature to create exogenous shocks. They are, instead, always reactions to the endogenous instability of the system. Such reactions are not always deterministically undertaken in obvious directions and size because they encounter inner conflicts: between public objectives, in divergent effectiveness in different areas of a heterogeneous society, because of side drawbacks closely connected to problems they tackle and because, after all, governments have to deal with the consensus and cohesion required in democratic societies as well as with the complication of the decision-making processes. Moreover, only after certain thresholds have been reached is it sometimes perceived that a process has progressed and can get out of hand.

5. Trust

A theoretical framework of public action must start from the general context dominated by uncertainty and from the state of operators' confidence. Economic decisions are not taken on strong anchors by operators, and those concerning demand are different from those concerning supply. Rationality in decisions is limited, and the knowledge of reality that individuals have is imperfect. In few areas can expectations about the future be traced to probabilistic schemes (if not subjective ones) or calculable risk; the majority are dominated by uncertainty (see Roncaglia, 2012). Depending on the case, exploratory, irrational, and imitative behaviors as well as routines and (partly) social and behavioral conventions have a role in the analysis. It is not just the type of behavior that is indefinable. The perception of a situation as a basis for decisions is weak (only the reductive idea about information and rationality that mainstream economics maintains can avoid these problems).[8]

If the above is true, the system is somewhat dominated by collective confidence, which influences the attitude and behavior of operators. Such confidence may depend on many exogenous factors. Today, for example, new elements of the economy have a negative effect on confidence [as, for example, globalization itself, the complexity of new technologies, the shortness of required reaction time, the weight of finance (involving more risk), the speed of technical progress, the rapidity of changes in the labor market, the fall in the quality of international governance, and more]. However, it is public action and the institutional structure that—by socializing many variables and providing the necessary anchoring—are decisive. They ultimately allow operators to deal with these aspects with more or less optimism and to make operators' confidence higher or lower and their way of looking at the future more open and less uncertain or, on the contrary, more dense with insecurity and more labile. Since the degree of confidence is the frame in which the whole economic process evolves, it follows that the task of the normative and operative aspects of public action is to turn economic policy in the direction of strengthening trust itself, dominating the complexity and reducing uncertainty. This is the key factor that governs growth and stabilization.

6. Remarks

Two considerations at the end. The alternative analytical framework can only be aimed at a *cultural* fallout. This basically entails the collective awareness that a society led by private profit produces social and economic uncertainty, a deep social economic divide, conflicting interests that find solution in the law of the stronger, market failures, and economic instability (and transformation)—all features that can be brought under control and governed in the collective interest only with the primacy of politics over economics (almost an opposite conclusion to that of orthodox economics).

This leads me to a second consideration that may appear unusual in an academic setting. Although it is true that reconstructing an alternative way of thinking is a disciplinary task, nevertheless, it aborts or changes meaning if it is a purely intellectual effort and does not occur with the participation of culturally committed political forces that feel this reconstruction is an integral part of their process of definition of their cultural identity.

Notes

1 The whole body of work of Roncaglia is food for thought concerning methodological and analytical issues including his seminal work, *The Wealth of Ideas* (Roncaglia 2005a). It is also worth reading *Why the Economists Got It Wrong* (2010), "What Do We Mean by Anglo-American Capitalism?" (2011), and *Il mito della mano invisibile* (2005b).

2 Many phenomena that have a causal direction from the standpoint of an individual operator present reversed causality at the aggregate level. A few well-known simple textbook examples can be cited: deposits determine loans for individual operators, while the opposite is true at the aggregate level; the same goes for the saving-investment relationship. What appears to be true in isolation may not be true in the aggregate, as, for example, also occurs in the relationship between decreases in wage costs and increases in profits for single firms, but not possibly for the economy as a whole. And so on.

3 This is a perspective that is opposite to the mainstream one. The latter states that one can draw inference with regard to the economy as a whole by studying a "representative" single agent (depicted as similar to the others, as abstract and utility maximizing). It relies on a mechanistic (econometric) analysis of aggregate phenomena (built on a database extended over a considerable length of time) for testing deductively derived propositions, as if the economy were stable and maintained identical parametric relationships over time. In that perspective, techniques and good software, not a thorough knowledge of reality, are needed.

4 "He must be mathematician, historian, statesman, philosopher in some degree" (Keynes, 1933, 173).

5 This implies that no variable is *parametrically* bounded in its movements and values to other variables, but is often determined by beliefs and conventions that dominate the behavior of operators. We can call this approach a "conventionalistic" one (meaning, for instance, that a given level of the exchange rate or inflation is compatible with a wide range of shapes and levels of the yield curve or vice versa). In this alternative analytical context, mathematical relations, formalized in a model, do not give a demonstration of anything, but can be sometimes a useful exercise that translate into the form of a model the ideas developed independently from the use of formal analysis; it can help (possibly) to extract the essence of these ideas and explore the ultimate abstract consequences, but the place of that model is in the Appendix of an essay. However, the exercise can be useful as long as one does not lose sight of the fact that it is a reductive operation, which can only be based on mechanistic relations and standardized reactions, and reduce to risk what is uncertainty (that is, the immeasurable as it were measurable).

6 These issues of method can be deepened in the essays contained in Becattini (1991a), especially in the essays of Becattini, Kregel, and Biasco. See also Roncaglia (2009).

7 I quote here as simple examples some basic spirals, such as wages-prices, inflation-exchange rate, or speculative bubbles, but many others can be brought out concerning more structural variables. Induced changes occurring during these spirals persist when they end. An inflationary process induces financial innovations (and redistribution of income); in a speculative bubble on the equity market firms strengthen their capital structure at low cost; a spiral of the exchange rate displaces sectorial production irreversibly, and so on. As the scale of a phenomenon increases, it reaches thresholds at which the operators' perception of it changes and therefore their behavior toward the phenomenon itself does, too. The conditions under which a spiral ends, can also bring irreversible changes.

8 If any decision implies a sequence of phases—that the perception of a situation leads to the evaluation of possible alternatives of actions, then to the decision itself, and finally to the application of a decision—in the *mainstream* approach the crucial phase is the third (the decision, i.e., the choice), while the others do not present problems. In other words, for *mainstream* economics what is crucial is which decision (rational and utility maximizing) is taken, once that the alternatives are evaluated on the basis of a complete information, which is perfectly deductible from reality. In a vision that is *not mainstream*, the crucial phase is the first, and this makes the others poorly definable.

References

Becattini, G., ed. 1991a. *Economisti allo specchio*. Firenze: Vallecchi.

———. 1991b. "Alla ricerca dell'antitesi." In *Economisti allo specchio*, edited by G. Becattini, 25–38. Firenze: Vallecchi.

Biasco, S. 1991. "Valori convenzionali delle variabili e metodo scientifico in economia." In *Economisti allo specchio*, edited by G. Becattini, 115–30. Firenze: Vallecchi.

Keynes, J. M . 1933. "Alfred Marshall." In *Essays in Biography*, vol. 10 of *The Collected Writings of John Maynard Keynes*, edited by D. Moggridge, 161–231. London, Macmillan, 1972.

Kregel, J. A . 1991. "La fine dell'economia politica keynesiana e la teoria della distribuzione." In *Economisti allo specchio*, edited by G. Becattini, 40–56. Firenze: Vallecchi.

Roncaglia, A . 2005a. *The Wealth of Ideas: A History of Economic Thought*. Cambridge: Cambridge University Press.

———. 2005b. *Il mito della mano invisibile*. Roma–Bari: Laterza.

———. 2009. "Sulla storia delle misure del prodotto e sul metodo dell'economia," *Rivista di storia economica* 25, no. 3: 383–88.

———. 2010. *Why the Economists Got It Wrong: The Crisis and Its Cultural Roots*. London and New York: Anthem Press.

———. 2011. "What Do We Mean by Anglo-American Capitalism?" *Adam Smith Review* 6: 283–89.

———. 2012. "Keynesian Uncertainty and the Shaky Foundations of Statistical Risk Assessment Models," *PSL Quarterly Review* 65, no. 263: 437–54.

Chapter Two

REFLECTIONS ON UNITY AND DIVERSITY, THE MARKET AND ECONOMIC POLICY

Jan Kregel

1. Introduction

The theoretical foundations of what has come to be called "market fundamentalism" suffer from an internal contradiction that renders it useless as a basis for economic policy. This is not a problem of abstraction or reliance on simplified models. It is the ubiquitous presence of the simultaneous assumption of uniformity and diversity. A simple example will illustrate the contradiction. Consider an airline ticket. Initially, it represented the provision by an airline to transport by air from point A to point B at a stipulated time and date in exchange for a posted fare. The service provided for a meal (usually rubberized chicken), transport of accompanying baggage and the right to sit in a seat. If you buy an airline ticket today, you may have to pay separately for the air transport, for the baggage transport, for the meal if you want one and even for the seat!

What is the "market" for airline tickets in which supply and demand is presumed to determine price? To answer that question it is necessary first to define the "commodity" that is being purchased in the market. As the example makes clear, the market is undefined until the commodity traded in the market is specified. Is there any economic basis for considering the separate services that now accompany air transport as separate commodities? And, more importantly, is there any economic basis for considering that the prices determined in separate markets are determined by a competitive process? Or are they, as Piero Sraffa has suggested in one of the most overlooked parts of his famous book, "joint products," which may be identified but for which there may be no separate production and thus no separate supply curve and no possibility of market or market price?

2. Prices and Markets: Theory and History from Smith to Schumpeter via Petty

This real-world example has a detailed theoretical history that is often ignored. Proponents of the superiority of market mechanisms consider a major benefit in what may be summarized as diversity. The market brings together diverse individual preferences to determine the quantities and prices of a wide range of commodities. These preferences and individual endowments are the given data that form the basis for the supply and demand functions, which in turn determine equilibrium prices that provide all the information required to permit maximum economic utility. Yet, closer inspection of this facade of diversity suggests that its general application requires a presumption of uniformity or homogeneity. Thus, just as the diversity of individual preferences is taken as the data of the economic landscape, the very definition of a commodity that elicits those preferences requires the presumption of uniformity.

Start with the question of how choice is exercised through free market exchange. Adam Smith provided the classic response to this question. In his *Theory of Moral Sentiments*, he noted that, our senses being limited, "they never can carry us beyond our own person, and it is by imagination only that we can form any conception of what are [others'] sensations" (1976, 9). "How selfish so every man may be supposed, there are evidently some principles in his nature, which interest him in the fortune of others, and render their happiness necessary to him, though he derives nothing from it except the pleasure of seeing it" (ibid.). This might be called the "Existential Diversity of Individuals." We might all have similar preferences, but no one would know it. The result, which Smith put forward in *The Wealth of Nations*, is that exchange takes place by means of each individual trying to please the imagined needs of others: altruistic hedonism. When Smith argues that "it is not from the benevolence of the butcher, the brewer, or the baker that we expect our dinner, but from their regard to their own interest," he is simply stating what he considered to be an incontrovertible fact that no individual can possibly act benevolently, given the impossibility of knowing the tastes and preferences of others. It is thus in one's own interest to imagine and try to discover the preferences of others. He then goes on to note that "though it may be true, therefore, that every individual even in his own breast, naturally prefers himself to all mankind, yet he dares not look mankind in the face, and avow that he acts according to this principle"; rather, "he must [...] humble the arrogance of his self-love, and bring it down to something which other men can go along with" (1976, 83). This Existential Diversity thus implies Existential Uncertainty about how one can best satisfy one's own needs since it relies on satisfying the unknowable needs of others. Thus, Smith argues that these needs can only be discovered through diversity and exchange. The market mechanism is thus a series of multiple bilateral exchanges between diverse individuals with diverse preferences, each seeking to serve their own needs by imagining and seeking to discover and satisfy the needs of others.

It is now necessary to identify what is exchanged between these diverse, self-interested individuals. Economists often speak of "commodity exchange," but if each individual has a different appreciation of what is exchanged, and if what is exchanged satisfies unknown wants, then each thing exchanged must be composed of different perceived characteristics—each of which would appeal to one or more of the diverse needs of diverse individual consumers. This means that there may be as many diverse "commodities" as individuals involved in each of the millions of exchanges that take place in the market, since each person evaluates them differently and considers them a different commodity because each satisfies a different need or preference. The market will thus be comprised of the bilateral exchanges of a multitude of unique commodities identified by their different characteristics.

Now, if all exchange is bilateral, what is the counterpart in these exchanges? The answer is usually other commodities, but traditional theory suggests that in a market economy, efficiency considerations should lead to the creation of an intermediary or standard commodity, usually called "money." But this raises another question of what commodity will serve as money.

The traditional answer is that it is a commodity that becomes uniformly accepted by reducing transactions costs, that is, it has a common property. Thus, the first condition for the existence of exchange is the existence of a commodity that does not represent diverse characteristics to each individual but satisfies a common need of all in exchange. Here begins the need of a functioning market economy to eliminate diversity and introduce uniformity.

Historically, precious metals, even though they have diverse particular characteristics, have been the commodity that served this purpose—but only when they are minted by a sovereign into coin to guarantee the required uniformity. But even in the case of minted coin, most economies that used metallic currency experienced the circulation of many different types of coinage, with different metallic content and different weight due to wear and tear and clipping. Thus, coins were in fact highly diverse, and were reduced to the underlying metal content by the application of a uniform market price. It is interesting that historically the difficulties in ensuring uniformity led to the adoption of a notional "unit of account," what Luigi Einaudi called "imaginary money," which was uniform by definition.

3. The Textbook Definition of the Perfect Competitive Market

The theoretical definition of a market found in any standard textbook would include the following characteristics:

1. a public gathering held for buying and selling commodities
2. a defined location for the purchase and sale of each commodity, for example, the soybean market
3. a single, equilibrium market price for each commodity traded in the location

Thus, what we usually mean by a market is a homogeneous geographical location, where buyers and sellers meet to exchange a single, uniform commodity, for a common uniform price expressed in a common uniform means of payment called money at specific periods of time. Indeed, the first markets in history were held at the pleasure of the sovereign in specified locations on specific days of the week with restricted participation. The diversity of continuous, bilateral free market exchange seems to have required uniformity, at least on the spatial and temporal levels. Exchange can only take place at specific times and specific places for well-defined commodities with uniform characteristics. Thus, while the benefits of free markets depend on diversity, the operation of these markets depends on uniformity.

The interesting point is that this problem is not new in economics. Indeed, it concerned one of the founders of modern political economy, William Petty, who was the first to confront this conundrum between diversity and uniformity. In his little book on Petty (Roncaglia, 1985), and then in his magnum opus *The Wealth of Ideas*, Alessandro Roncaglia notes that Petty was among the first to recognize that "the commodity is not the smallest existing unit of matter of which the economic universe is composed, but it is itself an abstraction" (2005, 64). Petty dealt with the "notions of commodity and market [… in] a brief essay written in the form of a dialogue, the "Dialogue of Diamonds":

> The protagonists of the dialogue are two: Mr. A, representing Petty himself, and Mr. B, an inexperienced buyer of a diamond. The latter sees the act of exchange as a chance occurrence, a direct encounter producing a bilateral relationship of bargaining conflict between buyer and seller, rather than a routine episode in an interconnected network of relationships, each contributing to the establishment of stable behavioural regularities. The problem is a difficult one because the specific individual goods included in the same category of marketable goods—diamonds in our case—differ the one from the other on account of a series of quantitative and qualitative elements, even leaving aside differing circumstances (of time and place) of each individual act of exchange. Thus, in the absence of a norm which might allow the establishment of a unique reference point for the price of diamonds, Mr. B considers exchange as a risky act, since it appears impossible for the buyer to avoid being cheated, in what for him is a unique event, by the merchant who has a more extensive knowledge of the market. In the absence of a web of regular exchanges, that is of a market, the characteristics and circumstances of differentiation mentioned above operate in such a way as to make each act of exchange a unique episode, where the price essentially stems from the greater or lesser bargaining ability of seller and buyer. (See Petty, 1899, 624–30: as quoted in Roncaglia, 2005, 63)

The existence of a market, on the contrary, allows transformation of a large part of the elements that distinguish each individual exchange from any other into sufficiently systematic differences in price relative to an ideal type of diamond taken as a reference point.

Thus the paradox of supply and demand as determinants of price: a uniform commodity is necessary for the creation of a market, but the uniformity that creates a commodity requires a market and a market price.

> There is thus a relationship between the emergence of a regular market on the one hand and, on the other hand, the possibility of defining as a commodity a certain category of goods, abstracting from the multiplicity of effective exchange acts, a theoretical price representative of them all. […] Petty's writings thus offer a representation of the process of abstraction leading to the concepts of market and commodity from the multiple particular exchanges that occur in the economy. (Roncaglia, 2005, 64)

Thus, for Petty, the market itself is an abstraction, in the sense that each individual act of exchange concerns a specific diamond, exchanged at a specific time and place, at a specific price. The market exists as a concept that is useful, indeed indispensable, to an understanding of the functioning of a mercantile and then a capitalistic economic system, precisely because it allows one to abstract from the myriad of individual exchanges a given set of relationships that can be considered as representative of actual experience and that can provide a guide to behavior. The same considerations apply to the concept of the commodity. In fact, reality is composed of an infinite number of specific individual objects. We group them into categories, such as diamonds, on the basis of some affinities to which we attribute central importance while ignoring elements of differentiation considered as of secondary importance. In other words, the commodity is not an atom of economic reality, but is itself an abstraction, which already implies a certain level of uniformity. The most opportune level of uniformity is determined by the extent of the interrelationships between the various acts of exchange. Thus, it is possible to consider different specific diamonds as the same commodity, with its own specific market, only because the separate exchanges of specific diamonds make plausible the hypothesis that they are the same good since they allow traders to reduce qualitative differences to quantitative price differences. The same process is required for consideration of a market for apples, or a fruit market, or the market for food in general: apples, fruit or food may be considered, in turn, as a commodity according to the level of aggregation thought to be most adequate, keeping in mind the relationships that come into play within the group of producers and within the group of buyers.

> Some abstraction is also necessary in formulating the concept of price so as to deal with the analytical problem of determining relative prices, namely exchange ratios between different commodities. Indeed a "price" corresponds to a "commodity"; it represents a multiplicity of values, each relative to an individual act of exchange, when such acts of exchange concern goods sufficiently similar among themselves as to be included under the unique label of the same commodity (as in the case illustrated above of the "price" of the "diamond"). Furthermore we have to delimit the set of acts of exchange to which we refer as the basis for our notion of price, relative to the time and space in which they take place. (Roncaglia, 2005, 66)

Thus, the theory of free markets requires markets to furnish the prices that render homogeneous the diversity of aspects of commodities, but a market can only exist if there are homogeneous commodities.
   This internal contradiction between uniformity and diversity is usually hidden behind the assumptions that are set out to define a perfectly competitive market, which are defined in textbooks as the existence of a single price for a given commodity:

1.   There are many suppliers, each with an insignificant share of the market—this means that each firm is too small relative to the overall market to affect price via a change in its own supply—therefore each individual firm is assumed to be a price taker.
2.   An identical, homogeneous output is produced by each firm—in other words, the market supplies homogeneous or standardized products that are perfect substitutes for each other. Consumers perceive the products to be identical and perfect substitutes.
3.   Consumers have perfect information about the prices all sellers in the market charge—so if some firms decide to charge a price higher than the ruling market

price, there will be a large substitution effect away from this firm, and vice versa, for those selling below the ruling price.

4.   All firms (industry participants and new entrants) are assumed to have equal access to resources (technology, other factor inputs), and improvements in production technologies achieved by one firm can spill over to all the other suppliers in the market.

5.   There are assumed to be no barriers to the entry and exit of firms in the long run—which means that the market is open to competition from new suppliers—and this affects the long-run profits made by each firm in the industry. The long-run equilibrium for a perfectly competitive market occurs when the marginal firm makes a normal profit only in the long term and each firm faces a horizontal demand curve for its output.

6.   There are no externalities in production and consumption, so that there is no divergence between private and social costs and benefits.

7.   There are no advantages or disadvantages from a geographical location, since all exchanges take place in a single location at the same time.

Thus, the definition of the competitive market eliminates the diversity that emerges from Smith's insistence on the individual assessments of one's own utility to be derived from each exchange and is replaced by perfect uniformity in all aspects of market exchange.

It is interesting that most economists did not fully accept these preconditions for the existence of competitive markets. For example, both Walras and Marshall used as referent financial markets where homogeneity assumptions appear to be satisfied—in particular, Walras's reference to the institution of the "auctioneer" operating a "call market" such as that used at the time in the Paris Bourse. Here exchanges took place at fixed periods, in a fixed place, for financial assets that were homogeneous. There is no difference in the multiple shares issued by a company or the debts, *rentes*, issued by a government. They are homogeneous by design, as is the market design. But more on this later. Walras believed that this example generalized to market exchange.

However, there were dissenters. For example, in his *Capitalism, Socialism and Democracy*, Joseph Schumpeter (1942) argued that the kind of competition that actually takes place in capitalistic economies is that associated with the creation of a "new commodity, the new technology, the new source of supply, the new type of organization (the largest-scale unit of control for instance)—competition which commands a decisive cost or quality advantage and which strikes not at the margins of the profits and the outputs of the existing firms but at their foundations and their very lives" (1942, 84).

For Schumpeter, it is the creation of diversity from existing production that provides for the benefits of the capitalist market system. But this also requires the continual creation of monopoly positions through the offer of better, different output, which provides for the "creative destruction" that produces wealth and accumulation in the economy. But, note that this is a different kind of diversity than that proposed by Smith, for it does not emanate from the idiosyncrasy of individual's preferences. It results from a change in the given data, and is thus much closer to the kind of process that Fag Foster had in mind. Schumpeter rejected the existence of "an entirely golden age of perfect competition" (ibid., 81). Yet, he maintained the Walrasian framework of equilibrium, in the belief that the market would eventually eliminate competitive advantages and return to stationary equilibrium, although in his later years he saw the advent of the large corporation as dimming the force of creation for destruction.

Somehow, economists seem able to live with the juxtaposition of the two principles of diversity and homogeneity—market efficiency that requires diversity, perfect competition that requires homogeneous products and Schumpeterian competition, which, again, requires differentiation to provide creative destruction.

There is a parallel to this argument at the macrolevel. A corollary of Sraffa's criticism of supply and demand theories of prices produced the Cambridge capital theory controversies in which mainstream economists put forward models in which a homogeneous capital good produced a homogeneous commodity in a model meant to show the operation of relative prices (which requires at least two prices) of capital and labor. But there is no market in which capital exchanges for labor; rather, there are only markets in which capital or labor-intensive goods compete.

4. The Diversity, Uniformity and Perfection of Financial Markets

It is now necessary to return to the market, where the assumption of homogeneity in support of perfect competition is said to be most naturally satisfied. Just to start, note that the entire mechanism of market efficiency that operates in financial markets is based on the difference between diversity and homogeneity in the form of the definition of alpha returns and beta returns. The former is idiosyncratic, and based on the diversity of an asset's returns, while the latter represents the market's uniform performance. The only justification for paying an asset manager is the ability to identify alpha returns, that is, returns that have not yet been homogenized by the market. Of course, once they are recognized, competition should cause conformity with market performance.

But, there is a more important example of this conflation of diversity and homogeneity. The very conception of an equilibrium market price requires diversity of expectations of the future movement in price on the two sides of a market exchange, since a buyer will only buy expecting a rise, and a seller will expect to avoid a decline in price. Equilibrium, and the determination of price, thus requires diversity of expectation, while rational expectations require full information and uniform assessment of all current information in prices. As the story goes, a Chicago finance professor will never bend down to pick up a $100 bill since he knows that in an efficient market someone will already have picked it up. Note that if everyone believes this, there should be a lot of $100 bills laying around on the streets of the South Side of Chicago!

Of course, note the implications of the idea that it is impossible to beat the market, so you should always buy the market. If there are no sellers, then it always goes up and by definition you cannot beat the market, but in order to have any transactions, you need sellers, and even in the presence of "liquidity" sellers (i.e., you need to sell to get money to pay the doctor bills), as long as they do not dominate, the market still cannot beat a market that only rises!

Finally, consider modern financial markets where financial innovation dominates. Now, just exactly what is *financial innovation*? As already noted, financial markets, pace

Walras, are based on the distinction between diverse, idiosyncratic alpha risks, and market or homogeneous beta risks. Things like consumer loans, auto loans, credit card loans, and especially home mortgages were all once considered iconic idiosyncratic risks. They were all essentially, idiosyncratically different, so that that the market process of uniformity and homogenization could not work. They could not be treated in the same way as bonds or shares. Every share of a given class issued by IBM is the same as any other, and any bond of a given class issued by IBM is the same as any other. A loan to John Smith to buy a Porsche is not the same as a loan to Adam Smith to buy a Chevrolet; a mortgage to John Smith to buy a house on Broadway is not the same as a mortgage to Adam Smith to buy a house on Park Place. They differ in terms of the borrower as well as in the underlying asset and the location that is being purchased. There is no way to compare the two, and thus there is no market and no market prices.

5. The Financial Engineers, Unbundling and Innovation

Or, at least that was the case until the financial engineers showed up. First, they challenged the idea of the uniformity of a bond by unbundling. A bond is not a bond; rather, it is a bundle of differentiated cash flows. The first coupon on, say, a thirty-year annual coupon bond is the same as a one-year bond. The second coupon is the same as a two-year discount bond, and so forth. A thirty-year bond can be split up into thirty-one separate cash flows (one for each coupon and one for the repayment of principal). Each can be traded, bought, or sold, sliced or diced in any shape or form. The market for thirty-year bonds is thus also thirty-one different underlying markets—more diversity and homogeneity and the possibility of earning from differences in the different markets.

But that still left the idiosyncratic risks. This was taken care of by the process of securitization. We can skip the consumer loans, the auto loans, and the credit card loans, and go straight to the mortgages. In the words of Lewis Ranieri (2000), who worked for Salomon Brothers and is credited with the creation of the collateralized mortgage assets that created so much difficulty in the current crisis, the "objective was to try to create a mortgage asset that was the equivalent of a bond, which was stripped of its idiosyncratic nature, of its diversity, to reduce the diverse mortgages to homogeneity."

> The goal was to create an investment vehicle to finance housing in which the investor did not have to […] know very much, if anything about the underlying mortgages. The structure of the deal was designed to place him or her in a position where, theoretically, the only decisions that had to be made were investment decisions. No credit decisions were necessary. The credit mechanisms were designed to be bullet-proof, almost risk-free. The only remaining questions for the investors concerned their outlook on interest rates and their preferences on maturities. (Ranieri, 2000, 38)

But,

> many of the factors that gave standard mortgage products high credit quality were missing in new mortgage products we devised. One such product was the GPM, to assist families that could not previously afford home ownership. This product is based on the principle

that inflation enables workers to get annual wage increases of 6 percent or more each year. The mortgage was designed with a rising payment schedule that gives credit for these wage increases. Therefore, a lender can qualify a borrower at a low monthly payment today and then step up the payment up 6 to 7 percent a year. This enables more households to qualify for mortgages. (ibid., 40)

This is a description of an adjustable rate subprime mortgage that came to dominate the mortgage market. Ranieri notes, however,

Unfortunately the GPM proved to be a failure […] because we overlooked a fundamental reality—everyone does not succeed. In fact some of us fail. Most simply get along. Therefore, a pool of GPM loans has default rates well above the actuarially allowable standard of three or four out of a hundred. Furthermore, if pay raises slowed or a recession occurred, defaults could be catastrophic. We learned that structures that depend on people succeeding and earning more each year do not follow the same actuarial trend as traditional mortgage products. […] A second new product that suffered from structural flaws was the adjustable rate mortgage (ARM). The early adjustable rate mortgages […] were designed to float within external market rates or a cost of funds index. However, when the interest rate index rose, which in turn increased the borrower's monthly payments, mortgagees protested the payment hike, and many defaulted on their mortgages. Securitization starts to break down as a concept when the issuer imposes on the investor the responsibility of analyzing the underlying collateral. As a general principle, we found that in order to successfully securitize an asset type, one must be able to predict the actuarial experience of defaults. Single family homes have an actuarial foundation. […] This problem could not be mitigated by insurance because the premium would be prohibitively expensive. (ibid., 40–41)

In simple terms, Ranieri is saying that his attempt to convert diversity into homogeneity failed. And as a result, there was no "commodity," no "market" and no efficient market "price." We could say that the fundamental theoretical error behind the subprime crisis was the failure to distinguish diversity from uniformity and the failure to realize that without a logical foundation for a uniform homogeneous commodity, there can be no market—and with no market, there can be no market prices to provide perfect information to inform decisions. The market was an imaginary construction, based on imaginary commodities, and decisions were based on imaginary prices. And on this basis, Foster would quickly tell us, maximum satisfaction clearly did not produce sustainability and the ability to continually be able to feed ourselves. More than simple regulations are needed to improve the operation of markets; institutions need to be reformed to restore viability to the financial system as a support for the financing of productive activity that provides employment and incomes.

But the real world keeps throwing up examples of the difficulties involved in resolving the paradox of uniformity and diversity. The scandal over the manipulation of the London Interbank Offered Rate (LIBOR) is an attempt to create a uniform, homogeneous rate of interest as a benchmark. But interbank lending takes place on a bilateral basis, between banks of diverse credit quality, of different amounts, at different times and places. LIBOR is an attempt to make these diverse bilateral exchanges appear as if it is the rate that would be created by the textbook definition of a competitive market producing a single price. Obviously, this could never be achieved, and the traders who manipulated the rate were working to their own advantage, but they were able to do so because of the paradox of diversity and uniformity.

6. Diversity, Homogeneity and the Fallacy of Composition in Current Economic Policy

Finally, consider the surprise that was caused when the subprime crisis produced impacts on real production and employment, producing the most serious disruption to economic activity since the Great Depression. Here, also, hides the paradox of individual diversity and homogeneity at work. Once the prices of mortgage securities were called into question, there was a uniformity of opinion on their values, which called into question the existence of markets in which to trade them. Not surprisingly, the imaginary prices soon proved to be just that, and financial firms were no longer willing to engage in borrowing and lending, resulting in a severe liquidity crisis and a drying up of funding for productive activities. Indeed, this is just an application of what was called the fallacy of composition. It is best understood by reference to the old story of the optimal behavior against the risk of fire in the movie house. For any single individual, there is an optimal path to the emergency exit. Each individual believes that it is possible to escape in case of fire. When fire breaks out, all individuals attempt to implement the optimal path, but none of them succeeds because they are all trying to execute the strategy at the same time. The same is true of financial institutions that believe that they have assets that can be converted at market prices into liquidity as required. But this implies the existence of diversity of opinion. When all hold the same view and that diversity disappears, there is no liquidity and everyone dies in the fire. Thus the importance of the central bank acting as lender of last resort, taking a diverse view and acting as a residual buyer when everyone is a seller—of becoming the market maker and the price maker.

And the same principle is at the basis of John Maynard Keynes's explanation of the impact of individual decisions on aggregate output. An individual can increase savings only if someone else is willing to take the opposite view. When everyone seeks to save to offset the losses incurred in the collapse of housing prices, there is no longer a diversity of views, and incomes will fall and stymie the attempt to recover from the crisis. Who will take the opposite view? Keynes's answer was that only the government had the ability to take a diverse view and dissave in order to allow the private sector to save. The government thus plays the same role as the central bank in providing the required diversity in the face of homogeneity of view: of being the buyer of last resort.

The current political discussion appears to be an attempt to introduce homogeneity in the behavior of all sectors of the economy: financial institutions are to reduce leverage to save and build up more capital, households are to reduce expenditures to increase savings to meet their losses from the housing collapse, the business sector is to reduce costs to improve profitability and the government is to reduce leverage by spending less to pay down debt. There is no longer the diversity that is required for a viable economy. But the lack of diversity is the characteristic of the command economy, and diversity the heart of economic survival.

References

Petty, W. 1899. "Dialogue of Diamonds." In *The Economic Writings of Sir William Petty*, edited by C. H. Hull, vol. 2. Cambridge: Cambridge University Press, Kelley Reprints, 1963.

Ranieri, L. S. 2000. "The Origins of Securitization, Sources of Its Growth, and Its Future Potential." In *A Primer on Securitization*, edited by L. T. Kendall and M. J. Fishman, 31–43. Cambridge, MA: MIT Press.

Roncaglia, A. 1985. *Petty: The Origins of Political Economy*. Armonk: M. E. Sharpe.

———. 2005. *The Wealth of Ideas: A History of Economic Thought*. Cambridge: Cambridge University Press.

Schumpeter, J. 1942. *Capitalism, Socialism and Democracy*. New York: Harpers.

Smith, A. 1976. *The Theory of Moral Sentiments*. Oxford: Clarendon Press.

Chapter Three

ENDING LAISSEZ-FAIRE FINANCE

Mario Tonveronachi

1. Introduction

In the current debates on financial reforms we often encounter the aphorism regarding the danger of fighting the last war. Because pervasive financial reforms are predominantly reactions to recent events, the perceived causes of the last crisis tend to attract the attention of reformers. Being right in fighting the last war requires the firm belief that the preexisting strategy was substantially sound, needing adjustments but not a radical redesign. Calling attention to the next war means trying to understand how the recent defeat was the product of a strategy based on the wrong understanding of the art of the war. If the previous financial regulatory framework were considered structurally unfit to contain the explosive effects of endogenous dynamic forces, a radical financial reform would be necessary. If the financial sector were considered as only part of the problem, further reforms should be called in.

The discussions that have arisen or been reignited by the recent crisis and the adopted or planned reforms have followed the two above strands. Reforms have tended to mend, not revolutionize, the previous regulatory framework. To a large extent they constitute a compromise between those calling for harsher measures and the milder position advocated by the industry, with both camps accepting the essentials of the previous approach. The other strand variously singles out structural weaknesses in the general design of public intervention, at international, regional and national levels.

Economists are accustomed to division. Another aphorism says that if ten economists are asked to interpret a passage of the Bible, they will produce ten different interpretations, eleven if one of them were John Maynard Keynes. However, in our case economists may be grouped in two significantly different clusters, so that our interest should lie in understanding what causes the main division. Keynes offers an explanation based on the ideas of past economists and political philosophers that should also apply to our subject, with politicians, financiers and the civil servants of regulatory and supervisory authorities among the main actors.

At the present moment people are unusually expectant of a more fundamental diagnosis; more particularly ready to receive it; eager to try it out, if it should be even plausible. But apart from this contemporary mood, the ideas of economists and political philosophers, both when they are right and when they are wrong, are more powerful than is commonly understood. Indeed, the world is ruled by little else. Practical men, who believe themselves to be quite exempt from any intellectual influences, are usually the slaves of some defunct economist. Madmen in authority, who hear voices in the air, are distilling their frenzy from some academic scribbler of a few years back. I am sure that the power of vested interests is vastly exaggerated compared with the gradual encroachment of ideas. Not, indeed, immediately, but after a certain interval; for in the field of economic and political philosophy there are not many who are influenced by new theories after they are twenty-five or thirty years of age, so that the ideas which civil servants and politicians and even agitators apply to current events are not likely to be the newest. But, soon or late, it is ideas, not vested interests, which are dangerous for good or evil. (1936, 383–84)

Section 2 follows Keynes's argument offering a discussion on the theoretical roots of the current approach to financial regulation and supervision. However, section 3 argues why, at least for the topic taken up in the present work, we may dare to disagree with the previous passage on the relevance of vested interests.[1] Section 4 presents an alternative approach to financial regulation based on Minsky's ideas. Section 5 briefly concludes.

2. The Theoretical Roots and Features of the Current Approach to Financial Regulation

History shows that capitalism may be blended with a large variety of political organizations, each summarily representing a different solution given to the public-private partnership. It is not a purely quantitative question just implying more of one term at the expense of the other. More or less of the public side of the relation implies a different quality of public intervention. Putting together received economic and political ideas, Keynes suggests in the previous passage that we cannot speak of science in the sense of applying purely deductive methodologies. Theoretical contributions are not an end in themselves; understanding of the functioning of the real system serves to design political and policy initiatives oriented to better social results. For example, Keynes mixes economic and political thinking when targeting a new balance between freedom and social justice (1931). His analysis on the inability of the laissez-faire system for producing convergence toward full employment is one aspect of the necessity of a political design capable of improving social justice.

The reference to Keynes is not meant to neglect other thinkers who, although in different ways, point to similar directions. For example, Henry Calvert Simons and Frank Knight, the guardians of liberal thought in the Chicago of the 1920s, argued that absolute economic freedom does not produce competition and social justice and asked for radical structural interventions by the state (Tonveronachi, 1982 and 1990). We may discuss at length policy issues that differentiate liberals like Keynes, Simons and Knight. However, the relevant fact is that they saw the state as the commanding molder of the system because markets do not produce the desired social results when these are defined according to openly stated political liberal principles and not through elegant but purely deductive theoretical propositions that help hide political preanalytical positions.

The latter is the case for the laissez-faire approach, a term that, following Keynes, is preferred to neoliberal or ultraliberal because it has nothing to do with the founding principles of liberal thought.[2] Its mission is to show, or to demonstrate in its jargon, that an anarchic economic system guided by a supernatural invisible hand is the best arrangement for producing a general optimum.[3] The eventual role of the state in the economy is to remove or weaken specific man-made imperfections defined in terms of discrepancies with respect to the anarchic model. However, even this supportive role of the state is looked upon with suspicion. The state is presented as full of political moral hazards and a myriad of other imperfections that miraculously disappear when the private governance of firms and markets collectively guided by the supernatural hand are considered. Following this logic, technical authorities (politically independent but well connected with the markets) should be the right solution.[4] The fact is that this approach does not pass the test of any reasonable scientific standard, which requires that the model must conform to reality, not vice versa. When uncertainty, money and financial markets are fully considered, the model collapses, but its policy prescriptions continue to be utilized "as if" the model were representing the optimal form of economic organization of the real world. Trying to force the real world to partially adapt to the anarchic model can only produce disasters. If these positions were to remain confined to academic circles, we would just sadly observe how much intelligence is being wasted. The problem is that for a variety of reasons, some of which are discussed in the next section, this approach is the (often covert) dominant foundation of economic policies. Financial regulation is a case in point.

Global finance requires the international harmonization of minimum regulatory and supervisory standards, the so-called regulatory level playing field. Weak home rules and supervision give an international bank competitive advantages, while, due to size and financial interconnectedness, its fragility puts the entire system at risk. Recipient countries must be convinced of the viability of foreign banks, as parents of local branches or as financial counterparties. Although specific financial regulatory measures are often considered issues to be left to technical experts, the overall regulatory design from which they descend requires an interpretation of the functioning of the economic system (Kregel, 2012a). In difference from the interwar period, in which the state in many countries played a direct role in designing the structure of the financial system, the spread of financial deregulation that accompanied the collapse of the Bretton Woods system and was sustained by a vibrant theoretical and policy counterrevolution confided in free markets to create efficient institutions, products and processes. Even when trying to flex their muscles in response to the recent crisis, the political leaders convened at the G20 reasserted that financial regulation should not limit the freedom of the private sector to innovate (G20, 2009a). Regulation should only impede the "excesses" that were considered the causes of the crisis (Geithner, 2009; G20, 2009b). In other words, the laissez-faire regime dictates its own market-based "best practices," defined as trying to hedge risks that any entity is free to assume in the quantity and quality that it desires. Technical authorities should then avoid excesses due to any single institution departing from those practices.

How does this apparently simple approach account for the increasingly complex, costly and ineffectual financial regulation and supervision, especially in the banking industry? The answer is, because interventions made according to the chosen representation of reality have produced an increasing disparity between desired and actual results. As occurred with the Ptolemaic cosmological theory, the attempt to fill the gap between new observations and the predictive power of the model led to the addition of adjustments that produced ineffectual complexity. Worse, our celestial finance is not immutable, but it is left free to introduce profit-seeking innovations that leave clumsy attempts at regulation in their wake. The simple observation that the passage to the regulatory laissez-faire system has gone in parallel with the increasing seriousness and frequency of financial crises (UNCTAD, 2015, ch. 2) should have finally alerted policy makers that something was profoundly wrong.

On the contrary, the G20 political reaction to the recent crisis has not been based on a change of paradigm. The self-criticism was limited to the identification of specific weaknesses of the previous regulation, which could be corrected by means of a more precise calibration of prudential regulation in Basel III and the addition of a new celestial sphere—macroprudential supervision.[5] The danger coming from the laissez-faire approach does not only come from the fallacy of composition of a microapproach. Because the sum of healthy banks does not necessarily produce a healthy banking system, a macro or systemic surveillance is necessary. The problem also lies in defining healthy banks according to their own profit-seeking risk metric. Fundamentally, the alternative is between policy makers designing a resilient financial structure and, as currently accepted, leaving the financial skeleton and its ex ante resilience to be dynamically molded by private interests.

Oblivious of the fact that financial laissez faire has increased the frequency and seriousness of crises, the new mantra of policy makers is that banking and financial crises have always existed, so that, interfering as little as possible with the privately induced financial dynamic, we must be prepared to manage crises in a nondisruptive way. Instead of further strengthening ex ante defenses, the main effort, made through the Financial Stability Board, has been directed at producing a regulatory standard for the swift resolution of failing systemic banks while shifting its costs from public finance to private investors. In reality, the purpose of switching from bail-out to bail-in appears that of limiting to some class of investors the number of voters damaged by a crisis. However, the possibility that the bail-in could produce disruptive domino effects has led to making its adoption contingent upon the absence of systemic threats. The resolution fund fed by the contributions of all banks would in this case at least partially substitute investors in the sharing of losses. The result is that investors are encouraged to prefer systemic intermediaries, thus increasing the existing too-big-too-fail distortions. Alternatively, if ex ante the nonactivation of bail-in is dubious, disruptive domino effects may ensue. In any case, the new resolution regime does not seem to solve the too-big-too-fail problem, as regulators want us to believe.

A further point of the regulatory response has been to endow supervisors with enhanced powers (Tonveronachi, 2010; Haldane, 2013). This might appear a bit farfetched given the criticisms leveled against precrisis supervisory practices as being too light touch and market friendly. Actually, all the crises experienced after the adoption of Basel's requirements have seen banks ex ante complying with that standard. In any case, if supervisors were cautious in their interventions, they were interpreting the spirit of a market-friendly regulation correctly. As an example, let us recall the message given by the Basel Committee of Bank Supervision (BCBS) when presenting the Basel II release (Caruana, 2004; Himino, 2004; Wellink, 2007). The aim, at least regarding large and sophisticated banks, was to align the regulatory capital to the economic capital that a bank autonomously computes following the industry's best practices.

A well-run bank chooses among the available methods for computing and hedging risks the one that best reflects its long-term interests. However, three questions should arise when taking the regulatory point of view: whether the long-term interest of well-run, but profit-seeking, banks coincide with the objectives that regulators should follow; whether best practices also mean socially reliable practices; and whether the ideas of what constitutes the industry's best practices coincide across national regulators and between them and banks, and how this relates to the attainment of the regulatory level playing field. To deal with these questions, a general outline of why and how banks are regulated according to the current laissez-faire approach is needed.

The why, at least as far as Basel is concerned, refers to stability. The first release of Basel only addressed large international banks that were considered efficiently run, but lacking the right incentive as far as capitalization was concerned. Because, for a variety of reasons, debt is preferred to capital, banks tend to save on capital, thus exposing themselves to the risk of insolvency when hit by unexpected losses, that is, losses larger than the statistically computed expected ones hedged by specific reserves. Therefore, a metric is needed to compute unexpected losses, and a decision must be taken on how much capital is required to cover them. When the BCBS speaks of best practices, it apparently refers to the methods for computing risks, reserving for itself the decision on the degree of their capital coverage. The latter has been set with capital per unit of assets not lower than 8 percent of the average risk weight. If, for example, the average risk weight is 50 percent, capital must cover unexpected losses for at least 4 percent of the total assets. However, the magic 8 percent does not emerge from some formal metric but apparently from the actual capitalization of a sample of international banks when, in the second half of the 1980s, the BCBS decision was made. Therefore, also regarding minimum capitalization, we have what is in essence self-regulation, because the reception of the *status quo ante* for the level of capitalization contradicts the regulators' premise that also well-run banks have strong long-term incentives to be undercapitalized, as the pre-1980s trend impressively shows. The capital buffers and the additional requirements for global banks introduced by Basel III as a reaction to the recent crisis introduce a new magic number, 2.5 percent, which we may suppose is again an empirical compromise with the industry. By the way, it is far from clear whether these additional requirements cover the increase in complexity, financialization and large banks' systemic footprint with respect to the period (the mid-1980s) when the previous 8 percent coefficient was decided.

The second crucial point concerns the methodology for computing the amount of risks to be hedged with capital. Starting from Basel I.5, regulation for the largest banks adopted the industry standard based on value at risk (VaR). Even if we were to allow that this is the best quantitative method available to banks, it does not necessarily represent a reliable solution for systemic stability purposes in an environment of risk complexity freely determined by banks.[6] In an uncertain world, quantitative methods filled with data taken from the past just produce educated guesses, while the real threat comes from estimated safe assets turning risky (Kregel, 2011; Roncaglia, 2012; Persaud, 2015). Furthermore, their reliability crucially depends on the complexity of risks managed within each institution, especially large ones, and on the complexity of the interrelations characterizing the financial and economic system. Because a quantitative method is a simplified representation of reality, its reliability decreases exponentially with the increase of complexity. Permitting a large variety of private interests to mold financial systems, the laissez-faire approach to regulation is responsible for the enormous increase of the financial complexity of the last decades, hence for the reduced relevance of the risk methodologies that it employs.[7]

As to whether the notions of best practices for regulators and for banks coincide, several factors point toward a negative answer. Laissez faire means the absence of internal and international barriers, leading to a global market in which institutions and products are free to operate and circulate. Competitive regulatory conditions mean that global actors are to be submitted to homogeneous rules. The regulatory level playing field and the common methodology then require that any bank facing the same data should produce homogeneous risk evaluation. Tests made after the inception of the recent crisis, asking several banks to use their internal models to compute the risk weights for the same banking and trading portfolios, have produced highly dispersed results. Because the internal model is what also guides a bank in computing its economic capital,[8] the result of the tests shows that we can hardly speak of an industry's common standard. In order to save the principle of the regulatory level playing field, the BCBS has reacted to the result of the tests by proposing restrictions to the typologies of internal models that banks are allowed to use. Apart from increasing procyclicality, for the majority of banks the adoption of this proposal would further distance their risk management and capital calculation made under the regulatory regime from what they would otherwise have chosen. The same line of reasoning applies to Basel's standardized methods for computing risk weights because they come from calibrations made on samples of smaller banks. In this case, too, we are led to suppose that the dispersion around the chosen coefficients is significant. By also adding various prudential multipliers and politically motivated demultipliers, regulators are increasingly asserting themselves to be the equivalent of good bankers.[9] The resulting complex set of incentives significantly affects, or distorts, banks' behavior and consequently the pricing of assets.[10] It should then come as no surprise that banks and other financial actors react, also through their freedom to innovate, to a distorted market-friendly regulation.

Beside apparently homogeneous rules not producing homogeneous results on risk weighting, other elements concur to further distort the international regulatory playing field. Most relevant are national discretions and heterogeneous accounting standards touching on crucial elements such as the components of regulatory capital, consolidation rules, the treatment of off-balance-sheet exposures, derivatives and provisioning. The increased relevance of Basel's Pillar 2, with its supervisory review and evaluation process (SREP), gives national authorities further room for distorting the playing field. The stress test exercises, which are a relevant aspect of the SREP, build on the doubtful and divergent internal risk metric discussed above, stressed with ad hoc scenarios. The markets, which should help supervisors discipline banks (Pillar 3), appear so confused by a complexity built on discretion and opacity that they often base their evaluations on simpler indicators, such as the unweighted leverage ratio and the Texas ratio. The current regulation also bends the playing field in favor of large banks, which are permitted to employ internal models that save on capital with respect to the standardized methods reserved for smaller banks. In addition, the latter do not have the means and power to react to a distorted regulation and to avoid diktats by supervisors.

Both private interests and regulation have thus concurred to create a mission impossible for bank management, markets and supervision. The thousands of pages of instructions that supervisors pour on bankers for regulatory compliance are the mark of the ineffectual complexity of supervision, not the solution.[11] Because the absence of public influence on financial structure also means the absence of a general and consistent design for regulation, regulatory interventions go after specific "excesses" defined in relation to what supervisors increasingly idealize as the best practices in the diverse branches of the financial system. Nonhomogeneous national or regional rulebooks and supervisory handbooks have thus become the official textbooks for good financial managers. However, risks are created globally, shifted and accumulated independently of the best intentions of national regulators and supervisors. What appears to be a heavily regulated system is actually a costly and distorted dysregulated one. Starting from the idea that freedom means competition and efficiency, the regulatory problem comes from its first principles, which leave financial institutions, especially global ones, free to innovate and create and take any type and amount of risks.

Ultimately, since the level international playing field is the necessary companion of global finance, the actual nonexistence of the first should lead to a profound reconsideration of the latter.

Financial laissez faire has also pushed up the systemic relevance of institutions that have increasingly become too big, too complex and too interrelated to be managed, supervised and resolved. In the current regulatory context, competitive conditions constrain financial actors to homogeneous rules, which do not include in any meaningful way limits to their market power.[12] As we observe generally, the adoption of the theory of contestable markets has meant looking for the misuse and not for the existence of market power. If nonnatural monopolies are often barred, especially those of foreign origin, oligopolistic markets dominated by a few large firms are the norm. This permits not only extreme cases of market manipulation, as the ones recently sanctioned, but also less glaring practices—helped by the basic cooperative nature of banking—that are difficult to prosecute. As Sylos Labini (1962) observed a long time ago, there is nothing wrong in principle with cartels; the judgment must rest on whether they serve general purposes. If, as we can easily observe, the extra returns created under the laissez-faire regime are seized within firms and the financial sector, or are utilized to finance larger and more fragile financial dimensions, they serve private (not general) interests. Even more worryingly, the concentration of market power serves to manipulate political decisions in order to sustain the laissez-faire regime from which that power derives. The distortion of democratic rules is what also differentiates a laissez-faire system from a liberal one.[13]

3. The Role of Vested Interests

The last sentence introduces the issue of vested interests, which include national interests.

Extrapolating Keynes's sentence cited in section 1 from its historical context we should be led to think that the laissez-faire policy counterrevolution was mainly the product of old or new modes of thought, not of vested interests. My doubts rest on how, if not supported by strong hands, nonscientifically based and weak theoretical and policy propositions could have gained such a dominant position outside a "lunatic asylum," borrowing the term from Keynes, and maintained it despite fierce criticism.

In the previous pages the terms "globalization," "global actors" and "global markets" have been used as synonyms of generalized cross-border activities. The term global refers to the almost-free international movements of goods, services, capital and firms, not to stateless entities. In the global laissez-faire system tensions may exist between the interests from which national politicians derive their legitimacy and the interests of national private economic and financial actors that are allowed to operate globally. From both points of view, the international arena is not a "natural" level playing field. Asymmetries in political and market power are the norm. Because the features of the global arena descend from a (noncomplete) set of common rules, the nature, or partial absence, of such rules is thus not neutral across the different actors. Formally, international political agreements have produced common rules. The question is why the outcome of these agreements were laissez-faire friendly rules and why current revisions do not contemplate radical changes notwithstanding the disasters they have produced.[14] In the short space of this chapter, I am not able to give a detailed answer. However, I will try to give a convincing one.

The starting point of the counterrevolution in financial regulation may be dated back to the 1970s, with the collapse of the Bretton Woods system (BWS). As the result of asymmetrical powers in the negotiation, an instance where Keynes's more reasonable plan succumbed to US interests, the BWS produced an asymmetrical system where the adjustment of current account imbalances was charged only to deficit countries. When, as Robert Triffin had foreseen, the US position exceeded the gold convertibility of its international reserve currency, the system collapsed and a new public order was not forged, also due to the illusion nurtured by some countries to force a symmetric multilateral arrangement. While external imbalances were multiplied and generalized by the two petrol shocks, the inability or unwillingness to reach a new supranational agreement left private international banks in charge of the job previously done by the International Monetary Fund (IMF), but on a more grandiose scale.[15] Flexible exchange rates with liberalized international financial flows were unable to eliminate large external imbalances, often increasing them. Substituting IMF loans with lending granted following private criteria, ex ante constraints on imbalances were replaced by ex post foreign debt and by financial and currency crises. The IMF de facto became the lender of last resort for funding the exit of foreign private capital, while imposing asymmetrical conditionality based on what was later named the Washington Consensus.[16]

Obviously, a system based on the international operation of private interests had to be based on market-friendly rules. Domestic financial deregulation and reregulation along microprudential lines permitted international inflows to be directed to real estate and securities sectors, fueling booms and bursts. The cause of a walk increasingly disseminated by systemic crises have been ascribed not to the model but to local realities not complying with the model, especially when those realities consisted of poor or emerging countries. Instead of considering the model as a pathology, the model was reasserted as the physiology that required to force the worldwide spreading of the financial laissez-faire system.

It would be rather naive to believe that the ideas purported by the academic resurrection, manipulation and elegant presentation of old theories were the autonomous spring that, after winning the minds and hearts of policy makers and managers, have led to the globalization of laissez faire. They were surely a means, but they were also forcefully nurtured by a flood of private funds that were directed at creating powerful think tanks and influencing the media and political elections and decisions.[17] It would be wrong to look at this as a conspiracy stemming from homogeneous and well-knit interests. More simply, it is the result of letting powerful private interests emerge, as Henry Simons denounced, and of the convergence of such interests on a few basic points regarding their global reach.

The consolidation of the system also produced the consolidation of a large set of dispersed "subordinated" vested interests. The market-friendly rules from which the laissez-faire system derives its existence and strength have been worked out with decades of efforts by international public and private institutions whose respectability depends on avoiding radical changes. These actors do not need much encouragement to defend the foundations of their past proposals and decisions, even after the recent crisis has hit the most developed countries, that is, the strategic center. The various IMF, World Bank, Organization for Economic Cooperation and Development, Basel Committee, International Organization of Securities Commissions, national regulatory and supervisory agencies and so on have not reacted by questioning the general design. As popular outrage recedes, minor lapses from the original design are being repaired (counterreforms). This while, by any serious analysis, financial fragility is higher than before the 2008 crisis.

4. An Alternative Approach to Financial Regulation

From the previous narrative, one main point emerges: the existing balance in the public-private partnership must be changed at the international and the national level. This implies in the first instance a radical rethinking of globalization.

Keynes, a liberal, criticized the extreme configurations of protectionism and globalization for international trade (proposed to keep finance firmly national) and reserved unfettered globalization to the circulation of ideas and tourism. His argument rests on the need to acquire degrees of freedom for directing policies toward national welfare

(Keynes, 1933).[18] Also the Clearing Union plan that he prepared ten years later for the Bretton Woods conference does not attribute any critical role to private international finance. Primarily interested in keeping unemployment low by public and private investments, Keynes was not friendly with financial rents. He would have criticized today's justification of international finance as permitting higher rents for rich countries' wealth owners coming from financing investments in less-developed countries. As Jan Kregel argues, this is just bad dynamic theory and unwillingness to learn a lesson from the experience of the last four decades. Setting up regional Keynes-type clearing unions could be a first step for designing new public governance that could progressively substitute private international flows (Kregel, 2015).

Making finance national would also dispense with the multitude of international regulatory standards that were set up to discipline international financial firms. Following Hyman Minsky, I have shown elsewhere (Tonveronachi, 2016) that the pursuit of the level international regulatory playing field does not take into account national specificities and physiological needs. Given different national conditions, homogeneous regulatory requirements lead either to fostering fragile and ever increasing financialization, or to insufficient credit growth. On the contrary, regulation should be used to pursue national objectives in conjunction with monetary and fiscal policies.

This comes from the fact that the long-term potential growth rate of bank assets, based on internal resources, depends on the share of retained profits, hence on the retention ratio, the return on assets and leverage (assets over own capital). While microprudential regulation tends to constrain the maximum value of leverage, the value of the other two variables comes from a complex set of private decisions and structural conditions. The resulting growth potential may then exceed or fall short of the potential growth of nominal national gross domestic product (GDP), a worrisome result if we think of finance as serving the economy. The impetuous and fragile growth of financialization and of financial firms' dimension over the last decades shows how and how far the laissez-faire system has grown in the absence of a public systemic design. The so-called macroprudential regulation spurred by the 2008 crisis falls short of adopting a systemic approach.

Following Minsky, financial regulation should pursue the objective of roughly equating the growth of bank assets and the growth potential of nominal GDP in the medium term. Minsky suggests that regulation should establish a common maximum leverage for all banks and then operate on the retention ratio to reach the desired balance. This Copernican revolution would disrupt the Ptolemaic G20 approach. In coordination with fiscal and monetary policy, financial regulation should look at national sustainable objectives, not at the international and national microprudential level playing field. National ownership of financial regulation would be consistent with Keynes's suggestion to keep finance national. Once downsized to exist only as national entities, the dimension, power and ownership structure of financial firms could be treated according to national preferences, without the latter spilling over to other countries.

Public authorities should take control of the main features of the entire design of the financial system, not just of the banks as defined in the current regulatory framework. Debt and its function should be the discriminating factors (Tonveronachi, 2016). The physiology of debt of financial firms is what Minsky calls the "acceptance function," which in the present institutional context means the credit created to serve a dynamic economic system. Debt should not be used just to amplify returns or losses. Funding via debt should be restricted to the acceptance function, that is, to what we can go on calling banks. Any financial firms using debt should be treated as a bank, and any nonbank financial contract should only be funded by shares. In this way, shadow banking and fictitious liquidity (Kregel, 2012b) would disappear as well as the necessity of burdening nonbank entities with capital and liquidity requirements. We could thus obtain simplicity and effectiveness instead of ineffective complexity.

5. Conclusions

As long as political boundaries persist, the "imperialism" of financial laissez faire is a harbinger of international and national political and economic problems. Keeping finance national (or regional) through Keynes-type clearing unions and reforming financial regulation along the previous lines is only part of a radical rethinking of global relations.

The attention devoted by the present chapter to vested interests comes from the necessity to properly consider the nontechnical difficulties that loom over alternative paths. Policy makers should realize however that the social and political climate nurtured by the global laissez faire of the last decades is making it difficult to avoid the fact that the next devastating crisis could bring back the fascist, and not the liberal, version of national interests.

Acknowledgments

Thanks are due to Jan Kregel and Elisabetta Montanaro for comments and suggestions on a previous draft of the paper. The usual caveats apply.

Notes

1 Given Keynes's previous stint in the India Office and his experience at the Versailles peace conference, later confirmed at Bretton Woods, it may be safe to assume that he did not include international relations among the vested interests referred to in the passage.
2 In the English idiom, liberalism and liberal political philosophy and constructions are not synonyms.
3 Converting the deus ex machina auctioneer into the *vulgata* of Adam Smith's invisible hand, the proponents of this approach try to gain respectability by referring to some past leading liberal thinker. As Roncaglia (2005, ch. 5) shows, this requires making violence both in the letter and the spirit of Smith's works. For a criticism of the traditional concept of equilibrium, see Kregel (2011).
4 A recent example is the introduction in the European Union (EU) of independent national fiscal councils whose function is to expose deviations from the market-friendly rules decided by the EU by national governments.
5 The absence of a defined set of principles and rules situates such macrofinancial interventions in the realm of discretionary supervisory action, patching the weaknesses of microprudential regulation, not of proper regulation. As discussed later in the section on an alternative approach to financial regulation, section 4, a truly macroprudential regulation might represent

a rupture if stemming from a different approach and, if dominating, not being dominated by the microprudential one.

6   Actually, the BCBS does not appear so sure of its reliability if it inserts in its capital computation "prudential" multipliers.

7   For a discussion on how much of this complexity is "fictitious," i.e., created by interests internal to the financial system and not to serve the economy, see Kregel (2012b).

8   Supervisors should verify that the internal model utilized for regulatory purposes coincides with the model used for the operational management of risks.

9   Worthy of attention is the work in progress of the newly created European single supervisory mechanism; see Lautenschläger (2016).

10 This point is made by Kregel (2012b), taking as an example Basel III's liquidity requirements. Shan et al. (2016) show that banks, especially large ones, have used credit default swaps not so much to improve their risk management but to lower regulatory capital. A recent BCBS revision of the market risk framework tries to address this type of regulatory arbitrage. This is just one of the many instances of the difficulty, if not impossibility, for regulators in calibrating their risk framework and of the unintended consequences of prudential regulation, in this case for increasing interconnectedness and systemic complexity.

11 The only beneficiaries of supervisory complexity are consultancy firms that are absorbing an increasing share of graduates in banking and finance.

12 Where they exist, national and local limits on the share of deposits may constrain local and regional banks, not global actors.

13 This point was forcefully made by Henry Simons (1948).

14 Goldbach (2015) offers an interesting analysis of the complex interplay of actors and interests affecting the layering of national and transnational rules and policy processes related to the Basel framework, and finally resulting in regulatory gaps. However, he fails to realize that the fundamental regulatory weakness resides in the basic design, with the gaps that he singles out not being different from what, according to the G20, caused the "excesses" that have led to the recent crisis.

15 This de facto ended the preoccupation that the IMF could crowd out private financial activity expressed by the American Bankers Association during the process leading to the US approval of the Bretton Woods agreement; see Morgan (1945).

16 For an in-depth analysis of the post-BW evolution, see Kregel (2008).

17 Admati (2016) contains a review of the literature on some of these issues. Interesting theoretical analyses are presented by Dal Bó and Di Tella (2003) and Dal Bó et al. (2006).

18 Although critical parts of Keynes's Dublin *Lectures* were politically motivated by his effort to present a compromise in the then-raging conflict between the United Kingdom and the recently independent Ireland regarding the latter's policy toward self-sufficiency, his argument for gradually shifting away from full globalization is based on the different world conditions with respect to the "imperialism" of the previous century. The full version of the *Lectures* is included in Emmett (2013).

References

Admati, A. 2016. "It Takes a Village to Maintain a Dangerous Financial System." Rock Center for Corporate Governance, Working Paper Series no. 219. Stanford: Rock Center for Corporate Governance.

Caruana, J. 2004. "Basel II—A New Approach to Banking Supervision." Remarks at the Fourth Annual International Seminar on Policy Challenges for the Financial Sector, *The Basel II—The International Banking System at the Crossroads*, Washington, DC, June 1. Available at http://www.bis.org/review/r040604c.pdf

Dal Bó, E., and R. Di Tella. 2003. "Capture by Threat," *Journal of Political Economy* 111, no. 5: 1123–54.

Dal Bó, E., P. Dal Bó, and R. Di Tella. 2006. "Plata o Plomo?: Bribe and Punishment in a Theory of Political Influence," *American Political Science Review* 100, no. 1: 1–13.

Emmett, R., ed. 2013. *Documents Related to J. M. Keynes: Institutionalism at Chicago & Frank H. Knight.* Bingley, UK: Emerald.

Geithner, T. 2009. *Written Testimony of the Secretary of the Treasury before the Joint Economic Committee, Financial Regulatory Reform.* US Department of the Treasury, November 19. Available at: https://www.treasury.gov/press-center/press-releases/Pages/tg413.aspx.

Goldbach, R. 2015. *Global Governance and Regulatory Failure.* Basingstoke: Palgrave Macmillan.

Group of 20 (G20). 2009a. "Enhancing Sound Regulation and Strengthening Transparency." Working Group 1, *Final Report*, March 25.

———. 2009b. *Leaders' Statement: The Pittsburgh Summit*, September 24–25.

Haldane, A. 2013. "Constraining Discretion in Bank Regulation." Speech given at the Federal Reserve Bank of Atlanta Conference, *Maintaining Financial Stability: Holding a Tiger by the Tail(s)*, April 9. Available at: http://www.bankofengland.co.uk/publications/Pages/speeches/2013/657.aspx.

Himino, R. 2004. "Basel II—Towards a New Common Language," *BIS Quarterly Review*, September: 41–49. Available at: http://www.bis.org/publ/qtrpdf/r_qt0409e.pdf

Keynes, J. M. 1931. *Essays in Persuasion.* London: Macmillan.

———. 1933. "National Self-Sufficiency," *The New Statesman and Nation*, July 8 and 15. Reprinted in *Activities 1931–1939: World Crises and Policies in Britain and America*. vol. 21 of *The Collected Writings of John Maynard Keynes*, edited by E. Johnson and D. Moggridge, 233–46. London: Macmillan and New York: Cambridge University Press, 1982.

———. 1936. *The General Theory of Employment, Interest and Money.* London: Macmillan.

Kregel, J. 2008. "Financial Flows and International Imbalances: The Role of Catching-up by Late Industrializing Developing Countries." Levy Institute Working Paper no. 528. Annandale-on-Hudson, NY: Levy Economics Institute of Bard College.

———. 2011. "Evolution versus Equilibrium: Remarks upon Receipt of the Veblen-Commons Award," *Journal of Economic Issues* 45, no. 2: 269–75.

———. 2012a. *Beyond the Minsky Moment: Where We've Been, Why We Can't Go Back, and the Road Ahead for Financial Reform.* e-book. Annandale-on-Hudson, NY: Levy Economics Institute of Bard College. Available at: http://www.levyinstitute.org/publications/beyond-the-minsky-moment-where-weve-been-why-we-cant-go-back-and-the-road-ahead-for-financial-reform.

———. 2012b. "Using Minsky to Simplify Financial Regulation." Research Project Report. Annandale-on-Hudson, NY: Levy Economics Institute of Bard College.

———. 2015. "Emerging Markets and the International Financial Architecture: A Blueprint for Reform." Levy Institute Working Paper no. 833. Annandale-on-Hudson, NY: Levy Economics Institute of Bard College.

Lautenschläger, S. 2016. "After One Year of European Banking Supervision, Have Expectations Been Met?" Speech at the Austrian Bankers' Business Lunch, Frankfurt, 13 January. Available at: http://www.ecb.europa.eu/press/key/date/2016/html/sp160113_2.en.html

Morgan, C. 1945. *Bretton Woods: Clues to a Monetary Mystery.* Boston: World Peace Foundation.

Persaud, A. 2015. "Reinventing Financial Regulation: A Blueprint for Overcoming Systemic Risk." VOX CEPR's Policy Portal. Available at: www.voxeu.org/article/blueprint-overcoming-systemic-risk.

Roncaglia, A. 2005. *The Wealth of Ideas: A History of Economic Thought.* Cambridge: Cambridge University Press.

———. 2012. "Keynesian Uncertainty and the Shaky Foundations of Statistical Risk Assessment Models," *PSL Quarterly Review* 65, no. 263: 437–54.

Shan, S., D. Tang, and H. Yan. 2016. "Regulation-Induced Financial Innovation: The Case of Credit Default Swaps and Bank Capital." Paper presented at the 27th Australasian Finance and Banking Conference, 2014. Available at: https://papers.ssrn.com/sol3/papers.cfm?abstract_id=2447328.

Simons, H. 1948. *Economic Policy for a Free Society.* Chicago: University of Chicago Press.

Sylos Labini, P. 1962. "Interrogatorio. Seduta 8 febbraio 1962." In Camera dei Deputati, *Resoconti stenografici degli interrogatori conoscitivi,* vol. 2 of *Atti della Commissione parlamentare di inchiesta sui limiti posti alla concorrenza nel campo economico,* 57–94. Roma: Servizio Studi Legislazione e Inchieste Parlamentari, 1965. Available at: http://legislature.camera.it/documenti/documentiParlamentari/ElencoDOC_1_12.asp?IdLegislatura=04|853#.

Tonveronachi, M. 1982. "Monetarism and Fixed Rules in H. Simons," *BNL Quarterly Review* 35, no. 141: 181–203.

———. 1990. "Teorie monetarie a Chicago." In *Il Pensiero economico: Temi, Problemi e Scuole,* edited by G. Becattini. Torino: Utet.

———. 2010. "Empowering Supervisors with More Principles and Discretion to Implement Them Will Not Reduce the Dangers of the Prudential Approach to Financial Regulation," *PSL Quarterly Review* 65, no. 255: 361–76.

———. 2016. "A Critical Assessment of the EU Monetary, Fiscal and Financial Framework and a Reform Proposal." FESSUD Working Paper No. 132. Leeds: Leeds University Business School.

United Nations Conference on Trade and Development (UNCTAD). 2015. *Trade and Development Report.* New York and Geneva: United Nations Conference on Trade and Development.

Wellink, N. 2007. "Basel II and financial institution resiliency." Remarks by Chairman of the Basel Committee on Banking Supervision at the *Risk Capital 2007* Conference, Paris, 27 June. Available at: http://www.bis.org/review/r070627a.pdf.

Chapter Four

DEMOCRACY IN CRISIS: SO WHAT'S NEW?

Michele Salvati

1. Introduction

Democracy is in crisis today, as many authoritative scholars remark. I, too, believe that democracy is now going through serious difficulties. However, I also believe that we can hardly hope to understand the nature of the crisis or come up with appropriate solutions unless we recognize that this form of government has, by its very nature, always been subject to crisis. It was in the direct democracy of the ancients, and it is in the representative democracy of modern times, both in the parliamentary democracy of notables with restricted suffrage in the nineteenth century and in the democracy of the great mass parties with universal suffrage in the twentieth century. And, again, it remains the case in our contemporary democracy dominated by the media and populist leaders. A couple of words of warning before getting down to the matter at hand. First, I use the term "crisis" inexactly, as it is widely used in journalism and even in academia—as a synonym for difficulties, frictions and the risk that democracy may turn into a political system that is no longer democratic. Secondly, my reference is to the present state of the democracies of the advanced capitalistic countries. Analysis of the state of democracy worldwide over the long period should be quite a different and more complex matter.

2. Back to Basics

The two basic reasons for crisis have been recognized since ancient times, lying in both participation in the democratic process—the "input" of democracy, as it were—and the results of that process, the quality of governments, the "output." Democracy has always been on the verge of crisis because its ideal of equality—equal political influence of all citizens in the government of the political community they belong to—has always been belied by reality. Indeed, it seems impossible for it to be fully implemented in societies— egalitarian as they may be—characterized by pronounced differences in wealth, prestige and power.[1] Such differences inevitably translate into differences in political influence. And crisis is always lurking since it is, indeed, rare to come anywhere even near the ideal of good government—government seen by the vast majority of citizens as a bringer of peace and general well-being, as depicted in Ambrogio Lorenzetti's superb fresco in Siena's city hall. Foreign wars and civil wars, social conflicts, indigence, unemployment and inequality are part and parcel of the history of many democracies, both ancient and modern. Until the mid-eighteenth century, in fact, the leading political thinkers were actually convinced that the ideal was unattainable given the irresponsible, demagogic forces democracy is subject to, preferring moderate forms of monarchy or oligarchy.

And yet the progress of democracy proved inexorable and, after the American and French revolutions, as parliamentary democracy evolved in the nineteenth century, the more affluent and influential classes came to the realization that the most extreme consequences democracy might have—expropriation of the few by the many—could be avoided. This might be achieved, for example, by restricting suffrage in the first place, and subsequently applying more refined instruments clashing less violently with the democratic ideal, such as abandoning the principle of pure proportional representation for the sake of governability. As for the output (the ideal of good government), the historical experience of the best democracies—the liberal democracies—showed that democratic government, if not exactly "good," was in any case possible and better than the nondemocratic forms. And so it was that democracy proceeded to become the most widespread political system globally, "the worst form of government, except for all the others," as Winston Churchill famously put it. But it is also a form of government whose quality can be maintained at an acceptable level only with a continuous, painstaking process of reformist maintenance.[2]

I began with the ABCs of the democratic crisis—the basic reasons why democracy has never succeeded, and never will, in fully standing by its promises of equality and good government—since otherwise the ongoing debate may give the impression that democracy is in crisis above all today. That today it is a "lost cause" (Mastropaolo, 2011), since democracy is "disfigured" (Urbinati, 2014) and harbors a "totalitarian vocation" (Wolin, 2008). That, unlike in the recent past, the system we know today is not even worthy of the name and should be termed differently, as "post-democracy" (Crouch, 2003) or something of the sort—as might be gleaned from the titles of some interesting books published recently. A vein of nostalgia runs through many of these texts: there is a widespread conviction that yesterday democracy was in rather better condition than it is today, and that, in particular, the old, ideological mass party—prevalent in Europe after World War II—was a far better tool for democracy than the media-dependent parties that succeeded it, ever subject to populistic or plebiscitary drifts.[3]

I, too, believe that the democratic systems of the advanced capitalistic countries have been going through a difficult phase as from the last two decades of the last century, but no more difficult than others faced in the more distant past. It is a state of affairs generated by deep-reaching structural changes, and we are hardly likely to find remedial indications by looking back to a happier recent past. Of the two major structural changes, the first—the international situation in which the individual national democracies are entangled—is, as we shall see, mainly operative on the output side. The second is a matter of the transformations (social, economic, cultural and technological) that all the national democracies have gone through in the last few decades. These affect the way the citizens are represented (the parties, in particular), the nature of the electoral processes and the principal features of the governments. Thus, the interest here is mainly on the input side.

Representative democracy, as historical experience shows, can function acceptably only within a "sovereign" and "national" state, where the government is able to decide on the main issues regarding the collective well-being of the citizens (*conditions of sovereignty*). It also requires that citizens are united by sufficiently strong bonds of "fraternity"—the third and all too often neglected term in the slogan of the French Revolution—for them to accept the majority decisions, even though they may have negative effects on relatively large segments of the population (*conditions of fraternity*). In the last two centuries the nation has been, and indeed remains, the most powerful means of bonding identities, able to produce conditions of "fraternity"—conditions that at least suffice for acceptance of the sovereign decisions taken by a democratic government. Having established so much, we must make do with a weak but realistic and widely accepted working definition of representative democracy, as proposed by Joseph Schumpeter (1943): faced with a range of candidates competing to govern (individual leaders, parties or coalitions), the citizens choose one with a majority vote. The performance of the chosen candidate will be judged in subsequent elections, in which the choice may be confirmed if the government has satisfied the citizens, or overturned it in the contrary case. And yet (objective) well-being and (subjective) satisfaction do not depend solely, and often not even mainly, on the actions of the government or the quality of the institutions of the single nation-state. They also—and increasingly—depend upon the conditions of the world economy and the economic and political relations the state has with the group of countries forming the international community. This community is certainly not democratic and is rife with relations of hegemony and dependence, and international institutions and rules, which the single states must bow to.

3. Good Government

For a long time after World War II—those "Glorious Thirty Years" up to the end of the 1970s—these relations, and the rules and institutions thereby engendered, saw extraordinary levels of well-being for the major advanced capitalistic countries, the countries we are mainly concerned with here. There is more than a grain of truth in the idea that nostalgia for the political systems of those times (and thus also for the great, stable mass parties that were prevalent then) was due more to the well-being that came with the spectacular economic growth than to their democratic quality, certainly far from perfect in many nation-states.

The turbulence of the 1970s was, however, followed by a very different phase at the international level, which saw growth slowing down in the advanced capitalistic countries. As from the end of the 1980s, this phase was destined to develop into the globalized capitalism we know today. At the national level, a great many countries tried to react with reforms to enhance the competitiveness of their economies and the efficiency of their public institutions, and all too often the reforms aggravated the living conditions of the less privileged classes, contributing in no small way to the unpopularity of the governments that implemented them. Again, there is quite a strong element of truth in the idea that part of the discredit befalling the democracy of our times is due more to these difficult external conditions than to a drastic deterioration in the quality of the democratic processes—more to the output than to the input of democracy. The basic reasons for the highly topical "crisis of democracy" are to be seen in a range of issues: lagging economic growth, unemployment and precarious employment, increasing inequality, disappointed hopes of continuous social progress, waves of immigration that wars and poverty in the less developed countries are driving onto the shores of the richer nations—all negative phenomena that the single nation-states are unable to cope with.

Thus, to the two broad causes of the difficulties of democracy, on the input side and on the output side, we should also add a *condition of context*, which lies at the origin of the difficulties that the single nation-states come up against in satisfying the aspirations of their citizens and guaranteeing them "good government." Many critics lament the loss of sovereignty of the single nation-states in the face of international finance, the great multinationals and even the supranational institutions themselves. Even where these external influences are most evident—and we will take a look at the state of affairs in the eurozone countries, where they are most felt—the difficulties that some national democracies are experiencing today are not due to a *loss of sovereignty*: they had not enjoyed greater sovereignty in the boom years, when it was easier for them to satisfy their citizens' aspirations. Today the individual democracies are troubled by two other phenomena. To begin with, there is the international economic policy regime, while at the same time in some cases they have inherited internal economic-institutional structures from a less complicated past, unsuited to international competition in a neoliberal, globalized context. In the case of the international economic policy regime there is little that a nonhegemonic country can do, while modifying the internal conditions of competitiveness is a formidable task that takes a very long time. However, democracy being a national matter, individual citizens focus their dissatisfaction on the governments of their countries, unable to recreate the more favorable conditions of the recent past. And democratic political competition often generates parties and movements that channel this discontent toward illusory objectives, accentuating the populistic-demagogic features that the critics of democracy have decried since the times of the ancient Greeks.

4. The Input of Democracy

So far we have confined our considerations to some problems concerning "good government," the second of the perennial reasons for the crisis of democracy that we mentioned at the outset. Reference here is to the radical structural modifications in the world capitalistic system—transition from the postwar period of growth benefiting the advanced capitalistic countries to neoliberal globalization creating difficulties for almost all the countries that had enjoyed the most success in the earlier period. However, interacting with this structural change on the output side is another—which has been particularly emphasized by the political analysts and commentators (namely a change on the input side)—of the forms of democratic participation and the ways in which the parties and governments respond to it. It is a change that has come about gradually, but by now, it is hard to see how the results could be reversed. This change has led from the great ideological mass parties of the postwar years to Richard S. Katz and Peter Mair's *Cartel Party* (1995), then to the media-dominated parties, geared to fight in the "democracy of the public" (Manin, 1995), and more recently to the great burgeoning of parties and movements with marked demagogic-populistic features, and increasing demagogic-populistic contamination of the traditional parties themselves.

The party that the older among us have known, the ideological mass party led by an oligarchy formally legitimized by a process of associative democracy (in reality not very democratic at all, as Robert Michels (1911) observed over a century ago), is not and cannot be the arena within which the opinions of the great mass of citizens are formed and the electoral intentions of most of the voters emerge. It has been eroded by virtually irresistible social, economic, cultural and technological transformations: the loosening of bonds and of the territorial, religious and cultural distinctions, which, as from the nineteenth century, had generated the traditional parties, together with a profound change in the class structure and the declining credibility of the ideological narratives that revolved around it. At the same time educational levels have risen sharply and society is subject to increasing individualization and fragmentation in terms of both interests and values pursued, while the mass media have grown to extremely powerful proportions, starting with radio, then the still-dominant television, and now also the Internet and social media. All these have played a part in bringing about, even in the most traditional parties, the transition from the oligarchy produced by associative democracy—remarkably stable as long as things went well—to the pronounced personalization of leadership. In short, the voters in their homes have become a nebulous "public," before which the party leaders (and more generally the political entrepreneurs) display their merchandise, with the hope of getting them to buy it, thereby getting their votes. That this entails risks of populism, demagogy and plebiscitary practices is beyond all doubt. But it is equally clear that there can be no going back to the (let me repeat, hardly very democratic) oligarchies of the mass parties, based on marked sociocultural rifts, ideological narratives (that used to be convincing) and, in the postwar years, an economic context of strong and steady growth.

The sociopolitical transformation processes I have outlined were already to be seen in the more advanced capitalistic countries well before the end of the boom years and the advent of a globalized, neoliberal system. Few, however, talked then of a crisis of democracy. Indeed, in the early 1990s—when Soviet communism was collapsing and before the negative social effects of neoliberalism and globalization began to make themselves felt seriously—public opinion was very different, showing a peak in the self-confidence of liberal democracy. Liberal, democratic capitalism had triumphed against its historical enemy, economic growth seemed to be going ahead without any significant snags and even the decline in voter turnout and ideological mobilization was seen more as a sign of a rational attitude on the part of the citizens than of a pathological disaffection for democratic politics. In short, it was the *End of History*, as Francis Fukuyama (1992) entitled his bestselling book.[4] This complacent attitude on the part of the political, economic and intellectual elites at the end of the millennium was destined to be short lived, and the turning point came with the American financial crisis of 2007–8 and the recession it caused worldwide.

The United States emerged from this crisis fairly soon, but the recession put an end to the self-satisfaction of the previous two decades and provoked widespread critical reflection on the negative consequences of financial deregulation and globalization. Reflection dwelt not only on the macroeconomic and financial aspects of the neoliberal system—the illusion that the financial markets can be self-regulating without needing the intervention of the public authorities—but above all on the growing distortion in the distribution of income in favor of the wealthier classes. The distortion had set in well before the crisis, as from the 1980s, but the major critical attention and political reactions came later on. This change in attitude inevitably led to renewed and redoubled criticism of the functioning of democracy, captured by the interests it should be regulating and indifferent to the living conditions of the classes it should be representing and defending: thus, the classical conflict between capitalism and democracy. On the left and the right alike, dissatisfaction with the policies of the elites—who had entrusted governance of the economy to technicians and the (alleged) experts—skepticism about policies of moderation and compromise and the attraction of the more extreme positions became rife in the years following on the Great Recession, and their consequences are still evident today. In the nomination process of the US presidential election, Bernie Sanders represented dangerous competition for Hillary Clinton on a quasi-socialist platform in the Democratic Party, while Donald Trump actually succeeded in obtaining the nomination of the Republican Party on a platform of extreme right-wing populism, and then in winning the presidential election. Such protagonists, such political outcomes had hardly been imagined in the times of the *End of History*.

5. The European Union

Europe shows a different and even more serious state of affairs, with the negative effects of globalized capitalism on the less competitive countries, firms and workers combining with a sharp acceleration in the institutional process of unification. The Maastricht Treaty of 1991 laid down both the basic constitution of the European Union (EU) and the rules of the monetary union, which was to come into force at the end of the century. Many hoped that, on the strength of this extraordinary constitutional revolution, Europe would be able to speak with one voice, and that this voice—given the political, economic and cultural weight of our continent—would be able to counter the more negative aspects of globalization for the less privileged classes of the advanced countries, tempering the individualistic-liberal model prevalent worldwide with the spirit of the "European social model." As is all too evident today, this hope has foundered: the explicit rules of Maastricht—applied to the countries belonging to the European monetary system—function in practice as a transmission belt and boost mechanism for those implicit in the world neoliberal system. There are two reasons for this: to begin with, it is a matter of constitutional rules enshrined in binding treaties and agreements, and, above all, the rules are upheld by the strongest countries in the Union, with Germany in the first place.

From an economic point of view, I believe that today the transition from "implicit" to "explicit," from rules and constraints self-imposed through a national democratic process or imposed from outside, makes no decisive difference. Even if released from observance of the Maastricht rules and the subsequent agreements, a competitively weak country would be led to behave as they prescribe, for it would come under the constraints of the globalized, neoliberal international system to which it belongs (Biasco, 2016, 163 ff.).

From a political point of view, however, subjection to the Maastricht rules and subsequent agreements makes a big difference, for it allows the Union authorities to intervene in the decision-making of the individual states continually and in considerable detail, highlighting yet further the limitations to their sovereignty. Greece, and indeed Italy, too, together with the economically weaker countries in general, exemplifies such intervention and the reactions it provokes. Of course, these are voluntary limitations of sovereignty, accepted on the basis of treaties freely undersigned, but the institutions imposing these constraints are not recognized as an authority whose decisions must be bowed to on the basis of a universally accepted criterion of legitimization. The Union is not a federal state endowed by a European demos with the authority to impose decisions taken democratically. The European Parliament is not a true parliament, and the European Commission is not a government answerable to it: the most important decisions are taken by the council of heads of state and government on the basis of power relations that do not depend on the will of the European citizens as a whole, expressed through a majority vote. It may be objected that even in a true federation the various state units experience strong constraints on their sovereignty and are subject to the decisions of the federation. However, the analogy is deceptive, and the shortcoming in the principle of democratic sovereignty in Europe is evident. In America, the citizens of the states are also citizens of the federation and vote for its government, thereby democratically controlling the controllers of their states. In short, what democratic power is taken from them at the state level is returned to them at the federal level. This is not the case in the EU, where the elections for parliament do not give the powers to control the true government of the Union democratically.

The reason for this state of affairs is no secret: the member states of the Union, and indeed the less numerous states belonging to the Eurogroup, are disinclined to forego their sovereign prerogatives any further and merge into a single, federal-type state. The identity-making bonds that join them, the "fraternity" necessary to accept democratic decisions at the European level, are far from sufficient.[5] And if we consider the time and conflicts it took even for countries enjoying highly favorable conditions to attain it in the past—here I am thinking above all of the history of the United States, in the eighteenth-century group of states showing marked linguistic, historical and cultural uniformity—it is hardly likely that such an objective can be attained within a foreseeable period in Europe. The "democratic deficit" of the Union is thus doomed to persist, and with it, the continual tensions between the decisions of the single sovereign states, taken democratically, and the rules that the Union seeks to impose. These tensions are generating populistic rebellion, as well as attempts at secession where possible (if the immediate costs are not too heavy), as in the case of a country that belongs to the Union but not to the European monetary system. Brexit has an important lesson to offer in this respect.

And yet, even if the constitution of the true federal state were possible, even if the levels of "fraternity" were strong enough to support a true sovereign state at the European level—this is a pure thought experiment, any such possibility being totally unrealistic today—it is highly questionable whether elimination of the democratic deficit that the Union suffers from would suffice to mitigate the protest behind the populist movements and the widespread impression of misgovernment. Actually, the protest is not against the democratic deficit nor against the deterioration in the input of democracy, but against its results on the output side—against unemployment, precarious employment, distribution of income perceived as increasingly unjust, poorer prospects of social improvement for most of the population and uncontrolled waves of immigration. Nor is there any certainty that the democratic government of the Union would yield satisfactory results for those suffering the negative consequences of the present phase of development. Even with a government responding to a true European Parliament, parties might predominate in supporting a policy of proceeding along the road of neoliberalism and globalization. This is the pattern that has been unfolding in the United States, and it might very well be the case in Europe. Ordo-liberalism, a variant of neoliberalism as it is understood today by the German elites, might well prevail against inevitably more complex and controversial positions favoring radical reform. (A European social model? A new Bretton Woods?—Where are the European political figures advancing realistic proposals on these issues?) They would also be fiercely opposed by the financial elites and all those benefiting from the present situation.

6. Crisis, Then, but Perhaps Not Unsurmountable: For Now

Rereading what I have written so far, I feel the need to make clearer in these closing remarks what marks my analysis out from that of the authors mentioned in the opening lines. Underlying the difference there is, in the first place, a different intellectual attitude, more as a realistic observer than political philosopher, more descriptive than normative, which leads me to appraise (and appreciate) democracy as it is (and as it has been at its best) more than as one might wish it to be in an ideal world. If this approach is coupled with a cultural background as an economist (together with studies in history, political science and international relations, all disciplines favoring a realistic more than normative attitude), I believe that my stress on the output side—the more limited capacity of today's democratic states to guarantee good government for their citizens—can readily be understood.[6]

As for the limitation of representative democracy solely to governments of nation-states where the conditions of "fraternity" suffice for acceptance of sovereign democratic decisions, and the difficulties encountered in extending these conditions on a larger scale, we need only look back over history to observe that this has always been the case, even in the past. And history shows us equally clearly that there have always been limitations to the sovereignty of nation-states, even if we confine our attention to the two centuries that saw forms of representative democracy in some of the more economically developed countries. As globalization and British hegemony advanced between the mid-nineteenth century and World War I, the financial system then prevailing at the international level, the gold standard, was no less binding and restrictive for the sovereignty of the single nation-states than the system in force today. The only exception seems to have been in the boom years with the Bretton Woods system, which created conditions for that extraordinary phase of growth and social inclusion that the developed capitalist countries went through after World War II. But was it really an exception?

Certainly not, at least in terms of the constraints on sovereignty that single countries had to undergo within an international financial and economic regime—even the Bretton Woods system entailed strong constraints. The exception was that these constraints followed an intelligent and long-sighted design, made possible by the extraordinary hegemony the United States found itself exercising after the war, and by the political and economic conceptions then prevailing among the Anglo-Saxon elites. And this has little to do with representative democracy or democratic government in the single states: power politics was in play, agreements and clashes occurred between states and political-ideological viewpoints and the economic convictions embraced by the international elites were Keynesian rather than neoliberal. These exceptional international conditions met with equally favorable economic conditions within the single states: many of them were on the threshold of an extraordinary technological transformation, which would ease transference to the mass Fordist-Taylorist industrialization of Europe and Japan that was already underway in the United States.[7] With hindsight, we can see that neither those internal economic conditions nor the geopolitical and ideological conditions prevailing after the war exist today. The countries that benefited in the boom years are now mature economies, the United States no longer enjoys the sort of hegemony it had in the postwar years and the ideas then prevalent among the leading international figures have been swept away by the neoliberal restoration that occurred at the end of the 1970s and led to the state of globalization in which we find ourselves today.

Today the shortcomings of democracy on the input side—in terms of the quality of democracy in the single nation-states—make themselves felt mainly in the difficulties experienced by the traditional parties faced with populistic-type reactions to the international economic regime now dominant, together with various (and usually more readily addressed) national causes. It is hard to predict future developments with the new patterns of representation already evolving in response to the social, cultural and technological influences mentioned above. However, comparison with the other great period of globalization, between the end of the nineteenth century and World War I, not to mention the period between the two wars, does not, I believe, suggest particularly dramatic outcomes. Dramatic consequences did ensue upon the crisis of democracy at the turn of the twentieth century and after World War I: today's democracy may be "disfigured," but it is not discredited as it was then. And today the populistic forces themselves are not explicitly pursuing demolition of parliamentary democracy but rather a form of parliamentary democracy they judge to be better. Moreover, at the geopolitical and cultural level the situation is more favorable. Despite the difficulties the EU is coming up against, it still constitutes extraordinary evidence of the possibility of building relations between states on foundations decidedly more peaceful, regulated and civil than had ever been the case in the past. This can also be said of the design of international economic and financial relations developed at Bretton Woods, upon which the conditions of well-being and social inclusion of the following 40 years were based. The design has since been erased, but the memory of it remains among all those involved in international relations today as a reminder that an intelligent long-sighted architecture for international economic-financial relations is in fact possible—memory that can prompt attempts at reconstruction on different bases.

Of course, the endemic and inevitable conflict between capitalism and democracy persists, often intensified in the phases of globalization and international expansion of capitalism.[8] Such conflict is inevitable because capitalism is at the same time a cause of crisis of democracy and a necessary condition for the very existence of representative liberal governments, as I have argued in various writings.[9] The conflict can, however, be moderated and regulated at both the level of the single democratic states and of the international relations between states.

Am I being too optimistic and idealistic? I do not think so. My viewpoint is based on the conviction that there is still room for reform at the level of the single national democracies, the EU and the world economic-financial and political system, and that it is useless turning to desperate remedies before desperate ills strike. But it is also based on the conviction that desperate ills may indeed strike and that—not yet, but in a not-too-distant future—democracy may be facing such trials as to threaten its very survival. Here I am thinking above all of the ecological disasters, demographic explosion and conflict over water and energy resources that threaten our planet.[10] Nevertheless, as long as Behemoth and Leviathan, the monsters of anarchy and absolute authority, can be kept at bay, I believe that democratic reformism is the best way to fight them off. This is the lesson I have learned from my master, Paolo Sylos Labini, and from his best pupil, Alessandro Roncaglia.[11]

Notes

1 As far as I know, nobody has written on this issue with greater elegance, passion and learning than John Dunn (2005). As will be seen below, however, I dissent from his radical conclusions.

2 This chapter contains a number of assertions for which the evidence may be lacking. It is based on my book *Capitalismo, mercato e democrazia* (2009a), where clarification and documentation can be found. This general reference obviates the need for numerous notes.

3 A vein of nostalgia that also runs through the fine posthumous volume by Peter Mair (2013).

4 Before the book came out, a homonymous article had made a great stir in *The National Interest* (Fukuyama 1989).

5 The best normative treatment of how to develop sufficient levels of "fraternity" is to be found in Ferrera (2015, chapter 4 and "Conclusion").

6 Even though they mostly refer to the American case, I found the insights of Achen and Bartels (2016) very useful.

7 Fuller analysis of these extraordinary conditions can be found in my essay in *Stato e Mercato* (Salvati, 2015).

8 Today it arises because of the competition from low-wage workers in less developed countries. As recent political events have clearly shown, it has become increasingly difficult for the less qualified workers of the advanced countries to maintain the standard of living they were used to. But possibly deeper trends are unfolding that risk leading us into lasting stagnation. This is the thesis of a book by Gordon (2016), which is causing quite a stir. More in general, I am indebted to Karl Polanyi (1944) for the work in his great book, and it should be evident from what I have been writing.

9 This is one of the basic theses of my book mentioned at the beginning of this essay (Salvati, 2009a). It is worth recalling for two reasons. First, there is the apparent paradox of capitalism as both obstacle to and necessary condition for representative democracy. Secondly, it has provoked considerable misgivings, especially for the Left, largely due to an unrealistic distinction between capitalism and a market economy. In the more recent literature, we

find representation of the conflict between capitalism and democracy less susceptible to the "reformist" reconciliation, which I still hold to be possible (see, for example, Streeck, 2013; Merkel, 2014; Crouch, 2016).

10 See my afterword (Salvati, 2009b, 325–26).

11 Numerous references might be cited, but for a cogent overview, see the anthology edited by Alessandro Roncaglia (2002).

References

Achen, C. H., and L. M. Bartels. 2016. *Democracy for Realists: Why Elections Do Not Produces Responsive Government*. Princeton, NJ: Princeton University Press.

Biasco, S. 2016. *Regole, Stato, uguaglianza: La posta in gioco nella cultura della sinistra e nel nuovo capitalismo*. Roma: Luiss University Press.

Crouch, C. 2003. *Postdemocrazia*. Roma-Bari: Laterza. (English edition: *Post-Democracy*. Cambridge: Polity Press, 2004.)

———. 2016. "Capitalism, Inequality and Democracy," *Stato e Mercato* 2: 159–82.

Dunn, J. 2005. *Setting the People Free: The Story of Democracy*. London: Atlantic Books.

Ferrera, M. 2015. *Rotta di collisione: Euro contro welfare?* Roma–Bari: Laterza.

Fukuyama, F. 1989. "The End of History?" *The National Interest* 16, Summer: 3–18.

———. 1992. *The End of History and the Last Man*. New York: Free Press.

Gordon, R. J. 2016. *The Rise and Fall of American Growth: The US Standards of Living since the Civil War*. Princeton, NJ: Princeton University Press.

Katz, R. S., and P. Mair. 1995. "Changing Models of Party Organization and Party Democracy: The Emergence of the Cartel Party," *Party Politics* 1, no. 1: 5–28.

Mair, P. 2013. *Ruling the Void: The Hollowing of Western Democracy*. London and New York: Verso Books.

Manin, B. 1995. *Principes du gouvernement représentatif*. Paris: Calmann-Lévy. (English translation: *The Principles of Representative Government*. Cambridge: Cambridge University Press, 1997.)

Mastropaolo, A. 2011. *La democrazia è una causa persa? Paradossi di un'invenzione imperfetta*. Torino: Bollati-Boringhieri.

Merkel, W. 2014. "Is Capitalism Compatible with Democracy?" *Zeitschrift für Vergleichende Politikwissenschaft* 8, no. 2: 109–28.

Michels, R. 1911. *Zur Soziologie des Parteiwesens in der modernen Demokratie: Untersuchungen über die oligarchischen Tendenzen des Gruppenlebens*. Leipzig: Werner Klinkhardt. (English translation: *Political Parties: A Sociological Study of the Oligarchical Tendencies of Modern Democracy*. New York: Hearst's International Library Co., 1915.)

Polanyi, K. 1944. *The Great Transformation*. New York: Farrar & Rinehart.

Roncaglia, A., ed. 2002. *Per la ripresa del riformismo*. Milano: Nuova Iniziativa Editoriale.

Salvati, M. 2009a. *Capitalismo, mercato e democrazia*. Bologna: Il Mulino.

———. 2009b. "Qualche nube all'orizzonte." In *Progetto 89: Tre saggi su libertà, eguaglianza, fraternità*, edited by A. Martinelli, M. Salvati and S. Veca, 317–28 (New edition). Milano: Il Saggiatore.

———. 2015. "Max Weber: Capitalismo, liberalismo, democrazia," *Stato e Mercato* 2: 229–61.

Schumpeter, J. A. 1943. *Capitalism, Socialism and Democracy*. London: Allen & Unwin.

Streeck, W. 2013. *Gekaufte Zeit: Die vertagte Krise des demokratischen Kapitalismus*. Berlin: Suhrkamp. (English translation: *Buying Time: The Delayed Crisis of Democratic Capitalism*. London and New York: Verso Books, 2014.)

Urbinati, N. 2014. *Democrazia sfigurata: il popolo fra opinione e verità*. Milano: Università Bocconi Editore.

Wolin, S. S. 2008. *Democracy Incorporated: Managed Democracy and the Specter of Inverted Totalitarianism*. Princeton, NJ: Princeton University Press.

Chapter Five

THE DEMOCRACY OF IDEAS: J. S. MILL, LIBERALISM AND THE ECONOMIC DEBATE

Marcella Corsi and Carlo D'Ippoliti

What I stated was, that the Conservative party was, by the law of its constitution, necessarily the stupidest party. Now, I do not retract this assertion, but I did not mean that Conservatives are generally stupid; I meant, that stupid persons are generally Conservative.[1]

1. Introduction

The main subject of this chapter is an eminent economist, John Stuart Mill (JSM), whom we dare say, our former supervisor, colleague and dear friend Alessandro Roncaglia, perhaps too hastily, somewhat overlooked throughout his long and successful career as an economist and historian of economic thought.

In his magnum opus, *The Wealth of Ideas*, Roncaglia (2005a) approvingly recalls JSM's analysis of individual behavior, from which our present analysis departs, but almost neglects *On Liberty* (JSM, 1859, henceforth OL), on which we focus here. The need to limit himself to core economic themes, and the necessity to summarize an impressive number of sources and authors in a single book, may explain this choice. However, as Roncaglia (2008, 27; our translation) stresses, "the conception of economics as a social science cannot be locked in the restrictive boundaries of disciplinary specialization," and we argue that JSM's not purely economic works still are a crucial foundation of modern liberal socialism and the associated economic policy stance—to which Roncaglia contributed especially in the Italian context.

As we attempt to show, JSM's treatment of the subject has many commonalities with Roncaglia's—the primacy of the moral dimension of social issues; the identification of the root (and main method) of democracy in the honest (as we will denote, "ethical") debate rather than in mere voting; a nuanced view of the individual and her agency; a political bet on education at 360 degrees (including the "training" of responsible citizens); and a rejection of the intellectual distortions of biased, conservative liberalism, too often incorrectly superimposed with classical liberalism.

Of course, JSM's analyses require crucial updating to consider an enormously changed social context. This, we hope, will occupy some of our and Roncaglia's time in the next few years.

2. The Moral Foundations of Liberalism

In the eighteenth century, it was commonplace to consider political economy a moral science, implying by moral not some *moralistic* sense of the word but the need to take reasonable, reasoned indeed, choices aimed at the improvement of mankind and society. From this perspective, JSM's approach departs from an Aristotelian notion of human flourishing, which will later be adopted by another economist that Roncaglia has approvingly cited, Amartya Sen (1999).

As is well known, JSM was a disciple of his own father and Jeremy Bentham, who gave an impetus to a consequentialist approach in ethics and legislation, whereby human actions are generally not considered as inherently good or bad, but they become so according to their consequences. At a first glance, this distinction seems to merely shift the judgment from the goodness of an action to that of its consequences, that is, it still requires an external definition of goodness. However, JSM underlines its revolutionary character for it makes morality a subject of rational debate and thus of democracy, whereas "an opinion on a point of conduct, not supported by reasons, can only count as one person's preference" (OL, 221), and as we discuss below, the fact that a preference may happen to be shared by many people, does not per se make it preferable.

As is well known, to Bentham the rational measure of goodness of any action's consequences is the greatest happiness of the greatest number of people. In his mature works, JSM conditionally approves of this definition, provided *happiness* is defined in a long-term, extensive sense of personal improvement: "I regard utility as the ultimate appeal on all ethical questions; but it must be utility in the largest sense, grounded on the permanent interests of man as a progressive being" (ibid., 224). In his posthumously published *Autobiography*, he describes the shift in his views with respect to the education Bentham and his father had given him:

> I never, indeed, wavered in the conviction that happiness is the test of all rules of conduct, and the end of life. But I now thought that this end was only to be attained by not making it the direct end. Those only are happy (I thought) who have their minds fixed on some object other than their own happiness; on the happiness of others, on the improvement of mankind, even on some art or pursuit, followed not as a means, but as itself an ideal end. Aiming thus at something else, they find happiness by the way. (JSM, 1873, 145)

This description of happiness informs JSM's (1861, 212) famous moral statement that it is better to be Socrates dissatisfied than a satisfied fool—not because of a religious or moral imperative to suffer, but precisely because mental and moral cultivation make us *happier*, provided happiness is properly distinguished from the immediate satisfaction of physical pleasures ("and if the fool isn't convinced, it is because he only knows half of the argument").

JSM not only modified Bentham's definition of the notion of "pleasures and pains" but also his approach on how to move from an individual to a social happiness (which only merits the name "utility"). While with the first generation of utilitarians social welfare, that is utility, was the mere sum of individuals' (un)happiness,[2] JSM was aware of how simplistic and biased this approach is. Our perception of happiness changes with our social interactions and modifications of the institutional context, which is what JSM calls our "social education," as well as with the development of habits and propensities, or our "self-education" (D'Ippoliti, 2011). Thus, the aim of public policy should be to create the conditions for elevated happiness, for human flourishing, of a vast majority of, if not all, people.

Since these considerations make it much more difficult to estimate the goodness of a specific individual action or public policy in a given context, JSM understood he had radically changed the original utilitarian approach, developing a "rule utilitarianism" whereby moral assessment usually applies not to a single act but to institutions and general rules of conduct—along Kantian lines—on the act as if it were to be applied as a general rule.

With his aim of generalized personal improvement, we still can consider JSM's approach as founded on a nuanced notion of political individualism. As he writes in *On Liberty*, "individuality is the same thing with development, and [...] it is only the cultivation of individuality which produces, or can produce, well-developed human beings" (OL, 267). Though, as common practice at the time, JSM was usually sparing of citations, it is evident that this approach is informed by, or at least recalls that of one of Roncaglia's favorite economists, Adam Smith. In some passages JSM ("without quoting Smith," Roncaglia, 2005a, 125) notices that each person "is the most interested person in his own well-being [...]; with respect to his own feelings and circumstances, the most ordinary man or woman has means of knowledge immeasurably surpassing those that can be possessed by any one else" (OL, 277).

However, differences between JSM's and Smith's approach abound. Thinking of the British environment of his time, JSM is very critical of the idea that human conduct is generally informed by feelings of sympathy. Comparing them to the "general habit" of the French, JSM laments "the way in which, among the ordinary English, the absence of interest in things of an unselfish kind, [...] causes both their feelings and their intellectual faculties to remain undeveloped" (1873, 61).

Interestingly, Schmoller (1900), the leader of the German Historical School, raised the same criticism against all British classical political economists, of not considering how generalized selfishness could be a peculiar feature of English society (D'Ippoliti, 2011). We doubt whether the other European populations (of that time or of our time) should be regarded as generally altruistic and other-regarding, but certainly the Anglo-Saxon influence on the economists of the rest of the world has by now made (especially mainstream) economists and their students much closer to the wicked and narrowly egotistic kind of person than Schmoller and Smith had in mind.

Truly, later JSM adds that "[i]n most other countries the paramount importance of the sympathies as a constituent of individual happiness is an axiom" (1873, 157), but in general he is much more willing to emphasize the wide diversity of people's motives and interests, and "all the multifarious causes which influence their wishes in regard to the conduct of others, [... s]ometimes their reason—at other times their prejudices or superstitions: often their social affections, not seldom their antisocial ones, [...] but most commonly [...] their legitimate or illegitimate self-interest" (OL, 221).

It hardly needs recalling here that JSM is very far from maintaining that people follow any sort of rational, be it self- or other-regarding, behavior: "I do not mean that they choose what is customary, in preference to what suits their own inclination. It does not occur to them to have any inclination, except for what is customary" (ibid., 265).[3] Thus, not only is sympathy just one among many motives of behavior, but it is not likely to be a major one. In contrast, Smith's liberalism and specifically his trust in the viability of free competition certainly impinges on his notion of sympathy as a ruler of moral conduct (set forth in his *Theory of Moral Sentiments*: Smith 1759), even though one should always recount how biased and far from Smith's view is the mainstream economic notion of an "invisible hand" (see, e.g., Roncaglia, 2005b).

The differences between Smith and JSM are not limited to the roots of their argument for liberalism but concern their overall policy stance too. In the *Wealth of Nations*, Smith proposes several forms of what today would be called public "intervention" in the economy, but his liberalism stopped short of the paternalistic aspects, for example, of JSM's call for an "education of the feelings" (1873, 115). As much as he draws a hierarchy between physical and mental pleasures, JSM deems self-interest neatly inferior to other-regarding behavior and argues that altruism and sympathy should be taught and cultivated (ibid., 277).

With respect to Smith and classical liberalism, Roncaglia (2005a, 121–26; 2005b) draws a much-needed distinction between selfishness and self-interest, clarifying that the latter is not necessarily in opposition to, and is quite often conjoint with public interest. However, JSM is obviously skeptical about the capacity even of this "enlightened self-interest" to bring about enough progressive social development. He specifically attributes this Smithian notion to his father, highlighting how this is one of the few things on which he later developed an autonomous, almost contrary, thinking:

> While fully recognizing the superior excellence of unselfish benevolence and love of justice, we [first-generation utilitarians] did not expect the regeneration of mankind from any direct action on those sentiments, but from the effect of educated intellect, enlightening the selfish feelings. Although this last is prodigiously important as a means of improvement in the hands of those who are themselves impelled by nobler principles of action, I do not believe that any one of the survivors of the Benthamites or Utilitarians of that day, now relies mainly upon it for the general amendment of human conduct. (JSM, 1873, 113–15)

Rather, in his view a social education of the feelings is necessary in order to allow society to attain the maximum utility it can achieve. Two major elements of this social education are democratic public debate and education in the strict sense, that is, a system of schooling as well as of higher education and research. Both topics deserve closer inspection both because *On Liberty* devotes the brunt of the argument to them, and because they play a crucial role in Roncaglia's thought as well.

3. A New Stage of Tyranny

From the multidimensionality of human motives and the dynamic feedback between behavior, habits and desires, JSM drew the necessity to modify Bentham's system into a rule utilitarianism. However, this complexity in the interaction between society and the individual implies even stronger consequences, that is, the recognition that rules themselves cannot be fixed and general but must evolve as society develops. Thus, JSM distances himself not only from specific aspects of his father's political philosophy (e.g., concerning women's right to suffrage) but also from his method in general.[4] He set forth to lay down not a set of model institutions but "principles from which the institutions suitable to any given circumstances might be deduced" (JSM, 1873, 169).

This relativism should more properly be recognized as historicism. JSM refers to French and German thinkers to highlight what he learned, partly in opposition to Bentham's and James Mill's deductive method:

> that the human mind has a certain order of possible progress in which some things must pre-
> cede others, an order which governments and public instructors can modify to some, but not
> to an unlimited extent; that all questions of political institutions are relative, not absolute, and
> that different stages of human progress not only *will* have, but *ought* to have, different institu-
> tions; that government is always either in the hands, or passing into the hands, of whatever
> is the strongest power in society, and that what this power is, does not depend on institutions,
> but institutions on it; that any general theory or philosophy of politics supposes a previous
> theory of human progress, and that this is the same thing with a philosophy of history. (Ibid.,
> 169; emphasis in original)

He provides a sketch of such a philosophy of history at the beginning of OL, where he describes a stage theory of "Civil, or Social Liberty." In many ways, this was also the way Smith decided to tackle the issue, central in his thought, of value in exchange and the division of labor.

According to JSM, in a first, rude stage of society, the imperatives of survival and security made it reasonable for the vast majority of society, unable to defend itself and its interests, to be subject to the strongest of its members, it being preferable to be exploited than predated. Evidently, from this stage dates the deep-rooted notion, taken in high consideration by contemporary populist movements, that the interests of the governed are different from, and often in opposition to, the interests of the governors. As civilization progressed, a struggle between liberty and authority ensued, in which the main aim of the liberal factions was to obtain limitations to the power of those who have authority—that is, constitutional checks. Then, in a third stage, this struggle evolved into one for voice and participation in the administration of common affairs, that is, democracy.

The evolution from tyranny to democracy is indisputably a positive development: not in itself (which would be a deontological ethical stance) but for the greater possibilities of human flourishing under democracy. JSM

> looked upon the choice of political institutions as a moral and educational question more
> than one of material interests. [… And he] thought the predominance of the aristocratic clas-
> ses, the noble and the rich, in the English Constitution, an evil worth any struggle to get rid
> of; not on account of taxes, or any such comparatively small inconvenience, but as the great
> demoralizing agency in the country. (JSM, 1873, 177)

However, democratization too has its drawbacks, against which it is necessary to establish countermeasures. As parliaments and governments grow to represent the will of the masses, according to JSM people in general would no longer feel them-selves different from and in opposition to the governing bodies. Thus, by his time (the fourth stage of development), democracies were engaged in, or at risk of, a reduction of the constitutional limits that were created in the previous stage, on account of the delusion that "[t]he nation did not need to be protected against its own will" (OL, 218).

Old-style liberals, thus, who understand liberty as protection from government inter-ference (which was very reasonable in Smith's time), were by JSM's time fighting the previous war. And neoliberals today, when we are probably in even a further stage of this dialectic development of liberty and authority, resort to such old-fashioned arguments that one wonders whether their plea for liberty in the oldest, pre-Smithian sense, is not in fact just a facade.

In a democracy, protection against the "tyranny of the magistrate" is not enough and is not even a priority, in the face of the looming threats of despotism. Indeed, the retrenchment of political or even constitutional checks in the name of efficiency (or today we would say "stability") paves the way to a further stage of the history of liberty, in which "the 'self-government' spoken of is not the government of each by himself, but of each by all the rest" (ibid., 219).

While being generally thrifty of citations, on this account JSM refers to an author who will later be amply lauded by Paolo Sylos Labini (whose relationship with Roncaglia needs no recounting here): Alexis de Tocqueville. At that point, JMS had already written two book reviews of Tocqueville's (1835) *De la Démocratie en Amérique*, and one could say the whole *On Liberty* is a reflection on Tocqueville's notion of the tyranny of the majority. In this fifth stage, the struggle between liberty and authority becomes one between the rights of minorities and the power of the majority.

However, consistent with his approach that institutions matter as a moral and edu-cational question, more than a material one, there is a specific aspect of the tyranny of the majority that JSM fears the most, "the tyranny of the prevailing opinion and feeling" (OL, 220). He repeatedly stresses that the free sway of society on aspects of an individ-ual's life that do not concern anyone else but the individual herself, consistently narrow the scope of individuality: "society has now fairly got the better of individuality" (ibid., 264), and that "at present individuals are lost in the crowd" (ibid., 268). This aspect of the tyranny of the majority is singled out by JSM in light of his theory of human flourishing as individual development, recalled above, from which descends the idea that in a demo-cratic society "the despotism of custom is everywhere the standing hindrance to human advancement" (ibid., 272).[5]

JSM traces back the tyranny of public opinion to some major long-term forces work-ing toward the leveling out of individual differences: the reduction in class differences of social position, the extension of education, improvements in the means of communica-tion, the increase in commerce and manufactures, and the ascendancy of the rule of public opinion in the political institutions of the state. In contrast, with a position that will be discussed in depth by Albert O. Hirschman (1977), JSM believes that "Europe is, in my judgment, wholly indebted to [... its previous] plurality of paths for its progressive and many-sided development" (OL, 274). Thus, he refers to an English translation of

Wilhelm von Humboldt (1851) to point out two measures necessary to allow people to remain "unlike one another; namely, freedom and variety of situations" (OL, 274). Jointly, freedom and variety allow us both to "experiment" lifestyles—about which JSM (1869) will reiterate, especially with respect to family arrangements and gender equality—and most of all to experiment pursuits and opinions, which are a necessary precondition for any change in practices.

4. Experimenting Diversity

According to JSM, a general trend of social development is the tendency to strengthen society and to diminish the power of the individual. This encroachment of individuality is supported "by some of the best and by some of the worst feelings incident in human nature" (OL, 227). We could say, some are instances of "disinterested" and some of "interested" intolerance.

Among the former, JSM mentions people's innate psychological tendency to seek agreement with each other. For example, "the religious belief [is] a case instructive in many ways [...]. So natural to mankind is intolerance in whatever they really care about, that [... w]herever the sentiment of the majority is still genuine and intense, it is found to have abated little of its claim to be obeyed" (ibid., 222).

Among the latter factors, JSM hints at social dynamics that will be taken up and dissected by another author to whom, incidentally, Roncaglia has not devoted many pages: Thorstein Veblen (1899). JSM notes that a "grand determining principle" of man's conduct is their understanding of the "supposed preferences or aversions of their temporal masters, or of their gods" (OL, 221). As a consequence, "[w]herever there is an ascendant class, a large portion of the morality of the country emanates from its class interests, and its feelings of class superiority" (ibid.).

Against these tendencies, JSM articulates a rational answer in favor of pluralism. Coherently with his rule utilitarianism, he does not appeal to notions of "abstract right, as a thing independent of utility" (ibid., 224). Rather, his argument is that "[m]ankind are greater gainers by suffering each other to live as seems good to themselves, than by compelling each to live as seems good to the rest" (ibid., 226). This is shown by the argument in favor of the liberty of thought and discussion (OL, chapter 2), from which the other liberties descend.

According to JSM, the peculiar evil of silencing the expression of an opinion is that it is robbing the entire human race: "those who dissent from the opinion, still more than those who hold it" (ibid., 229). Indeed, the peculiarity of JSM's defense of free public discussion is that, by giving up the argument based on the absolute right of minorities, he has to show that freedom of discussion not only benefits those who hold a minority view but also is for the greatest advantage of the greatest number of people—that is, of those who hold the mainstream view too. Indeed, according to JSM, minorities are in a relatively better position in a debate: "[t]here are many reasons, doubtless, why doctrines which are the badge of a sect retain more of their vitality than those common to all [...]; but one reason certainly is, that the peculiar doctrines are more questioned, and have to be oftener defended" (OL, 249).

As he summarizes at the end of chapter 2, the argument is divided into four steps:

1. Any silenced opinion may be true.
2. Even if an error, the silenced opinion may contain "a portion of truth."
3. Even if, instead, the received opinion were the whole truth, unless it is contestable and actually contested, those who believe it will not fully understand it, and will not grasp the grounds on which it is based, and its significance.
4. All uncontested ideas become sterile and die out, preventing the development of their very doctrine.

To express the injustice of silencing other opinions, JSM recalls the Smithian image of "judges without hearing the other side" (ibid., 233). However, his argument (especially points 1. and 2. above) directly descend from his theory of logic and understanding (as laid out in his *System of Logic*: JSM, 1843). He departs from the obvious observation that all silencing of discussion is an assumption of infallibility (OL, 229). However, "it is not the feeling sure of a doctrine (be it what it may) which I call an assumption of infallibility. It is the undertaking to decide that question *for others*" (ibid., 234; emphasis in original).[6] He does not focus on experts or single "great thinkers", who had always been found even "in a general atmosphere of mental slavery" (ibid., 243). Rather, freedom of thinking is indispensable for the "average human beings" in order to attain the highest mental stature which they are capable of.

With words that foreshadow aspects of Karl Popper's approach, JSM stresses the need for any theory to be "contendible," to use an economic term, if it is to be rationally— even though provisionally—relied upon:

> Complete liberty of contradicting and disproving our opinion, is the very condition which justifies us in assuming its truth for purposes of action; on no other terms can a being with human faculties have any rational assurance of being right [...]. The whole strength and value, then, of human judgment, depending on the one property, that it can be set right when it is wrong, reliance can be placed on it only when the means of setting it right are kept constantly at hand. [...] The beliefs which we have most warrant for, have no safeguard to rest on, but a standing invitation to the whole world to prove them unfounded. [...] This is the amount of certainty attainable by a fallible being, and this the sole way of attaining it. (Ibid., 231–32)

It is noteworthy that JSM does not believe inference is a sufficient ground to bring an individual closer to the truth. He relies on an argument that more recently would be built on by the postmodern movement, especially in the economics field by McCloskey (1985):

> A quality of the human mind, the source of everything respectable in man either as an intellectual or as a moral being [... is] that his errors are corrigible. He is capable of rectifying his mistakes, by discussion and experience. Not by experience alone. There must be discussion, to show how experience is to be interpreted. [...] Very few facts are able to tell their own story, without comments to bring out their meaning. (OL, 231)

According to JSM, the only way in which we can make some approach to knowing a subject, is by hearing what can be said about it by persons of every variety of opinion and by studying "all modes in which it can be looked at by every character of mind" (ibid., 232). This argument is very close to that put forward, with respect to the economic debate, in chapter 1 of Roncaglia (2005a). Thus, it seems fit to analyze in greater depth the specific scope of liberty of scientific discussion in JSM's approach.

5. Open Debate as Scientific Morality

In the twin essays on "Coleridge" and "Bentham," JSM (1838, 1840) stresses his conviction that on every subject on which difference of opinion is possible, the truth usually depends on a balance to be struck between two sets of conflicting reasons. However, he notes that it is in the very nature of conversation in the social sciences to be cast in terms of a debate:

> Even in natural philosophy, there is always some other explanation possible of the same facts […]. But when we turn to subjects infinitely more complicated, to morals, religion, politics, social relations, and the business of life, three-fourths of the arguments for every disputed opinion consist in dispelling the appearances which favour some opinion different from it. (OL, 244)

Thus, he holds in great esteem the methods of Socratic dialectics, or school disputations in the Middle Ages (another topic that features prominently in Roncaglia, 2005a).

He deems discussion so essential to a real understanding of moral and human subjects that if one had no opponents, it would be "indispensable to imagine them, and supply them with the strongest arguments which the most skillful devil's advocate can conjure up" (OL, 245).[7]

Thus, a fair, rational and even moral approach to science is necessary. Open and free debate is a chief ingredient for it, but it also relies on the good faith of the debaters. While not neglecting his numerous scientific contributions, Roncaglia has always remembered with great emphasis the strong morality of his master and friend, Sylos Labini (see, for example, Roncaglia, 2006, 2008, 2016; Roncaglia and Corsi, 2007). Thus, we think it would be significant to report here JSM's conclusions on the topic:

> condemning every one, on whichever side of the argument he places himself, in whose mode of advocacy either want of candour, or malignity, bigotry, or intolerance of feeling manifest themselves; but not inferring these vices from the side which a person takes, though it be the contrary side of the question to our own: and giving merited honour to every one, whatever opinion he may hold, who has calmness to see and honesty to state what his opponents and their opinions really are, exaggerating nothing to their discredit, keeping nothing back which tells, or can be supposed to tell, in their favour. This is the real morality of public discussion. (OL, 259)

It is straightforward to see how far from this standard of morality is the notion of the "marketplace of ideas." In fact, in OL, JSM discusses a similarly "evolutionist" theory, of the survival of the "fittest" ideas. He considers the radical argument of those who maintain that truth may justifiably be persecuted, because in the long run persecution cannot possibly have the best of it. (With reference to our own recent work, we can think of those who do not today see the current spread of biased research evaluation procedures as a great devil.) In principle, they cannot be charged with being intentionally hostile to the reception of new truths, though "we cannot commend the[ir] generosity" (ibid., 237). However, according to JSM, this view of the subject is in fact "mostly confined to the sort of persons who think that new truths may have been desirable once, but that we had enough of them now" (ibid.). This is because "the dictum that truth always triumphs over persecution, is one of those pleasant falsehoods. [...] Persecution has always succeeded, save where the heretics were too strong a party to be effectually persecuted. [...] It is a piece of idle sentimentality that truth, merely as truth, has any inherent power denied to error" (ibid., 238).

JSM talks, in general, of any sort of heretical ideas, including in matters of religion. Thus, he recognizes that the above argument is extreme, as capital and other penal punishments for heretics were by his time almost extinct. However, he notices that even if harsher punishments were still in place, "the chief mischief of the legal penalties is that they [would] strengthen the social stigma. It is the stigma which is really effective" (ibid., 241).

Mere social intolerance kills no one and does not completely root out any opinion, but induces men to disguise their opinions and/or to abstain from active efforts for their diffusion. At best, it creates "a convenient plan for having peace in the intellectual world," preserving a sphere of intellectual debate in which almost any opinion survives, though separate from the sphere of public debate in general, in which prevailing opinions remain undisturbed. "But the price paid for this sort of intellectual pacification, is the sacrifice of the entire moral courage of the human mind" (ibid., 241–42).

In accordance with the need to highlight the losses for the majority as well as the minority, JSM asks who can compute what the world loses in the multitude of promising intellects combined with timid characters (ibid., 242). He adds, even if the heretical view were completely wrong, since it does not have to stand a proper discussion, it is prevented from spreading too much, but it will never totally disappear either.

But social stigma has much more serious consequences, which seem to us reminiscent of the current predicament of many contemporary schools at the margins (or the frontiers) of the economic mainstream:

a state of things in which a large portion of the most active and inquiring intellects find it advisable to keep the general principles and grounds of their convictions within their own breasts, and attempt, in what they address to the public, to fit as much as they can of their own conclusions to premises which they have internally renounced, cannot send forth the open, fearless characters, and logical, consistent intellects who once adorned the thinking world. [...] Those who avoid this alternative, do so by narrowing their thoughts and interest to things which can be spoken of without venturing within the region of principles, that is, to small practical matters. (Ibid., 242)

We do not think that the epidemic of "economic" papers in top journals, dealing with the football World Cup, child obesity or dating partner choice (all relevant, though not really economic topics), deserves further comment.

6. The Economic Debate

It is customary to associate British classical political economists with free-trade policies and a "small government" approach. In many writings, Roncaglia has shown how
biased and misleading this characterization is, for example, with respect to Adam Smith's
thought. In JSM's case, too, it is more correct to talk about liberal socialism—a position
personally shared in broad terms by Roncaglia—than unqualified liberalism, in a traditional sense. In his *Autobiography*, JSM describes his gradual process of adding qualifications and distancing himself from his father's thought,[8] and attributes a significant shift
in his political views to his slowly evolving relationship with Harriet Taylor.[9] He describes
his, or rather their, ideals toward the end of his life as follows:

> The social problem of the future we considered to be, how to unite the greatest individual
> liberty of action with an equal ownership of all in the raw material of the globe and an equal
> participation of all in the benefits of combined labour. [...] Both these classes [workers and
> employers] must learn by practice to labour and combine for generous, or at all events for
> public and social purposes, and not, as hitherto, solely for narrowly interested ones. But the
> capacity for this has always existed in mankind, and is not, nor is ever likely to be, extinct.
> Education, habit, and the cultivation of the sentiments will make a common man dig or
> weave for his country, as readily as fight for his country. (JSM, 1873, 239)

JSM refused to embrace or support several socialist proposals, on account of their foreseeing strong social control over the individual, or "social machinery" that JSM considered inefficacious or impractical. However, he favored the spread of socialist propaganda
because the proclamation of such ideals of human society could prompt more efforts to
improve society and bring it closer to the ideal (JSM, 1873, 175).

In OL, he is very explicit in ruling out that liberty in the economic field is on a par
with the sort of "capital L" liberty—civil, political, of thought, of discussion, of experimental lifestyles—he defends in the essay. Concerning the former, he does advocate a
general competitive system, but not on the high moral ground on which he had argued
for the latter. In the economic domain, any restraint on individuals' liberty always affects
that part of their conduct that, if need be, society is perfectly competent to restrain.
Legitimacy arises because individual action in the economic domain produces effects on
other people and on society in general: "trade is a social act" (OL, 293). Thus, restraints
to free competition "are wrong solely because they do not really produce the results
which it is desired to produce by them" (ibid.).

For example, concerning taxation, JSM considers the case of indirect taxation, stating
that "every increase of cost [of a commodity] is a prohibition, to those whose means do
not come up to the augmented price; and to those who do, it is a penalty laid on them for
gratifying a particular taste" (ibid., 298). However, he immediately adds,

> but it must remembered that taxation for fiscal purposes is absolutely inevitable; that in most
> countries it is necessary that a considerable part of that taxation should be indirect; that the
> State, therefore, cannot help imposing penalties, which to some persons may be prohibitory,
> on the use of some articles of consumption. It is hence the duty of the State to consider, in the
> imposition of taxes, what commodities the consumers can best spare. (Ibid.)

Thus, he lists three cases in which objections to "government interference" are reasonable and the liberal stance should be upheld (ibid., 305). First, the obvious case, is when the private sector can operate a certain activity better than the government. In the second case, though government action may be more efficient or effective, it is nonetheless desirable that a certain activity be delegated to the citizens, "as a means of their own mental education" (ibid.). Again,

> these are not questions of liberty [...] they are questions of development. [...] These things [are] parts of national education; as being, in truth, the peculiar training of a citizen, the practical part of the political education of a free people, taking them out of the narrow circle of personal and family selfishness, and accustoming them to the comprehension of joint interests, the management of joint concerns. (Ibid.)

Limitations to government action in the private sphere of the economy, or even in the administration of certain public businesses, are a form of *social education*, as Tocqueville had already suggested in the case of the jury system in the United States, which in JSM's view made Americans generally more aware of public concerns through their involvement in the administration of justice. Once again, the centrality of one's life experience in shaping one's personal development (and thus motives, passions and interests) emerges as a prime consideration for JSM: "[t]he worth of a State, in the long run, is the worth of the individuals composing it; and a State which postpones the interests of *their* mental expansion and elevation, to a little more of administrative skill [...] will find that with small men no great thing can really be accomplished" (ibid., 310; emphasis in original).[10]

Finally, the third case for limiting government power in JSM's view is the need to prevent the creation of an all-encompassing public administration, which poses a greater threat to social development the more it is efficient and it attracts the ablest individuals. "Under this *régime*, not only is the outside public ill-qualified, for want of practical experience, to criticize or check the mode of operation of the bureaucracy, but [...] no reform can be effected which is contrary to the interest of the bureaucracy" (ibid., 306–7; emphasis in original). JSM cites the Chinese example of how a perfect administrative machine may reduce citizens' propensity for self-help, and how bureaucracy degenerates into "pedantocracy."[11] Against this risk, he does not propose the administration of public affairs by private, for-profit companies, but rather the extension of federalism and decentralization, creating a sort of geographical pluralism and experimentation within the nation, and even competition among local administrations. "What the State can usefully do, is to make itself a central depository, and active circulator and diffuser, of the experience resulting from many trials" (ibid., 306).

In conclusion, JSM's liberalism is clearly alien to modern reinterpretations of neo-liberalism. He himself explains that acquaintance with French (socialist) literature, especially the St. Simonians, significantly influenced his thinking (JSM, 1873, 175). Indeed, in several of JSM's writings we find indications of one possible source of the bias in contemporary mainstream economics, namely its strong Anglo-Saxon roots:

> In England, from the peculiar circumstances of our political history, [...] there is considerable jealousy of direct interference, by the legislative or the executive power, with private conduct;

not so much from any just regard for the independence of the individual, as from the still subsisting habit of looking on the government as representing an opposite interest to the public. [... T]here is a considerable amount of feeling ready to be called forth against any attempt of the law to control individuals in things in which they have not hitherto been accustomed to be controlled by it; and this with very little discrimination as to whether the matter is, or is not, within the legitimate sphere of legal control. (OL, 222–23)

7. Conclusions

To conclude, we highlight a final connection between JSM and Adam Smith, this time in the latter's concept of the "vanity of the philosopher." This is the idea that we are all born equal and that differences between people mostly arise from their education, upbringing and life experiences—and that if looking at a less noble workingman the philosopher does not realize this intuition, it must be due to his vanity.

In his *Autobiography*, JSM defines Benthamism not as a school but rather as the approach of a group of people, mostly surrounding his father, who shared a combination of Bentham's point of view with that of classical political economy. He added, concerning politics, an almost unbounded confidence in the efficacy of representative government and complete freedom of discussion, and in psychology, their "fundamental doctrine was the formation of all human character by circumstances, through the universal Principle of Association, and the consequent unlimited possibility of improving the moral and intellectual condition of mankind by education. Of all [their] doctrines none was more important than this, or needs more to be insisted on" (JSM, 1873, 107–11).

Perhaps not by chance Smith, too, when recognizing the drawbacks of an extended division of labor, identified education as a main corrective. The similarities between the two thinkers are not limited to the political centrality they attribute to education: they extend to how education should be organized. It is here, we would argue, that their treatment diverges from our and Roncaglia's convictions.[12]

With an aim to preserving variety and experimentation, JSM followed Smith in thinking that

> if the government would make up its mind to *require* for every child a good education, it might save itself the trouble of *providing* one. [...] A general State education is a mere contrivance for moulding people to be exactly like one another [...]. An education established and controlled by the State should only exist, if it exist at all, as one among many competing experiments, carried on for the purpose of example and stimulus (OL, 302; emphasis in original).

Yet again, this classical liberal approach, minimalist as it may be, still falls short of several much more extreme and dangerous positions upheld by contemporary neoliberals.

In the Italian context, they argue for a complete liberalization of the whole education and training sectors, abolishing State quality and contents requirements on schools and universities as well as renouncing any legal value for educational attainments. Such calls, which undoubtedly resonate with certain economic interests, cannot be based on any notion of liberty. As JSM notes, "[a]ll attempts by the State to bias the conclusions of its citizens on disputed subjects, are evil; but it may very properly offer to ascertain and certify that a person possesses the knowledge requisite to make his conclusions, on any given subject, worth attending to" (OL, 303).

As JSM highlights, it is one thing to prevent the state from exercising an improper influence over opinion, and it is a completely different thing to have the state certify that an opinion was acquired after due study. To safeguard this distinction, JSM notes, the knowledge required for passing an examination—which would then lead to a legally valid certification—should always be confined only to facts and "positive science."

This, of course, is much more complicated in fields, such as the social sciences, in which even the definition, conceptualization and analysis of "social facts" may be disputed. But this competition of points of view does not prevent the objective assessment of a student's (or a colleague's) competence in the social field. Rather, to properly evaluate one's competence, it is necessary to turn to the history of thought: "[t]he examinations on religion, politics, or other disputed topics, should not turn on the truth or falsehoods of opinions, but on the matter of fact that such and such an opinion is held, on such grounds, by such authors, or schools, or churches" (OL, 303).

More than in formalization and empirical applications, it is in the history of thought that economics and the other social sciences can most properly be the object of teaching and can look for "facts"—notwithstanding what several "scientific-minded" colleagues think. Alessandro Roncaglia has explained this to generations of statistics students, and we plan to do the same.

Notes

1 John Stuart Mill (1866), *Parliamentary Debates*, 3rd ser., vol. 183, col. 1592 (31 May).
2 Alas, this is as well the position of several, if not most, contemporary mainstream economists. This is but one of the several destructive criticisms by Roncaglia against mainstream economics (on which see, e.g., Roncaglia 2010) and a major reason for studying classical authors in search of a different, more useful, path of economic thought.
3 Thus, for example JSM explains several forms of behavior that may at first glance look like hypocrisy, as in fact instances of cognitive dissonance: "[a]ll Christians believe that the blessed are the poor and humble, and those who are ill-used by the world; [...] that if they would be perfect, they should sell all that they have and give it to the poor. They are not insincere when they say that they believe these things. [...] But in the sense of that living belief which regulates conduct, they believe these doctrines just up to the point to which it is *usual* to act upon them" (OL, 249; emphasis added).
4 Referring to James Mill's essay on *Government*, he writes, "[m]y father's premises were really too narrow [...]. Identity of interest between the governing body and the community at large, is not, in any practical sense which can be attached to it, the only thing on which good government depends" (JSM 1873, 165).
5 Notice that, as shown by fads and fashions, this does not imply immobility of tastes and habits; however, "when there is change it shall be for change's sake, and not from any idea of beauty or convenience; for the same idea of beauty or convenience would not strike all the world at the same moment [...]. It is not progress that we object to; on the contrary, we flatter ourselves that we are the most progressive people who ever lived. It is individuality that we war against" (OL, 273).
6 JSM makes a specific point of great topicality in the context of today's debate on social media: "in proportion to a man's want of confidence in his own solitary judgment, does he

usually repose, with implicit trust, on the infallibility of 'the world' in general. And the world, to each individual, means the part of it with which he comes in contact" (OL, 230).

7 JSM mentions the fate of most religions as a relevant example, but his own experience may be more telling. In his *Autobiography* he informs the reader that, at the height of his productive years, the gestation of his *Principles of Logic* had been especially difficult. However, in a later chapter he adds, "during the rewriting of *Logic*, Dr. Whewell's *Philosophy of the Inductive Sciences* made its appearance; a circumstance fortunate to me, as it gave me what I greatly desired, a full treatment of the subject by an antagonist, and enabled me to present my ideas with greater clearness and emphasis as well as fuller and more varied development" (JSM 1873, 231).

8 Indeed, he writes that James Mill "wrote on no subject which he did not enrich with valuable thought, and excepting the *Elements of Political Economy*, a very useful book when first written, but which has now for some time finished its work, it will be long before any of his books will be wholly superseded" (JSM 1873, 213).

9 "Our opinions were now far more heretical than mine had been in the days of my most extreme Benthamism. In those days [...] the notion that it was possible to get rid in any considerable degree of the flagrant injustice involved in the fact that some are born to riches and the vast majority to poverty, I reckoned chimerical; and only hoped that by universal education, leading to voluntary restraint on population, the portion of the poor might be made more tolerable. In short, I was a democrat but not the least of a Socialist. We were now less democrats than I had formerly been, [... and] our ideal of future improvement was such as would class us decidedly under the general designation of Socialists" (JSM 1873, 239).

10 Incidentally, it is worth recalling that in *The Subjection of Women* JSM does not deny that in his time women were often considered to be generally more selfish than men, an accusation often put forward by opponents to the extension of suffrage. Rather, he explained this tendency with the obligation imposed on them since infancy, to only consider and care for their most inner circle of affections and nothing else (D'Ippoliti, 2011).

11 Some of his predictions in such a situation seem especially foresighted: "the absorption of all the principal ability of the country into the governing body is fatal, sooner or later, to the mental activity and progressiveness of the body itself. [...] The official body are under the constant temptation of sinking into indolent routine, or, [... to the opposite] of rushing into some half-examined crudity which has struck the fancy of some leading member of the corps" (OL, 308). For a relevant example, one could think of Italy's agency for the evaluation of universities and research.

12 Of course, not entirely. See, for example, the following passage, in which JSM defends "[t]he position [he] took up, vindicating the high educational value alike of the old classic and the new scientific studies, [...] and insisting that it is only the stupid inefficiency of the usual teaching which makes those studies be regarded as competitors instead of allies" (1873, 287).

References

D'Ippoliti, C. 2011. *Economics and Diversity*. Abingdon: Routledge.

Hirschman, A. O. 1977. *The Passions and the Interests: Political Arguments for Capitalism before Its Triumph*. Princeton, NJ: Princeton University Press.

Humboldt, W. von. 1851. *Ideen zu einem Versuch, die Grenzen der Wirksamkeit des Staates zu bestimmen*. Breslau: E. Trewendt.

McCloskey, D. 1985. *The Rhetoric of Economics*. Madison: University of Wisconsin Press.

Mill, J. 1825. "Government." In *Supplement to the Encyclopaedia Britannica*, 1–32. London: J. Innes.

Mill, J. S. 1838. "Bentham." In *Essays on Ethics, Religion, and Society*, vol. 10 of *The Collected Works of John Stuart Mill*, edited by J. M. Robson, 75–115. Toronto: University of Toronto Press, 1969.

———. 1840. "Coleridge." In *Essays on Ethics, Religion, and Society*, vol. 10 of *The Collected Works of John Stuart Mill*, edited by J. M. Robson, 116–64. Toronto: University of Toronto Press, 1969.

————. 1843. *A System of Logic, Ratiocinative and Inductive*. In *A System of Logic. Part I and Part II*, vols. 7–8 of *The Collected Works of John Stuart Mill*, edited by J. M. Robson. Toronto: University of Toronto Press, 1969.

————. 1859. *On Liberty*. In *Essays on Politics and Society. Part I*, vol. 18 of *The Collected Works of John Stuart Mill*, edited by J. M. Robson, 213–310. Toronto: University of Toronto Press, 1977.

————. 1861. "Utilitarianism." In *Essays on Ethics, Religion, and Society*, vol. 10 of *The Collected Works of John Stuart Mill*, edited by J. M. Robson, 203–60. Toronto: University of Toronto Press, 1969.

————. 1869. *The Subjection of Women*. In *Essays on Equality, Law, and Education*, vol. 21 of *The Collected Works of John Stuart Mill*, edited by J. M. Robson, 259–340. Toronto: University of Toronto Press, 1984.

————. 1873. *Autobiography*. In *Autobiography and Literary Essays*, vol. 1 of *The Collected Works of John Stuart Mill*, edited by J. M. Robson, 1–290. Toronto: University of Toronto Press, 1981.

Roncaglia, A. 2005a. *The Wealth of Ideas: A History of Economic Thought*. Cambridge: Cambridge University Press.

————. 2005b. *Il mito della mano invisibile*. Roma–Bari: Laterza.

————. 2006. "Paolo Sylos Labini, 1920–2005," *Banca Nazionale del Lavoro Quarterly Review* 59, no. 235: 3–21.

————. 2008. "Il socialismo liberale di Paolo Sylos Labini." In *Libertà, giustizia, laicità: In ricordo di Paolo Sylos Labini*, edited by A. Roncaglia, P. Rossi and M. L. Salvadori, 27–57. Roma–Bari: Laterza.

————. 2010. *Why the Economists Got It Wrong*. London: Anthem.

————. 2016. "L'etica dell'economista," *Moneta e Credito* 69, no. 273: 7–19.

Roncaglia, A., and M. Corsi. 2007. "A proposito di 'Salveminiani e machiavellici': Un commento a Michele Salvati," *Il Mulino* 56, no. 430: 361–65.

Schmoller, G. 1900. *Grundriß der allgemeinen Volkswirtschaftslehre*, 2 vols. Leipzig: Duncker & Humblot.

Sen, A. 1999. *Development as Freedom*. New York: Oxford University Press.

Smith, A. 1759. *The Theory of Moral Sentiments*. London: Millar.

Tocqueville, A. 1835. *De la Démocratie en Amérique*, 2 vols. Paris: Pagnerre.

Veblen, T. 1899. *The Theory of the Leisure Class: An Economic Study of Institutions*. New York: Macmillan.

Chapter Six

TURGOT AND THE DIVISION OF LABOR

Peter Groenewegen

1. Introduction

It is well known that Anne Robert Jacques Turgot (1727–1781) was an outstanding polymath. He after all worked in many fields of thought, was a polyglot in his command over ancient and modern languages and was recorded in history as a sound administrator, fiscal reformer, major Enlightenment figure and skilled writer on applied and theoretical economics. At the 2003 Turgot Conference held at Caen and Lantheuil, many papers were presented on Turgot the translator, the political and moral philosopher, the sociologist and the philosopher of history, the linguist, the poet, the student of probability and, especially, the reformer, the lawmaker, the statesman and administrator and the profound economic theorist.

Turgot's many biographers have also commented invariably on his broad scientific aptitude, his wide philosophical interests, his experiments in chemistry, physical and mathematical study and his abiding interest in history, sociology, philosophy, political science and political economy, both in its theoretical ramification and as an applied science designed to secure major reforms and improvements. These wider talents, on the exercise of many of which he left specific writings, major or minor, make him a generalist, an eighteenth-century "Renaissance man," a true product of the Enlightenment who tried to understand all and to elaborate the mysteries of science—natural and especially social—in letters, memoranda, short papers and occasionally even short books.

Turgot's personal library likewise demonstrates his enormous breadth of interests. As catalogued by Takumi Tsuda (1974), it is easy to indicate its scope by summarizing the table of division of the library by subject matter. Not surprisingly, given his early education and training, it contained many theological works and a substantial collection of works on jurisprudence. The last embrace much material on the laws of nature and of the people. Turgot's history collection ranged from ecclesiastical history to ancient history, modern history, national history (especially that of France, Germany, England and Spain) and literary history. The sciences and the arts were well represented. In the order of this table, they included philosophy, ethics, morals, economics, education and metaphysics, while natural history covered the literature of agriculture, medicine, mathematics, chemistry, pharmacy, surgery, astronomy and optics. Works on the arts covered architecture, painting, sculpture, music, dance and the military arts. The section on belles lettres lists works such as grammars and dictionaries, writings on ancient and modern languages (that is, Latin, French, Italian, German, Flemish and English) and books on rhetoric and poetry drawn from many countries, as well as novels and books on philology. Well-represented languages among the books of this immense library were Latin, Italian, Spanish and English, with French, not surprisingly, dominating the collection. This was the library of a nonspecialist, of a widely cultured person, interesting himself in virtually every aspect of intellectual activity: the type of library expected of a true figure of the Enlightenment.

Yet Turgot was also a convinced believer in the importance of specialization, as demonstrated by the many advantages of the division of labor he noted in his writings. For Turgot, these advantages were a crucial feature of economic, social and human development. Nevertheless, few essays have been published that explicitly tackle the importance of specialization and division of labor in Turgot's work. I myself know of only one article exclusively devoted to this topic (that is, Ravix, 1992, esp. pp. 42–48). This perhaps makes it useful to briefly examine three aspects of Turgot's treatment of specialization and the division of labor. The first concerns Turgot's discussion of the necessary link between inequality, the division of labor and the progress of knowledge and wealth. This linkage is concisely raised in some of Turgot's early writings, in particular his important 1751 "Letter to Mme. de Graffigny," inspired by his reading of her *Lettres péruviennes*. The second aspect dwells on Turgot's discussion of the division of labor and economic progress, with particular reference to its implications for capital accumulation and the division of society into specific classes. This he sketched with great elegance in his famous *Réflexions sur la formation et la distribution des richesses*, completed in November 1766 and published in several versions during his lifetime. The third aspect of Turgot's treatment of the division of labor arises from Turgot's attempts to grapple administratively with securing some major benefits for contemporary society from his reform of the corvée and his attempt at reforming the *milice*.

Aspects of Turgot's generalist spirit therefore arise even in his discussion of the advantages (and costs) of specialization and the division of labor. After all, the three aspects of his treatment of the division of labor to be discussed reveal Turgot the political and moral philosopher, Turgot the economist and sociologist of progress and Turgot the administrator and social reformer actively seeking to enhance the economic welfare for the communities that he was called upon to administer during the most historically significant parts of his life. These were his intendancy of Limoges (1761–74) and his brief service to Louis XVI as minister (1774–76), first of the navy, and then of finance as *contrôleur-général*.

Turgot's main concern was with the social division of labor, or the division of professions, to use the expression Turgot himself tended to use. The manufacturing division of labor at best featured marginally in his concise analysis of the subject in his 1766 *Réflexions*, particularly in its shoe manufacturing examples, which are quoted below in section 3 of this chapter. Presenting a broad aspect of Turgot's economics of production is also a fitting tribute to Alessandro Roncaglia, whose economic contributions are celebrated in this collection of essays published in his honor.

2. Inequality and the Division of Labor

Turgot's observations on inequality and the division of labor in his Letter to Mme. de Graffigny commenced with his defense of the unequal "distribution of ranks so characteristic of contemporary society." Contrary to what Zilia, Mme. de Graffigny's heroine in the *Lettres péruviennes*, appears to think, Turgot argued succinctly that the unequal distribution of ranks in society is a most important matter, a proposition he claimed rather easy to justify. Turgot did this in three paragraphs. These directly link inequality with the division of professions (the social division of labor) because such a division in turn implies differences in skills and aptitudes for specific tasks, which create differences in remuneration and, ultimately, in class structure.

As done more fully in his later *Réflexions* (see section 3, below), Turgot linked the division of labor with capital, and the division of contemporary commercial society into owners of capital on the one hand, and propertyless "hands" (or laborers), on the other.

Turgot's subtle argument in his Letter sees inequality as rooted in human existence, caused by the different endowments of skills and abilities that nature has bestowed on individuals. Of particular interest in these paragraphs is his interpretation of what were to become the first two of the three basic objectives of the 1789 French Revolution: liberty, equality and fraternity. Turgot, however, did not deal with fraternity in this context, and perceived liberty and equality as mutually inconsistent and virtually unattainable in combination. Complete freedom of property, the manner in which Turgot generally interpreted freedom or liberty, entailing as it did specialization and the division of labor, is inimical to equality for reasons previously stated. However, Turgot's manner of putting the argument is so interesting that it can be extensively quoted:

[Inequality] is necessary, because men are not at all born equal; because their strength, their mind, their passions, invariably break the temporary balance between them, which laws may be able to place there; because all men are born in a state of weakness which makes them dependent on their parents and creates undissolvable ties amongst them. Families unequal in skill or strength double the causes of inequality; war between savages assumes a chieftain. What would become of society without this inequality of ranks? Everyone would be reduced to bare necessities, or rather, there would be a multitude of people who are not assured of them. It is impossible to work without having some tools, and the means of subsistence prior to the harvest. Those who do not have the knowledge or the opportunity to acquire them, do not have the right to deprive those who have deserved, earned or acquired them through their work. If the lazy or the ignorant deprive the industrious and the skilled [of these resources], every type of work would be discouraged. Poverty would become universal. It is most just and useful for all, that those who lack either mind or the good fortune, lend their arms to those who know how to use them, who are able to give them a wage in advance and to guarantee them some share in the future product. Their subsistence is then assured, but so is their dependence. It is not unjust that those who have invented a productive employment and who have provided their fellow workmen with the food and the necessary implements for existence, who only have free contracts with this, keep the best part [of the produce] as the price of their advances, they need to work less, and enjoy more leisure. This leisure puts them in the position to reflect longer, further increasing their knowledge, what they are able to save from their share, justly the best share which they need to obtain from the product, increases their capital and ability to launch other enterprises.

Inequality was born in this way, and grows even more among the most virtuous and moral people. It may have, and frequently has had, many more additional causes, and every stratagem through which it is desired to depart from the State, amounts to a relapse into inequality. But it is not an evil, it is fortunate for mankind, a benefit for those who have weighed up with as much kindness as wisdom, all the elements which enter into the human mind. Where would society be if things were not like this and if everyone would only till his own small field? It would [then] be necessary that everyone also build his own house, and makes all his clothes by himself. Every man would rely on himself alone, and on the products of the small plot which form his environment. Of what would the inhabitants of the soil live if they produced no wheat at all? With what would they transport the produce from one country to another? The least among peasants enjoys a multitude of commodities, often gathered from very different climes. I presume the least was provided: a thousand hands, perhaps a hundred thousand, have worked for him. The division of professions necessarily leads to the inequality of ranks. Without this division, what perfects the useful arts? What succors the weak? What extends the knowledge of the mind? What gives to mankind and to nations that education as much specialised as general which forms habits? Who peacefully will arbitrate quarrels? Who will place a brake on the ferocity of some and protection for the weakness of others? Liberty!—I speak of it while longing for it. Mankind is perhaps unworthy of thee. Equality—they long for it, but they cannot attain it.

Oh, that Zilia once more weigh up the converse benefits of savages and civilized man. Preference for savages is a ridiculous declamation! Until she refutes it, until she demonstrates that the vice we look upon as induced by good breeding are the lot of the human mind, that those who have no gold at all are as miserly as those who have it, because men everywhere have a liking for property [and] for the right to preserve it, a covetousness which brings about an ability to accumulate products from it. (1751a, 785–86; my translation)[1]

It may be noted that an earlier work by Turgot (1750, 43) differs slightly from the argument just presented. It explicitly stated that "barbarism makes all men equal." However, it also developed the argument that progress, especially once a surplus has arisen in agriculture, permits a division of classes—that is, property owners and workmen—and a division of the professions, which in turn creates "towns, trade, the useful arts" and so on.

Subsequently, Turgot's *Plan for a Discourse on Universal History*, which probably dates from early 1751, modified the statement about barbarism just quoted. Turgot there altered his opinion as follows: "among barbarous peoples, this inequality could not be very great" (1751b, 89).

However, when labour is divided according to man's aptitudes, which is in itself very advantageous, since everything is done better and quicker. The unequal distribution of goods and social responsibilities means that the majority of men who are employed in rough and lowly work, are unable to make the same progress as other men, to whom this distribution gave leisure and the means of advancing themselves. (Ibid.)

The link between inequality and the division of ranks, and progress, capital accumulation and the division of labor, was therefore one that Turgot had already put forward while in his early twenties. The view of stadial progress, that is, the so-called four stages theory he also developed at this time, was totally inconsistent with the elevation of savage society to which some of his noted contemporaries were rather prone. The notion of the noble savage and the happiness of the savage state were not propositions to which Turgot could easily subscribe given his views that progress in the growth of wealth, requiring a division of labor and an accumulation of capital, necessarily implied inequality. After all, the class structure of modern commercial society was that of property owners (of land and capital) and propertyless wage laborers, an explicitly unequal distribution of wealth. When Turgot again pondered this subject 15 years later in his famous *Réflexions sur la formation et la distribution des richesses*, this is satisfactorily elaborated for both the agricultural stage and the subsequent (in time) more superior commercial stage. This links the argument immediately to that presented in the next section of this chapter.

3. Turgot's *Réflexions*

Turgot's economic analysis in his *Réflexions* begins with a reminder that equality in landownership, giving each person a piece of land just sufficient to produce his subsistence, is a picture of society that has never existed, and never could exist (1766, 43). The reason advanced for this is simply that the various types of soil cannot produce everything (ibid., 45) and that therefore a single individual was unable to provide for his basic wants of food, clothing and shelter. An exchange economy with a division of professions is inevitable. Moreover, given the long-term nature of preparing raw materials for use, and the complexity of this process, some division of this preparation is essential, if things are to be efficiently produced. Turgot's example in the *Réflexions* of the preparation of hides for shoe production, illustrates this clearly:

> What labourer could attend to all the detail necessary in this operation which continues for several months, sometimes for several years? If he could, would he be able to, for a single hide? What a loss of time, space, materials, which might have served either at the same time or successively to tan a large quantity of hides! And even if he did succeed in tanning a single hide, he needs only one pair of shoes: what will he do with the rest? Shall he kill an ox to make his pair of shoes? Shall he cut down a tree to make a pair of wooden shoes? The same thing may be said concerning all the other wants of man, who, if he were reduced to his own field and his own labour, would waste much time and trouble in order to be very badly equipped in every respect, and would also cultivate his land very badly. (Ibid., 45)

If wants are to be adequately met, the need for exchange brings labor contracts into the picture, enabling labor to be sold for commodities. Once again, the benefits of this are linked to the division of labor. A laborer for hire, "by devoting himself to a single kind of labour, succeeded much better in it" (ibid., 45). Turgot then connected the argument to the division of labor into social classes. An agricultural society yields three social classes. The class of owners gains a share of the product without working, their price for letting others use their property in land for productive purposes.

The class of "cultivators" organizes the farming of the land by providing implements and the necessary working capital. Thirdly, there is a class of laborers who work for their subsistence wage, the outcome of competition in the labor market (ibid., 49). The second and third class are active in the production of wealth; the first class, who as Turgot (ibid., 49–50) explains, have inherited their right to landed property, won in the distant past by their remote ancestors. They use their leisure "for the general needs of the Society, such as wars, and the administration of justice," either as a form of voluntary personal service or, more likely, for payment from the state (ibid., 49).

Progress transforms this class arrangement of responsibility sharing characteristic of an agricultural society into that of a commercial, capital-using society. This takes place once sufficient capital has accumulated to enable highly productive capitalistic farming methods. Property ownership of the land is here completely divorced from the management of production on that property. Such a situation, or higher stage of development, assumes an already wealthy country where capital-using techniques can be applied to agriculture as well as to every other type of production from the relative abundance of capital this implies (ibid., 55).

The arrival of commercial society, that is, a fully-fledged exchange economy, gives opportunities for an even wider application of the division of labor, combined as it can now be with capital-using productive processes. Such a society, as Turgot (ibid., 64–65) put it, "greatly facilitates the separation of the different labours among the different members of society." This remark is combined with the view that the growing surplus from improved agricultural production facilitates the accumulation of "moveable wealth" or capital, which in turn is described "as an indispensable prerequisite for all lucrative work" (ibid., 64–65).

The last proposition takes Turgot's argument into discussing the various "employments" of capital. This allowed him to elaborate further on the preparation of leather, an example previously used to illustrate the advantages of the division of labor. As Turgot put it,

I have already mentioned the preparation of leather of which shoes are made: whoever has seen the workshop of a tanner, cannot help feeling the absolute impossibility of one, or even several poor persons providing themselves with hides, lime, tan, utensils, etc. and causing the buildings necessary for the Tanner to be erected, and of their living for several months until their leather was sold. In this Craft, and in many others, must not those that work at it have learned the trade before they venture to touch the materials, lest they should spoil them in their first attempts?

Here is another indispensable advance. Who then will collect the material for the work, the ingredients, the tools necessary for the process? Who is to construct canals, markets, and buildings of every kind? Who will enable that great number of workmen to live until their leather is sold, of whom none individually would be able to prepare a single hide, considering moreover the profits of the sale of a single hide could not furnish subsistence for any of them? Who will defray the expenses for the instruction of Pupils and Apprentices? Who will maintain them until they are sufficiently instructed, guiding them gradually from an easy labour proportionate to their age, to works that demand the utmost strength and ability? It will be one of those Owners of *capitals*, or moveable accumulated values, who will employ them partly in advances for the construction of the establishment and the purchase of materials, partly for the daily wages of the Workmen who labour in the preparation of them. It is he who will wait for the sale of the leather to return to him not only all his advances, but also a profit sufficient to compensate for what his money would have been worth to him, had he turned it into the acquisition of an estate, and moreover, the wages due to his labour and care, to his risk and even to his skill; for surely, if the profits were the same, he would have preferred living without any exertion on the revenue of the land which he could have purchased with the same capital. As fast as his capital returns to him by the sale of the products, he uses it for new purchases to furnish and maintain his Manufactory by this continual circulation; he lives on his profits, and lays aside what he can spare to increase his capital, and to direct it to his business, thereby increasing the amount of his advances, in order to increase his profits even more. (Ibid., 70)

The more advanced model of the *Réflexions* neatly interrelates progress, division of labor and accumulation of capital in the transition from agricultural to commercial society. In commercial society, the associated class distinctions create an additional property-owning class—the owner of capital or movable riches who, like the owners of land at both the stages of development, can live off of the revenue from their property (interest and profit) without necessarily having to work. The emphasis in the *Réflexions*, that "magnificent performance" as Joseph Schumpeter (1954, 325) called it, and the praise of which Alfred Marshall had anticipated (Groenewegen, 2003). Inequality remained an important feature of this account, but is no longer the major rationale for this more elaborate account of the division of labor by the "mature" Turgot (cf. Groenewegen, 1987, 902) for a more succinct account in the context of the notion of the division of labor).

4. Turgot's Reforms of the Corvée and the *Milice*

More than half a century ago, I wrote in my master of economics thesis on the economics of Turgot, that Turgot's administrative activities in seeking to abolish the corvée and reforming the *milice* were two closely related reform policies. Both these reforms were designed to prevent disturbances to the ordinary activities of the peasant by enabling him to concentrate more fully on his agricultural tasks. If responsibilities for road making and military transport were taken out of his hands, and the system of conscription were more orderly conducted, it would be the peasant and his income that benefited. At the same time, roads would become of better quality since skilled labor was used in constructing them, while military transports would be more efficiently organized by paid servants of the state, and conscripts would be selected with the least amount of disorientation for the rural community.

These tax reforms reduced the hardship suffered by the peasant by abolishing those taxes that peasants traditionally paid with their own labor time. Their abolition therefore came clearly within the scope of agricultural reform in general. The removal of these imposts, as Turgot explained, enhanced the efficiency of the peasant, by enabling peasants to concentrate on their agricultural activity without having their labor sidetracked by its compulsory contribution to road works as well as the provision of military services. More positively, the abolition of these taxes could be said to increase the welfare of society by raising agricultural output.

This statement about the objectives of Turgot's reforms of the corvée and the *milice* failed to mention the analytical foundations on which they rested. These were the advantages from upholding a rigid division of professions to enable peasants to concentrate on their agricultural work without the disruption of periodical road service, and the use of their carts, draft animals and their labor for military transports, and the temporary removal of peasants from their land when they attempted to avoid the risk of being conscripted for military service under the *milice*. A sample of Turgot's administrative writings on these policies needs to be briefly examined to assess the extent to which he himself explicitly relied on this type of theoretical argument to justify his approach in his policy statements on reforming the corvée and the *milice*.[2]

Take first the *milice*. Turgot wrote several memoranda and letters on this imposition during the early 1770s. One set of observations together with a letter to the appropriate minister on this subject (October 1, 1771) have unfortunately been lost, according to Anne-Robert-Jacques Du Pont in the notes he inserted when editing the set that was preserved (Turgot, 1773, 115fn2 and 120fn2). This was a letter (dated January 8, 1773) to the Marquis de Monteyard as minister of war in which Turgot set out his many objections to administering this levy and the steps to be taken to secure its real reform. Inequities in its implementation that arose from indivisibilities in the tax base (that is, the local community from which military conscripts were to be secured by means of a so-called lottery) was one such critical observation offered by Turgot (1773, 117). Moreover, Turgot noted the regional population disruptions generated by those seeking to escape the tax when the annual levy was rotated among different communities over the years. This created an incentive for those liable to the *milice* (young men of a designated age) to leave their community when it was its turn to furnish military recruits, by escaping to a village unaffected by the *milice* for that year (ibid., 118). Replacing the system of direct recruiting for the army—by either commuting the *milice* to a money tax whose revenue could be devoted to hiring soldiers or by administering the *milice* with less emphasis on compulsion—were the specific reform options supported by Turgot.

Turgot's major criticism of the levy rested on equity grounds. Inequities arising from indivisibilities in the tax base have already been mentioned. The widespread exemptions—particularly for those with money or those able to rely on protection from the influential—were the major inequities Turgot identified in this context. For Turgot, it was much better to depend on the welfare benefits from voluntary service, even if this had to be paid for by additional taxes on the peasants and villages affected. As Turgot (ibid., 125–26) put it, "Why oppose that a person essential for [the maintenance of] his family, puts in his place a person who would carry out this service with pleasure? Contributions [like the *milice*] are always less onerous when they are perfectly freely and voluntarily made."

In his final paragraph of observations, Turgot (ibid., 129) also noted that reform would likewise free the local intendant and his staff from much unnecessary and unpleasant labor, more usefully bestowed elsewhere. Turgot added that there were other arguments on this subject, some of them apparently lost subsequently. Perhaps these may have pointed out what Turgot had omitted in his 1773 memorandum: the overwhelming case for reforming the *milice* and the compulsory provision of military transport and services by peasants, from the standpoint of rigorously applying the principle of the division of labor, so badly violated in the existing, erroneous policies.

Turgot's case for abolishing the corvée was most succinctly made in his preamble to the Edict of February 1776, which intended to abolish it for France as a whole. After reminding the people of the valuable services to agriculture, manufacturing, commerce and government rendered by good roads for enhancing transport and communication, Turgot claimed that these benefits could be more efficiently procured by means of financing road construction directly rather than through imposition of the corvée as an indirect tax in the form of labor services (1776, 287–88). The enforced labor by peasants on road work without payment constituted a particularly pernicious form of what Turgot described as "double taxation." Moreover, it lowered the incentives for the conscripted labor to carry out its tasks with vigor and due care. This form of tax in kind was far better commuted into a money tax. Road building and associated construction would then be left to a group of entrepreneurs specializing in this type of activity, skilled in directing a paid workforce solely employed in this activity. This clearly enabled the work to be carried out more effectively. In addition, a money tax could also be more equitably assessed on every class of society, given that some of those currently exempt benefited greatly from using the roads (ibid., 291–92). In provinces where such reforms had already been made—Turgot's former province of Limoges was a good example—the benefits of this reform in the form of better roads were clearly visible, as were those from removing the inconvenient period of road conscription by those forced to pay the corvée (ibid., 293–94). To remove the temptation to divert to other purposes some of the revenue levied by the money tax for replacing the corvée, Turgot proposed that this revenue should be specifically tied to the objectives of road and associated construction for which it was imposed. Although this preamble to the act implementing the abolition of the corvée mentioned the advantages of a specialized labor force for road construction, the principle of the general benefits of specialization and division of labor was not explicitly invoked. Perhaps Turgot believed it unnecessary to state such an obvious truth to the learned audience of magistrates to whom the text of the preamble to the Edict was explicitly addressed.

Despite Turgot's omission of explicitly justifying these reforms of removing onerous taxation in kind from the peasantry by appealing directly to the advantages of specialization and the division of labor, this rationale was clearly appropriate to the reform of both the *milice* and the corvée. Turgot's proposed reforms would have left peasants in peace to carry out their own work in the fields without the interruptions from transferring their labor to tasks for which they were not necessarily suited and to which other, more specialized, labor ought to be directed for the sake of efficiency. Equity arguments were likewise part of Turgot's explicit rationale for these measures, but the efficiency argument from the division of labor was clearly also important for him, even if only implicitly appealed to by him in this context.

5. Conclusions

Turgot, the generalist, as demonstrated by the many intellectual topics he pursued, also upheld the tremendous importance of specialization of professions and the division of labor in many of his economic and administrative writings. After all, Turgot portrayed specialization and division of labor as indispensable to development and progress, whether historically, economically, or socially contemplated. As shown in the previous sections of this chapter, his economic writings, especially his most important one, the *Réflexions sur la Formation et la Distributions des Richesses* (1766), portrayed both the social and the manufacturing division of labor, while some of his policy proposals, especially those for reforming the corvée and the *milice* at both the provincial and the national level, could be described as resting on the productivity consequences from introducing a division of labor (see section 4). On this topic, as in many other parts of economics, he was a true classical economist who, like some of his contemporaries, placed this type of evaluation of labor organization at the forefront of his economic analysis. It is this type of classical economics that also inspired Alessandro Roncaglia to make some of his contributions to economic literature.

Notes

1 Available in French at http://gallica.bnf.fr/ark:/12148/bpt6k57291/f5.image.
2 Some useful background to these reforms is provided by Dakin (1939, chapter 5) and by Poirier (1999, 91–94 and 283–88).

References

Dakin, D. 1939. *Turgot and the Ancient Régime in France*. London: Methuen.
Groenewegen, P. 1987. "The Division of Labour." In *The New Palgrave: A Dictionary of Economics*, vol. 1, edited by J. Eatwell, M. Milgate and P. Newman, 901–7. London: Macmillan.
———. 2003. "Marshall and Turgot." Paper presented at the International Conference *Turgot (1727–1781), Our Contemporary: Economics, Administration and Government in the Enlightenment*, May 7–10. Caen and Lantheuil: Institute National d'Etudes Demographiques, Société des Amis de Turgot and University of Caen.
Poirier, J.-P. 1999. *Turgot*. Paris: Perlin.
Ravix, J. T. 1992. "Division du Travail, Échange et Production: Retour à Adam Smith et Turgot," *Economies et Société* 16, no. 3: 35–50.
Schumpeter, J. A. 1954. *History of Economic Analysis*. London: Allen and Unwin.
Tsuda, T. 1974. *Catalogue des livres de la bibliothèque de Turgot*. 3 vols. Tokyo: Institut d'Etudes Economiques, Université Hitotsubashi.
Turgot, A. R. J. 1750. "A Philosophical Review of the Successive Advances of the Human Mind." In *Turgot on Progress, Sociology and Economics*, translated and edited with an introduction by R. L. Meek, 41–59. Cambridge: Cambridge University Press, 1973.
———. 1751a. "Lettre à Mme de Graffigny." In *Œuvres de Turgot*, vol. 2, edited by E. Daire and H. Dussard, 785–94. Paris: Guillaumin, 1844.
———. 1751b. *On Universal History*. In *Turgot on Progress, Sociology and Economics*, translated and edited with an introduction by R. L. Meek, 61–118. Cambridge: Cambridge University Press, 1973.

———. 1766. *Reflections on the Formation and Distribution of Wealth.* In *The Economics of A. R. J. Turgot,* edited and translated with an introduction by P. Groenewegen, 43–95. The Hague: Martinus Nijhoff, 1977.

———. 1773. "Lettre au Ministre de la Guerre sur la Milice." In *Œuvres de Turgot,* vol. 2, edited by E. Daire and H. Dussard, 115–29. Paris: Guillaumin, 1844.

———. 1776. "Edit du Roi qui supprime les corvées, et ordonne la confection des grandes routes à prix des argents." In *Œuvres de Turgot,* vol. 2, edited by E. Daire and H. Dussard, 287–98. Paris: Guillaumin, 1844.

Chapter Seven

AGRICULTURAL SURPLUS AND THE MEANS OF PRODUCTION

Gianni Vaggi

1. Introduction

I have often asked myself why Appendix D of Piero Sraffa's (1960) book does not mention Sir William Petty, though his works are abundantly present in Sraffa's library (see De Vivo, 2014). Maybe some of the friends working on Sraffa's papers will satisfy my curiosity.

The question has not to do with the "corn model" but with the existence of an "economy which produces more than the minimum necessary for replacement" (Sraffa, 1960, 6).

To my knowledge Petty was the first author to clearly spell out the importance of the existence of a surplus of necessaries (see below section 3). Whether it is made of corn, agricultural products, subsistence goods or basic commodities, the concept of a physical surplus is at the core of Sraffa's investigation. In Sraffa's *Production of Commodities* (parts 1 and 2), the physical quantities of both the inputs and the outputs are given and are not related to prices; this is a fundamental assumption. From chapter 2 onward there is also a physical surplus, and "the right-hand side of the resulting sum-equation (or gross national product), will contain, besides all the quantities which are found on the left-hand side (or means of production and subsistence), some additional ones that are not" (ibid., 6).[1]

This chapter offers a quick overview of the story of the role agricultural surplus and of the theory of wealth from mercantilism to Smith. Section 2 examines mercantilism, while section 3 deals with Petty and Cantillon. Section 4 examines the contribution of Francois Quesnay, and section 5 presents some elements of Adam Smith's view of wealth.

Moreover this chapter provides an opportunity to examine the scope and method of the early political economists up to Smith. The classical political economists tackled the issue of the wealth of nations, and some notions they elaborated are still of crucial importance in today's debates on development economics.

In particular, agricultural surplus is a puzzling issue for development theories and policies. As for theoretical issues: set yourself in a low-income country in sub-Saharan Africa, and some decisive questions do arise. Is agricultural productivity above bare subsistence a necessary condition for economic growth? Successful economic growth requires a process of structural change in the composition of the gross domestic product, which should include fewer primary commodities and be comprised of more and more medium and high-technology manufactures (see Chang, 2002). But then why bother about improvements in food production? All the more so, when we see that the share of employment in agriculture is declining and, in developing countries, most of the people are working in the service sector too. Where should W. Arthur Lewis's "disguised unemployed" people move to when leaving the primary sector (see Lewis, 1954)?

2. Mercantilism and the Balance of Trade

It is commonly believed that mercantilists defined national wealth as precious metals, but this is a limited and distorted view of their approach to the theory of wealth. As early as the 1620s, most mercantilists did not regard precious metal as wealth in itself.[2] Mercantilism could well accept a definition of wealth in terms of commodities, as was the case from Thomas Mun onward. Mercantilists did not identify wealth with precious metals but defined it in terms of species: commodities required for satisfying people's wants. In his dispute with Gerard de Malynes about the devaluation of the currency, Mun clearly speaks of wealth as being made up of commodities, either necessities (which he calls natural wealth) or "manufactures and industrious trading with forraign commodities," which he calls artificial wealth (Mun, 1623, 7; see also pp. 71–73). Flows of international currency describe a modification of national wealth, but they are not the cause of this change. Only a favorable balance of trade can increase national wealth. In the end, it is the trade balance and not the capital flows that determine a change in a country's wealth. In modern terminology, we could say the current account side of the balance of payments determines the size and the sign of the financial account.

Money could even be exported, if this were a way to improve the trade balance and then to increase English treasure (see ibid., 14). The level of interest rates and the strength of the domestic currency have no direct influence on the wealth of a nation. Interest rates may influence the cost of the circulating capital and hence the competitiveness of domestic products on international markets.

Of course, the mercantilists tried to show that the "balance of trade theory" would benefit all social classes, above all the landlords and the sovereign, not only the merchants.

Mercantilism has often been defined as the political economy of the merchants, but the merchants became producers and entrepreneurs, and this fact led to the development of the "cottage industry" (see Rubin, 1979, 31). In the sixteenth century, the role of a merchant and of a capitalist-entrepreneur coexisted in the same person, as the story of the English clothing industry shows. The merchant-producers asked the government to protect domestic industry from foreign competitors, and this led to the emergence of the protectionist variation of mercantilist thought.

However, the emergence of a class of producers that was separate from that of the merchants, together with the strengthening of competition in international markets, led to conflicting interests between the merchants on the one side and the landowners and producers (the clothiers) on the other (see Appleby, 1978, 190–94).

The merchants' gain derives from buying cheap and selling dear (see Mun, 1623, 26; Appleby, 1978, 161), and national wealth is the outcome of the country's successes at the expenses of her trading partners. During the seventeenth century, this analytical framework successfully interpreted and guided the growth of the English and Dutch economies, thus proving to be an adequate paradigm for explaining the economic successes of the two countries.

The balance of trade theory of wealth was not unanimously accepted throughout the seventeenth century. As early as 1623, Edward Misselden wrote that "trade hath in it such a kind of natural liberty in the course and use thereof as it will not induce to be forced by any. If you attempt it, it is a thousand to one that you leave it worse than you found it" (quoted in Hutchison, 1988, 22). Toward the end of the century, authors like Nicholas Barbon, Douglas North and Henry Martyn praised the role of large markets and of consumption expenditures in increasing the wealth of a nation. Not only did they regard wealth as commodities and not as an amount of precious metal, but they also believed these commodities were designed to satisfy people's needs and to make their life more enjoyable and were not necessarily geared toward the export markets.

However, these critiques did not lead to the abandonment of the "balance of trade theory" of wealth. The early free trade views that emerged between 1696 and 1713 were defeated also because of the role played by John Locke during the debate on the value of money (see Appleby, 1978, 230–32 and 248–52). Appleby's explanation is quite convincing, but there is also the fact that in the early eighteenth century no theory of wealth capable of being an alternative to the "balance of trade theory" had yet emerged.

The definition of wealth began to change during the course of the seventeenth century, but by itself this modification did not lead to the abandonment of the "balance of trade theory" of wealth.

3. Petty and Cantillon

3.1 Sir William Petty

In this short history of agricultural surplus, Sir William Petty plays an important role. Petty underlines the use-value aspect of goods and singles out the peculiar role of the agricultural sector, which, by producing a surplus of necessaries, provides the basis for the development of both the population and of manufacturing. In a famous example, Petty assumes that 100 men produce food and clothing for a thousand. In his 1662 *Treatise of Taxes and Contributions*, Petty (1662, 30: emphasis and bold added) writes the following:

> If there be 1000. men in a Territory, and if 100. of these can raise necessary food and raiment for the whole 1000. If 200. more make as much commodities, as other Nations will give either their commodities or money for, and if 400. more be employed in the ornaments, pleasure, and magnificence of the whole; if there be 200. Governors, Divines, Lawyers, Physicians, Merchants and Retailers, making in all 900. the question is, since there is **food enough for this supernumerary 100. also**, *how they should come by it?*

Leave aside for the moment Petty's question, which is emphasized by the second italics. Agriculture maintains all other economic activities, because its output is larger than the inputs required in its own production. Agricultural surplus implies that some individuals produce food and other necessaries in excess of their own needs, and therefore there is subsistence for others, a fact that allows manufacture, trade and other activities to arise. The very existence of activities different from the agricultural ones is proof that there is a surplus in agriculture, since this sector maintains all other economic activities. It is thanks to the surplus of necessaries that societies can diversify their activities and the structure of employment.

Petty's other important notion is that of social division of labor, which is quite obviously a twin concept to that of an agricultural surplus. The very question at the end of the previous passage is an example of the way in which Petty tries to analyze contemporary society—everyone must have a role in it, and her/his entitlement to receive part of the produce must bear some sort of relation to this role. Hence, how the 100 supernumerary "*should come by it?*" How can they survive? In which way might the extra subsistence, on top of that appropriated by the other 900 men, reach them? What is the type of mechanism that allows them to receive the available food and raiment? Petty indicates five possible, and not very pleasant, options: "begging, [...] stealing, [...] to starve, [...] be put to death, [....] be given away to another Nation" (ibid., 30).

Of course, the last option reminds us of migration flows, a growing phenomenon that in less than 20 years has brought international remittances to be three times larger than international aid (see Capelli and Vaggi, 2016, 226). The question that closes the quote above indicates that in the type of society Petty has in mind, people are entitled to subsistence depending on their role and function inside the social organization. Petty does not progress to explicitly saying that individuals will share subsistence according to their contribution to national wealth, in a sort of functional distribution of income approach, but the existence of the question poses a very modern problem about the production and distribution of wealth.

The surplus of the economy springs out of the primary sector, but it is the manufacturing sector that can take advantage of the technical division of labor. This is another important element in the process of modification of the mercantilist theory of wealth.[3] Petty (1676, 260) believes that there is a type of technological division of labor that allows for a reduction in the cost of production of commodities: "for as Cloth must be cheaper made, when one Cards, another Spins, another Weaves, another Draws, another Dresses, another Presses and Packs; than when all the Operations above-mentioned, were clumsily performed by the same hand."

This passage anticipates by one century the Smithian theory of wealth and the famous example of the 18 operations of the "trade of the pin-maker" in the opening chapter of the *Wealth of Nations* (see Smith, 1776, I.i.3). Lower production costs lead to lower prices, as described in the famous example of watches in the 1682 work *Another Essay on Political Arithmetick* (see Roncaglia, 1977, 93–94).

Petty links up the way in which commodities are produced to their value. In the *Treatise of Taxes and Contributions*, he has the famous sentence about labor and land being the father and mother of wealth (see Petty, 1662, 68); hence, "all things ought to be valued by two natural Denominations, which is Land and Labor" (ibid., 44).

Later on in the *Treatise*, Petty seems to highlight a sort of labor theory of value when he underlines that "dearness and cheapness" depend "upon the few or more hands requisite" to produce necessaries (ibid., 90).[4]

Notwithstanding all his valuable and very modern insights into the production process, Petty does not produce a theory of national wealth that could be an alternative to the "balance of trade" one.

He discusses the technological division of labor but does not give any explanation of how it is possible to achieve that surplus in the production of "food and raiment," which is at the basis of the organization of society.

3.2 Richard Cantillon

Richard Cantillon was a non-French author whose work first appeared in France. In the first chapter of the *Essai sur la Nature du Commerce en General*, entitled "De la Richesse," Cantillon writes, "The Land is the Source or Matter from whence all Wealth is produced. The Labour of man is the Form which produces it: and Wealth in itself is nothing but the Maintenance, Conveniences, and Superfluities of Life" (1755, 3).

In this passage there are all the ingredients for a theory of wealth that could provide an alternative to the mercantilists' balance of trade theory. Land is there, but above all Cantillon mentions the productive powers of labor. Cantillon follows Petty in saying that land and labor are the two original sources of production and of value. Wealth is clearly defined as produced commodities, and all products designed to satisfy the wants of individuals—both for necessaries and for luxury goods—are equally regarded as wealth.

As Petty, Cantillon also believes that part of the population maintains all the people of a country: "it is shown that the Labour of 25 grown persons suffices to provide 100 others, also grown up, with all the necessaries of life" (1755, 87).

Thus, leaving aside the children and the elderly, who amount to 50 people, at least another 25 adults can be employed as soldiers and domestic servants, and also to create the things necessary for life (ibid.). This implies that "the State will be deemed rich in proportion to this increase of work" (ibid.), even if there is no increase in subsistence goods.

However, two pages later Cantillon writes that if the 25 extra workers "were employed to produce permanent commodities," which includes all the raw materials and the work needed to transform them "into Tools and Instruments for the use of man," then "the state will not only appear to be richer for it but will be so in reality" (ibid., 89).

Here Cantillon hints at the difference between commodities that are going to be used as inputs for further production and those that will be consumed. It looks like a rudimentary division of economic activities into productive and sterile ones.

Cantillon clearly shows that agriculture is the most important among all human activities, since it provides subsistence for all the people of the country. As in Petty, the surplus element appears in terms of the number of people who can be maintained by those employed in the production of necessaries. It is the productivity of agriculture that allows provisions for the extra 75 people. However, as in Petty, Cantillon does not give any explanation for the existence of the agricultural surplus and of what determines its size. He assumes that the 25 individuals generate more products than what is needed for their subsistence.

Cantillon highlights the role of the entrepreneurs: the farmers are true entrepreneurs, who by their advances and by their work enhance the productivity of the soil. The role of the farmer is completely different from that of the landlord. It is the farmer who organizes and coordinates agricultural production, and he is an undertaker who bears the risks of the activity (ibid., 47 and 49; see also Murphy, 1986, 255–57). As compensation for these risks and for his coordinating activity, the farmer obtains one-third of the produce of the land, while he uses another third for the subsistence of his workers. The last third is the landlord's rent.[5] Cantillon's "three rents theory" emphasizes the crucial role played by the agricultural entrepreneur, and it anticipates Smith's view of the value of the social product as being made up of three different distributive shares. In a sense this theory answers the question posed by Petty with the 100 supernumerary men—the output is entirely distributed according to the functions of the different groups in the process of production.

However, Cantillon did not produce a new satisfactory theory of wealth. With regard to mercantilism he often uses ambivalent expressions. Gold and silver are only a way to measure wealth and in particular to compare the wealth of different countries (see Cantillon, 1755, 89 and 91). However foreign trade is always the main way of increasing the wealth of a country and its population (see ibid., 233, 235 and 237).[6] In the best mercantilist tradition, he writes that precious metals must enter the country not as a result of the sale of primary commodities but "in exchange for the Labour of the People, such as Manufactures and articles which contain little produce of the soil" (ibid., 91). According to Cantillon, it is also necessary to discourage the consumption of foreign manufactured goods (see ibid., 91 and 239), and the products of domestic industry should be sent abroad using the country's ships (see ibid., 239 and 241).

Cantillon follows Petty's indication that the land and labor involved in the production of a commodity are the basis for its "intrinsic value" (ibid., 29). The measurement of this value depends on the solution to the problem of finding a "par or relation between the Value of Land and Labour" (ibid., 31). According to Cantillon, this is a fundamental problem that has been posed but has not been solved by Petty.

Notwithstanding his emphasis on the role of the farmers, on the importance of having a surplus in the production of necessaries and on the influence of production on the value of commodities, Cantillon fails to provide an alternative to mercantilism. I believe this failure depends on the fact he did not provide an explanation of how the 25 persons could produce necessaries for a hundred; Cantillon lacks an analysis of the causes of wealth. He fails to relate agricultural surplus to the process of economic growth (see Murphy, 1986, 261), and there is little analysis of the role of capital in the process of production.

4. Quesnay: A Story of Oxen and Horses—the *Avances*

"Le fondement de la société est la subsistance des hommes,"[7] writes François Quesnay in the 1765 "Le droit naturel" (in Quesnay, 2005, 1: 122). Societies are based on people's subsistence. The full title of the essay is "Observations sur le droit naturel des hommes réunis en société", and here Quesnay refers to organized human societies and to the principles that allow them to exist and (hopefully) to prosper, a theme that will also constitute the main topic for Smith's inquiry. It is important to underline that this is not abstract speculation, because the starting point of Quesnay's investigation is what he regards as the major issue of his time: why is France so backward vis-à-vis prosperous England? This is one of the most challenging questions of the period, and this is what leads Quesnay to try to understand the causes of wealth and then to suggest policies that could overcome French backwardness.

This way of proceeding highlights a method that will become typical of classical political economy. This approach to economic facts is duly called "political," not because it investigates the way in which people express their political orientation, but because it directly tackles a policy issue. The starting point of the analysis is not represented by an abstract theoretical debate but by the most pressing problem of contemporary societies. For Quesnay, this problem is France's sluggish growth and the continuous social and economic crises that during the first half of the eighteenth century have led to several defeats by England.

The 1756–57 articles written by Quesnay for the *Encyclopédie* tell part of the story, and they are an example of the use of that comparative historical method that characterizes classical political economy. "Hommes," "Grains" and "Fermiers" focus on the comparison of France and England.

Quesnay's starting point is the contention that trade is just an exchange of value for equal value; therefore, no surplus can be created in exchange: trade is a sterile activity (see "Sur les Travaux des Artisans," in Quesnay, 2005, 2: 983).

Thus Quesnay focuses on agricultural production and finds that France is a much poorer country than England because her agriculture is less productive. England's superiority in the cultivation of corn is explained by the fact that in England the farmers use the best available techniques of cultivation, while the French cultivators employ older techniques of production.

In the 1756 essay "Fermiers," there is the story of oxen and horses that provides an example of comparative economic analysis. In England, rich farmers use horses that pull a plow with an iron spade, while in France the poor sharecroppers plow their fields with a plow pulled by oxen and with a wooden spade (see Quesnay, 2005, 1: 129–30). Hence the productivity per hectare is higher in England than in France, notwithstanding the more fertile soil of the latter.

The most famous aspect of physiocracy is the contention that only agriculture is productive, while industry, along with trade, is a sterile occupation. However, the activities taking place in the primary sector are not productive simply because nature provides them with a gift. Being part of the primary sector is a necessary, but not sufficient, condition of productivity. It is the existence of a physical surplus that bestows the quality of "productive" on the labor employed in agriculture. Quesnay regards only those agricultural activities whose output is considerably higher than their inputs as sources of surplus and wealth, such as large-scale cultivation, which characterizes agriculture in England and in the northern provinces of France (see "Fermiers," in Quesnay, 2005, 1: 149–51). But where does the surplus come from? Why are those agricultural activities generating a surplus, while the rest of French cultivation is barely at a subsistence level?

In England and in the northern provinces of France, cultivation takes place under the supervision of rich farmers who can rent large amounts of land, and above all they employ large advances in the process of cultivation. These advances are made up of both circulating and fixed capital (see "Analyse," in Quesnay, 2005, 1: 549 and 552). It is the use of a large capital stock that allows England to adopt the best available techniques of production.

In small-scale cultivation, like *métayage*, crop-sharing cultivators are poor; they cannot afford the advances necessary to make agriculture really productive, and they hardly have a surplus on top of the expenses of cultivation. It is the existence of a large stock of capital that allows cultivation to be productive. Surplus is not a gift of nature but the result of modern and efficient techniques of production.

Quesnay emphasizes the role of fixed capital in increasing the productivity of cultivation. Thanks to a large stock of *avances primitives*, it is possible to create a modern and prosperous agriculture.[8] Horses are a necessary type of fixed capital, in order for the most advanced agricultural techniques of Quesnay's time to be adopted, as the best technology is embodied in the most modern type of capital equipment.

Industry is sterile largely because of its lack of fixed capital; industrial activities are carried on by poor artisans, who can only recover their production expenses, that is to say their wages and the costs of raw materials (see "Sur les Travaux des Artisans" in Quesnay 2005, 2: 982–83).

Quesnay singles out a theory of wealth based on capitalistic agriculture where we can identify some logical steps.

1. Focus on the subsistence sector, as Petty and Cantillon did;
2. define national wealth as the annual flow of agricultural output;
3. separate the gross output from the advances and define the net product;
4. explain how to achieve the most productive type of techniques in the subsistence sector;
5. the best technology is identified with large-scale cultivation, which is characterized by a 100 percent ratio between the surplus and the *avances annuelles* (circulating capital);[9]
6. fixed capital is the element that allows for the use of the best techniques of production.

Points four through six provide the new theory of the causes of wealth. In particular, point six links the new principle of wealth to productivity and technical progress. The accumulation of capital in the most productive sector (the only productive one for Quesnay) is an important point on which Smith will build his own theory of wealth. Smith will more clearly describe that *surplus-profit-investment-productivity nexus*, which is no longer limited to the subsistence sector and which by and large still explains the rise and fall of nations.[10]

This approach to economic analysis is also known as the "surplus approach," because the size of surplus relative to the capital invested becomes the decisive indicator of past successes and future potentialities. Petty and Cantillon underline the existence of a physical surplus of necessaries, while Quesnay shows that the size of the surplus depends on the technology adopted and the amount of capital employed. Quesnay provides a clear analytical link between the notions of surplus and reproduction.[11] However, in Quesnay it is reproduction that takes the fore, because the future physical surplus depends on the quantity and the quality of the new means of production. With Quesnay, we move from the emphasis on a surplus of subsistence commodities to the role of commodities in the process of capital accumulation.

But now come the policy and political challenges. How can the French cultivators command enough fixed capital to be able to implement the most productive type of cultivation? In modern terminology, how can French agriculture reach the frontier of the production possibility set and not stagnate inside it?

For Quesnay, this is not a purely technical issue. The two techniques correspond to two different modes of cultivation and to two different ways of describing the social settings in agriculture—*fermage* and *métayage*—which distinguish the *grande culture* in England from the *pétite culture* in France. With some simplification, we can say that we have two different social relationships of production: a capitalistic one and a feudal one.[12] This is an example of how classical political economy, in this case Quesnay, never isolates the technical and economic features of society from politics and history.

Policies must enter the picture, and they should transform the poor sharecroppers into rich farmers by helping the cultivators become rich and accumulate fixed capital.

In the final part of a note to "Maxime XX" of the *Maximes générales du gouvernement économique d'un royaume agricole*, Quesnay writes, "PAUVRES PAYSANS, PAUVRE ROYAUME" (see Quesnay, 2005, 1: 592, emphasis in original).[13]

To move toward large-scale cultivation, the physiocrats advocate two major reforms: the single tax on rents and the so-called laissez-faire policies for corn trade. The former is advanced by the Marquis de Mirabeau in the 1760 *Théorie de l'Impot*, written under the supervision of Quesnay. The two physiocrats try to convince the landlords of the advantages of their proposed tax reform. This reform should replace an old system that imposes many different taxes on the cultivators and on the gross products of agriculture with a single tax on rent, the only disposable part of agricultural output. Therefore, the cultivators would pay less in taxes because the revenues of the Kingdom would be supported by the new tax on landlords' rent. However, according to Mirabeau and Quesnay, in the end landlords will benefit from accepting to pay taxes in place of the cultivators. The latter would reinvest the money saved for taxation into larger and better techniques of cultivation, which would lead to increases in the productivity of agriculture and to higher surplus and rents in the future. Needless to say, the reform was never implemented, but the *Théorie de l'Impot* saw Mirabeau sent to the Bastille, from where he was released thanks to Madame de Pompadour, only to be exiled for a few months to southern France.

Between the end of 1763 and the first months of 1764, Controlleur Général Bertin had already favored the exportation of some products of agriculture, and on July 18, his successor, de L'Averdy, proclaimed some edicts that allowed the free export of all kinds of corn by sea and land (see Weulerrse, 1910, 2: 222–24). But in 1770, the edicts were revoked by the new Controlleur Général, Terray. This is the only physiocratic recommendation adopted by the French rulers. In the physiocratic analysis of the origin of wealth, the liberalization of corn trade is the starting point for the increase in the prosperity of the country (see Mirabeau, 1769, 47–48).

It is worth recalling that contrary to Turgot, the physiocrats are not in favor of unlimited free trade; rather, they just want to allow the French cultivators to sell their corn where it is more convenient, either at home or abroad. The physiocrats oppose the import of manufactured products. In a sense, it is a kind of export-led model of accumulation but with exports being limited to the products of the primary sector. Today, there is a debate in many developing countries on how to transform incomes that derive from the export of primary commodities into a process of structural change that could reduce dependence on commodity exports and lead to sustained economic growth. The debate is particularly vibrant in Latin America and Africa (see, for instance, Cimoli and Porcile, 2011).

The physiocratic attempt to reform the economic policy of the ancien régime failed for social and political reasons (see Fox-Genovese, 1976, 11 and 238–42). Physiocracy was looking for a utopian alliance between the farmers, the landed aristocracy and the sovereign against the merchants and the bureaucrats, such as the tax collectors—the *fermiers généraux* violently attacked by Mirabeau in the *Théorie de l'Impot* (see Mirabeau, 1760, 102–8).

The failure of physiocratic policies has little to do with their analytical structure; however, there are analytical flaws in Quesnay's analysis of the causes of wealth. Capital accumulation and technical progress in agriculture are the causes of national wealth, and both depend upon the reinvestment of a farmer's profits. However, in physiocracy the profits of the cultivators represent a magnitude of uncertain existence and unstable size, as a farmer's profits depend on the existence of a difference between the "firsthand" price of corn—which is a market price subject to frequent and large fluctuations—and the fundamental price (see Vaggi, 1987, 80–86). The firsthand price is the selling price of corn for the farmer, while the fundamental price is the unit cost of production of corn. Free exportation should increase the fundamental price without affecting the firsthand one, thus leaving a higher profit for the French cultivators.

This may be a good description of the working of corn markets at the time of Louis XV, but this notion of profit can hardly sustain a long-run theory of growth based on the accumulation of capital in agriculture. In Quesnay's economics, profits are a sort of hybrid magnitude. On the one hand, they depend on market prices, which are subject to wide fluctuations and appear as a short-run phenomenon; on the other hand, profits are the source of capital accumulation and economic development, which are typical long-run factors, and for this reason they must be exempted from taxation. The two elements can hardly coexist.

5. Smith and the Division of Labor

Smith's *Wealth of Nations* provides a full-fledged alternative to the mercantilist "balance of trade theory" of wealth. The causes of national wealth are the "Improvements in the Productive Powers of Labour," as we read in the title of book 1, and these improvements depend on the "Division of Labour," which is the title of chapter 1 of book 1 (Smith, 1776: I.i.1). At the very beginning of the *Wealth of Nations*, Smith provides the answer to the question of the causes of wealth, and there is no need to limit his answer to the production of subsistence commodities and to agriculture.

The first three chapters of the *Wealth of Nations* are amazing. There the technological division of labor coexists with the social one. The pinmaker is in paragraph 3 of chapter 1, and in the next paragraph we read that "the separation of different trades and employments from one another seems to have taken place in consequence of this advantage" (ibid., I.i.4).

The increases in labor productivity that derive from the technological division of labor open the way to the specialization of the different branches of trade, also known as the social division of labor.

In chapter 2, we find the famous "triple B" example: the butcher, the brewer and the baker, from whose own interest, and not from their benevolence, we expect our dinner (see ibid., I.ii.2). Here the division of labor that Smith is talking about is clearly the separation of arts and branches, of trades and occupations, into different activities and sectors.

The next paragraph reads, "In a tribe of hunters or shepherds a particular person makes bows and arrows [...] with more readiness and dexterity." He finds that by exchanging these products for cattle or for venison he can get more of both "than if he himself went to the field to catch them" (ibid., I.ii.2).

It is then in his interest to specialize in "the making of bows and arrows" and to become an armorer. In the same way, someone will become a "house-carpenter," another a "smith" and still another "a tanner or dresser" (see ibid., I.ii.3).[14]

However, in order to specialize in one specific trade and to abandon other activities, each worker needs to be sure that he will sell his surplus produce. He must have "the certainty of being able to exchange all that surplus part of the produce of his own labour, which is over and above his own consumption (ibid.; see also Smith, 1762–63, 351–52).

And this is why chapter 3 tells us that the division of labor is limited by the extent of the market (see Smith, 1776, I.iii).[15]

If we add the accumulation of capital in book 2 (see ibid., II.iii), we obtain a virtuous circle of economic growth that can be described as follows (see Stathakis and Vaggi, 2006, 13):

Surplus $\Rightarrow$ profits $\Rightarrow$ savings $\Rightarrow$ investments [$\Leftarrow$ expected rate of profit] $\Rightarrow$
capital stock increases $\Rightarrow$ (structural change *and* division of labor) [$\Leftarrow$ extent of the market] $\Rightarrow$ increases in labor productivity $\Rightarrow$ increases in surplus and profits.

However, two points are worth noticing.

First, Smith is well aware of the importance of having an agricultural surplus, as a very efficient production of subsistence commodities seems to be a sort of prerequisite for the social division of labor and for the rise of manufactures. As a matter of fact, Smith clearly says that from the point of view of society as a whole, the social division of labor that leads people to specialize in specific economic activities requires a surplus of agricultural products (see Smith, 1776, I.ix.c.7); therefore, agriculture must be productive in Quesnay's sense. He also adds that it is the surplus produce of the country that maintains the towns (see ibid., III.i.2).

For this reason, capital must be invested in agriculture in order to have an abundance of food. In book 2 we read, "Unless capital was employed in the production of rude produce to a certain degree of abundance, neither manufactures nor trade of any kind could exist" (ibid., II.v.4).

And on the next page: "The capital employed in agriculture [...] is by far the most advantageous to the society" (ibid., II.v.12).

Second, Smith is very cautious in his description of the relationships between rich and poor nations. He does not think that the latter ones will always necessarily benefit from free trade (see Myint, 1977, 246–48). In the so-called "Early Draft of Part of the Wealth of Nations" he writes, "It is easier for a nation, in the same manner as for an individual, to raise itself from a moderate degree of wealth to the highest opulence, than to acquire this moderate degree of wealth; money, according to the proverb, begetting money, among nations as among individuals" (Smith, 1763, 579: point 42).

There is no automatic mechanism that guarantees the catching up, or convergence, of the poorer countries to the level of income of the rich ones. On the contrary, wealthy nations have an interest in trading among themselves because of their rich markets, rather than with poor countries—England should trade with France rather than with Portugal (see Smith, 1763, 578: point 40). Smith lists several impediments facing poor countries when they have to undertake the first steps of a development process. The most significant of these impediments is "that a nation is not always in a condition to imitate and copy the inventions and improvements of its more wealthy neighbours; the application of these frequently requiring a stock with which is not furnished" (ibid., 579: point 42).[16]

Quite often, poor countries do not have the resources to adopt the same techniques of production of the rich ones. Productivity increases and technical progress depend on the accumulation of capital. Of all the impediments, the lack of capital goods is the hardest to overcome.

In the next point of the "Early Draft," Smith stresses the importance of agriculture and of its productivity. He writes, "That the cultivation of land depends upon the proportion which the stock of those who cultivate it bears to the quantity of land to be cultivated" (ibid., 579: point 43).

This passage seems to owe a lot to Quesnay's emphasis on the role of capital in modern cultivation.

6. Conclusions

In our brief description of the views of wealth up to Smith we have moved from trade to the surplus of necessaries, on to the role of technology in cultivation and then to capital accumulation in the productive sectors of the economy. A surplus production of food and basic goods is a necessary condition for the division of labor, and this condition can only be achieved by investing enough capital in the agricultural sector.

Concepts such as surplus in the production of necessaries, backward agriculture, reproduction, productive and unproductive labor and, of course, capital accumulation are still of crucial importance in present-day discussions.[17] Between winter 2015 and spring 2016, Ethiopia experienced a serious famine in the northern part of the country. Many countries in Africa are in an endemic condition of food vulnerability. The huge granaries that one can easily see outside some capital cities in Africa witness a situation in which stocks of cereals have to be kept aside in order to face times of scarcity. Goal number two of the Sustainable Development Goals, which were approved by the United Nations General Assembly in September 2015, reads, "End hunger, achieve food security and improved nutrition, and promote sustainable agriculture," and target 2.3 asks for a doubling of agricultural productivity by 2030 (see UN, 2015).[18]

The method of investigation of classical political economists relied a lot on comparative economic history and a long-run approach to the evolution of societies. Both issues represent major challenges for present-day theories and views on development. Unfortunately, few modern development economists seem to be aware of the analytical wealth of classical political economy and of how far this wealth could contribute to dealing with modern challenges.

Notes

1 Subsistence commodities should always be part of wages; on this problem, see Roncaglia (1975, chapter 4). Here I do not discuss the issue of the measurement of this surplus but I simply recall that a bundle, a vector, of physical commodities does exist.

2 On the defeat of the so called "bullionism," see Appleby (1978, 202).

3 A wider discussion of Petty's view on the division of labor is in Aspromourgos (1986, 29–32).

4 This point is dealt at length in Roncaglia (1977, chapter 8).

5 The limits of Cantillon's concept of profit have been examined elsewhere (see Vaggi, 1990, 1–2).

6 Herlitz regards Cantillon as the most rational supporter of mercantilism (see Herlitz, 1988, 25).

7 The subsistence of men is the foundation of society.

8 Quesnay's ideal economy has been defined as a sort of agrarian capitalism (see Hoselitz, 1968, 661–62).

9 This is the ratio that characterizes large-scale cultivation and is assumed to be the one in operation in the 1759 *Tableau économique* (see "*Extrait des économies royales de M. De Sully*," in Kuczynski and Meek, 1972, 6).

10 According to some of the best explanations of Asian economic growth, the above nexus is one of the major economic mechanisms that help to understand the East Asian miracle (see, for instance, Wade, 1990 and UNCTAD, 1996).

11 On the tableau as an early linear production model, see the very interesting paper by Van den Berg and Steenge (2016).

12 On some precapitalistic modes of production in agriculture, see, for instance, Bhaduri (1983, chapter 4).
13 The *Maximes generals...* were published in the 1767 in the *Physiocratie* by Pierre Samuel Du Pont de Nemours. A similar text is in the note to *maxime* XIV in the *Extrait des économies royales de M. De Sully*, in the third edition of the *Tableau économique*, in the first months of the 1759 (Kuzcynski and Meek, 1972, 10).
14 Notice that the division of labor is a typical feature of a civilized state vis-à-vis a primitive one. On the four stages theory in Smith and in the eighteenth-century debates in France, see Meek (1976). Turgot, too, provides a very interesting analysis of the division of labor (see the chapter by Peter Groenewegen (2017) in this book).
15 On Smith's view about international trade and the sale of a growing output, the so-called vent for surplus argument, see Myint (1977).
16 Remember that Smith uses the term "stock" where we now use "capital."
17 For a description of the different views on the division of labor of some classical authors and their relationship to modern development issues, see Sai-wing Ho (2016).
18 In sub-Saharan Africa, agricultural output per person is now only slightly higher than in the early 1960s.

References

Appleby, J. 1978. *Economic Thought and Ideology in Seventeenth-Century England*. Princeton, NJ: Princeton University Press.
Aspromourgos, T. 1986. "Political Economy and the Social Division of Labour: The Economics of Sir William Petty," *Scottish Journal of Political Economy* 33, no. 1: 28–45.
Bhaduri, A. 1983. *The Economic Structure of Backward Agriculture*. London and New York: Academic Press.
Cantillon, R. 1755. *Essai sur la nature du commerce en general*. Reprint edited by H. Higgs, London: Frank Cass, 1959. Capelli, C., and G. Vaggi. 2016. "Why Gross National Disposable Income Should Replace Gross National Income," *Development and Change* 47, no. 2: 223–39.
Chang, H.-J. 2002. *Kicking Away the Ladder: Development Strategy in Historical Perspective*. London: Anthem Press.
Cimoli, M., and G. Porcile. 2011. "Global Growth and International Cooperation: A Structuralist Perspective," *Cambridge Journal of Economics* 35, no. 2: 383–400.
De Vivo, G. 2014. *Catalogue of the Library of Piero Saffa*. Torino and Milan: Fondazione Luigi Einaudi and Fondazione Raffaele Mattioli.
Fox-Genovese, E. 1976. *The Origins of Physiocracy*. Ithaca, NY: Cornell University Press.
Groenewegen, P. 2017. "Turgot and the Division of Labor." Chapter 6 in this volume.
Herlitz, L. 1988. *Ideas of Capital and Development in Pre-Classical Economic Thought*. Institute of Economic History Report 7. Goteborg: Institute of Economic History.
Hoselitz, B. F. 1968. "Agrarian Capitalism, the Natural Order of Things: François Quesnay," *Kyklos* 21, no. 4: 637–63.
Hutchison, T. 1988. *Before Adam Smith*. Oxford: Blackwell.
Kuczynski, M., and R. L. Meek, eds. 1972. *Quesnay's Tableau Economique*. Edited for The Royal Economic Society. London: Macmillan.
Lewis, W. A. 1954. "Economic Development with Unlimited Supplies of Labour," *Manchester School* 22, no. 2: 139–91.
Meek, R. L. 1976. *Social Science and the Ignoble Savage*. Cambridge: Cambridge University Press.
Mirabeau, V. R. 1760. *Théorie de l'Impot*. The Hague: Benjamin Gibert. Reprint Aalen: Scientia Verlag, 1972.
———. 1769. "Suite de la Seizième lettre de M.B. A M*** et la Quatrième sur la Stabilité de l'Order Légal." In *Ephémérides du citoyen*, vol. 2. Paris: Didot.

Mun, T. 1623(?). *England's Treasure by Forraign Trade*. London: Thomas Clark, 1664. Reprint New York: Augustus M. Kelley, 1986.

Murphy, A. E. 1986. *Richard Cantillon: Entrepreneur and Economist*. Oxford: Clarendon Press.

Myint, H. 1977. "Adam Smith's Theory of International Trade in the Perspective of Economic Development," *Economica* 44, no. 175: 231–48.

Petty, W. 1662. *A Treatise of Taxes and Contributions*. London: Brooke. Reprinted in *The Economic Writings of Sir William Petty*, edited by C. H. Hull, vol. 1. Cambridge: Cambridge University Press, 1899.

———. 1676. *Political Arithmetick*. London: Clavel and Mortlock, 1690. Reprinted in *The Economic Writings of Sir William Petty*, edited by C. H. Hull, vol. 1. Cambridge: Cambridge University Press, 1899.

Quesnay, F. 2005. *François Quesnay—Ouvres économique complètes et autres texte*, edited by C. Théré, L. Charles and J-C. Perrot. 2 vols. Paris: INED—Institut Nationale d'Études Démographiques.

Roncaglia, A. 1975. *Sraffa e la teoria dei prezzi*. Roma–Bari: Laterza. (English edition: *Sraffa and the Theory of Prices*. Chichester: John Wiley, 1978).

———. 1977. *Petty: la nascita dell'economia politica*. Milano: Etas Libri.

Rubin, I. I. 1979. *A History of Economic Thought*. London, Ink Links. (Originally published in 1929 in Russian).

Sai-Wing Ho, P. 2016. "Linking the Insights of Smith, Marx, Young and Hirschman on the Division of Labour: Implications for Economic Integration and Uneven Development," *Cambridge Journal of Economics* 40, no. 3: 913–39.

Smith A., 1763. '*Early Draft' of Part of the Wealth of Nations*, in *Lectures on Jurisprudence*. Reprint edited by R. L. Meek, D. D. Raphael and P. G. Stein. Oxford: Oxford University Press, 1978.

———. 1762–63. *Lectures on Jurisprudence. Report of 1762–63*. Reprint edited by R. L. Meek, D. D. Raphael and P. G. Stein. Oxford: Oxford University Press, 1978.

———. 1776. *An Inquiry into the Nature and Causes of the Wealth of Nations*. Reprint edited by R. H. Campbell, A. S. Skinner and W. B. Todd. Oxford: Oxford University Press, 1976.

Sraffa, P. 1960. *Production of Commodities by Means of Commodities*. Cambridge: Cambridge University Press.

Stathakis, G., and G. Vaggi. 2006. "Economic Development and Social Change: The Classical View and the Moderns." In *Economic Development and Social Change: Historical Roots and Modern Perspectives*, edited by G. Stathakis and G. Vaggi, 1–25. Abingdon: Routledge.United Nations (UN). 2015. *Transforming Our World: The 2030 Agenda for Sustainable Development*. September 25–27. Geneva: United Nations. Available at: https://sustainabledevelopment.un.org/.

United Nations Conference on Trade and Development (UNCTAD). 1996. *Trade and Development Report*. Geneva: United Nations.

Vaggi, G. 1987. *The Economics of François Quesnay*. London: Macmillan.

———. 1990. "The Classical Concept of Profit Revisited." In *Perspectives on the History of Economics Thought*, edited by D. E. Moggridge, vol. 3. Aldershot: Edward Elgar.

Vaggi, G., and P. Groenewegen. 2003. *A Concise History of Economic Thought*. Basingstoke: Palgrave Macmillan.

Van den Berg, R., and A. Steenge. 2016. "*Tableaux* and *Systèmes*: Early French Contributions to Linear Production Models," *Cahiers d'économie politique: Histoire de la pensée et theories* 71: 11–30.

Wade, R. 1990. *Governing the Market: Economic Theory and the Role of Government in East Asian Industrialization*. Princeton, NJ: Princeton University Press.

Weulersse, G. 1910. *Le mouvement physiocratique en France (de 1756 à 1770)*. 2 vols. Paris: Alcan Editeur. Reprinted Paris: Mouton, 1968.

Chapter Eight

THE ROLE OF SRAFFA PRICES IN POST-KEYNESIAN PRICING THEORY

Geoffrey Harcourt

1. Introduction

Alessandro Roncaglia has been analyzing Piero Sraffa's contributions and how they fit into the context of the developments of economic theory since the time of the classical political economists on. In particular, he has concerned himself with how the structure of Sraffa (1960) prices in *Production of Commodities by Means of Commodities* are to be interpreted in relation to both Sraffa's (and our) predecessors and as a contribution to modern economic theory. In his comprehensive volume on Sraffa in Tony Thirlwall's important series, *Great Thinkers in Economics*, Roncaglia (2009) identifies three major interpretations of what Sraffa has done and where he may have wished developments of his contributions to go: a Smithian interpretation, a Ricardian interpretation and a Marxian interpretation. Along with his mentor, Paolo Sylos-Labini, Roncaglia places himself in the Smithian stream. He identifies Heinz Kurz and Neri Salvadori especially in the Ricardian stream and Pierangelo Garegnani especially in the Marxian stream.

While I greatly respect his arguments and provision of evidence in the public domain, I want to argue here that the Marxian stream is the most appropriate one, both for interpreting Sraffa's own views and inclinations and for providing relevant theoretical developments to aid our understanding of the structure of, and processes at work in, the modern capitalist world. In arguing this I am comforted by the fact that, for example, the late Krishna Bharadwaj, whose understanding of Sraffa and his works was second to none, Giancarlo de Vivo, the late Pier Luigi Porta and Luigi Pasinetti are in overall agreement with such a take on these important matters.

Many years ago I published an exploratory and speculative paper, "Marshall, Sraffa and Keynes: Incompatible Bedfellows?" (Harcourt, 1981). Its principal objective was to examine the role of the concept of a center of gravitation in the contributions of these three great political economists. I pointed out that Alfred Marshall was trapped in a dilemma partly of his own making, partly because his principal method of analysis was akin to that of classical physics, while his "vision" of the society he was observing and analyzing was of an evolving organic system. The Mecca of economists was therefore biology, not physics.

Marshall wished to have a theory of long-period normal prices that included as ingredients normal profits and normal wages. His time periods—market period, short period, long period—were used to establish his theory. He argued that they could merge imperceptibly one into another and could be short or long according to the immediate purpose at hand, and actual or potential according to the realism of the factors locked up in the ceteris paribus pound in any particular case. He vacillated between whether they were actual or potential, sometimes naming periods of calendar time as illustrative of what he had in mind, wishing to have it both ways. That is to say, he wished his normal prices to be real centers of gravitation, making sense of observations in historical time, yet he knew that if he simultaneously had in mind an economy moving forward through time with technical progress and accumulation occurring, there were puzzles associated with arguing that they could be revealed from observations on actual prices. He in fact says that it is only in the stationary state that the actual and normal coincide, can be "convertible terms" (Marshall, 1890, 372).

He never solved his conundrum—hence his use of time-period analysis became less and less satisfactory and illuminating, the longer the period (or run) he had in his sights. Moreover, he was not able to draw on a consensus of views from the evolutionary biologists of his time because there was none. After his death, as Neil Hart has shown (2012, 2013), evolutionary theory itself moved more toward a consensus among evolutionary biologists and allowed great strides forward to be made by modern evolutionary economists.

While John Maynard Keynes was very much a Marshallian in method, even in *The General Theory*, he was not as handicapped as was his mentor because for most of the time he was analyzing short-period systemic problems. There, I argued, the application of the concept of a center of gravitation provided a useful shortcut for establishing illuminating theory and providing sensible and realistic policy proposals. The concept had a part to play in the Keynesian context of short-period rest states (and, possibly, even longer sustained rest states associated with deep and sustained depressions), a view I believed could be supported from Keynes's own writings and by Jan Kregel's (1976) classic interpretation of them.

When I wrote in 1981, there was an ongoing debate concerning whether the concept should or should not be maintained in a Marxian and/or post-Keynesian analysis of a modern capitalist economy moving forward through time. I argued that their natural place was in the theory of pricing that characterized important sections of such economies, in the normal cost-pricing hypothesis and the connection of price making with the investment decision. In particular, I thought then, and I do so now, that there may be a role for the concept of the natural rates of profits and of wages—that they are macroeconomic concepts associated with the working of the system as a whole, imposing themselves as norms on group behavior within the system.

Similarly, if we accept the snapshot view of what Sraffa was doing—as Roncaglia has long argued and which the emerging evidence from the unlocking of the Sraffa archives more and more establishes—Sraffa too is not be deviled by Marshall's conundrums.[1] Recently, Ajit Sinha (2013) has argued that the uniform rate of profits in Sraffa's system is not necessarily based on Smithian (natural prices), Marxian (prices of production) and

Marshallian (normal long-period equilibrium prices) centers of gravitation, but is instead a mathematical property of Sraffa's system. I think there is merit in this argument; however, it is certainly not one that has been accepted by other Sraffa watchers. Indeed, there is much hostility to it.

Be that as it may, I want to argue that there is a similarity between the role that the dominance of the sphere of production over the sphere of distribution and exchange in Karl Marx's analysis, and the role that Sraffa prices play in modern price theory, especially if allied with the promising methods and advances associated with the development of the cyclical growth models of Richard Goodwin (1967) and (late) Michał Kalecki (1968). Put together, I shall argue that we potentially have a structure that overcomes the inability of the mainstream structure to link the short period with the long period because the theory of the medium period in between is incoherent, to say the least.[2]

Moreover, it is unclear whether the long period is an actual state but a theoretical concept, as Marshall sometimes had it, or a stretch of historical time in which changes in the capital stock, methods of production and the supplies of different types of skilled labor are occurring. Suppose, though, that the role of the long period is interpreted as the gathering together of expected long-term forces and factors that have an impact on decisions made in the short period. Then, if this is accompanied by the impacts of expected short-term factors, we may analyze how activity and so on is established short period by short period, run by run, over actual historical time.[3]

The proponents of the long-period method—Pierangelo Garegnani, Heinz Kurz, Neri Salvadori and others—while they have always stressed that they want an apparatus with which to handle the interrelationships of persistent forces, have never been able to incorporate the two most characteristic sustained and persistent forces—an inescapable environment of fundamental uncertainty and continuous technical changes—into their formal analytical structures. In contrast, the approach outlined here does, I argue, allow us to start to tackle these problems, and Sraffa's contributions are a vital, central part of what may evolve.

2. Marx's Role

First, let me sketch the relevant role of Marx's analysis for our discussion. The person who has set this out most explicitly is Donald Harris (1975, 1978). Drawing on Marx's distinction between the sphere of production and the sphere of distribution and exchange, and on the synthesis associated with Joan Robinson and her circle's writings on generalizing *The General Theory* to the long period, Harris provided a diagrammatic analysis that clearly brought out the logical dominance of the sphere of production over the sphere of distribution and exchange. His analysis also revealed how the realization problem identified by Marx, then by Keynes and, independently and in a more appropriate setting of Marx's schemes of reproduction, by Michał Kalecki, is solved in the sphere of distribution and exchange.

Common to Adam Smith, David Ricardo, Marx and Sraffa is the central core concept of the surplus—its creation, extraction, distribution and use—and the implications that follow from these processes. Harris shows how the *potential* surplus available for accumulation and other uses is the outcome, period by period, of the relationship between the current state of the class war between the capitalists and the wage earners and the existing methods of production in the current capital stock, itself the outcome of past accumulation associated with the use of previous realized surpluses. The potential surplus is the ultimate source of the potential size of profits and the rate of profits realized in the sphere of distribution and exchange—that is one of the core meanings of Marx's labor theory of value (Harcourt and Kerr, 1996). On the one hand, realization of the surplus depends on the factors determining aggregate investment expenditure (a relationship between expected profitability and planned accumulation), and, on the other hand, the relationship between actual accumulation and actual profitability, itself associated with the impact of the distribution of income between profits and wages on aggregate saving.

For the present purposes, the moral to be drawn is that the relationships in the sphere of production dominate and determine what may happen in the sphere of distribution and exchange without there being any need for a complete one-to-one mapping from the actual size of the potential surplus onto the corresponding sizes of profits and the rate of profits. I argue that exactly the same features are present in Sraffa's system of prices in relation to the determination of the sizes of markups on costs and their corresponding prices in the multinational oligopolistic market structures of the modern world.

In Harcourt (1981, 261), I noted the puzzles that hound the concept of prices of production when trying to incorporate them as operational concepts in the analysis referred to above. The dynamic nature of capitalist development, with the embodiment of technical changes through investment expenditure, may be so rapid in most periods (runs) as to not allow sufficient historical time for centers of gravitation of a lasting nature to be formed. There is not the time, as Joan Robinson put it, for traders to become familiar with what is the norm through actual experience, so that when their bearings are cut loose, they are all at sea, rudderless, as are also the overlooking economists. The factors needed to be held constant theoretically so as to allow the centers of gravitation they imply to be ultimately struck are in fact changing so fast that there is not the time needed for their ultimate values to be established. I still do not see how John Eatwell's (1979, 2) statement that the forces that determine the centers of gravitation are the most dominant, systematic and persistent, and that "[whether] this centre of [gravitation] is a temporal constant, or takes different values through time, does not affect the essence of the method," overcomes this puzzle.

3. Effects of Systemic Constraints

Many political economists have analyzed the overall systemic constraints imposed by macroeconomic characteristics of the economy, constraints that create the environment in which individual decision makers have to make decisions about prices and especially about the sizes of markups. These systemic constraints relate to both overall levels of aggregate demand prevailing at any moment of time (arising from the interplay of real, monetary and financial factors) and from the relationships in the sphere of distribution and exchange outlined above. They result in the formation of norms, of ranges of behavior within which it is possible to make choices.

Within this aspect of the analysis, I have in mind the links between discretion over price setting and the need to raise internal finance for planned accumulation. These ideas are especially associated with Jim Ball (1964), Al Eichner (1973, 1976), Adrian Wood (1975) and Peter Kenyon and myself (1976). My conjecture is that the Sraffa prices at each moment of time are both the systemic and individual industry and firm constraints within which these decisions have to be made.

In the long-period interpretation of Sraffa prices, the long-period structure of prices is seen to be in the outcome of persistent processes. Is this not inconsistent with, or at least unable to cope with, the impact of continuous technical change and fluctuations in aggregate demand on the economy and on the structure of Sraffa prices? The snapshot view overcomes this but, of course, carries with it the danger that if the characteristics of the snapshots vary widely from period to period because of the impact of changing levels of activity and technical variations in investment to labor and investment to output ratios, the establishment of general norms that guide behavior will not occur.

This last consideration brings to the surface a problem that plagued Keynes, his ultimate despair of ever being able to find a definite unit of time with which he could handle the analysis of all the interrelated processes he had emphasized in the development of his revolutionary theory of the workings of a monetary production economy in *The General Theory* and afterwards. He decided therefore never to push any particular piece of analysis very far past its starting point, so as to get the central message across. In his 1937 lectures, as Kregel (1976, 213) has documented, Keynes said that if he were to write the book again, he would start with the factors responsible for existence, as we would say now, in order "to distinguish the forces determining the position of equilibrium from the technique of trial and error by means of which the [entrepreneurs discover] where the position is" (1937, 182). The upshot is that instability and indeterminateness may persist in certain historical time periods, in a sense the analogue of modern general equilibrium theorists finding multiple positions of equilibrium in many parts of their analysis.

That certain time periods are characterized by instability or even crisis is, of course, not a surprising inference to be drawn from any relevant theoretical structure and approach to the analysis of economic systems. (That it was *not* an inference of the dominant theoretical structure is a major criticism of its failure to predict the recent global financial crisis (Harcourt, 2010).) Certainly, I do not think Sraffa would have been either surprised or dismayed by such an inference. I also conjecture that these suggestions fit well into, indeed supplement sensibly, the structures of Goodwin's and (late) Kalecki's cyclical growth models.

The contributions of other great thinkers from the last century are also relevant here. I start with Dennis Robertson. One of his criticisms of what he saw as the Keynesians attempting to sustain full employment and attain a steady rate of growth arose from his understanding of the real business cycle he argued formed the foundations for the processes at work in modern economies. He pointed out that when we consider a interrelated production economy—which has different lengths of gestation periods for the construction of machines in different sectors and their accompanying methods of use, and different economic lifetimes of their operation—it is just not possible to conceive that the aggregate outcome of their operation would be either full employment of labor over time or steady growth of output over time (Anyadike-Danes, 1985). In his 1975 book on Keynes, Hyman Minsky discerned in Keynes's approach an endogenous cyclical mechanism that not only took in Robertson's insights but also added to the real story a sophisticated analysis of the interrelationship of real monetary and financial factors associated with Keynes's insistence that the latter be included right from the start of the analysis. These contributions are complementary to the Goodwin/Kalecki growth cycles, which contain both theories of accumulation and the distribution of income that are as much Marxian as Keynesian and that spell out the implications in the sphere of distribution and exchange of the dominance of the sphere of production mentioned above. Moreover, Goodwin ultimately brought together the aggregate analysis of Keynes with the production interdependence insights of Sraffa and Wassily Leontief (see Goodwin and Punzo, 1987; Goodwin had made major separate contributions to both these two approaches over his lifetime).

I understand that Sraffa, unlike some of his followers, had great respect and liking for Kalecki, as did Maurice Dobb. In the late 1930s, Sraffa worked with Kalecki on pricing in UK manufacturing industries. Goodwin (1983, chaps. 7 and 8) also was influenced by and wrote on Sraffa's approaches, so it is pleasing that these three great original political economists may and should be agreeably brought together in a deeper understanding of the processes at work in modern capitalism.

Notes

1 I pointed out that Sraffa did not object to the use of Marshall's method in appropriate settings, but he did object to Marshall's use of it in conjunction with supply and demand functions and curves.
2 On this, see Nevile, Harcourt and Kriesler (2015, especially pages 109–10), and Solow's (1997 and 2000) wise comments on the issues.
3 For the distinction between the concepts of period and run, so often now regarded as interchangeable, see Harcourt (2012).

References

Anyadike-Danes, M. K. 1985. "Dennis Robertson and Keynes's *General Theory*." In *Keynes and His Contemporaries*, edited by G. C. Harcourt, 105–23. London: Macmillan.
Ball, R. J. 1964. *Inflation and the Theory of Money*. London: Allen and Unwin.
Eatwell, J. L. 1979. "Theories of Value, Output and Employment." Thames Papers in Political Economy. London: Thames Polytechnic.
Eichner, A. S. 1973. "A Theory of the Determination of the Mark-up under Oligopoly," *Economic Journal* 83, no. 332: 1184–200.
———. 1976. *The Megacorp and Oligopoly*. Cambridge: Cambridge University Press.
Goodwin, R. M. 1967. "A Growth Cycle." In *Socialism, Capitalism and Economic Growth: Essays Presented to Maurice Dobb*, edited by C. H. Feinstein, 54–58. Cambridge: Cambridge University Press.
———. 1983. *Essays in Linear Economic Structures*. London: Macmillan.

Goodwin, R. M., and L. F. Punzo. 1987. *The Dynamics of a Capitalist Economy: A Multi-Sectoral Approach.* Cambridge: Polity Press; Oxford: Basil Blackwell.

Harcourt, G. C. 1981. "Marshall, Sraffa and Keynes: Incompatible Bedfellows?" *Eastern Economic Journal* 7, no. 1: 39–50. Reprinted in *On Political Economists and Modern Political Economy: Selected Essays of G. C. Harcourt,* edited by C. Sardoni, 250–64. London and New York: Routledge, 1992.

———. 2010. "The Crisis in Mainstream Economics." *Real-World Economics Review* 53, June, 47–51. Rev. version in *Macroeconomics and the History of Economic Thought: Festschrift in Honour of Harald Hagemann,* edited by H. M. Kramer, H. D. Kurz and H.-M. Trautman, 183–90. London and New York: Routledge, 2012.

———. 2012. "On the Concepts of Period and Run in Economic Theory." In *Classical Political Economy and Modern Theory: Essays in Honour of Heinz Kurz,* edited by C. Gehrke, N. Salvadori, I. Steedman and R. Sturn, 257–65. London and New York: Routledge, 2012.

Harcourt, G. C., and P. Kenyon. 1976. "Pricing and the Investment Decision" *Kyklos* 29, no. 3: 449–77. Reprinted in *On Political Economists and Modern Political Economy: Selected Essays of G. C. Harcourt,* edited by C. Sardoni, 48–66. London and New York: Routledge, 1992.

Harcourt, G. C., and P. Kerr. 1996. "Marx, Karl Heinrich (1818–1883)." In *International Encyclopedia of Business and Management,* edited by M. Warner, 3388–95. London: Routledge. Reprinted as "Karl Marx, 1818–83," in G. C. Harcourt, *50 Years a Keynesian and Other Essays,* 157–68. Houndmills, Basingstoke, Hampshire: Palgrave Macmillan, 2001.

Harris, D. J. 1975. "The Theory of Economic Growth: A Critique and a Reformulation," *American Economic Review, Papers and Proceedings* 65, no. 2: 329–37.

———. 1978. *Capital Accumulation and Income Distribution.* Stanford, CA: Stanford University Press.

Hart, N. 2012. *Equilibrium and Evolution: Alfred Marshall and the Marshallians.* Houndmills, Basingstoke, Hampshire: Palgrave Macmillan.

———. 2013. *Alfred Marshall and Modern Economics: Equilibrium Theory and Evolutionary Economics.* Houndmills, Basingstoke, Hampshire: Palgrave Macmillan.

Kalecki, M. 1968. "Trend and Business Cycle Reconsidered," *Economic Journal* 78, no. 2: 263–76.

Keynes, J. M. 1936. *The General Theory of Employment, Interest and Money.* London: Macmillan. Reprinted as *The General Theory of Employment, Interest, and Money,* vol. 7 of *The Collected Writings of John Maynard Keynes.* London: Macmillan, 1973.

———. 1937. "'Ex Post and Ex Ante.' Notes from Keynes' 1937 Lectures." Reprinted in *The General Theory and After. Part II: Defence and Development,* vol. 14 of *The Collected Writings of John Maynard Keynes,* 179–83. London: Macmillan, 1973.

Kregel, J. A. 1976. "Economic Methodology in the Face of Uncertainty: The Modelling Methods of Keynes and the Post-Keynesians," *Economic Journal* 86, no. 342: 209–25.

Marshall, A. 1890. *Principles of Economics.* London: Macmillan.

Minsky, H. P. 1975. *John Maynard Keynes.* New York: Columbia University Press.

Nevile, J. W., G. C. Harcourt, and P. Kriesler. 2015. "Macroeconomic Policy for the Real World: A Post-Keynesian Approach," *Economic Papers* 34, no. 3: 108–17.

Roncaglia, A. 2009. *Piero Sraffa.* Basingstoke: Palgrave Macmillan.

Sinha, A. 2013. "On the Notion of Equilibrium or the Center of Gravitation in Economic Theory." In *The Oxford Handbook of Post-Keynesian Economics,* Vol. 1: *Theory and Origins,* edited by G. C. Harcourt and P. Kriesler, 101–21. New York: Oxford University Press.

Solow, R. M. 1997. "Is There a Core of Usable Macroeconomics We Should All Believe In?" *American Economic Review* 87, no. 2: 230–32.

———. 2000. "The Neoclassical Theory of Growth and Distribution," *Banca Nazionale del Lavoro Quarterly Review* 53, no. 215: 349–81.

Sraffa, P. 1960. *Production of Commodities by Means of Commodities: Prelude to a Critique of Economic Theory.* Cambridge: Cambridge University Press.

Wood, A. 1975. *A Theory of Profits.* Cambridge: Cambridge University Press.

Chapter Nine

CLASSICAL UNDERCONSUMPTION THEORIES REASSESSED

Cosimo Perrotta

1. Introduction

Underconsumption theories maintain that capitalist accumulation has an inner tendency to make demand permanently fall short of the increase in production. According to Michael Bleaney (1976), we cannot speak about an underconsumption view before the nineteenth century, because only Adam Smith separated consumption and investment expenses. Bleaney is partially right, but things are more complex. Such a separation already existed in the writings of other Enlightenment authors (see Perrotta, 2004, chap. 11), and more clearly in the physiocrats, who wanted a right balance between consumption and investment expenses. However, François Quesnay—like Pierre le Pesant de Boisguilbert and Richard Cantillon before him—still saw investment, exchange and circulation as depending on landlords' consumption. What he lacked was the idea of accumulation as a steady growth of investments and profits in all sectors. It was only Smith who introduced this concept by opposing—rather than just distinguishing— unproductive consumption and investment. This changed political economy as a whole.

Later, Smith's hostility to unproductive consumption and his unconditional support of investment raised doubts among underconsumption economists. But only a few, like William Spence, tried to revive the physiocratic approach (see below). On the contrary, Smithian followers criticized the physiocrats on this issue. J. B. Say ironically wrote, "Many people […] have imagined that to encourage consumption means fostering production. The Economists [the Physiocrats] seized this idea and made it one of the main principles of their doctrine."[1] Even more sarcastic was James Mill (1808, 75–80) when criticizing Spence and the physiocrats for defending landlords' consumption. Despite this, Jacob Hollander's (1928, lxxix–lxxx) idea of tracing back the underconsumption view to the physiocrats appears inappropriate.

However, Smith's commitment for saving drove to neglect the importance, for accumulation, of consumption increase, and of the consequent increase in skill. About productivity growth, Smith only relied on the opposite process: division of labor. The idea that accumulation only consisted in a growing division of labor led economists to uncritically accept the first industrial revolution, where mechanization was decreasing the need for skilled labor and was pushing wages down to the subsistence level. Classical authors assumed these conditions as unavoidable economic laws. Thus, when the periodical crises first appeared, it was practically impossible for economists to avoid an uneasy alternative: either denying the importance of the crises and maintaining that accumulation could go on indefinitely (this was the position of Say, David Ricardo, even Karl Marx, and their respective followers) or stating that capitalist accumulation was destined to reach a standstill (underconsumption theses). The perspective of a stationary state was the *trait-d'union* between the two views. This alternative excluded the prospect that many Enlightenment authors had hinted at, that is, a steady investment in human capital.

The enormous literature about the classical debate on underconsumption still leaves some issues unclear. Here we are set to argue the following.

First, since the 1930s two wrong interpretations of underconsumption have generated great confusion. One—best expressed by Gottfried Haberler—mistakes underconsumption for a simple element of the trade cycle. The other, attributable to John Maynard Keynes, improperly reduces underconsumption to hostility toward saving and extends this supposed attitude to mercantilists (see below, section 2).

Recognizing the two interpretations of underconsumption are very different from one another, we only examine the authors who started to publish in the period 1800–20, when the main features of the debate were implemented (section 3). In particular, the two main representatives, J. C. L. Simonde de Sismondi and Thomas Malthus, unawares, radically diverge as to the causes and the remedies of the periodical crises. However, all underconsumption authors failed to convincingly propose an alternative accumulation model (see section 4).

However, the critics of underconsumption answered the following question: where the increasing final consumption goods were to be employed productively without causing gluts (section 5).

Critics show that in the long run Say's law suggests a prospect of indefinite increase of new needs and new goods (section 6). However, the question remains: who will consume these goods? In real experience, they have been absorbed by skilled labor, which—since then—has been growing more and more. But the economists of 1800–20 never grasped this process. Since their debate was the blueprint of the economists that followed, the right solution never emerged.

2. The Two 1930s Misleading Approaches

Originally the underconsumption approach refers to a long-term, structural process that involves the nature of capitalist accumulation.[2] But in the 1920–1930s, an interpretation prevailed that considered underconsumption as connected to the trade cycle, that is, to a short-term process.[3]

Haberler was appointed by the League of Nations to investigate the nature of economic crises. Not surprisingly, he discards as simplistic the view that business cycles were due to underconsumption, but he does not distinguish between the two processes (Haberler, 1937, 118ff). All the leading figures of that period share his approach, from Joseph Schumpeter to Friedrich Hayek, Lionel Robbins and so on, and Keynes (1936, chap. 22: respectively 196 and 202–3) himself discusses underconsumption within the trade-cycle analysis.

In the end, these authors have the same view of the classical critics of underconsumption, who reduced the latter to a temporary unbalance between production and consumption in some sectors.[4] The only difference is that for the classical critics gluts were a casual, unpredictable phenomenon, while for the moderns it was a cyclical, necessarily superable, passage. The latter view shows that long-term capitalist accumulation and its possible breakdown have been canceled in the neoclassical framework. It has been reduced to an invariable alternation of upswings and downswings.

Haberler does ask himself, What do secular processes—like demographic variations, increase in stock and technical progress (which were the very objects of the classic debate)—have to do with business cycles? He answers, nothing (1937, 121–22), but he does not deduce that underconsumption and trade cycles are separate issues. He rather concludes that the view of long-term crises is wrong. Since then, most of the literature on underconsumption has followed Haberler's steps.[5] Today there is a growing attention to "medium-term" crises, but it seems too timid a compromise.

In the same years Keynes gives importance to the underconsumption approach, but suggests that it simply opposes excessive saving. He cites many authors who, according to him, support an increase in consumption and state that parsimony hinders development. However, Keynes neglects the difference between hoarding and saving. Before the mercantile economy, hoarding was widespread; it was coherent with a static economy, where occasions for investment did not exist. Saving, in contrast, arose with commercial economy. It was due to the tendency—opposite to hoarding—to invest wealth. This tendency aimed at a productive use of wealth, not to devote it to wars and ostentatious luxury.

Then, contrary to what Keynes suggests, the pre-Smithian authors he mentions[6] are favorable to saving. Also they support consumption for very different reasons, neither of which can be labeled as an underconsumption attitude. Barthélemy de Laffemas (1597) supported the consumption of silk in France because he pressed for an import substitution policy, not for an alternative to saving.[7] William Petty, Samuel Fortrey and Friedrich von Schrötter, in supporting luxury, expressed the seventeenth-century commonplace that "the luxury of the rich gives work to the poor" (see also below). This statement, however, did not mean an opposition to saving and investment. At the end of the seventeenth century, Nicholas Barbon and John Cary praised increase in consumption, but it was in order to encourage domestic demand. The same attitude is to be found in Bernard Mandeville, the main representative of Free Thinkers' economics. Mandeville actually appears closer to Keynes's interpretation; however, his polemic target was not saving but rather the Christian ethics of renunciation.[8]

In the eighteenth century the favor toward an increase in consumption augmented, but, again, not as a dismissal of saving. Contrariwise, such an increase was seen as a powerful factor of accumulation. Most authors, Smith included, supported high wages. Some of them praised high wages because they allowed a higher skill and increase in productivity. In general, Enlightenment authors—except physiocrats—were in favor of comfort for the productive classes, but bitterly attacked the unproductive ostentatious luxury of the aristocrats, which kept wealth away from investment (see Perrotta, 2004, ch. 11).

3. Differences among Underconsumption Authors

In underconsumption authors there is a tension between the need for saving in order to secure investment and production, and the want for a sufficient level of demand, which can grant an outlet to products. The latter concern prevails; however, it is expressed in very different ways.

Canard defines as "superfluous" all labor that goes beyond the production of bare necessities. Superfluous labor produces luxuries, whose consumption is also superfluous, that is unproductive. Ceteris paribus, the level of luxury is in proportion of the industry of a people. We need—he writes—a balance in the advantages provided respectively by the three sources of income (land, capital and labor). The sum of the advantages provided by one of these sources is always proportioned to the sum of exigible (i.e., exchangeable) superfluous labor that has created it. When luxury consumption exceeds what is produced by superfluous labor, it is consuming the very sources of incomes (Canard, 1801, 15–16, 80).

Spence uses Quesnay's defense of landlords' luxury to support his own underconsumption view. His treatment reminds us of the old idea that "the luxury of the rich gives work to the poor." This idea was widespread among Free Thinkers and seventeenth-century mercantilists.[9] In Quesnay and Mirabeau such an attitude appears in the view that distribution is put in motion by landlords' consumption (about which Quesnay approves the *luxe de subsistance*, which fosters agricultural production, while he condemns the *luxe de décoration*, which refers to manufactured products) (Quesnay, 1766, 895 and 1767, 580; Mirabeau, 1769–71, 200–203).

Spence uses this approach against Smith's defense of parsimony. If all people saved, he says, no one would consume the industry's products. The rule of thrift does not hold for landlords' consumption. Without the latter, incomes and consumption of the other classes would diminish. However, Spence (1807, 29–36) acknowledges that an excessive consumption diminishes reproduction. Besides, differently from Quesnay, he prefers the luxury of durable goods, which increases national wealth (ibid., 35).

The Earl of Lauderdale, one of the most important authors, attacks Smith and shows a radical aversion to saving and thrift. Saving is not the basis of accumulation. An excess of it can even drive to stagnation, while generating both excess of investment and lack of demand. Besides, the increase of machines diminishes capital returns. The driving force of accumulation is an increase in consumption, while demand should be supported even through a public debt. Lauderdale also attacks the sinking fund.[10]

His main argument is that economists (especially Smith) confuse private and public wealth, since they consider the latter as the sum of private riches. This is wrong, although both types of wealth have the same three sources (land, capital and labor) (Lauderdale, 1804a, chap. 2, esp. pp. 39–41 and 1804b, 34–47). Private wealth is measured on the basis of its value, which is determined by scarcity. For an individual, the scarcer it is, the greater a good's value, and the greater the owner's wealth. In contrast, public wealth is calculated on the basis of its utility for society; otherwise, we should think that the less water a society disposes of, the richer it grows, which is absurd. Lauderdale goes on by providing other amusing paradoxes to prove that thrift or prodigality produces different effects for individuals and for society. Private thrift makes a man richer, because it increases his income. But general thrift makes society poorer (Lauderdale, 1804a, 8–10, 39–45 and 208–9: passim, and 1804b, 20–34: passim). Every prodigal man—he complains while quoting Smith—is regarded as a public enemy, and every thrifty person as a public benefactor (Lauderdale, 1804a, 41).

Note that the same argument had been used by Barbon and, forcefully, by Mandeville. It was then repeated by Keynes, as a criticism of excessive saving (see above). Keynes, however, does not mention Lauderdale. Malthus used many of Lauderdale's reflections.[11] However, he rightly criticized Lauderdale about his belief that consumption can substitute for saving in propelling accumulation (Malthus, 1820, 314).

In 1821, an anonymous author put forward a brilliant criticism to Malthus's underconsumption view (*Inquiry*, 1821, 39–41ff). He also noted that if profits go down because of the increasing demand for labor, accumulation does not slow down. Entrepreneurs simply adapt themselves to lower profits (ibid., 28–31).

The year after, John Cazenove, who edited the second, posthumous, edition of Malthus's *Principles*, wrote a tract in support of Malthus. Capital accumulation, differently from Lauderdale's opinion, "does not necessarily diminish consumption […] but merely changes the direction of it", that is, changes it from unproductive to productive. Accumulation however "augment[s] the supply in relation to the demand" (Cazenove, 1822, 2). If demand does not increase, profits drop. In contrast, prodigality increases the proportion of demand to supply and raises the rate of profit (ibid., 3–5). Thus he calls for a due balance between productive and unproductive consumption. Cazenove always identifies necessaries with wage goods and comforts with luxuries. He takes the classical view to the extreme—from which underconsumption derives—that a gradual increase of workers' comfort is not a realistic prospect.

The Rev. Chalmers maintains that Smith and Say imply the idea that an infinite expansion of capital exists. But they are wrong.[12] Also the increase in capital has its limits, as it is proved by Malthus and Ricardo's analyses on fertile land (Chalmers, 1832, 60–65, 249fn, passim). Thus there can also be too many machines in existence, because excessive saving depresses the profit rate (ibid., 65–69ff.). Chalmers maintains that the expenditures of landlords and the clergy foster trade; however, while landlords do not give any service in exchange to the community, the clergy does (ibid., 252).

Charles Ganilh always seems to be swinging between the idea that saving on one's own consumption is necessary to generate capital and the conviction that any consumption increases production.[13] However, he criticizes Say's law because, he says, excesses in production do exist.[14] Yet he often repeats that production always adapts itself to effective demand, as the production of material objects adapts to the production of services (Ganilh, 1815, vol. 1: 315–17; vol. 2: 24–25). Besides, it is not true, as Malthus believes, that industrial nations are short lived; on the contrary, they are richer than the agricultural ones (ibid., vol. 1: 321–23).

4. Malthus and Sismondi vis-à-vis Periodical Crises

When periodical crises started affecting the market in the early nineteenth century, underconsumption authors interpreted them not as short-term phenomena but rather as the consequence of a long-term tendency of capitalist accumulation to overproduction.

Malthus is the most important underconsumption author, and his analysis on the subject is direct. Two premises are needed. First, Malthus shares Ricardo's view about the different trend between profit and rent. With the increase of accumulation, profit tends to diminish while rent tends to increase. However, Malthus (1820, bk. 1, chap. 3, sec. 1) believes that rent is not a consequence of monopoly but rather of a specific quality of the soil, because land is able to sustain more people than those needed for its cultivation (this reminds the physiocrats). Besides, since land revenue never drops with an increase in cultivation, it represents a source of enjoyments for all (ibid., sec. 9: 215–17).

Regarding the second premise, Malthus says wage levels depend on the customs of different peoples. In some countries, workers are used to consume all production in excess of bare necessities to raise children (that is, in the increase of population). In other, more refined, countries workers use this surplus for comfort.[15] Customs determine the subsistence level, which can be different in different countries. However, wages always tend to stabilize themselves at the given subsistence level due to the competition between workers. For example, if technical progress causes a sudden increase in the resources for workers, the subsistence level remains stable, because habits change much more slowly than accumulation. The consequence is that the increase in productivity only causes population growth (ibid., bk. 2, chap. 1, sec. 3).

However, according to Malthus, a stable increase in the consumption levels of productive workers cannot be an incentive for accumulation. First, because workers prefer indolence rather than working more to consume more; second, because an increase in productive workers' consumption would erode profits and extinguish the incentive to invest (ibid., 314–15, 319–20 and 326). This conviction was shared by the other classical economists, and it led them to the theory of wage fund.

Malthus's conclusion is that when accumulation grows faster than demand, the consequent surplus of goods causes gluts on the market because workers cannot absorb such a surplus even if they increase their habits of consumption (because habits change slowly) or through the increase in population, as Ricardo maintains, because this increase requires 16 or 18 years to arrive to the labor market (ibid., 319–20).[16]

Malthus interprets capital accumulation as a transformation of a part of the unproductive workers (he says, workers employed in personal services) into productive workers. Thus, when accumulation goes on rapidly, it generates a surplus of goods without increasing the demand for final consumption (ibid., 360 and 398).

In terms of social classes, Malthus maintains that capitalists tend to save in order to invest, so their consumption cannot match the increase in products. Workers cannot significantly increase their consumption without hindering profits, then accumulation. Finally, landowners' consumption does not always suffice to absorb the excess of goods; only unproductive workers' consumption can eliminate gluts, so they should not be reduced in number by accumulation. It is the latter that should be slowed down (ibid., 404–5).

Ricardo, adds Malthus effectively, often speaks as if saving were an end, not a means. It is erroneous to say that there are no limits to saving and investment. It is even dubious that man's desires are unlimited (ibid., 401–2).[17] Malthus (ibid., 316ff) also criticizes Say's law and the authors who support it (Mill, Ricardo, John R. McCulloch).

Like Malthus, Sismondi (1819, 51 and 90) agrees with Smith that saving is the very basis of accumulation. In his most mature economic work, the *Nouveaux principes*, he effectively describes the insurmountable tension hidden in accumulation. The only natural end of accumulating the fruits of labor, he says, is happiness. There is a real increase in wealth only when national happiness increases (ibid., 51). However, with accumulation going on, the number and the types of products increase, while workers get poorer and poorer. This is the cause of crises, which increase in number and violence. This means that in rich nations accumulation is determined not by needs but rather by the abundance of capital. This is why it overcomes consumption and produces "a cruel poverty" (ibid., 367–68).

The arguments Sismondi uses in his powerful picture are, unawares, double-faced. On the one hand, he complains that workers are paid too little, so they cannot buy the excess of what is produced. In a sense, they are deprived of the major part of the result of their own work. Instead of working to satisfy their own needs, they work for the luxury of the rich. Instead of working in order to rest, they work to make some others rest (ibid., 78–80; see also Sismondi, 1820–27, 396–97). On the other hand, capitalists tend to produce too much so that production is no longer aimed at satisfying the needs of the producers (Sismondi, 1819, 75–76; see also Sismondi, 1820–27, 401–2).

Then, Sismondi opens a prospect for a solution: if workers were to get a bigger share of social wealth, they could have access to luxury goods (comforts). The latter's increase is unlimited, while the increase of necessary goods is limited by natural needs. However, he states—like Malthus—that in order to overcome gluts, unproductive laborers are needed (Sismondi, 1819, 77–78). The last three chapters of the book describe the mechanism of workers' expulsion caused by accumulation and explain how workers need a social protection (ibid., 312–68).

Sismondi's (1820–27) answer to his critics is an effective synthesis of his view of capital accumulation.[18] The first essay is an acute criticism of Say's law, which Robert Torrens had largely used against Sismondi's book. Among other things, he notes that a total compensation of production and consumption would be possible if there were only basic goods, and all people were forced to always consume the same things. But, since superfluous goods exist, any variation fancied in one individual's consumption would create a break in the general equilibrium between production and consumption (ibid., 390). In another point—against the thesis that crises are never general but are only due to inconsistencies between single sectors—Sismondi observes that when gluts alternate among the different sectors, the result is equal to a permanent excess in production, that is, a general glut or saturation (ibid., 402–3; he often repeats these terms.)

In the second essay, Sismondi criticizes Ricardo and Say for being in favor of an indefinite increase in productivity and in production, despite the gluts caused by the overproduction. He stresses he is not against technical progress, which increases productivity and makes a part of labor superfluous. Rather, he is against the "modern organisation of society, which does not protect workers from excessive competition" (ibid., 433). Following Malthus, he shows examples of the ancients who, as a way to prevent overproduction, provided employment through the implementation of public works. He concludes that he is not able to find out which is the right way to organize production, but he tries to show economists that the present way is wrong (ibid., 440–48).

In his last economic work Sismondi states that while other economists try to speed accumulation up, he tries to slow it down. He adds that intellectual workers are also redundant in those times and that the poor must be discouraged from trying to change their social condition through intellectual labor. Society has to watch that everyone develops his intelligence in proportion to his proper social status (Sismondi, 1837–38, tome 2, essay 13: 149 and 191–92). Of course, this proposal is disastrous. It would impede any economic and civil progress.

Despite his confusion and contradictions, Sismondi best shows the basic difficulty in which classic economists are caught. Their accumulation model is based on the assumption that final productive consumption cannot increase but to the detriment of investment. This hypothesis necessarily drives to the impossibility of accumulation itself in the long run.[19]

Malthus and Sismondi seem unaware of the deep difference between their own analyses about the causes and remedies of the crises. As to the causes, both authors accept capitalist accumulation, but they see in it a distortion of the natural aim of production, that is, consumption. However, Sismondi attributes this flaw mainly to low wages and the consequent lack of demand. Malthus sees the limit in the tendency to transform all wealth in capital, without leaving the due room to comforts and luxuries (which, he implies, are external to investment logic). Then, for Malthus the lack of demand mainly comes from insufficient unproductive consumption.

The remedies are even more distant. Sismondi asks to move part of the surplus—generated by accumulation—from profits to wages. This would also slow accumulation down. Malthus, more radically, asks to move part of the surplus from investment to unproductive consumption and unproductive labor.

In the end, underconsumption authors are not able to show an alternative to accumulation's shortcomings. Besides, their forecast of a failure of accumulation has been disproved by experience.

5. Criticisms of Underconsumption Theories

In those years the discussion was very intense, with comments, replies and rejoinders made to one another in the shortest time.

Mill (1808, 75–80) sarcastically criticizes Spence for his praise of landlords' luxury. He, says Mill, does not even distinguish between landlords' unproductive consumption and entrepreneurs' productive consumption (ibid., 68–69). Mill exposes at length Say's law (ibid., 81–88), which he expresses in an extreme (and certainly wrong) version: production of commodities creates a market for its own commodities (ibid., 81). Mill (1821), like many others, repeats Smith's sentence "That which is annually produced is annually consumed,"[20] but he suggests a "Say's law interpretation" of it (see also the following section of the same book).

Colonel Torrens, against Sismondi, argues that consumption capacity necessarily grows along with production capacity.[21] He also bitterly criticizes Robert Owen as if the latter were an economist, not a social reformer. Owen had written that technical progress produces more goods than the present structure of society allows its population to consume. Torrens's (1819, 74) answer is based on Say's law: "The supply of one set of commodities constitutes the demand for another." However, Owen did not refer to underconsumption; he was strongly favorable to technical progress and to the increase of (cheaper) goods. He referred to the enormous inequality of incomes, and he was right (see Owen 1815 and 1818).

Say criticizes Lauderdale's thesis that saving can damage production, and says that Lauderdale supports waste.[22] He untiringly repeats that products are exchanged only with products, services included.[23] This would mean that production cannot exceed consumption. He also repeats that it is impossible that all products be in excess at the same time, and, in the chapter devoted to criticize Sismondi, adds, "If each man produces much, each man will consume much" (Say, 1828–29, vol. 1: 345, vol. 2: 210). What was later called Say's law is best expressed in his chapter "On the *débouchés*" (1803, book 2, ch. 15) and in his letters to Malthus (Say, 1820), especially the first. The most frequent argument opposed to the underconsumption view by Say and all the followers of his law is that "to save is to spend," although in another way. Then, overproduction is impossible.

Ricardo (1820, 234) appears scandalized about Malthus's solution to the problem (unproductive workers will absorb the surplus). He too appeals to Say's law: "Mr. Malthus never appears to remember that to save is to spend" (ibid., 245); and "as I think that demand depends only on supply, the means of obtaining abundance of commodities can never I think be otherwise than beneficial" (ibid., 198).

Ricardo (1821, 343–44) also suggests that the surplus will be absorbed by the population's increase (for Malthus's answer, see above). Morton Paglin has noted that Ricardo's argument holds only in the long run (1961, 134–50), but there are more cogent objections. If an increase in resources would automatically cause an increase in population (as both Malthus and Ricardo believe), then the scarcity of land would stop accumulation. Besides, even in that period this automatic consequence was not considered certain. Torrens (1808, 83–84: note B) challenges Malthus's law of population because, he writes, Ireland is much poorer, but also much more prolific, than England.

Moreover, Ricardo himself is not so sure that accumulation would absorb the increase in the working population. In the chapter on machinery, added in the last edition of his *Principles*, he changes his mind (due to John Barton's objection)[24] and admits that—especially in sudden technical changes—an increase in profits and rent, consequent to the increase in productivity, can make net produce (income) rise, while gross produce relatively diminishes. This can make some workers redundant, because a part of the previous wage fund can be destined to unproductive (personal) consumption rather than to investment (Ricardo, 1821, ch. 31). However, in order to sugar the pill, Ricardo (ibid., 475–77) adds, the more the rich consume in the service of menial servants, rather than in luxuries, the more workers will be employed in new jobs.[25] This is a curious conclusion for a fierce enemy of unproductive labor. In any event, McCulloch and Torrens criticized Ricardo's change of mind.[26] Besides, Ricardo here neglects the fact that production of luxuries also creates jobs and, moreover, productive jobs, if their products are sold.

6. Conclusion: Diversification of Goods as the Driving Force of Accumulation

In conclusion, both parties failed to show a credible employment of the surplus, which could allow accumulation to go on. In the historical experience, such an employment was the investment in human capital. It is the growing increase in comforts, education and skill of the producers that is the driving force of secular development. In our debate we can find several authors who hint at this kind of development process, but such suggestions never became a real analysis because they were at odds with the postulates of the respective views.

Sismondi, for instance, calls for increasing wages (but also for hindering technical progress). Wage increase has actually been the main process that has driven accumulation during 150 years. However, Sismondi does not connect this process with the most important consequence of it, that is, an increase in productivity due to skill. In the short run, wage growth increases demand and avoids gluts; it also increases productivity to some extent, due to comforts. But in the long run, wage growth allows workers' children to go to school and acquire skills, and thus it supports a proper investment in human capital.

For Mill (1824, 38–41), the education of workers in knowledge and intelligence is necessary both for their happiness and for the higher productivity it allows. Mill, however, does not connect these statements with the analysis of accumulation. The latter remains based on the postulate of subsistence wages.

Differently from Sismondi, Malthus praises technical progress and its main consequence: making commodities cheaper and cheaper.[27] However, he says, if it arrives at the point of producing an overabundance of goods, it leads to lower profits. It is true, as Smith (1776, 164–65) states, that comforts have no certain limits, but Malthus (1820, 401–2) writes that there are limits to saving and investment.

As to Ricardo, Samuel Hollander (1983) a variable-wage interpretation in opposition to George Stigler's fix-wage interpretation of Ricardo's model (wages fixed at the subsistence level). However, for Ricardo, accumulation is always pressed by the increase in the cost of subsistence goods, due to the decreasing productivity of land. This limit makes comforts actually unattainable for workers.

In any case, the crucial point is Say's law. In the short run, this law does not provide evidence for its postulate,[28] and ends by denying the evidence of crises. To say that crises are simply due to temporary imbalances among sectors, not to lack of demand, is not a solution. Imbalances are due to a lack of demand considered as a whole. Actually, nearly always (at least in this period) the law is expressed as a false syllogism. Moreover, there is a sort of trick in saying that "to save is to spend." There is a big difference between the two types of spending, whether for final consumption or for investment. The first absorbs production, and the second generates more production, so the proportion between the two matters.[29]

Ronald Meek has argued that Say's law is far from being the analytical basis of Ricardian economics, as Keynes maintains. Although Ricardo uses it for answering Malthus, he does not attribute real importance to it. On the political level, Meek (1950) adds, things change. Ricardo and his disciples were keen to defend capital accumulation against rent, while Malthus had the opposite interest.

Nevertheless, in a very few cases the representation of Say's law lets us dimly see a real prospect of long-run development. Say and Ricardo both state, against Malthus, that human needs are unlimited. Say (1828–29, tome 2: 210–13) declares, "You cannot say that production is in excess until all people are provided of all things and nobody has anything more to desire." He soon adds that the fulfillment of needs cannot be limited to elementary needs; it must also involve nonmaterial needs, which are unlimited. Ricardo (1821; 1810–13, 44–45, letter 19, September 16, 1816), like Malthus, quotes Smith, but completely adheres to his opinion that needs are unlimited. He adds that it is the increase in capital that pushes the inclination for "luxuries" of any kind.

However, no supply can be unlimited unless it continually varies its products. The diversification of goods is the driving force of accumulation. The two authors are well aware of this fact. Say (1803, bk. 1, chap. 15: 92) states, "In order to encourage industry, mere consumption is not sufficient. We need foster the development of taste and needs which generate among people the desire of consuming." And Ricardo (1821, 343–44) writes, "If every man were to forego the use of luxuries, and be intent only on accumulation [i.e., to investment in labor], a quantity of necessaries might be produced, for which there could not be any immediate consumption. Of commodities so limited in number, there might undoubtedly be an universal glut."

This was a decisive achievement. But why is it that these economists never connected it with the increase in productivity of human capital? Because the conditions of the time appeared to deny any connection of the kind. An enormous gap divided factory work and professional labor, workers' wages and the incomes of the intellectual labor. Of course, even then, there was a connection between the increase in consumption and the increase in productivity of human capital. Factory machines were invented, built up, checked and repaired by skilled producers. The same happened for the organization of labor as well as of trade and for the various aspects of business.

However, this kind of labor was unnoticed; there was no room for it in the classical accumulation model. One could think that as technical progress went on, the role of skilled and technical labor would appear more and more central. Unfortunately, the two decades we have examined were the blueprint for the following economics on our subject. When the concept of human capital was finally acquired, one-and-a-half centuries had passed and economic categories were radically changed. Very few people still used to think in terms of accumulation and productive consumption.

Notes

1 Cited, in French, by J. Hollander (1928, lxxix).
2 For a different view, see Paglin (1961, 116–17).
3 Schneider (2008, 456–57), too, notes this incongruity.
4 See Torrens (1821, 399–430) and also Torrens (1819, 75–76).
5 See, for example, Dow (1977) and Kates (1998, chap. 6).
6 See Keynes (1936, chap. 23, sec. 7: 222–24).

7 See Laffemas (1597) and my introduction to his English translation.
8 For all these authors, see Perrotta (2004, chaps. 9 and 11). Keynes himself is more moderate than the attitude he wrongly attributes to pre-Smithian authors. He writes, "At the same time we must recognise that only experience can show how far the common will, embodied in the policy of the State, ought to be directed to increasing and supplementing the inducement to invest; and how far it is safe to stimulate the average propensity to consume, without foregoing our aim of depriving capital of its scarcity-value within one or two generations" (Keynes, 1936, ch. 24, sec. 2: 377).
9 For example, Houghton (1677, 261–62), Mandeville (1705, 25 and 1714, 107ff) and Voltaire (1738, 358).
10 See Lauderdale (1804a, especially ch. 4 and 1804b, 59ff). On the sinking fund, see Lauderdale (1829, 79–117).
11 See also Paglin (1961, 118–19).
12 Chalmers (1832, 249; chaps. 1 to 5). See also, in general, Chalmers (1808).
13 See, for example, Ganilh (1809, 1: 97–127 and 252–73; 1815, 2: 413–44; 1835, 304–18).
14 See Ganilh's (1826, 159–61) entry "Consommations."
15 Malthus (1820, bk. 1, chap. 4, sec. 2: 223–31; bk. 2, chap. 1, sec. 2: 311–14; bk. 2, chap. 1, sec. 3: 318–20). See also Torrens (1815, 62–64).
16 The author of *Inquiry* (1821, 19–23) agrees with Malthus. Salim Rashid (1977, 226–27) grasps that the solution to underconsumption consists in new consumption goods, but he erroneously attributes this view to Malthus. He also believes that, for Malthus, one of the remedies to gluts is "the redistribution of wealth from the rich [...] to the poor, who had an abundance of wishes yet to fulfil." However, from his words it appears that the supposed redistribution is in fact an increase in the number of workers hired for the leisure of the rich (ibid., 232–33). Nor does Malthus ever attribute to workers the wish to increase and vary their comforts, as Rashid thinks (ibid., 229–30).
17 See the clear synthesis given by Paglin (1961, 117).
18 It consists of a short introduction and a conclusion, written for the 1827 edition, and two essays first appeared, respectively, in 1820 and 1824.
19 Patten (1899, 317) maintains that after landlords were defeated by capitalists—due to the Free Trade policy adoption—James Mill's extreme defense of profits (against rent) went to the detriment of workers.
20 It is the title of section 2 in chapter 4.
21 Quoted in detail by Sismondi (1820–27, first article).
22 See Say (respectively, 1803, bk. 1, chap. 11, fn93: 72–73 and 1820, 72: second letter).
23 See Say (1803, bk. 1, chap. 15: 87–88; 1820: first letter, and 1828–29, part 3, chap. 2: 341–42).
24 See Barton (1817, 40–45; 1814–17, 182–88).
25 St. Clair (1957, chaps. 11–13, esp. 256–57) drives to the extreme Ricardo's arguments, ending by deforming them.
26 McCulloch (1821, 102–3) had repeated the argument of the previous Ricardo's edition. His refusal of Ricardo's self-criticism is—it seems—in the *Edinburgh Review*, n. 69. See Torrens (1821, Preface: xi–xii fn). For the positive effects of technical progress on labor, see also Torrens (1834, 33–44).
27 This is also stressed by Bonar (1885, 296).
28 See also O' Brien (1975, 353).
29 See also Faucci and Pesciarelli (1976, 57–64: "Introduction").

References

Barton, J. 1814–17. "Population Growth and National Strength (third essay)." In *Economic Writings*, vol. 1. Regina, Sask.: Lynn Publishing Company, 1962.
———. 1817. *Conditions of the Labouring Classes of Society*. London: Arch.

Bonar, J. 1885. *Malthus and His Work*, 2nd ed. London: Allen & Unwin, 1924.

Bleaney, M. 1976. *Underconsumption Theories*. London: Lawrence and Wishart.

Canard, N.-F. 1801. *Principes d'économie politique*. Paris: F. Buisson.

Cazenove, J. 1822. *Considerations on the Accumulation of Capital*. London: Richardson.

Chalmers, T. 1808. *An Inquiry into the Extent and Stability of National Resources*. Edinburgh: Oliphant & Brown.

———. 1832. *On Political Economy*. Glasgow: Collins; New York: Appleton.

Dow, L. A. 1977. "Malthus on Sticky Wages, the Upper Turning Point and General Glut," *History of Political Economy* 9, no. 3: 303–21.

Faucci, R., and E. Pesciarelli, eds. 1976. *L'economia classica: Origini e sviluppo (1750–1848)*. Milano: Feltrinelli.

Ganilh, C. 1809. *Des systèmes d'économie politique*. 2 vols. Paris: Xhrouet, Déterville, Lenormant, Petit.

———. 1815. *La théorie de l'économie politique, fondée sur les faits résultats des statistiques de la France et de l'Angleterre*. 2 vols. Paris: Déterville.

———. 1826. *Dictionnaire analytique d'économie politique*. Paris and Brussels: Ladvocat.

———. 1835. *Principes d'économie politique et de finance*. Paris and Strasbourg: Levrault.

Haberler, G. 1937. *Prosperity and Depression: A Theoretical Analysis of Cyclical Movements*, rev. ed. Geneva: League of Nations, 1939.

Hollander, J. H. 1928. "Introduction." In D. Ricardo, *Notes on Malthus' "Principles of Political Economy*," edited by J. H. Hollander and T. E. Gregory. Baltimore: Johns Hopkins Press.

Hollander, S. 1983. "On the Interpretation of Ricardian Economics: The Assumption Regarding Wages," *American Economic Review* 73, no. 2: 314–18.

———. 1995. "Malthus as Physiocrat: Surplus Versus Scarcity." Reprinted in *Literature of Political Economy. Collected Essays II*, ch. 18. London and New York: Routledge, 1998.

Houghton, J. 1677. "England's Great Happiness." Reprinted in *A Select Collection of Early English Tracts on Commerce*, edited by J. R. McCulloch, 251–74. London: Political Economy Club, 1856.

Inquiry. 1821. *An Inquiry into Those Principles, Respecting the Nature of Demand and the Necessity of Consumption*. London: Hunter.

Kates, S. 1998. *Say's Law and the Keynesian Revolution*. Cheltenham: Edward Elgar.

Keynes, J. M. 1936. *The General Theory of Employment, Interest and Money*. London: Macmillan.

Kolb, F. R. 1972. "The Stationary State of Ricardo and Malthus: Neither Pessimistic nor Prophetic." Reprinted in *David Ricardo: Critical Assessments*, edited by J. Cunningham Wood, 1: 235–50. London and Sydney: Croom Helm, 1985.

Laffemas, B. 1597. *Reiglement général pour dresser les manufactures en ce royaume et couper le cours des draps de soye et autres marchandises qui perdent et ruynent l'État*. Paris: Claude de Monstr'oil and Jean Richter. English translation: *General Regulation for the Establishment of Workshops*. London: Anthem Press, 2016.

Lauderdale, J. M. 1804a. *An Inquiry into the Nature and Origin of Public Wealth and into the Means and Causes of Its Increase*, 2nd ed., greatly enlarged. Edinburgh: Constable & Co.; London: Longman, Hurst, Rees & Orme, 1819.

———. 1804b. *Observations by the Earl of Lauderdale, on the Review of his Inquiry into the Nature and Origin of Public Wealth. Published in the VIII Number of the Edinburgh Review*. Edinburgh: Constable & Co.; London: Longman, Hurst, Rees & Orme.

———. 1829. *Three Letters to the Duke of Wellington on the Fourth Report of the Select Committee of the House of Commons, Appointed in 1828 to Enquire into the Public Income and Expenditure of the United Kingdom: In Which the Nature and Tendency of a Sinking Fund Is Investigated and the Fallacy of the Reasoning by Which It Has Been Recommended to Public Favour Is Explained*. London: Murray.

Malthus, T. R. 1820. *Principles of Political Economy*, 2nd ed. London: Pickering, 1836.

Mandeville, B. 1705. "The Grumbling Hive: Or, Knaves Turn'd Honest." In *The Fable of the Bees: Or, Private Vices, Publick Benefits*, edited by F. B. Kaye, 1: 17–37. Oxford: Clarendon, 1924.

———. 1714. "Remarks." In *The Fable of the Bees: Or, Private Vices, Publick Benefits*, edited by F. B. Kaye, 1: 58–251. Oxford: Clarendon, 1924.

McCulloch, J. R. 1821. "The Opinions of Messrs Say, Sismondi and Malthus on the Effects of Machinery and Accumulation, Stated and Examined," *Edinburgh Review* 35, no. 69: 102–23.

Meek, R. 1950. "The Decline of Ricardian Economics in England," *Economica n.s.* 17, no. 65: 43–62. Reprinted in *Economics and Ideology and Other Essays*, 51–74. London: Chapman and Hall, 1967.

Mill, J. 1808. *Commerce Defended*. London: Baldwin.

———. 1821. *Elements of Political Economy*, 3rd ed. London: Bohn, 1844.

———. 1824. "Education." In *Encyclopaedia Britannica*, 6th ed. (signed G. G.). London: Encyclopaedia Britannica.

Mirabeau, V. 1769–71. *Les Économiques*, 3 vols. Amsterdam: no publisher.

O'Brien, D. P. 1975. *The Classical Economists*. Oxford: Clarendon.

Owen, R. 1815. *Observations on the Effect of the Manufacturing System*, 2nd ed. London: Longman, Hurst, Rees, Orme & Brown, and others, 1817.

———. 1818. *Two Memorials on Behalf of the Working Classes*. London: Longman, Hurst, Rees & Orme.

Paglin, M. 1961. *Malthus and Lauderdale. The Anti-Ricardian Tradition*, reprint. Clifton, NJ: A. M. Kelley, 1973.

Patten, S. 1899. *The Development of English Thought*, reprint. New York and London: Garland, 1974.

Perrotta, C. 2004. *Consumption as an Investment*. New York and London: Routledge.

Quesnay, F. 1766. "Sur les travaux des artisans: Second Dialogue." Reprinted in *François Quesnay et la Physiocratie*, 2: 885–912. Paris: INED, 1958.

———. 1767. "Despotisme de la Chine." Reprinted in *Oeuvres économiques et philosophiques de François Quesnay*, edited by A. Oncken, 563–660. Paris: Peelman and Francfort: Baer, 1888.

Rashid, S. 1977. "Malthus's Model of General Gluts." In *Thomas Robert Malthus: Critical Assessments*, edited by J. Cunningham Wood, 3: 224–38. London and Sydney: Croom Helm, 1986.

Ricardo, D. 1810–23. *Letters to Malthus*, edited by J. Bonar. Oxford: Clarendon, 1887.

———. 1820. *Notes on Malthus' "Principles of Political Economy."* Reprint edited by J. H. Hollander and T. E. Gregory. Baltimore: Johns Hopkins Press, 1928.

———. 1821. *Principles of Political Economy and Taxation*. London: Murray.

Say, J.-B. 1803. *Traité d'économie politique*, 6th ed. Paris: Guillaumin, 1841.

———. 1820. *Lettres à M. Malthus*. Paris: Bossange.

———. 1828–29. *Cours complet d'économie politique pratique*, 2nd ed. Paris: Guillaumin, 1840.

Schneider, M. 2008. "Underconsumption." In *The New Palgrave Dictionary of Economics*, 2nd ed., edited by Steven N. Durlauf and Lawrence E. Blume, 456–60. Basingstoke: Palgrave Macmillan.

Sismondi, J.-C.-L., Simonde de. 1819. *Nouveaux principes d'économie politique, ou de la richesse dans ses rapports avec la population*. Paris: Delaunay.

———. 1820–27. "Éclaircissemens relatifs à la balance des consommations avec les productions." In *Nouveaux principes d'économie politique, ou de la richesse dans ses rapports avec la population*, 2nd ed., vol. 2: 369–464. Paris: Delaunay, 1827.

———. 1837–38. *Études sur l'économie politique*. 2 vols. Paris: Treuttel et Würtz.

Smith, A. 1776. *An Inquiry into the Nature and Causes of the Wealth of Nations*, 5th ed., edited by E. Cannan. London: Methuen, 1904.

Spence, W. 1807. *Britain Independent of Commerce*. In *Tracts on Political Economy*, 1–92. London: Longman, Hurst, Rees, Orme & Brown, 1822.

St. Clair, O. 1957. *A Key to Ricardo*, reprint. New York: A. Kelley, 1965.

Torrens, R. 1808. "The Economists Refuted." Reprinted (with separate pagination) in *The Principles and Practical Operations of Sir Robert Peel's Bill of 1844: Explained and Defended*, 2nd ed. London: Longman, Brown, Green, Longman & Roberts, 1857.

———. 1815. *An Essay on the External Corn Trade*. London: Hatchard.

———. 1819. "Mr. Owen's Plans for Relieving the National Distress." In *The Economists Refuted and Other Early Economic Writings*, edited by P. Groenewegen. Sydney: University of Sydney, 1984.

————. 1821. *An Essay on the Production of Wealth.* London: Longman, Hurst, Rees & Orme.

————. 1834. *On Wages and Combination.* London: Longman, Hurst, Rees & Orme.

Voltaire. 1738. "Observations sur MM. Jean Law, Melon et Dutot; sur le commerce, le luxe, les monnaies et les impots." Translated from French: "Osservazioni su John Law, Melon e Dutot." In Voltaire, *Scritti politici.* Torino: UTET, 1964.

Chapter Ten

ON THE "PHOTOGRAPH" INTERPRETATION OF PIERO SRAFFA'S PRODUCTION EQUATIONS: A VIEW FROM THE SRAFFA ARCHIVE

Heinz D. Kurz and Neri Salvadori

1. Introduction

Alessandro Roncaglia in his book *Sraffa e la teoria dei prezzi* (1975), an English version of which was published as *Sraffa and the Theory of Prices* (1978), put forward the view that Sraffa's systems of price equations are best interpreted in terms of a "photograph" taken of the economic system at a given moment of time or, rather, a snapshot of a cycle of production of the system. He wrote,

> The determination of prices was studied at a given moment of time, given the prevailing technology. [...] In other words, the classical economists' analysis of prices examined the situation of a given economic system at a given moment in time, much like a photograph of the system at an instant in time.

He added,

> In this way all the economic variables which were not the object of analysis could be considered as given. Theoretical investigation could concentrate attention on the "virtual" movement of specific variables and on the relations between these variables as if they were being considered "isolated in a vacuum." In the case of *Production of Commodities by Means of Commodities* the choice of variables to be analysed has fallen on the relations that exist between prices of production and the distributive variables, the wage rate and the rate of profits. (Roncaglia, 1978, 21)[1]

This short contribution revolves around the metaphor of "photograph" and its possible meaning(s) in Sraffa's preparatory papers leading up to his 1960 book and the book itself. We proceed in the following way. We ask, first, whether, and if so, when Sraffa came across the metaphor in the literature and used it himself (section 2). Next we draw the attention to another, but closely related, metaphor Sraffa used: "the man from the moon," and its possible relation to David Ricardo's activities in Parliament (section 3). Then we discuss a statement by Maffeo Pantaleoni in one of his books that Sraffa annotated. His annotations throw some light on the materialist or objectivist approach Sraffa was keen to develop in the late 1920s and at the beginning of the 1930s (section 4). Then we reflect upon the relationship between Sraffa's analysis in his 1960 book and what he called "the standpoint [...] of the old classical economists from Adam Smith to Ricardo" (1960, v) in the theory of value and distribution (section 5). The metaphor of the photograph reappears in Sraffa's correspondence with a German student in 1968, and its meaning there is precisely the one implied by Sraffa's characterization of the classical as opposed to the marginalist approach in the theory of value and distribution. The way Roncaglia uses it is similar (section 6). The paper concludes with a few final observations (section 7).

2. Sraffa and the Metaphor of "Photograph"

In Sraffa's hitherto unpublished manuscripts and notes and in his annotations in books and papers, kept at Trinity College Library, Cambridge, the term "photograph" appears a couple of times in different contexts. We do not know whether Roncaglia came across the term when he and John Eatwell took stock of Sraffa's papers in the 1970s, before Sraffa appointed Pierangelo Garegnani as his literary executor, who with the help of Krishna Bharadwaj produced the first catalogue of Sraffa's papers.[2] Here we provide, first, a reference to the term photograph in a book by Cunynghame that Sraffa had read and annotated. Next, we turn to his preparatory notes for his 1960 book, which he began to compose as early as November 1927, but had to interrupt beginning in 1930 because of his appointment to the editorship of Ricardo's works and correspondence by the Royal Economic Society. He resumed the work on what he called "my book" in 1942, but had to interrupt it once more after the discovery of Ricardo's correspondence with James Mill, and finally was able to put together the book from his old notes from 1955 to 1958. Finally, we consider the use of the metaphor in Sraffa's correspondence.

2.1 An Annotation in One of Sraffa's Books

The term photograph is probably first mentioned in the context of Sraffa's critical scrutiny of marginalist, or demand and supply, theory, with the focus on market equilibrium. In 1904, Henry Cunynghame had published *A Geometrical Political Economy, Being an Elementary Treatise on the Method of Explaining Some of the Theories of Pure Economic Science by Means of Diagrams*. The book is in Sraffa's library (item 2243) and is annotated by him. There is reason to presume that Sraffa read it at an early time. In his treatise, Cunynghame stresses right at the beginning, "All the curves mentioned in this book are intended to be applicable to *states of equilibrium*, reached after temporary oscillations have ceased; or rather, since all things are in a state of perpetual flux, as *instantaneous photographs* taken at times *when the market conditions are normal*" (1904, 3; second emphasis added).

In the margin of this passage, Sraffa put a straight line. By straight lines, he typically signaled the relevance of a passage from the point of view of his own studies at the time or approval of the proposition contained in it. The important thing to note here is that the photograph under consideration has been taken at the right moment, that is, when the economic system is in a "state of equilibrium" or, somewhat less stringent, when "market conditions are normal." As anyone who has ever used a camera to catch a moment or a particular situation knows, the art consists in pushing the trigger button at the "right moment." Missing it gives a picture that does not catch in full what the photographer was interested in seeing and in the extreme nothing of interest at all. Obviously, "hitting the moment" presupposes that the photographer already has an idea of the object to be caught and seeks to catch it when it materializes. Cunynghame's wording makes it very clear that the trigger button of the camera must not be pressed arbitrarily, that is, at any time, but precisely when equilibrium or normal market conditions obtain. Since they will hardly ever be realized in actual fact, it should also be clear that the photograph cannot be taken to capture the realized state of markets in an actual economy but refers to an idealized state, one that is hypothetically in equilibrium or exhibits normal market conditions. In Marshallian partial equilibrium theory, the point of reference is the intersection between a demand and a supply function, as Cunynghame stresses. The photograph thus conveys the image the photographer has in his mind of a very particular situation in the market. It does not portray reality as it is, but as the photographer thinks it is, focusing attention on the magnitudes in terms of which certain phenomena (relative prices and income distribution) can be explained.

Cunynghame (1904, 3) then asks whether there is a difference between a Marshallian short and a long-period analysis and opines, "It does not seems to me, nor do I understand Professor Marshall to say (see *Principles of Economics*, bk. 5, chap. 4, p. 416, 1890 ed.), that there is any fundamental difference between short-period and long-period curves." Interestingly, there is also a straight line along this passage in Sraffa's copy of the book. What did Sraffa wish to express by annotating the passage in this way at the time when he annotated it? We cannot know for sure, but will put forward some considerations that might perhaps contain a clue to grasping what he probably had in mind. However, we will postpone this discussion and first turn to documents from Sraffa's unpublished papers.

2.2 Sraffa's Unpublished Papers

Difference vs. Change

In a manuscript of several pages entitled "Difference vs. Change," contained in a folder with the title "After 1927," which can safely be assumed to have been written in the first period of his constructive work (1927–30), Sraffa made an attempt to clear up what he considered to be a fundamental confusion in the theory of value. Immediately below the document's title he added, "(simultaneous) (succession in time)," the former bracketed term obviously relating to "Difference" and the latter to "Change." He wrote,

> The general confusion in all theories of value (except Marx probably) must be explained by the failure to distinguish between two entirely distinct types of questions and the universal attempt of solving them both by one single theory.

The two questions are:

1) What determines the [*difference* in the (?)] values at which various commodities are exchanged in a given market on a given instant?
2) What determines the *changes* in the values of commodities at different times? (e.g. of *one* commodity). (Sraffa Papers, D3/12/7/115; Sraffa's underlinings are italicized here)[3]

Sraffa, after some deliberation, concluded, "The first problem gives rise to a geometrical theory, the second to a mechanical one" (Sraffa Papers, D3/12/7/117). With regard to the first problem/theory he adds that "its object is, as it were, the *photograph* of a market place" and that it "must be solved by the theory of value. The second, I think, can only be solved by the theory of industrial fluctuations. All the old confusion between cause and measure of value is connected with the mixing up of the two questions" (ibid.; emphasis added). Against the background of this distinction, he then argued that Marshall's theory "can only be understood as an attempt to solve the first question in terms of the second" (ibid.). What about Marx's theory? Sraffa observed that Karl Marx wanted to tackle both problems in terms of a single theory by focusing attention on what is common to all commodities. Marx asked, first, if today coal exchanges for boots at a given ratio, "what is the common element, the substance which enters in equal quantity in the two things, hidden behind the widely different appearances?" He asked, secondly, if a year ago the exchange rate was different, "what is the difference, hidden behind the identical appearance of these two pairs of boots, which makes them different in exchange?" Sraffa then added, "this way of putting the distinction is confusing. If the 'common substance' is drawn in for the first case, it is clear that as it explains the equality in the first case, it will explain the difference in the second. Besides the making of the first a matter of equality and of the second a matter of difference, is a purely verbal trick [...]" (Sraffa Papers, D3/12/7/118).

What to make of this? First, the metaphor of photograph is again invoked with regard to markets and the relative prices solving the corresponding equations. The theory has to capture the constellation of forces responsible for the observed prices, and the picture shot is supposed to expose them. As regards the search for a "common substance," Marx's (in)famous *tertium comparationis*, the question is, of course, what it is and what its properties are, whether it is unique, whether it can be known independently of solving the equations of production, whether it remains the same when time goes by and so on. As regards intertemporal (and also interspatial) comparisons, there seems to be no presumption that there is a common substance "embodied" in commodities produced at different times, the "substance," if any, is rather bound to change over time.

In this document, the metaphor of a photograph appears to be invoked as an alternative to that of a motion picture: a single photograph can highlight elements one might easily lose sight of when confronted with a quick sequence of snapshots as in a film, but the dynamic aspects can, at least partially, be lost.

Working Capital

In a note entitled "Working capital," stemming from November 1927, Sraffa reflected on a lecture by John Maynard Keynes he had attended, in which Keynes had argued that "Circulating capital is exceedingly small." After some deliberation Sraffa concluded that "W.[orking] capital is exceedingly small because it is the photograph of what exists at any one moment, not of what has been spent during the period." Hence the metaphor of the photograph is misleading in the present context or, rather, it provides only very limited information that can easily be misread. If the whole picture of the social process of production is taken into account, firms turn out to have a huge working capital. Sraffa explains, "Nobody holds stocks. What matters is to have ready command over stocks, to be able to rely with certainty upon possibility of procuring it. But this is *money*. Firms have an enormous working capital because they have money. This *is* capital […]" (Sraffa Papers, D3/12/11/37; emphasis in original).

Sraffa here refers to the distinction between stocks and flows. Clearly, a photograph can only depict stocks, but as Sraffa's eventual treatment of fixed capital using the joint-products method shows, stocks may be represented as a sequence of flows and actually this representation is much more useful. Once again the question is asked how much a single photograph can show or explain compared to a motion picture, but in the present context a photograph is clearly inferior, because it may provide a distorted picture of reality.

Time, Labor, Value

Finally, we turn to a manuscript of three pages dated "Oct. 1929," in which Sraffa discusses anew what a theory of value has to accomplish (Sraffa Papers, D3/12/13/1 [1–3]). At the time he wrote it, he had already elaborated the method of reduction of prices to dated quantities of labor and felt that the Böhm-Bawerkian concept of "period of production" could be employed as an alternative to his equations. We transcribe the manuscript in full.

Sraffa introduces the issue in the following way: (Sraffa Papers, D3/ 12/ 13/ 1[1]-[3]; here words underlined once are italicized and words underlined twice are underlined once and italicized).

The real question is:

Given the situation of an / (number of) / industry / (completely integrated vertically) / *at one instant* (i.e. given all physical, chemical, etc. connotations[4] and measurements of the situation, but excluded all economic connotations, especially values, utilities, productivities, etc.), and assuming all men exactly alike to one another (both for wages they receive, and value they add to the product), is it possible to deduce the value of its product per unit of time?

Or, is the above possible, given the same data for, *not* an instant, bur for *a period of time*, such that all the different operations should be performed within it? (more exactly: such a proportion of them that the defect should be smaller than any assigned proportion.) (This would be, roughly, a year in agriculture; but one day, or perhaps one hour in case of continuous shifts, in the motor industry).

He goes on:

As regards labour, the answer is simple enough: so far as it is concerned, value will be proportional to the number of workers employed.

It is with capital that difficulties arise: for, while for labour we have defined a measure by assuming all workmen to be equal, we have no such measure for capital: *it is composed of heterogeneous objects*, which cannot be measured, "qua" capital, by number or weight, etc.

How to deal with this problem?

Suppose the above difficulty is overcome by measuring capital as accumulated labour; i.e. adopting the *second* question [sic! The reference ought to be to equation, meaning the approach in terms of periods of production rather than simultaneous equations], and assuming that all the various acts of labour are performed within a period of production, and that their order of succession is known.

Thus, "time" is part of our assumptions, i.e. they are not instantaneous: but it is a peculiar time, or perhaps only a part of time. It admits only of cyclical change, i.e. it is a sort of circular time: changes take place, but only recurrent changes, which periodically lead back to the original position: no permanent, or "true," change is allowed.

With these assumptions we can go as far as the second equations [i.e., with a surplus], and also introduce rent (to some extent: but we must assume knowledge of wages (*or* of rate of interest). To dispense with the last knowledge, we must pass to the "marginal" analysis: and this involves knowledge (and possibility) of possible changes—different from anything that actually occurs, in the course of the "steady process." How can this difficulty be overcome?

Sraffa continues:

Clearly, we must reduce *all* the data to things that actually happen, excluding inexistent possibilities. Only such things are measurable, and can enter the theory as "knowns," or "constants"; and, in reality, only really happening things can be real causes and determine effects.[5]

This notion of time is important: it really substitutes "instantaneous photographs" as opposed to ordinary time. It is only a part of ordinary time, it has only some of its connotations: it includes events, / also different events, / but not change of events. It enables us to compare two simultaneous, but not instantaneous, events—just as if they were "things."

It is, in effect, equivalent to the physicist's *dt*, as understood by Russell (Outline of Phil. [1927], p. 122)[6]—a time in which effects follow causes, but so closely that there is no room either for dispersion or for entering of foreign influences: *dt* does this by differentiation (making the time so short as actually to leave no room for change in circumstances: the cause & effect are perfectly contiguous—nothing is in between)—our "time" does this by "assuming" away all changes, (i.e. "coeteris paribus"? no: by positing the problem in the form of finding the conditions of repetition indefinitely, or even once).

This conception of time enables us to take into account, not only *stocks* (as the instantaneous view does) but also steady or cyclical *flows* (which that does not), while still using the geometrical model. (italics added)

Once again, photograph and motion picture are contrasted, but now, with reference to a repetitive or self-replacing process, an appropriately redefined concept of the former is considered to capture adequately the case under consideration. The kind of photograph Sraffa speaks of cannot be arbitrary, and, strictly speaking, it cannot be a one-shot snapshot but rather a picture (or sequence of pictures) that contains all the necessary information concerning an entire period of the production of commodities by means of commodities. It conforms to Roncaglia's snapshot of a cycle of production of the system.

3. Another Metaphor: The "Man from the Moon"

Interestingly, Sraffa employed also another metaphor as a shorthand to describe the same thing: the "man from the moon." The note in which he used it was composed presumably toward the end of the early period of his work, that is, in 1929 or 1930. He characterized his first and second equations (in ink) in the following way:

The significance of the equations is simply this: that if a man fell from the moon on the earth, and noted the amount of things consumed in each factory and the amount produced by each factory during a year, he could deduce at which values the commodities must be sold, if the rate of interest must be uniform and the process of production repeated. In short, the equations show that the conditions of exchange are entirely determined by the conditions of production. (Sraffa Papers, D3/12/7/87)

This note is interesting for several reasons. First, while it does not refer to a photograph, it contemplates on what an impartial observer, coming from another planet, would see on earth and what he could infer with regard to relative prices and the rate of interest. He would see physical quantities of things (inputs) being transformed into other things (outputs). A photograph would have the task to show these quantities. It would not show the rate of interest and relative prices: these would rather be the result of the impartial observer's mental work, seeking to find a system of relative prices that support the distribution of the social surplus in terms of a uniform rate of interest across all productive activities. This condition is superimposed on what could be seen in a photograph and reflects particular social institutions or "rules of the game," such as free competition. From this it follows that the photograph metaphor is of limited use only, because it is unable to capture the essence of the problem at hand: the observer's projection of given social conditions onto a given physical scheme of production and establishing the implications that follow from them (interest rate, prices).

Second, presumably in 1942 when Sraffa resumed his constructive work and reread his old notes, he added (in pencil) "Man from the Moon" and also put two straight lines along the passage in the margin. These additions evoke two remarks. First, characterizing the situation under consideration with reference to the man from the moon echoes an event that took place in British Parliament on the occasion of a debate on agricultural distress on May 30, 1820. In the debate Ricardo is reported to have said that, "because he consulted the interests of the whole community, he would oppose the corn-laws" (1820, 49). A Mr. Brougham, the Member for Winchelsea, who supported the agriculturalists' motion in favor of additional protective measures, qualified Ricardo's argument as if it came from a man who "had dropped from another planet" and lived in an "Utopian world" (ibid., 56).[7] The reference to the "man from the moon" may thus be seen as a metaphor designed to indicate the need to take a detached point of view, to see things as they are and not through the tinted glass of some particular interest group. What was badly needed was an objectivist perspective rooted in indubitable facts, such as the productive transformation of things, that is, commodities, and not a partisan outlook on matters.[8]

Third, and closely related to what has just been said, one has to stay away from existing explanations of income distribution and relative prices and make a fresh start. The man from the moon was by definition in the lucky position of being unaffected by received doctrines (marginalist theory or the labor theory of value) and could seek a new solution to an old problem. This solution, Sraffa implied, the man from the moon could easily find because of his unprejudiced point of view—he is in fact taken to see at a glance what some economists do not see at all and others see only vaguely, namely, that the rate of interest and relative prices follow from the given conditions of production. Economic theory may be a formidable tool that allows us to grasp aspects of a complex subject matter, but it may also mislead or bedazzle us.

The metaphor of the man from the moon can be seen as a development of the metaphor of the photograph. In our interpretation both are steps in Sraffa's search for a nonsubjectivist, objectivist explanation of relative prices and income distribution, which was at the heart of Sraffa's research program. We have put forward ample evidence from Sraffa's papers in support of this interpretation and refrain from repeating ourselves here. The interested reader is asked to consult Kurz and Salvadori (2004, 2005), Gehrke and Kurz (2006), Salvadori and Signorino (2007) and Kurz (2012). We rather reflect upon the issues at hand around an annotation in one of Sraffa's book we have not mentioned up until now that provides a welcome foil for our discussion.

4. Interpreting Sraffa's Approach vis-à-vis a Statement by Pantaleoni

We now turn to Sraffa's annotations in the second edition of Maffeo Pantaleoni's *Principii di economia pura*, published in 1894 (see Sraffa's Library, item 2302), a book he was familiar with and had read at an early time of his career as an economist.[9] Pantaleoni writes, "La ragione quindi per fermarsi soltanto sulla utilità delle cose come una funzione della loro quantità, e non altresì sulla loro utilità come una funzione dei nostri bisogni, o una funzione delle loro proprietà fisico-chimiche, *sta esclusivamente nella maggior fecondità di questo concetto*" (1894, 99–100; emphasis added).[10]

Sraffa puts two straight lines in the margin of this passage, signaling it to be very important. The question is why? We know that from an early time onward he doubted the alleged "superior fecundity" of marginal utility theory that Pantaleoni extolled. What were the reasons the latter gave in support of it, and could they be sustained in Sraffa's view?

When singling out marginal utility theory as the best option available to economists, Pantaleoni had to show that alternative approaches to the theory of value and distribution were untenable or at any rate inferior. Sraffa was especially interested to hear what Pantaleoni had to say against attempts to see the values of commodities as rooted in the "physical-chemical properties" of commodities. Why did Pantaleoni think that the values of commodities, that is, "things" (*cose*), could not be explained in this way? Pantaleoni saw such approaches as carrying over John Dalton's atomic theory straight away to the sphere of economics. However, Pantaleoni was convinced that this was not possible. Dalton's atomic theory is based on two laws: (1) the law of the conservation of mass and (2) the law of definite proportions or constant composition: in any given chemical compound, the elements are always combined in the same proportion by mass. Are commodities not just embodiments of well-specified amounts of various things, elements or atoms "productively consumed" when produced? The analogy with chemical compounds is indeed close at hand. Water, for example, is both a chemical compound and typically also a commodity and can be represented by $2H_2O = 2H_2 + 2O$. It is always "produced" in the same way by combining elements H and O in a given composition. If this analogy were to extend to all commodities, then all commodities could be conceived of in terms of the elements constituting them.

Pantaleoni disputed the second of the two laws, the law of constant composition, because in economics one and the same commodity can typically be produced not only in one way but also in different ways involving different proportions of the physical–chemical elements out of which the commodity is made. This follows from two facts. First, producers are commonly faced with a choice among a set of alternative methods of production to produce the same commodity, which is known as the choice of technique problem. Second, even if there would be only a single method available, workers who operate the method could be fed, clothed and housed in different ways, again implying that the object they produce may be conceived as exhibiting, or "embodying," different physical–chemical compositions.

These observations are obviously correct and must not be ignored. They speak against the possibility of carrying atomic theory over to economics in a straightforward manner, and Sraffa was perfectly aware of this. But did this mean that the physical cost approach to the theory of value and distribution had to be entirely abandoned in favor of marginal utility theory, as Pantaleoni concluded, or could it serve as the starting point of a theory that could be given a coherent form and was possessed of a great fecundity? And what can be said about the coherence, or otherwise, of the marginalist theory of value and distribution? Was it really possessed of a superior fecundity, as Pantaleoni opined?

Here we cannot provide detailed answers to the two questions raised. We ask the reader to consult some works of ours in which we dealt with them in greater detail (see Kurz, 2012, 2016; Kurz and Salvadori, 2005; Salvadori and Signorino, 2007). Here it suffices to point out the following. First, in case Dalton's atomic theory could directly serve as the foundation of the theory of value, the distinction between short and long period would collapse, because natural laws hold at any moment of time and the production of any commodity would always consist in the transformation of well-specified amounts of energy and mass into a new form of energy and mass.[11] Photographs taken at any instant of time of this process would always show the same picture. This explains perhaps why in the early phase of his constructive work Sraffa vacillated as to the importance of the distinction between long and short period.[12]

Second, in November 1927 Sraffa began to elaborate his "first" equations relating to an economic system without a surplus, that is, a system in which no more is produced of the different commodities than is consumed productively (means of sustenance of workers and means of production). In a document entitled "Physical Costs & Value," contained in a folder "Nov. [1927]," he noted as regards the values determined in terms of his simultaneous equations,

When I say that the value of a product is "determined" by the *physical volume of commodities used up in its production*, it should *not* be understood that it is determined by the value of those commodities. This would be a vicious circle, because the value of the product is equal to the value of the factors [...].

What I say is simply that the numerical proportions between amount of factors and amount of product *is*, by definition, the absolute value of the product. (Sraffa Papers, D3/12/11/101, first emphasis added, "not" is underlined twice in the original)

And in a document contained in the same folder, he also talked of "physical value" (Sraffa Papers, D3/12/11/75).

Sraffa also made it clear that the physical cost approach to the theory of value was not his discovery or invention, but was anticipated in earlier works. What he, Sraffa, did was simply to provide a consistent formulation of the approach (followed by its extension to systems with a surplus, without and with fixed capital, joint production proper and scarce natural resources). The physical cost approach, he surmised, was foreshadowed, for example, in the just price doctrine of the canonists, but it essentially derived from the "*veduta essenzialmente fisiocratica, che il valore sia una quantità intrinseca degli oggetti, quasi una qualità fisica o chimica*," as he put it in a document composed in the summer of 1929 (Sraffa Papers, D3/12/12/7).[13] He was on the lookout for traces of the physical cost approach in the classical authors and encountered many of them. The perhaps most remarkable statement in this regard he came across was contained in the third edition of James Mill's *Elements of Political Economy*, in which Mill stated, "The agents of production are the commodities themselves [...] They are the food of the labourer, the tools and the machines with which he works, and the raw materials which he works upon" (1826, 165). In summer 1929, Sraffa stated explicitly that he was keen to elaborate an "atomic analysis" (Sraffa Papers, D3/12/13/16[9]), and in August 1931, in a critical retrospect, he characterized his previous analytical efforts as having been concerned with developing "an entirely objective point of view," which is "the natural science point of view" (Sraffa Papers, D3/12/7/161[3]).[14]

Before we proceed, the following deserves to be stressed. In terms of his first equations Sraffa was able to show convincingly that Pantaleoni's rejection of an approach based on the physical–chemical properties of things (i.e., commodities) was not well grounded. In the case of the no-surplus economy, which is the realm of pure necessity, this approach was the only one capable of explaining "necessary prices," that is, those prices that allow the self-replacement of the system. The question then was whether the approach could also be successfully carried over to the with-surplus case, and for a while Sraffa appears to have been convinced that it could. This was possible, he thought, by extending the realm of necessity to include it. He felt that this could be accomplished by distinguishing between *natural costs*, on the one hand, and *necessary social costs*, on the other, which implied interpreting the surplus (profits) as a necessary social cost levied upon workers by the capitalist society. Extending the "natural science point of view," Sraffa insisted, implied that "we shall have to adopt *that definition which makes the scale of absolute values identical with what it was when there was no surplus*" (Sraffa Papers, D3/12/6/14; emphasis added). In this way the logic applying to values in the case of production for subsistence was taken to apply also to the with-surplus case. This necessitated reducing the surplus—that is, an "effect" for which there had to be "sufficient cause" (as Sraffa wrote in Sraffa Papers, D3/12/7/161)—to some "cost" or other. Interest, Sraffa at the time insisted, reflects some objective necessity, rooted in some objective "social" as opposed to "natural" obstacles that have to be overcome: "*Interest appears thus as the necessary means of overcoming an obstacle to production. It is a social necessity* as distinguished from the material necessity of, say, putting coal into a locomotive that it may do its work" (Sraffa Papers, D3/12/18/11; emphases added).[15]

If this extension of the natural science point of view was admissible, a purely physical cost of production approach to the theory of value would have been possible. Alas, it was not as Sraffa found out toward the end of the first period of his constructive work. Here we need not dwell on the reasons that prompted Sraffa to abandon the undiluted natural science point of view he at first had endorsed, see therefore Kurz (2012, 1546–51). It suffices to mention that he saw very clearly that with a choice of technique and flexible consumption patterns of workers the Law of definite proportions could not be carried over to economics and the problem of income distribution could not be reduced to one of necessary cost.[16]

5. Production of Commodities by Means of Commodities

We now turn to Sraffa's 1960 book, the upshot of his earlier efforts. In the book we do not encounter the metaphors "photograph" and "man from the moon," but it becomes abundantly clear what the equations mean and that they are designed to reformulate in a logically consistent way the approach to the theory of value and distribution of the classical economists. Sraffa in fact states explicitly in the preface of the book that the "standpoint" he takes "is that of the old classical economists from Adam Smith to Ricardo, which has been submerged and forgotten since the advent of the 'marginal' method" (1960, v). And he also specifies very clearly how in his view the "method" of the classical authors differs from that of the marginalists: in the former "no changes in output and (at any rate in Parts I and II) no changes in the proportions in which different means of production are used by an industry are considered, *so that no question arises as to the variation or constancy of returns*." He adds, "The investigation is concerned exclusively with such properties of an economic system as do not depend on changes in the scale of production or in the proportions of 'factors'" (1960, v; emphasis added). In other words, the classical economists investigated a *given system of production*. That is, they were keen to establish its properties as regards the distribution of income and relative prices. This method, Sraffa maintained, was in marked contrast to the marginalist method:

> The marginalist approach requires attention to be focused on change, for without change either in the scale of an industry or in the "proportions of the factors of production" there can be neither marginal product nor marginal cost. In a system in which, day after day, production continued unchanged in those respects, the marginal product of a factor (or alternatively the marginal cost of a product) would not merely be hard to find—it just would not be there to be found. (Ibid.)

This is a warning to his readers: marginal products and marginal costs are analytical objects, not observable ones. In fact, even in a stationary state, the observer could calculate the marginal product of a factor or the marginal cost of a commodity, provided that infinitesimal changes *were* (counterfactually) assumed, but obviously no observer can experience them. Things are different with respect to what Wicksteed called "spurious" margins. Sraffa explained, "The most familiar case is that of the product of the 'marginal land' in agriculture, when lands of different qualities are cultivated side by side" (ibid.). In this case two different objects are envisaged by the observer, and the difference between them defines the increments implicit in the concept of margin. This concept of margin was actually introduced by the classical economists. Sraffa reminds us, "P. H. Wicksteed, the purist of marginal theory, [...] condemns such a use of the term 'marginal' as a source of 'dire confusion'" (ibid., v–vi).

The production equations Sraffa then discusses in chapters 1 and 2 of the book are actually variants of those he had elaborated in the late 1920s. Sraffa describes technology by listing industries, where each industry is considered as fully described by the list of inputs it employs and the list of outputs it produces. Where do these data come from? Sraffa (1960) is silent about this. However, many remarks from the unpublished manuscripts (among them those mentioned in the above) clarify that these data are supposed to have been directly observed, as it is the case with the man from the moon. As regards the prices he determines for given real wages (conceived as an inventory of commodities), he stressed explicitly that "such classical terms as 'necessary price,' 'natural price' or 'price of production' would meet the case" (ibid., 9). In the with-surplus case, these prices involve a uniform rate of profits on the value of the capital goods advanced in each industry of the economy. When Sraffa in chapter 12 of his book discusses the choice of technique problem, he starts from the premise that the choice "will be exclusively grounded on cheapness" (ibid., 83). The prices are seen to be the outcome of the cost-minimizing behavior of producers: "At any given level of the general rate of profits, the method that produces at a lower price is of course the most profitable of the two for a producer who builds a new plant" (ibid., 81).

Finally, we draw attention to Sraffa's correspondence after the publication of his book. Interestingly the "photograph" metaphor reappears in it once and confirms the meaning we discussed in the above: its purpose is to draw attention to the classical approach, which is fundamentally different from the marginalist one, and to emphasize its objectivist character revolving around the concept of physical costs and its development.

6. Sraffa's Correspondence

In February 1968, Sraffa received a letter from a German student, Rüdiger Soltwedel, asking him about the meaning and purpose of his equations, which were a riddle to him, having been educated in the marginalist mode of thinking. In Sraffa's reply of March 1, 1968, the metaphor of photograph is used again:

> As regards your own interpretation, I must say frankly that you have gone astray the moment you speak of "equilibrium" or of "elasticity of factor supply": all the quantities considered are what can be observed by taking a photograph. There are no rates of change, etc. This point of view was that of the classical economists (e.g. Ricardo), whereas supply & demand curves were introduced in the middle of the 19th century. Economists are now obsessed with them and cannot think without them. My chapter V, which gives you such a headache, could be understood as an attempt to solve a problem set by Ricardo, and which I described in my Introduction (sections IV & V) of Vol. I of the *Works of Ricardo*, 1951. (Sraffa Papers, C 294, 2)

In this letter the metaphor of the photograph is used precisely in the sense expounded in the preface of Sraffa's 1960 book when specifying the difference between the classical and the marginalist approach to the theory of value and distribution. The classical economists from Adam Smith to Ricardo explained the rate of profits (the real wage rate) and relative prices in terms of a given system of production in use and a given real wage rate (a given rate of profits). The sense also conforms to the one given by Roncaglia: we do have on the one hand a set of given facts (*explanans*) and on the other a set of magnitudes (wage rate, rate of profits, relative prices) whose relationships are to be determined (*explanandum*). These relationships define the "mathematical properties" (Sraffa, 1960, 23) of the system of production under consideration and thus how a change in one variable (e.g., the wage rate) implies corresponding changes in the other variables (the rate of profits, prices).[17]

7. Concluding Remarks

In this chapter we scrutinize the metaphor of "photograph" and the related one of "man from the moon" in Sraffa's papers leading up to his 1960 book, in his annotations in his books and in his correspondence. We show that the main purpose of the first metaphor was to emphasize the most important distinguishing feature of the classical approach to the theory of value and distribution as compared with the marginalist one. While the former analyzes a given system of production with regard to its properties concerning income distribution and relative prices, the latter confronts the given system with an imagined adjacent system, as is reflected in concepts such as marginal productivity and marginal cost. The metaphor of the photograph was meant to express the focus on a given system and the absence of changes in outputs and factor input proportions. The metaphor of the man from the moon was meant to express the data from which the classical theory of value and distribution starts its reasoning, which differ markedly from the marginalist data: given quantities of commodities as inputs (including means of subsistence of workers), on the one hand, and outputs, on the other. "Natural prices" or "prices of production" are fully determined in terms of these givens. In this context it is perhaps interesting to point out that up until the final stage of preparing his manuscript for print, Sraffa tinkered with the idea of giving the book the title "Production of Commodities by Commodities." This is fully in accordance with the man from the moon metaphor and expresses well the objectivist nature of the analysis. We touch upon the relationship between Sraffa's analysis and "a purely natural science point of view" by commenting on a statement in a book by Pantaleoni, Sraffa had annotated. Finally, we show that Roncaglia's use of the metaphor of photograph is in the spirit Sraffa had intended.

Acknowledgments

We are grateful to Christian Gehrke, Bertram Schefold and Alex Thomas for valuable comments on an earlier draft of this paper.

Notes

1 Roncaglia reiterated these statements in Roncaglia (2009).
2 The catalogue now typically used is the one elaborated by Jonathan Smith, archivist of Trinity College Library; see http://www.trin.cam.ac.uk/SRAFFA. In the following, all references to Sraffa's papers are to it and the labeling convention it uses.
3 He inserted a note written in all probability in the same period, which reads, "Perhaps the two questions are better enunciated thus: (1) differences in value of two commodities at one time (2) changes in value of one commodity at two times (value in terms of commodities in general: whence Ricardo's troubles for finding an 'unchanging measure of value,' which in the first question is not involved.)"
4 In the margin he adds, "including wages, or not?"
5 When Sraffa at the beginning of the 1940s discovered that Bortkiewicz (1906, 970–71) had enunciated essentially the same principle, he henceforth spoke of Bortkiewicz's "dictum"; see Gehrke and Kurz (2006, 115–18).
6 The reference is obviously to Russell (1927).
7 He reiterated this characterization on March 7, 1821; see Ricardo (1821, 85).
8 As Sraffa put it in a note written "after 1927" (and probably in 1930, after Sraffa had been appointed to the editorship of Ricardo's works and correspondence), "we are looking for the objective ground of value, and not for what the producers or their accountants, or the economists regard as sensible" (Sraffa Papers, D3/12/7/27). This specification of the aim of his investigation is to be found in the context of a critical discussion of the labor theory of value.

9 When Pantaleoni died in 1924, Sraffa published an obituary in *The Economic Journal* signed as P. S. (Sraffa, 1924), in which he called him "the prince" of economics in Italy—a characterization with ambivalent meanings, including a reference to the prince in Machiavelli's treatise *Il Principe*. Pantaleoni had contributed an important essay on the role of power in economics and on the relationship between the strong and the weak (Pantaleoni, 1898). He was a towering figure in Italian economics around the turn of the century. A propagator of Marshallian economics in Italy and a staunch advocate of markets and competition, he toward the end of his life leaned toward fascism.

10 English translation: "Therefore the reason to focus attention only on the utility of things as a function of their consumption, and not also on their utility as a function of our needs and wants or a function of their physico-chemical properties, *rests exclusively with the greater fecundity of this concept.*"

11 We here ignore that possibility that some fractions of the amounts of inputs will not enter in full the output, but get dissipated into the environment.

12 This is just another example reflecting Sraffa's vivid interest in whether and what the natural sciences had to offer to the economist who sought to elaborate an objectivist or materialist approach to the problem of value and distribution. If Dalton's atomic theory could be applied in a straightforward manner to economics, which according to Sraffa it could not, the commodity composition of each and every "thing" would be knowable and fixed, and production at any point in time would *always* reflect this composition. A sequence of instants, that is, a period whatever its length, would not give a different picture of chemical compounds. It would always be true, for example, that $2H_2 + 2O$ would give $2H_2O$. In this case the distinction between short and long run would not add anything to our understanding. However, in economics things are different precisely because an economy that gravitates toward a cost-minimizing long-period position typically changes the way in which commodities are being produced and thus the commodity composition of inputs that enter them. This is so, because in the short period the methods of production actually employed are typically not fully adjusted to the other data of the classical approach to value and distribution (real wages and gross output levels).

13 English translation of the Italian phrase: "essentially physiocratic point of view that value is a quantity that is intrinsic to the objects, almost a physical or chemical quality."

14 In Sraffa (1960, 3) we will eventually read that the values solving the first equations "spring directly from the methods of production"; in his papers he also used the (Ricardian) term "absolute values" with regard to the case under consideration.

15 It deserves mention that this idea was still present when in the summer of 1942, Sraffa, after having read his old notes, resumed his constructive work and jotted down a list of topics (regarding the planned contents of the book he was to write). It contains, among other things: "2) With profits—everything a necessity." (Sraffa Papers, D3/12/15/1)

16 For a discussion of the steps Sraffa took as a consequence of this, see Kurz and Salvadori (2005), Gehrke and Kurz (2006) and Kurz (2012).

17 Interestingly enough, the uniqueness of the standard commodity is here related only to its role as an invariable measure of value, but this is suggested as a way to understand the latter, that is, a way to relate it to a practical consideration and not to the abstract tool that is used to prove many of the propositions in the first part of the book.

References

Bortkiewicz, L. v. 1906. "Der Kardinalfehler der Böhm-Bawerkschen Zinstheorie," *Schmollers Jahrbuch* 30: 943–72.

Cunynghame, H. 1904. *A Geometrical Political Economy: Being an Elementary Treatise on the Method of Explaining Some of the Theories of Pure Economic Science by Means of Diagrams.* Oxford: Clarendon Press.

Gehrke, C., and H. D. Kurz. 2006. "Sraffa on von Bortkiewicz: Reconstructing the Classical Theory of Value and Distribution," *History of Political Economy* 38, no. 1: 91–149. Reprinted in H. D. Kurz and N. Salvadori, *Revisiting Classical Economics: Studies in Long-Period Analysis*, 142–92. Abingdon: Routledge, 2015.

Kurz, H. D. 2012. "Don't Treat Too Ill My Piero! Interpreting Sraffa's Papers," *Cambridge Journal of Economics* 36, no. 6: 1535–69.

———. 2016. *Economic Thought: A Brief History*. New York: Columbia University Press.

Kurz, H. D., and N. Salvadori . 2004. "Man from the Moon: On Sraffa's Objectivism," *Économies et Sociétés* 35: 1545–57. Reprinted in H. D. Kurz and N. Salvadori, *Interpreting Classical Economics: Studies in Long-Period Analysis*, 120–30. Abingdon: Routledge.

———. 2005. "Representing the Production and Circulation of Commodities in Material Terms: On Sraffa's Objectivism," *Review of Political Economy* 17, no. 3: 413–41. Reprinted in *Piero Sraffa: The Man and the Scholar: Exploring His Unpublished Papers*, edited by H. D. Kurz, L. L. Pasinetti, and N. Salvadori, 249–77. Abingdon: Routledge.

Marshall, A. 1890. *Principles of Economics*. London: Macmillan.

Mill, J. 1826. *Elements of Political Economy*, 2nd ed. London: Henry G. Bohn.

Pantaleoni, M. 1894. *Principii di economia pura*, 2nd ed. Firenze: Barbera.

———. 1898. "An Attempt to Analyse the Concepts of 'Strong and Weak' in Their Economic Connection," *Economic Journal* 8, no. 30: 183–205.

Ricardo, D. 1820. "Agricultural Distress." Speeches given in the House of Commons, May 12, 25 and 30, 1820. In *Speeches and Evidence: 1815–1823*, vol. 5 of *The Works and Correspondence of David Ricardo*, edited by P. Sraffa with the collaboration of M. H. Dobb, 47–57. Cambridge: Cambridge University Press, 1952.

———. 1821. "Mr. Gooch's Motion for a Committee on Agricultural Distress." Speech given in the House of Commons, March 7, 1821. In *Speeches and Evidence: 1815–1823*, vol. 5 of *The Works and Correspondence of David Ricardo*, edited by P. Sraffa with the collaboration of M. H. Dobb, 81–91. Cambridge: Cambridge University Press, 1952.

Roncaglia, A. 1975. *Sraffa e la teoria dei prezzi*. Bari: Laterza. (English edition: *Sraffa and the Theory of Prices*. Chichester: John Wiley, 1978).

———. 2009. *Piero Sraffa*. Basingstoke: Palgrave Macmillan.

Russell, Bertrand. 1927. *An Outline of Philosophy*. London: George Allen and Unwin.

Salvadori, N., and R. Signorino. 2007. "Piero Sraffa: Economic Reality, the Economist and Economic Theory: An Interpretation," *Journal of Economic Methodology* 14, no. 2: 187–209. Reprinted in H. D. Kurz and N. Salvadori, *Revisiting Classical Economics: Studies in Long-Period Analysis*, 70–92. Abingdon: Routledge, 2015.

Sraffa, P. 1924. "Maffeo Pantaleoni," *The Economic Journal* 34, no. 136: 648–53.

———. 1960. *Production of Commodities by Means of Commodities: Prelude to a Critique of Economic Theory*. Cambridge: Cambridge University Press.

Chapter Eleven

ON THE EARLIEST FORMULATIONS OF SRAFFA'S EQUATIONS

Nerio Naldi

1. Introduction

When I was a student, I read Alessandro Roncaglia's illustration of Piero Sraffa's con-tribution to the theory of prices, and some years later it was on his advice that I went to Cambridge and had a rather quick look at some of the papers Sraffa had left to Trinity College. At that time, in 1996, my interest was limited to the lectures Sraffa had delivered in Perugia at the beginning of his academic career, but following Roncaglia's suggestion, I realized how rich and fascinating the large and multifarious body of the Sraffa Papers was.[1] Roncaglia knew very well what I would have found—between 1972 and 1975, as recorded in Sraffa's diaries, he had met Sraffa about a hundred times, he had been discussing with him his own work and Sraffa's writings and had spent many hours in his rooms, studying and ordering his papers, under his supervision.

Since that travel to Cambridge, much of my time has been taken by research on the Sraffa Papers, and what is discussed in this chapter is only one of the many themes enshrined in them. Indeed, following the very opening propositions of *Production of Commodities by Means of Commodities*, as summarized by Roncaglia in his 1975 book—"in the first instance Sraffa demonstrates that when 'commodities are produced by separate industries' in a system of subsistence production ('which produces just enough to main-tain itself'), 'there is a unique set of exchange values which if adopted by the market restores the original distribution of the products and makes it possible for the process to be repeated; such values spring directly from the methods of production'" (quotation is from the 1978 English version, p. 4)—we are led to the focus of this chapter: was not starting an analysis of price determination, as Sraffa did in the first section of his 1960 book, from "an extremely simple society which produces just enough to maintain itself" (p. 3) quite an original departure in the history of economic thought? As a matter of fact, neither such sources as the *Tableau Èconomique* or Karl Marx's schemes of simple repro-duction nor earlier sources as we can find in the writings of Richard Cantillon, John Law and William Petty describe a subsistence, extremely simple or primitive society as that to be found in the opening propositions of *Production of Commodities*. How did Sraffa come to introduce that case?

To answer the questions we have just asked, we will turn to a slightly different one, concerning the origins of Sraffa's approach and of the schemes he employed in *Production of Commodities*. Indeed, during the two decades that have followed the opening of the papers of Sraffa to the public of scholars, the question of how he had come to conceive the schemes that in 1960 appeared in his book has been answered in different and sometimes contrasting ways. Three main interpretations have been put forward. A first interpretation indicated Marx's *Theories of Surplus Value* and the reproduction schemes contained in the second volume of Marx's *Capital* as Sraffa's main source of inspiration (de Vivo, 2000 and 2003; Gilibert, 2001 and 2003).[2] Another interpretation has called attention to Sraffa's reading of contemporary economists and to his interest in natural sciences (notably atomic physics and chemistry) as influences that may have led him to describe production processes as he did with his schemes (Kurz and Salvadori, 2004 and 2005; Gehrke and Kurz, 2006; Kurz, 2012). Thirdly, it has been argued that Sraffa's schemes have been an offspring of an endogenous evolution that his thought would have gone through in the summer of 1927 (Garegnani, 2004 and 2005).

The latter interpretation, independently of specific weaknesses or merits of the others, has the advantage of pointing to a sequence of documents that allow formulation of a hypothesis concerning a precise line leading Sraffa toward his equations. According to the view put forward by Pierangelo Garegnani (2004 and 2005),[3] Sraffa, in his 1925 and 1926 articles on cost curves, had conceived of classical authors as sharing the essential features of the demand and supply approach to value and prices developed by Alfred Marshall as the cornerstone of his *Principles*. In the summer of 1927, however, he would have recognized that their conception was altogether different. Then, in November 1927, in the process of elaborating upon some aspects of his new reading of the classics, he would have come across what he called his equations[4] and would have realized that they opened a new way to the analysis of price determination.

Garegnani grounded the part of his interpretation relating to the results reached by Sraffa in the summer of 1927 on a set of notes drafted by Sraffa as a basis for the lectures he had agreed to deliver in Cambridge during the coming Michaelmas term.[5] In particular, Garegnani stressed that, in the opening pages of those notes, classical economists were depicted as interested in a "philosophical", or "pre-scientific", approach where value was understood as expression of "a relation of commodities as a whole to mankind" and of the "primitive notion that there had to be somewhere or other one single ultimate cause of value" (Sraffa Papers, D3/12/3/9–10 [A4/4iv–v]). Such a "primitive notion" was counterposed to what was described as a more properly scientific interest in the explanation of relative or individual prices, which had been developed by modern theorists (Sraffa Papers, D3/12/3/10, 12 [A4/4iv, vi]). Shortly afterward, however, according to Garegnani, Sraffa, drafting the same notes, would have recognized the general importance of the classical authors' search for an "ultimate cause" or an "ultimate standard" of value.[6] Indeed, he came to state that also contemporary theories of value could not avoid having recourse to an "ultimate standard" or "common measure" of value (Sraffa Papers, D3/12/3/17 [A4/4xiii], D3/12/3/41–42 [A4/14ii–iii]; see also Garegnani, 2005, 461–64).

In this chapter, we accept this general outline of the development in Sraffa's thought in the summer of 1927 and concentrate our attention on some of its features and on aspects of Garegnani's interpretation of subsequent developments. However, before shifting our focus to the points we wish to discuss, we advance a few qualifications to Garegnani's approach to the prelectures. To start with, we would stress that the content of Sraffa's 1925 and 1926 articles and of the prelectures (manuscript D3/12/3 [A4]) suggest that at that time—even though he had directed his critique almost exclusively against contemporary economists—Sraffa's knowledge of the classical authors and of Marx was comparable to his knowledge of more recent literature.[7] Secondly, we would say that, until a number of questions are addressed, we cannot take for granted that the structure of the prelectures closely reflects the evolution of Sraffa's thought in the summer of 1927. Indeed, it should be considered whether that manuscript, as we know it, might be better described as reflecting an arrangement intentionally designed by Sraffa to suit didactical purposes. Furthermore, it must be noted that only six out of more than eighty sheets that form the prelectures (Sraffa Papers, D3/12/3/1–7 [A4/2–A4/4iii]) had been numbered by Sraffa himself.[8] This fact is particularly important if we want to assess the relationship between the order of the sheets that we now may observe and the order in which they had been written, or the likelihood that some parts of the prelectures may have been removed by Sraffa himself to different folders and are now kept in other sections of the Sraffa Papers. Finally, it should also be considered whether other manuscripts in the Sraffa Papers could have been written in the same period (i.e., in the summer of 1927).

Be that as it may, our present focus is not directed toward Garegnani's approach to the general structure of the prelectures. We rather focus on the part of Garegnani's interpretation dealing with the more specific question of pointing out the spring, if we may say so, that may have led Sraffa to write the earliest formulation of his equations.

Our analysis begins with detailed consideration of a part of the prelectures that, according to Garegnani, marks the onset of Sraffa's new understanding of the classical approach (Garegnani, 2005, 464; see also 461–63) and, pointing to the possibility of reducing all inputs of a given production process to what Sraffa called an absolutely necessary commodity, identifies a line that he would have followed in his subsequent research up to the earliest formulation of his equations (Garegnani, 2005, 465). With regard to this document, we argue that it contains additional information (not mentioned by Garegnani) that is crucial to understanding the origins of Sraffa's equations (section 2). Furthermore, we show that the manuscript that, according to Garegnani, would reflect the steps that in November 1927 would have led Sraffa precisely to his equations, are susceptible to a different interpretation (section 3). A short digression allows us to consider the grounds that may support the hypothesis that it was exactly toward the end of November 1927 that Sraffa wrote the earliest formulations of his equations (section 4). Finally, we point to other manuscripts that may more closely reflect Sraffa's transition from the prelectures and from the conception of an absolutely necessary commodity to his equations (section 5).

2. The Spring of Sraffa's Equations: The "absolutely necessary commodity" and the "community that produces just what is sufficient to keep it going"

In order to start our discussion of how the exploration of the reduction of the inputs of a given production process to an absolutely necessary commodity may have led Sraffa to write his equations, the part of the prelectures that contains the relevant sentences must be quoted in full:[9]

Physical real costs

This conception would be tenable only if all the commodities considered (or at least one of them) had, each of them, no possible substitute (and therefore were absolute necessaries, since luxuries are naturally substitutes among themselves). But if commodities have substitutes, there is no more "one" real cost composed of a series of various quantities of commodities, which don't require a common measure: so soon as there are substitutes, there is an infinite number of combinations of the different commodities, which satisfy the condition of maintaining life and efficiency of the producers. [*But in a community that produces just what is sufficient to keep it going would there not be only one combination which satisfies the above condition? it would be "the cheapest"*] How are we to choose between these combinations? It is of course impossible to choose between *1 kg of bread + 1/2 kg of meat* and *1/4 kg of bread + 1 kg of meat*, unless we introduce the common measure of their value—and that would beg the question. It should be remarked that if this difficulty (of no substitutes) were overcome and an absolutely necessary commodity found, the difficulty of reducing to a common measure the various things factors entering into real cost would solve by itself. In effect, *it would be easy to find the cost of all the other things in terms of the necessary one, and thus by going back enough in the genealogy of production, (and stopping along each branch so soon as we have resolved it into our necessary commodity) we might find exactly the total amount of wheat corn (if this were the ideal necessary commodity, which it is not) that has actually entered into the production of, say, this book, and covers entirely its cost of production, at the exclusion of any other commodity.* (This is true: it is just as true as saying that a man has not a drop of blood that does not come from a man called A...: in fact if we followed each branch of his genealogy up to when we find an A... and stopped there in each case, this would happen. In the case of corn the process would be different, because at each step backwards we would find a part of cost being wheat and the other not, and setting aside the first, while going on analysing the latter, this non-wheat residue would ultimately be reduced to practically nothing—would have zero as limit.)

There is however something to be said for this conception of real cost. It is true that there is an infinite number of combinations of commodities which would be "the minimum" necessary to support permanently a labourer working 8 hours a day at a given standard of efficiency. But this difficulty arises only in so far as we *abstain from using a unit of measure for the different commodities*, and *simply say that the real cost of producing a given article is a given set of diverse commodities*—and *this would be an "ultimate" conception if there were no possible substitutes for those commodities.* This not being the case, we must find a unit of measure for cost: the necessity for this unit arises, not from a desire of actually measuring—it is prior to it, and is required even for thinking of cost. The best measure available is the amount of various commodities that is required to support during an hour, ~~or day or year~~ a average common labourer: if there are many of such sets of commodities, we can choose the one that can be produced with a minimum of labour (this is ambiguous!). Of course, not all individuals in one trade require the same amount of necessaries, and persons in different trades require different amounts—and to this extent our measurement is inexact, and real cost is slightly different (in excess or deficiency) from number of hours of labour. I contend however that the amount of necessaries varies much less between different workers, than vary a) their disutilities, b) their wages.

Thus to Ricardo's T. V.,[10] based on amount of labour, two interpretations can be given: 1) the subjective psycholog., disutility one, 2) the objective physical, necessaries of existence one. He probably had not always clear in mind the distinction, but I believe that the latter is the one that underlies his T. V. (Sraffa Papers, D3/12/3/44–47 [A4/16iii–vi]; spelling and words underlined or crossed out as in original manuscript; smaller case indicates words Sraffa inserted above the line; sentences within square brackets were written by Sraffa, within square brackets, on the left hand margin of the sheet; emphasis added)

The passages we have just reproduced appear in the prelectures at a point where Sraffa had already recognized that also more recent theories of value must rely upon an ultimate standard and had already criticized the possibility of employing to such an effect either Léon Walras's, Carl Menger's and William Jevons's utility or Marshall's real costs. Here Sraffa considers an alternative conception: physical real costs. The relevant passages, however, even though opening as if something had already been said about such an alternative conception, are not preceded by any real introduction nor contain it themselves, and no author is mentioned as proponent of the conception. Nevertheless, it can clearly be gathered that physical real costs are opposed to what Sraffa had just described as psychological standards ("All the ultimate standards we have considered up to this point are psychological," Sraffa Papers, D3/12/3/42 [A4/16i]). On the contrary, as the text soon reveals, physical real costs refer to a conception that describes production processes as sets of commodity inputs—and, to do this, also labor inputs have to be expressed as a set of commodities "which satisfy the condition of maintaining life and efficiency of the producers" (Sraffa Papers, D3/12/3/44 [A4/16iii]).[11] The latter set is described as an absolutely necessary commodity, and, as Sraffa put it, once such a commodity had been identified,

it would be easy to find the cost of all the other things in terms of the necessary one, and thus by going back enough in the genealogy of production (and stopping along each branch so soon as we have resolved it into our necessary commodity) we might find exactly the total amount of corn (if this were the ideal necessary commodity, which it is not) that has actually entered into the production of, say, this book, and covers entirely its cost of production, at the exclusion of any other commodity. (Sraffa Papers, D3/12/3/44–45 [A4/16iii–iv], underlining as in original manuscript)

This would answer the question of the existence of an ultimate standard or of a common measure of value, and would allow to express the value of any commodity by a definite magnitude.

We might try and identify the sources of this conception (see, for instance, documents kept in folders D3/12/2, D3/12/42 and D2/4), but what we wish to stress is that, according to Sraffa, an obstacle would stand against the possibility of reaching a general solution by this route: the existence of substitutes would make it impossible to identify an absolutely necessary commodity and would imply that the physical real costs conception, in Sraffa's words, is not tenable (Sraffa Papers, D3/12/3/44 [A4/16iii]). Sraffa, however, suggests that this outcome could be avoided by confining the analysis within a special case or by pursuing an approximate solution. In general, a bundle of commodities could be used to the same purpose that should have been served by the absolutely necessary commodity. This would allow us to obtain an approximate solution, and, according to Sraffa, even though not exact, this solution would be more precise than any measures of value based on disutility or wages. The special case, in contrast, is outlined by Sraffa in the note appended on the left-hand margin of sheet D3/12/3/44 [A4/16iii]: within the boundaries of "a community that produces just what is sufficient to keep it going,"[12] the problems posed by the existence of substitutes could be sidestepped and the physical real costs approach could lead to an exact determination of the value of individual commodities by reducing their inputs to different amounts of the absolutely necessary commodity.

If this can be taken to be the stage reached by Sraffa in the summer of 1927 in terms of positive explanation of the values of individual commodities,[13] we may stress that it contains elements pointing toward three crucial directions: (1) the description of production processes as lists, as we may call them, or sets, as Sraffa put it, of quantities of diverse commodities representing the real cost of producing a given article; (2) the identification of the case of an economy that barely "keeps going"—that is, an economy that produces no surplus above the replacement of the means of production it employs; (3) the reduction of the production process of any individual commodity to a hypothetical absolutely necessary commodity.

The importance we attribute to these three elements, or directions, stems from their similarity with two features of *Production of Commodities*: the way industries, or production processes, are described and the distinction between production for subsistence and production with a surplus. On this basis, it may be natural to conclude that Sraffa's equations and the schemes that characterize *Production of Commodities* may be seen as an evolution from the prelectures.

But recording these similarities does not necessarily have to mark the end of our inquiry into the origins of Sraffa's equations: a more detailed conjecture concerning the line in the development of Sraffa's thought from the prelectures to the early formulations of his equations may be put forward. More precisely, we consider information on how, starting from the identification of a physical real costs approach and from the three elements mentioned above, Sraffa may have moved toward the definition of a system of simultaneous equations whose solution would have allowed him to determine exchange values, as in *Production of Commodities*, with no need to reduce the production process of each commodity to a hypothetical absolutely necessary commodity.

The importance of the third element is notable because we expect it to indicate the precise analytical direction taken by Sraffa in November 1927: in order to reduce production processes to a hypothetical absolutely necessary commodity, he most likely could have tried to describe them analytically, following the idea that they could be seen as sets of inputs. And he could have done this for the special case of an economy that barely keeps going. Indeed, it is reasonable to say that if he had not identified a case within whose boundaries the problems posed by the existence of substitutes could have been sidestepped, he would have had little or no incentive to pursue the reduction of the production process of an individual commodity to a hypothetical absolutely necessary commodity—a direction that he had otherwise described as untenable.[14]

3. Writing the Equations: Garegnani's View

As we have just seen, in order to attempt a reconstruction of the development of Sraffa's analysis from the prelectures to his equations, we may take as starting point the idea that in the summer of 1927 (or between the summer and November 1927) he decided that, at least in a special case, pursuing the reduction of the various inputs entering into the production process of a given commodity to an absolutely necessary commodity would have been consistent with the logic of economic analysis and would have delivered an exact result for the value of each commodity. We may then accept Garegnani's hypothesis that, approximately around mid-November 1927,[15] he decided to delve deeper into that reduction and see how it could actually be accomplished. Indeed, some notes, identified as items D3/12/6/1(1–6) [C XVI 1i–vi] and kept in a folder that is headed in Sraffa's hand "Winter 1927–28", have been described by Garegnani (2005, 465) as the locus of "a resumption of the argument [Sraffa] began [in the prelectures] about the 'necessary commodity.'" Garegnani, however, did not provide a detailed illustration of the relevant documents. For this reason, we now proceed to consider their structure and content.

Item D3/12/6/1(1) [C XVI 1i] is the first sheet of a series of six manuscripts (numbered 1–6 by Sraffa himself) and bears a sort of heading, most likely added by Sraffa while reconsidering this and other sets of notes sometime after they had been written. The heading ("Equations for whatever surplus") may be justified by the fact that, while sheet 1 depicts a case where the surplus is nil, sheets 2–5, although focused on a case of positive surplus (just like sheet 6), adopt a notation that does not imply that the magnitude of the surplus be positive, negative or nil. The first sheet is crossed out, most probably by Sraffa—but, whichever meaning we may attach to this, its full text must be reproduced and discussed:

$$A = \Sigma a = a_1 + a_2$$
$$B = \Sigma b = b_1 + b_2$$

$$A = a_1 + b_1 \qquad A - a_1 = b_1 = a_2$$
$$B = a_2 + b_2 \qquad B - b_2 = a_2 = b_1$$

$$x = ax + bx$$
$$y = ay + by$$

$$x = ax + ay$$
$$y = bx + by$$

$$x = ax + a(bx + by) = ax + abx + aby$$
$$\quad = ax + abx + ab(bx$$

$$x = ax + ay$$

The first statement we can make about these equations is that they are visibly consistent with two of the elements, or directions, we have singled out above: no surplus is produced,[16] and each production process may be seen as described by a list of commodities.[17] But the content of the manuscript elicits further observations.

1. The three sets of equations where outputs appear to be expressed as A and B and inputs as a_1, b_1, a_2 and b_2 and the two sets where x and y express both outputs and inputs resemble schemes that can be found in several other manuscripts kept in the section of the Sraffa Papers (D3/12) that collects the main body of documents relating to the preparation of *Production of Commodities*.

2. The writing of the third of these sets of equations[18] seems to stop on the verge of the determination of its solution, and we may presume that the absence of such a result follows from the absence of a distinction between each variable and its coefficient (i.e., between each commodity and its quantity, or each quantity and its value).[19]

3. The two subsequent sets of equations[20] can be seen as containing an attempt to introduce exactly the distinction just mentioned.[21] In this case, a simple substitution would provide a solution and determine the exchange ratio between x and y, but such a route is not pursued.

4. Indeed, the second of the latter sets of equations[22] is developed into what may be interpreted as an attempt to calculate such solutions by what we would call full input substitution,[23] which would be a reduction of the production process of commodity x to a single input.[24]

5. But the attempt (whether we interpret it as a formal method to solve the system or as a reduction) is soon abandoned.[25] The reason why it is abandoned is not clear, but we can say that, if we take it to be a reduction to an absolutely necessary commodity, we must acknowledge that it contains a peculiarity: the substitution performed by Sraffa amounts to an attempt to eliminate input y from the production process of x. This, in terms of reduction, would imply that y is not the absolutely necessary commodity—which should then be x—but calculating the amount of x directly and indirectly employed to produce x would be of no use to establish the value of commodity x except in terms of the ordinary commodity y. On the contrary, if x was taken to be the absolutely necessary commodity, to establish the value of y in terms of the absolutely necessary commodity, Sraffa should have pursued an attempt to eliminate input y from the production process of y: he should have substituted the equation for y into the production process of y itself.[26]

To sum up, it is not obvious that the document contains an attempt at calculating exchange values by means of a reduction to an absolutely necessary commodity, as maintained by Garegnani. In our view it could be more appropriately understood as aimed at calculating relative exchangeable values with only an incidental relation to such a reduction.[27]

The next sheet (item D3/12/6/1(2) [C XVI 1ii]) clearly contains an attempt to calculate the solutions of the system of equations in a more general case: three commodities and three equations are considered; no specific numerical value is given to the coefficients; the magnitude of the surplus is not tied to being positive, negative or nil. Furthermore, we may also note another important difference from the previous sheet: input coefficients are now both explicitly introduced and distinguished one from another. This suggests that the reason to abandon the systems in sheet D3/12/6/1(1) rested in the way the systems had been written, rather than in the way their solution, or a reduction (if any), had been attempted. The new system reads as follows:

$$(\text{or} = \text{or} <)$$

$$x = a_1 x + b_1 y + c_1 z \qquad x > \textstyle\sum ax \qquad 1 > \textstyle\sum a$$

$$y = a_2 x + b_2 y + c_2 z \qquad y > \textstyle\sum by \qquad 1 > \textstyle\sum b$$

$$z = a_3 x + b_3 y + c_3 z \qquad z > \textstyle\sum cz \qquad 1 > \textstyle\sum c^{28}$$

As a matter of fact, a solution is pursued following the same route as in document D3/12/6/1(1): the method of full input substitution is applied by eliminating input z from the production process of x, which comes to be expressed in terms of x and of y (because no substitution is being done for y). The process, therefore, cannot be properly considered as a reduction to an absolutely necessary commodity.

We reproduce only the first and the second stages of this process:

$$x - a_1 x = (1 - a_1)x = b_1 y + c_1 z$$

$$(1 - a_1)x = b_1 y + c_1(a_3 x + b_3 y + c_3 z)$$

After a number of steps, in the last line of sheet D3/12/6/1(2), Sraffa wrote the limit for the polynomial (dubbed S) he had obtained for x, but he also added, "no, S still contains x". Indeed, this should come as no surprise, because, just as in the previous sheet, what he had been doing was eliminating z, not x. Sraffa's remark may reveal that he meant to find the value of x/y. Alternatively, if, following Garegnani, we interpreted this manuscript as an attempt to reach a reduction to an absolutely necessary commodity, we should conclude that Sraffa could not see the proper way of doing it.

Be that as it may, the same calculations are further pursued in sheet D3/12/6/1(3), alas!, to no better effect. But in manuscript D3/12/6/1(4), following a note placed at the bottom of the previous sheet,[29] Sraffa started them again after having defined a new system of equations, with different coefficients:

$$x = \frac{1}{a_1}x + \frac{1}{b_1}y + \frac{1}{c_1}z \qquad \textstyle\sum \frac{1}{a} < 1$$

$$y = \frac{1}{a_2}x + \frac{1}{b_2}y + \frac{1}{c_2}z \qquad \sum \frac{1}{b} < 1$$

$$z = \frac{1}{a_3}x + \frac{1}{b_3}y + \frac{1}{c_3}z \qquad \sum \frac{1}{c} < 1$$

After a number of transformations, in the subsequent sheet (D3/12/6/1(5)) a result is reached where y/x is expressed as ratio between two polynomials in the coefficients a_1, a_2, a_3, b_1, b_2, b_3, c_1, c_2, c_3. This—if document D3/12/6/1(1–6) had been (as suggested by Garegnani) directly stemming from the prelectures—might have been expected to be heralded by Sraffa as a new and particularly important result, and should have marked a pause in his reflection. Yet he placed no emphasis on it, nor did he seem to regard it as satisfactory: in manuscript D3/12/6/1(6), apparently believing that in this way a "mistake" could be amended,[30] he explicitly introduced a magnitude representing a positive surplus product into equations elaborated from the previous system. But the ensuing calculations are interrupted before reaching any result. Assuming that in these manuscripts Sraffa was not pursuing a reduction to an absolutely necessary commodity and that his aim was the determination of x/y, we may ask why he discarded exactly that result in order to take into account a positive surplus. Our explanation runs as follows: equations in documents D3/12/6/1(2–5) had been originally conceived of as an attempt to describe a case of positive surplus. Then Sraffa realized that the systems he had written and the solution he had reached for x/y would also apply to cases where the surplus could be negative or nil. For this reason, in sheet D3/12/6/1(6) he would have developed a system where a positive surplus was explicitly introduced. And for the same reason he would have introduced a correction in the initial definition of the system in sheet D3/12/6/1(2) by adding "(or = or <)" (this, indeed, appears to be an addition introduced after the system had already been written).

To end this long discussion we may put forward our conclusion: contrary to what had been suggested by Garegnani (2005, 465), documents D3/12/6/1(1–6) [C XVI 1i–vi] do not stem directly from the prelectures and do not contain an attempt to develop a reduction to an absolutely necessary commodity. These documents could more likely reflect an attempt to generalize results concerning the solution of systems of equations that Sraffa had already reached for cases of both no surplus and positive surplus. Furthermore, the fact that in these documents Sraffa seems to experiment with different ways of introducing input coefficients may be interpreted as a sign that the results that he had already reached were not obtained using general coefficients such as a_1 and b_1 but only within systems written using numerical coefficients. This would be consistent with the presumption—based on an entry in his pocket diary, which will be considered in the next section—that by the end of November 1927, he had already produced an early outline of his systems for the cases of no surplus and positive surplus, and solved at least the first, and it would also be consistent with the fact that documents D3/12/6/1(1–6) are kept in a folder headed "Winter 1927–28" (i.e., we may assume that Sraffa wrote them after November 1927). This would also explain why in those documents, as we have seen, while pursuing the solution of the system, Sraffa, having once attained that result, started working it out again from scratch, as if the determination of such solutions had been of little importance. Indeed, we may presume that what he wanted to do in the winter of 1927–28 was to determine solutions (i.e., exchange ratios) within an analytical framework that satisfied some requirements of generality and in the context of an economy producing a positive surplus. Finally, we may suppose that, revising his notes some months or some years later, Sraffa found documents D3/12/6/1(1–6) of some interest exactly for the feature that, originally, he had seen as a mistake: they contained a scheme that could describe cases where the surplus could be positive, negative or nil—hence the heading he put, most likely only at that time, on the first sheet: "Equations for whatever surplus."

4. End of November 1927

As we have just hinted at, there are reasons to maintain that, by the end of November 1927, Sraffa had already outlined systems of equations for the cases of no surplus and positive surplus (what at that time he called "first equations" and "second equations") and had reached a solution at least for the former case. This statement rests on several sources, first among them an annotation in Sraffa's pocket diary under the date of Saturday, November 26, 1927: "K approves 1st eq." (Sraffa Papers E1),[31] but the whole context of Sraffa's activities in that period deserves to be considered.

Sraffa had moved to England at the beginning of July 1927 to prepare himself for the lectures he had agreed to deliver at the University of Cambridge beginning in the coming October, but early autumn marked a period of special uneasiness for him. On September 22, he replied to Angelo Tasca, who had asked him to contribute some articles to an Italian communist journal printed in France, "Excuse me for not doing anything for *Lo Stato Operaio*; in 15 days lessons begin, and I am discovering that giving lessons in English is far more difficult" (Fondo A. Tasca, Archivio Fondazione Feltrinelli, Milan). Indeed, two weeks later, according to what Keynes wrote to his wife, Sraffa asked "whether he could not suddenly become ill and run away" (King's College, Modern Archive Centre, JMK/PP/45/190/3/233, J. M. Keynes to L. Lopokowa, October 8, 1927). On October 15, he certainly was still working hard to prepare his lectures: on that day he wrote to Tasca that if in his letter he had been repeating the same thing a dozen times it was because he had "much work to do" ("Mi scusi la forma di questa lettera, in cui devo aver ripetuto una dozzina di volte la stessa cosa: ho molto lavoro," Fondo A. Tasca, Archivio Fondazione Feltrinelli, Milan). But three days later, the *Cambridge University Reporter* announced that Sraffa's lectures were postponed to the next term (Marcuzzo, 2005, 428 and 446fn8). Quite naturally, after learning that the beginning of his lectures on the theory of value was to be delayed, Sraffa may have stopped working on their preparation for a while. Furthermore, at the end of October he found himself unexpectedly exposed to the rigor of the fascist laws called *leggi eccezionali*. Following the publication of a letter on Antonio Gramsci's detention he had sent to the *Manchester Guardian* (probably on October 21), he became potentially subject to measures to punish anti-Italian activities abroad: because of a mistake by the newspaper's staff, his name had appeared in the index of the letters published on that day. In that contingency, he certainly had to devote some time to try to cover up the mistake and monitor its developments, which we may take to have led him to return to the preparation of his lectures not earlier than the beginning of November.[32]

In this context, it is plausible that when he went back to the notes he had been drawing during the previous months, he reconsidered also those on physical real costs and that—with some months ahead before the beginning of the new term—he tried to elaborate on that conception. This might have happened sometime in November. The hypothesis that identifies precisely the second half of November 1927 as the time when Sraffa came to conceive of his equations is supported by a number of specific facts. First of all, as we shall see, one of the documents we consider most relevant in tracing the earliest formulations of Sraffa's equations (D3/12/2/32 [A1/27ii]) has been annotated by Sraffa himself as taken from a folder headed "End of Nov. 1927" and was written on the back of the second page of a letter that Sraffa could not have received earlier than November 23.[33] Secondly, at the end of November Sraffa was presenting to Keynes his "first equations," presumably as a result he had reached very recently. This may be inferred from two sources. On the one hand, under the date of Saturday, November 26, 1927, Sraffa noted in his pocket diary, "K approves 1st eq". On the other hand, in a letter sent to his wife on Monday, November 28, 1927, Keynes wrote about Sraffa's excitement,

> On Sunday[34] I had a long talk with Sraffa about his work. It is very interesting and original […] Sraffa is in so much intellectual ferment and excitement about his ideas since I said that I thought there was something in them that he walks very fast up and down his room all day thinking about them. It is impossible for him to write them down, because as soon as he thinks about them, he has to start walking again. He is now inclined to give up his Christmas visit to Italy so that he can be able to continue in these courses for several weeks more. (King's College, Modern Archive Centre, JMK/PP/45/190/3/268–9, J. M. Keynes to L. Lopokowa; emphasis in original).[35]

5. Writing the Equations: A Different View

Let us sum up the conclusions reached so far. On the one hand, we have suggested that in November 1927 Sraffa may have reconsidered the notes he had written in the summer of 1927 (the prelectures), and we have seen that by November 26 (most likely not long before that date) Sraffa had already conceived of and solved an early formulation of his "first equations," and had at least conceived of his "second equations." On the other hand, we have provided new evidence to support the hypothesis that Sraffa's earlier steps toward writing his equations may had been rooted in the prelectures and in the way he had discussed the conceptions of physical real cost and of an absolutely necessary commodity. However, following an analysis of their content and of their likely dating, we have argued that the manuscripts singled out by Garegnani as the closest link between the prelectures and Sraffa's equations did not reflect a development directly stemming from the prelectures and were not meant to serve as a starting point to pursue a reduction of production processes to quantities of an absolutely necessary commodity directly and indirectly employed in those very processes.

In our view, manuscripts reflecting earlier steps in the development from the prelectures to the "first" and "second equations" may indeed—as maintained by Garegnani—be expected to contain systems of equations meant to pursue a reduction to an absolutely necessary commodity, but those systems should also show the characteristics—not stressed by Garegnani—of depicting outputs as the result of the combination of sets of commodities and of starting the analysis from a case of production with no surplus. Furthermore, the same systems—as implied by the structure of the documents examined in section 3—should also show the additional characteristic of describing production processes by specific numerical examples rather than by more general notation.

The Sraffa Papers contain several manuscripts that match these requirements, but, looking for candidates to fit the role of earliest analytical elaboration, two items may be singled out: manuscripts D3/12/2/32 and D3/12/2/34 [A1/27ii, iv]. These manuscripts, which discuss a no-surplus case, may then be associated to two other documents: manuscripts D3/12/2/33 and D3/12/2/35 [A1/27iii, v], which seem to have been written at the same time as items D3/12/2/32 and 34. All these manuscripts are kept among items dating to the 1940s and 1950s, but on one of them (manuscript D3/12/2/32) Sraffa annotated, "(From folder headed: 'End of Nov. 1927')." Furthermore, as already mentioned in section 4, above, that document is written on the back of the second page of a letter sent from Britain to Sraffa's address in Milan and dated November 19, 1927. Presumably, Sraffa received that letter, forwarded from Milan to Cambridge, between November 22 and 24. This would imply that manuscripts D3/12/2/32–35 could not have been written more than a couple of days before November 26—the day when Sraffa showed his "first equations" to Keynes.

The schemes contained in manuscripts D3/12/2/32 and 34 employ an *A, B* notation similar to that in item D3/12/6/1(1). Here, however, as numerical coefficients are used, quite naturally each input and each output is associated to two magnitudes identifying each commodity and its quantity.

Both manuscripts D3/12/2/32 and D3/12/2/34 elaborate on the same system of equations:[36]

$$10A - 3A + 7B + 4C$$

$$20B = 6A + 5B + 1C$$

$$15C = 1A + 8B + 10C$$

In sheet D3/12/2/32, the equations are arranged exactly as we have written them.[37] They are then followed by a few calculations scattered throughout the page, which we reproduce in a single column:

$$\frac{4}{5}A + \frac{32}{5}B$$

$$7A - \frac{4}{5}A = 7B + \frac{32}{5}B$$

$$\frac{31}{5}A = \frac{67}{5}B$$

$$\boldsymbol{A = \frac{67}{31}B}$$

$$B = \frac{31}{67}A$$

$$C = \frac{63}{67}A$$

$$7A = 4C + \frac{6A + 1C}{15}7$$

$$7A - \frac{42}{15}A = \frac{63}{15}A = \frac{67}{15}C$$

$$\boldsymbol{A = \frac{67}{63}C}$$

$$7B = \frac{217}{67}A$$

$$4C = \frac{252}{67}A$$

$$4C + 7B = \frac{469}{67}A = 7A$$

The solutions for A in terms of B and for A in terms of C (emphasized here in bold) are placed by Sraffa within circles, and it seems clear that Sraffa's attention was focused on solving the system.[38]

In sheet D3/12/2/34 we find the same equations as in D3/12/2/32, but they are arranged in a row.[39] Under each equation we find approximately the same calculations that appear, scattered, in document D3/12/2/32. Those calculations are now accomplished more systematically, as if to put in good order and check what in the other manuscript had been jotted down too quickly. The calculations lead to solutions by ordinary substitution (i.e., applied, just like in the calculations in item D3/12/2/32, after eliding the presence of the same variable when it appeared on both sides of each equation), and they stop when the values of B and C in terms of A are found:[40]

$10A = 3A + 7B + 4C$	$15C = 1A + 8B + 10C$	$20B = 6A + 5B + 1C$
$7A = 7B + 4C$	$5C = 1A + 8B$	$15B = 6A + 1C$

$$7A = 7B + \frac{4}{5}A + \frac{32}{5}B$$

$$C = \frac{1}{5}A + \frac{8}{5}B$$

$$B = \frac{6}{15}A + \frac{1}{15}C$$

$$7A - \frac{4}{5}A = 7B + \frac{32}{5}B$$

$$C = \frac{1}{5}A + \frac{8}{5}\left(\frac{6}{15}A + \frac{1}{15}C\right)$$

$$\frac{31}{5}A = \frac{67}{5}B$$

$$C = \frac{1}{5}A + \frac{48}{75}A + \frac{8}{75}C$$

$$31A = 67B$$

$$C - \frac{8}{75}C = \frac{1}{5}A + \frac{48}{75}A$$

$$B = \frac{31}{67}A$$

$$\frac{75 - 8}{75}C = \left(\frac{15}{75} + \frac{48}{75}\right)A$$

$$\frac{67}{75}C = \frac{63}{75}A$$

$$67C = 63A$$

$$C = \frac{63}{67}A$$

Arranging equations in a row and repeating previously scattered calculations are quite unusual features in the Sraffa Papers. We propose to interpret them as signs of Sraffa's surprise in the face of a result he had reached somewhat unexpectedly. A surprise that would have induced him to reconsider what he had just done. In general, the characteristics of manuscripts D3/12/2/32 and D3/12/2/34 that we have just considered allow us to interpret them as the earliest documents reflecting Sraffa's work on his equations, if not the very earliest steps of their elaboration.

How did Sraffa come to write and solve the equations in documents D3/12/2/32 and D3/12/2/34? The hypothesis that we want to put forward is consistent with Garegnani's suggestion: Sraffa wrote those equations in order to lay down the groundwork of an attempt to calculate a reduction to an absolutely necessary commodity. Indeed, in these documents, the two of the crucial elements singled out in section 2, above, as outlining the stage reached by Sraffa in the summer of 1927 in terms of explanation of the values of individual commodities via a reduction to an absolutely necessary commodity (i.e., the description of production processes as lists of quantities of commodities and the identification of the case of an economy that produces no surplus) can be recognized.

The fact that no attempt to calculate a reduction (the third of the elements, or directions, singled out in section 2) may be found in these manuscripts does not necessarily weigh against our interpretation: the description of a no-surplus economy's production processes would have been a necessary step toward such a reduction, but once Sraffa had written down that description as a set of equations representing additions of quantities of inputs, the possibility of solving the system and determining exchange ratios may have immediately appeared to his eyes as the likely outcome of the application of straightforward algebraical logic.[41] Indeed, following such logic would have allowed Sraffa to see that the solution of the system could produce exchange ratios between commodities with no need to reduce inputs to an absolutely necessary commodity.

To sum up, if Sraffa had taken such a step, we may expect that a reduction to an absolutely necessary commodity would have immediately fallen outside his analytical horizon, while, at the same time, a question concerning what would happen if there were a positive surplus would have emerged. Indeed, we find no document that may be associated with such a reduction (save, possibly, for those, dating to a later period, pointed out by Garegnani and discussed in section 3, above), but an attempt to answer the question concerning a positive surplus may be immediately recognized in manuscripts D3/12/2/33, 35 [A1/27iii, v].

Manuscript D3/12/2/33 shows the following system and calculations:[42]

$$10A + 4A = 3A + 9B$$
$$12B = 7A + 3B$$

$$14A = 3A + 9B$$
$$12B = 7A + 3B$$

$$11A = 9B \qquad A = 9/11B$$
$$9B = 7A \qquad A = 9/7B$$

The latter results are accompanied by a big question mark and by the following annotations: "V. Chini p 41 (*le equazioni sono contraddittorie quindi non esiste alcuna soluzione*) *Le equaz. devono essere non contraddittorie indipendenti.*"[43] We may presume this to have been the earliest formulation of Sraffa's equations for the case of a positive surplus: he had not yet introduced any distributive variable, and he noticed that the system could not be solved. The train of thought they reveal confirms that this document had been written at a very early stage of Sraffa's work on his equations, but it must certainly be subsequent to documents D3/12/2/32, 34.[44]

Document D3/12/2/35 [A1/27v] contains a further attempt to deal with the same difficulty:[45]

$$11A = 3A + 9B$$

$$13B = 7A + 3B$$

$$S = 1A + 1B$$

$$S = 1A + \frac{7}{10}A = \frac{17}{10}A$$

$$A = \frac{9}{8} B$$

$$B = \frac{7}{10} A$$

Also in this case Sraffa faced—and could not solve—the same problem he had met in the previous document. Accordingly, beside the three equations he wrote: "These are contradictory, whether S equal or not to zero."

6. Conclusions

In this chapter we have examined the evidence put forward by Pierangelo Garegnani to support his thesis that Sraffa came to conceive his equations within a process started from the recognition that a conception of physical real cost was at the root of the classical economists' approach to value. According to Garegnani, Sraffa's equations emerged from an attempt to elaborate on that conception and, in particular, on the possibility of placing the concept of absolutely necessary commodity at the basis of value determination.

We have argued that this contention has solid foundations, but that some of its parts may be significantly enriched, while others need deep revision. More precisely, our analysis has developed three main points:

1. We have shown that the text of the manuscript dating from the summer of 1927 and dubbed by Garegnani prelectures reveals a deeper and stronger relationship to Sraffa's earliest formulations of his equations (in particular, of his "first equations") than suggested by Garegnani himself. This relationship rests on the fact that identifying the case of an economy that produces no surplus is a significant part of the analysis of the reduction to an absolutely necessary commodity developed in the prelectures and on the fact that the description of production processes and of bundles of commodities that we can find in that part of the prelectures is very close to what we can find in Sraffa's earliest formulations of his equations.

2. We have argued that the document that, according to Garegnani, illustrates the moment when Sraffa again took up (in November 1927) the concept of absolutely necessary commodity and the way it led him to write his equations is more likely to reflect a slightly subsequent stage in the development of Sraffa's work and does not necessarily refer to a reduction to an absolutely necessary commodity.

3. We have put forward the hypothesis that another document, also kept among the Sraffa Papers, may illustrate that crucial turning point in the development of Sraffa's thought when he first came to write the earliest formulation of his equations and see how they might have opened a new way to value determination.

If we compare the results on value determination achieved by Sraffa in late November 1927 to the stage his analysis of physical real cost had reached in the summer of 1927, we may see that, in a single stroke, he had solved, or wiped away, at least four problems that had been stressed in the prelectures. First, individual values, or prices, did not have to rely on other individual values to be taken as already known, leading to circular reasoning. Second, no absolutely necessary commodity had to be singled out or defined. Third, by representing economic activity through a sort of photographic picture, to turn to a metaphor already used by Roncaglia in his 1975 book, where outputs and inputs (including workers' consumption, which had been substituted for their labor time) were taken as given, the question of the existence of substitutes was also eliminated. Fourth, no hypothesis as to an ultimate cause or common measure of value had to be introduced. The overall result, as Sraffa later put it, was that "the equations show that the conditions of exchange are entirely determined by the conditions of production" (D3/12/7/87 [A7/29iii]).

Acknowledgments

Many thanks are due, with no further implication, to Giancarlo de Vivo, Saverio Maria Fratini, Andrea Ginzburg, Heinz Kurz, Maria Cristina Marcuzzo, Arrigo Opocher, Annalisa Rosselli, Jonathan Smith, Attilio Trezzini, the institutions mentioned in the paper and their staff, and to Lord Eatwell, who granted his permission to quote from the Piero Sraffa Papers.

Notes

1 The Piero Sraffa Papers are kept at the Wren Library, Trinity College, Cambridge (catalogue available at https://janus.lib.cam.ac.uk/db/node.xsp?id=EAD%2FGBR%2F0016%2FSRA FFA).
2 This interpretation is criticized in Kurz (2012 and 2015) and in Kurz and Salvadori (2015); see also de Vivo and Gilibert (2013).]
3 See also Garegnani, 1998.
4 As we shall see, in November 1927 Sraffa dubbed "first equations" and "second equations" his schemes describing cases of economies producing no surplus and positive surplus.
5 The relevant notes are currently identified by the catalogue of the Piero Sraffa Papers with the reference number D3/12/3. Garegnani most plausibly argued that that document—kept in a folder headed by Sraffa "Notes London, Summer 1927 (Physical Real Costs etc.)"—may be taken to reflect Sraffa's first attempt to prepare a text he would have used to deliver the lectures on advanced theory of value he was expected to start in Cambridge in October 1927. Those lectures, however, were delayed, first to the next term, then to the subsequent academic year, and came to be based on a different set of notes. For these reasons, document D3/12/3 [A4] was dubbed by Garegnani "pre-lezioni" or "prelectures" (Garegnani, 2004 and 2005). In this chapter we follow the same convention (after reference to the catalogue of the Sraffa Papers we add, in square brackets, the reference number of the earlier catalogue, prepared by Khrisna Bharadwaj and Pierangelo Garegnani soon after Sraffa's death—this should facilitate comparisons with the hybrid notation that appears in Garegnani's 2004 and 2005 articles).

6   In the prelectures, even though Sraffa clearly illustrates the difference between the two concepts (see D3/12/3/36, 41), "ultimate cause" and "ultimate standard" of value tend to be treated as synonyms (see also Sraffa Papers, D2/4/3(19) and D3/12/7/120, where Sraffa states that this was how the two concepts were treated by classical authors).

7   From one of his letters to his sister-in-law (letter from A. Gramsci to T. Schucht, March 24, 1929; Gramsci and Schucht, 1997, 332), we know that before being arrested, Gramsci owned a copy of the same edition of Marx's *Theories of Surplus Value* (the 1924–25 French edition), which is now kept among Sraffa's books and which Sraffa certainly used. This information and a statement in a letter sent by Sraffa to Tatiana Schucht ("Of course, there is the *Histoire des doctrines économiques*, in 8 small volumes, that Nino knows," letter from P. Sraffa to T. Schucht, June 21, 1932; Sraffa, 1991, 74: our translation) allows us to argue that before November 1926, Sraffa too had already owned that book and that he had talked about it with Gramsci.

8   A pencil note in square brackets at top of document D3/12/3/8 [A4/4iv] reads, "From here on numeration on top is by PG", where PG certainly means Pierangelo Garegnani.

9   Garegnani (2005, 465) quoted about a third of the following passages.

10   Read: theory of value.

11   It may also be stressed that a wage basket was described by Sraffa as "1 kg of bread + 1/2 kg of meat" (D3/12/3/44 [A4/16iii]); we will return to this point in note 36, below.

12   This sentence closely resembles the phrase used in *Production of Commodities*: "an extremely simple society which produces just enough to maintain itself" (we may also note the absence of any reference to an economy's *net product* or *surplus*).

13   We assume that the note in D3/12/3/44 [A4/16iii], which may be compared with other annotations on the margins of the prelectures, was written in the summer of 1927 or, at the latest, between that period and November 1927.

14   Reducing production processes to a hypothetical absolutely necessary commodity in the more general case described in D3/12/3/44-46 [A4/16iii-v] would have required a much more complex analytical apparatus and presented little or no chance in actually comparing the approximation it could have delivered with those implied by alternative methods mentioned by Sraffa himself in the same sheet.

15   We further consider this hypothesis below.

16   $A = a_1 + a_2$
$B = b_1 + b_2$
and
$x = ax + bx$
$y = ay + by$

17   See note 36, below.

18   $A - a_1 = b_1 = a_2$
$B - b_2 = a_2 = b_1$

19   The lack of that distinction can be recognized in other documents, e.g., D3/12/5/2 [A6/1i], D3/12/11/54 [E2/48], D3/12/11/84 [E2/74i] and D3/12/11/87 [E2/75].

20   $x = ax + bx$
$y = ay + by$
and
$x = ax + ay$
$y = bx + by$

21   The set of equations referred to in point (2) above could be associated to Marx's conditions of simple reproduction. But, given that they are abandoned with no further elaboration and that Sraffa immediately moved to consider another set of equations, we may gather that such a similarity with Marx's conditions of simple reproduction was either not noticed or taken to be of no interest by Sraffa.

22 $x = ax + ay$
    $y = bx + by$

23 This amounts to applying the method of substitution before eliding the presence of the same variable on both sides of the equation representing the production process of an input. This method leads to reach a solution by an infinite number of steps. Ordinary application of the method of substitution (i.e., eliding the presence of the same variable on both sides of the relevant equation) would lead to a quicker solution.

24 This would correspond to what Sraffa had written in the prelectures: "by going back enough in the genealogy of production [...] and stopping along each branch so soon as we have resolved it into our necessary commodity" (D3/12/3/44 [A4/16i]). Two notes kept in folders respectively dated "December 1927" and "Winter 1927–28" touch on the relationship between method of substitution and reductions (see D3/12/10/71 [E3/26] and D3/12/6/4 [CXVI 3i]).

25 The repetition of equation $x = ax + ay$ at the end of the document may reflect the intention, also abandoned, of starting a new attempt to solve the system.

26 Few steps, just like in the case developed by Sraffa, would have clearly shown the pattern of the solution: $y = (b+b^2)x + b^2y = (b+b^2+b^3)x + b^3y$.

27 A reduction of production process of x to x itself may be recognized in an already quoted sentence in the prelectures: "In the case of corn [...] at each step backwards we would find a part of cost being wheat and the other not, and setting aside the first while going on analysing the latter, this non-wheat residue would ultimately be reduced to practically nothing" (D3/12/3/45 [A4/16iv]). Strictly speaking, however, the context in which this sentence appeared was not that of a reduction intended to determine the value of a commodity, but that of an illustration of the mechanics of reduction as such. A reduction intended to determine the value of a commodity had appeared few lines earlier in the same sheet of the prelectures, and in that case production process of y was appropriately reduced to x: "we might find exactly the total amount of [...] corn (if this were the ideal necessary commodity, which it is not) that has actually entered into the production of, say, this book, and covers entirely its cost of production at the exclusion of any other commodity" (D3/12/3/45 [A4/16iv; underlining as in the original manuscript).

28 Here Sraffa also notes, "what if $(x - a_jx) > \sum ax$.?"

29 Most likely, this note, referring to the calculation of limits of a numerical series, had been inspired by what Sraffa had read in the section on geometrical progressions in a book by Mineo Chini explicitly mentioned in other manuscripts. The book, *Corso speciale di matematiche. Con numerose applicazioni. Ad uso principalmente dei chimici e dei naturalisti* (see de Vivo 2014, 89; see also note 43, below), is still kept in Sraffa's library. Chini's *Corso speciale* was an introductory handbook based, as Chini himself stated in its preface, on university-level teaching experience of the mathematics needed by students who were to engage in experimental sciences; the latter characteristic, together with examples and exercises distributed throughout the text, mainly relating to chemistry and to natural sciences in general, justified the subtitle of the book. We may presume that Sraffa (who owned the sixth edition of the book, issued in 1923, while a subsequent edition was issued in 1926) bought it between 1923 and 1926, i.e., in the years he was starting his academic career (he began teaching at the University of Perugia in academic year 1923–24, and in March 1926 he moved to the University of Cagliari). It would not be surprising if that book had been recommended to Sraffa by Ettore Molinari, professor of chemistry at Bocconi University (Sraffa's father was the rector of that university) and a prominent figure of the Anarchist movement, or by his son, Alessandro Molinari, who had graduated from Bocconi University in 1920 with a thesis on Russian Soviets (when, in June 1922, Piero Sraffa was appointed director of the Labor Office of the Province of Milan, Alessandro Molinari was director of the Labor Office of the Municipality of Milan, and they certainly were acquainted with each other).

30 The manuscript reads: "The mistake has been not make it explicit in the initial equations that product is greater than total factors. Therefore here they are written again" (D3/12/6/1(6); underlining as in original manuscript).

31 Read: Keynes approves first equations.

32 Seemingly, Italian authorities failed to associate the letter, which had to be published anonymously, with the name of Piero Sraffa (see Naldi, 2005, 387–89; 2008, 17; Lattanzi and Naldi, (2015, 17–18)).

33 For the first page of that letter, see item D3/12/5/32 [A6/13] (it may also be noted that manuscript D3/12/5/33 [A6/14i] is dated by Sraffa "2.12.27"). This point is further considered below.

34 Most likely: Saturday, November 26, 1927.

35 Keynes attributed Sraffa's excitement to his own approval of his ideas; we assume that at least in part that excitement came from the fact that those ideas reflected results he had reached very recently. A fact at variance with Keynes's description may also be stressed: in those days Sraffa drafted many notes, including a long one (D3/12/4/15–16 [A5/14i–ii]) relating at least in part to the content of the very conversation with Keynes of November 26, which is explicitly mentioned in it (this document, bearing the title "Metaphysics," has been often quoted; for its full text see Naldi (2016, 120–21). Furthermore, Sraffa most likely did not leave England during Christmas vacations because—after his letter on Gramsci's detention—he was in danger of being arrested by the Italian police or, eventually, of being refused permission to reenter in Britain, as had already happened in January 1923: see Naldi (2005, 380–81 and 388–89).

36 Gehrke and Kurz (2006, 97fn6) suggested that this notation, where heterogeneous quantities such as a_j and b_j or $7B$ and $4C$ are straightforwardly added together, may reflect Sraffa's familiarity with chemical formulas. In our view, a more direct explanation may be attained by observing the passage reproduced from the prelectures, where a wage basket was described as "1 kg of bread + 1/2 kg of meat" and the real cost of producing a given article as "a given set of diverse commodities" (D3/12/3/44–46 [A4/16iii–v]). On such a basis, Sraffa may be expected to have initially treated the magnitudes that appear in the equations as strictly physical quantities, linking them by the signs + and =.

37 On the top of the sheet Sraffa wrote, "(From folder headed: 'End of Nov. 1927')" and "Without surplus" (the two phrases seem to have been written at different times).

38 Other calculations, mainly located on the bottom of the page, were crossed out by Sraffa and are not reproduced here.

39 On the top of the sheet Sraffa wrote, "No surplus (stesse equazioni)" ("No surplus (same equations)").

40 We doubt that this fact may be interpreted as a sign that Sraffa was treating A as absolutely necessary commodity (such an interpretation would be at variance with the fact that the value of B in terms of A is calculated from the equation describing the production process of A). Other calculations, located on the bottom of the page, were crossed out by Sraffa and are not reproduced here. On the back of this sheet Sraffa wrote another system of equations where no surplus was considered, but crossed it out. The system (which is reminiscent of that in item D3/12/6/1(4)) is the following:

$$A = \frac{1}{4}A + \frac{1}{3}B + \frac{1}{4}C$$

$$B = \frac{1}{4}A + \frac{1}{2}B + \frac{1}{2}C$$

$$C - \frac{1}{2}A + \frac{1}{6}B + \frac{1}{4}C$$

41 There is no reason to doubt that Sraffa immediately saw that the solutions could be under-
    stood as exchange ratios and as values. Indeed, in a manuscript kept in a folder headed by
    Sraffa "Winter 1927–28 Looms, etc." we read, "[the equations] have infinite sets of solutions
    […] the solutions of each set are proportional. These proportions are univoche. These pro-
    portions we call ratios of Absolute values. They are purely numerical relations between the
    things A, B […]." (D3/12/5/2 [A6/1i]; our insertions within square brackets). The same point
    emerges even more clearly from manuscripts kept in a folder headed by Sraffa "Winter 1927–
    28": "these are still homogeneous equations and give us only ratios between unknowns: this
    is satisfactory for values, but is it for R? It will give us the ratios between R and our apparent
    unknowns a, b […]. Now these are only «one unit of measure of each commodity» (1 bushel of
    wheat, 1 ton of coal etc) […]. If this were unsatisfactory, we could put the equations in a form
    which shows explicitly that our real unknowns are values" (D3/12/6/17–18 [C XVI 4ii, iii]).
    Accordingly, he introduced "[unknowns] $V_{a/b}$ The value of A in terms of B, etc" (D3/12/6/18
    [C XVI 4iii]; our insertions within square brackets; see also D3/ 12/ 11/ 89, 101).
42 On the top of the sheet Sraffa had also annotated the following: "Try negative surplus (loss)"
    and "Surplus only in A ~~with two unknowns~~ there are two solutions Why?" (the different sen-
    tences seem to have been written at different times).
43 "See Chini p 41 (equations are contradictory therefore no solution exists) Equations must be
    non contradictory independent." "Chini page 41" certainly refers to the book by Mineo Chini
    already mentioned in note 29, above. For other references to Chini's book in the Sraffa Papers,
    see Kurz (2012, 1545–47).
44 We may also recall that, if on November 26 Sraffa recorded that he had shown to Keynes his
    "first equations" (i.e., his scheme for the case of no surplus), he certainly had already defined a
    set of "second equations" (i.e., a case of positive surplus).
45 On the top of the sheet Sraffa had annotated, "Surplus «a separate industry»."

References

de Vivo, G. 2000. "Produzione di merci a mezzo di merci: note sul percorso intellettuale di Sraffa."
    In *Piero Sraffa: Contributi per una biografia intellettuale*, edited by M. Pivetti, 265–95. Roma: Carocci.
———. 2003. "Sraffa's Path to *Production of Commodities by Means of Commodities*. An Interpretation,"
    Contributions to Political Economy 22, no. 1: 1–25.
———. 2014. *Catalogue of the Library of Piero Sraffa*. Torino and Milano: Fondazione Luigi Einaudi
    and Fondazione Raffaele Mattioli.
de Vivo, G., and G. Gilibert. 2013. "On Sraffa and Marx: A Comment," *Cambridge Journal of
    Economics* 37, no. 6: 1443–47.
Garegnani, P. 1998. "Sui manoscritti di Piero Sraffa," *Rivista Italiana degli Economisti* 3, no. 1: 151–56.
———. 2004. "Di una svolta nella posizione teorica e nella interpretazione dei classici in Sraffa
    nei tardi anni Venti." In *Convegno internazionale Piero Sraffa*, Atti dei Convegni Lincei, 159–94.
    Roma: Accademia Nazionale dei Lincei.
———. 2005. "On a Turning Point in Sraffa's Theoretical and Interpretative Position in the Late
    1920s," *European Journal of the History of Economic Thought* 12, no. 3: 453–92.
Gehrke, C., and H. Kurz. 2006. "Sraffa on von Bortkiewicz: Reconstructing the Classical Theory
    of Value and Distribution," *History of Political Economy* 38, no. 1: 91–149.
Gilibert, G. 2001. "Gramsci, Sraffa e il secondo libro del *Capitale*." In *Marx e Gramsci: Memoria e
    attualità*, edited by G. Petronio and M. Paladini Musitelli, 159–72. Roma: Manifestolibri.
———. 2003. "The Equations Unveiled: Sraffa's Price Equations in the Making," *Contributions to
    Political Economy* 22, no. 1: 27–40.
Gramsci, A., and T. Schucht. 1997. *Lettere (1926–1935)*, edited by A. Natoli and C. Daniele.
    Torino: Einaudi.

Kurz, H. D. 2012. "Don't Treat Too Ill My Piero! Interpreting Sraffa's Papers," *Cambridge Journal of Economics* 36, no. 6: 1535–69.

———. 2015. "Sraffa's Equations 'Unveiled'? A Comment on Gilibert." In *Revisiting Classical Economics: Studies in Long-Period Analysis*, edited by H. D. Kurz and N. Salvadori, 192–224. Abingdon: Routledge.

Kurz, H. D., and N. Salvadori. 2004. "Man from the Moon: On Sraffa's Objectivism," *Économies et Sociétés* 35: 1545–57. Reprinted in *Interpreting Classical Economics: Studies in Long-Period Analysis*, edited by H. D. Kurz and N. Salvadori, 120–30. Abingdon: Routledge, 2007.

———. 2005. "Representing the Production and Circulation of Commodities in Material Terms: On Sraffa's Objectivism," *Review of Political Economy* 17, no. 3: 69–97.

———. 2015. "On the Beginnings of Sraffa's Path to *Production of Commodities by Means of Commodities*: A Comment on de Vivo." In *Revisiting Classical Economics: Studies in Long-Period Analysis*, edited by H. D. Kurz and N. Salvadori, 226–44. Abingdon: Routledge.

Lattanzi, E., and N. Naldi. 2015. "Documenti su Piero Sraffa all'Archivio Centrale dello Stato e all'Archivio Storico Diplomatico (Documents on Piero Sraffa at the Archivio Centrale dello Stato and at the Archivio Storico Diplomatico)." Centro Sraffa Working Papers no. 12. Roma: Centro di ricerche e documentazione Piero Sraffa. Available at: http://www.centrosraffa.org/cswp_details.aspx?id=13

Marcuzzo, M. C. 2005. "Piero Sraffa at the University of Cambridge," *European Journal of the History of Economic Thought* 12, no. 3: 425–52.

Naldi, N. 2005. "Piero Sraffa: Emigration and Scientific Activity (1921–1945)," *European Journal of the History of Economic Thought* 12, no. 3: 379–402.

———. 2008. "Archival Research and the Reconstruction of Piero Sraffa's Intellectual Biography: An Interim Report." In *The Keynesian tradition*, edited by R. Leeson, 4–41. Basingstoke: Palgrave Macmillan.

———. 2016. "Sulle conversazioni fra Sraffa e Wittgenstein." In *Sraffa e Wittgenstein a Cambridge*, edited by G. Cospito, 113–39. Pisa: Edizioni della Normale.

Roncaglia, A. 1975. *Sraffa e la teoria dei prezzi*. Bari: Laterza. (English edition: *Sraffa and the Theory of Prices*. Chichester: John Wiley, 1978).

Sraffa, P. 1925. "Sulle relazioni fra costo e quantità prodotta," *Annali di economia* 2, no. 1: 277–328. (English translation by J. Eatwell and A. Roncaglia: "On the Relations between Costs and Quantity Produced." In *Italian Economic Papers*, vol. 3, edited by L. L. Pasinetti, 322–63. Bologna: Il Mulino and Oxford: Oxford University Press, 1998.)

———. 1926. "The Laws of Returns under Competitive Conditions," *The Economic Journal* 36, no. 144: 535–50.

———. 1960. *Production of Commodities by Means of Commodities: Prelude to a Critique of Economic Theory*. Cambridge: Cambridge University Press.

———. 1991. *Lettere a Tania per Gramsci*, edited by V. Giarratana. Roma: Editori Riuniti.

Chapter Twelve

NORMAL AND DEGENERATE SOLUTIONS OF THE WALRAS-MORISHIMA MODEL

Bertram Schefold

1. A Controversial Model

The Walras-Morishima model is here reconsidered in the perspective of the Cambridge Debate on the theory of capital. This is a preparatory exercise in a specific context. On the one hand, it is related to the attempt to demonstrate that the Cambridge critique concerned not only the surrogate production function but also general equilibrium as well (Garegnani, 2011; Schefold, 2008 and 2011). On the other hand, the contribution is related to the attempt to investigate the conditions under which a surrogate production function can be approximated despite the occasional occurrence of reswitching and reverse capital deepening (Han and Schefold, 2006; Schefold, 2013). I hope that a later work will build on the foundations laid here and that this focus will fit in with the interests of the group of friends of Alessandro Roncaglia who dedicate this Festschrift to him in appreciation of his distinguished academic career.

Walras's model of capital formation has always been controversial (for an overview of the debates, see Roncaglia, 2005, 342). The observation that Walras's model of capital formation links up with the problematic of the production function goes back to Piero Garegnani (1960). A pointed application of Garegnani's analysis was made in John Eatwell's (1987) contribution to *The New Palgrave Dictionary of Economics* on Walras's theory of capital: Eatwell endeavored to show that in general the production of only one capital good was compatible with normal profits on the cost of production and the availability of endowments in arbitrary proportions. But, with only one capital good available in the subsequent period, the system could not reproduce itself. He linked this insight to the broader claim that, apart from narrow exceptions, the neoclassical theory of distribution can explain the rate of return on capital only, if only one capital good is available. For the amount of capital and the rate of profit are needed to determine the cost of production in the long run and to derive normal prices, but normal prices also serve to measure the amount of capital as the aggregate value of capital goods. The circular determination of prices is possible in an equilibrium of the classical type, where distribution is exogenously given, but if distribution is endogenous and depends on the supply of, and the demand for, factors of production, these have to be measured before formulating the schedules of supply and demand, or else the long-period method must be abandoned. The quantity of capital is unambiguous in models with only one capital good, and so Eatwell's analysis seemed to confirm a general hypothesis of a deficiency of neoclassical theory in an important representative case: the Walrasian model, although set up to show how many capital goods reproduce themselves, is certain to result in a uniform rate of profit only, if there is only one capital good, but then the system can in general not reproduce itself in the subsequent long period.

The interest in the Walras-Morishima model thus derives from the fact that it represents a neoclassical model of capital formation with a uniform rate of profit. However, it has been recognized that the Walrasian system in its original form cannot be solved in general, because the given endowments are incompatible with the general rate of profit—inequalities have to replace equalities, and different types of solutions become possible (some with normal prices, some not), which have not yet been analyzed fully. The aim of this chapter is to provide more insight into the nature of the different solutions, focusing on the conditions for "normal" solutions with a uniform rate of profit and such that all capital goods are produced so that some form of reproduction of the system is possible. The analysis of the Walras-Morishima model has been complemented by the presentation of a hybrid in which the reproduction of the capital goods is assured, because their quantities are determined endogenously, while the labor supply remains exogenous. This hybrid model may be used to illustrate problems of classical, neoclassical and Keynesian economics, and its analysis has also led to new insights about the improbability of reswitching and the certainty of Wicksell effects (Schefold, 2016).

The Walras-Morishima model first appeared in the *Zeitschrift für Nationalökonomie* in 1960 (Morishima, 1960). The paper was reprinted with few changes in Michio Morishima (1964) and taken up again in Morishima's (1977) book on Walras's economics but with modifications that we cannot take up here, since they concern wider aspects of the interpretation of Walras. The model has been discussed by others, in particular, as stated, by Eatwell (1987) in *The New Palgrave Dictionary of Economics*. Morishima's proof of the existence of equilibrium has been examined and corrected in small detail by Jan van Daal (1998). For a broad historical account, see Donald Walker (1987). I received an essential stimulus from the book by Fabio Petri (2004) on capital theory. Garegnani was the first to insist on the contradictory nature of Walras's approach: one hypothesis on which the theory is built (the arbitrary composition of the endowments) is incompatible with the determination of a system of equilibrium prices with a uniform rate of profit.[1]

The model contains n consumption goods with prices $\mathbf{p}$, m capital goods with prices $\mathbf{u}$, labor (all of one kind in our simplification) with wage rate w and the rate of interest (equal to the rate of profit) r. We neglect depreciation and assume that all capital goods are used up during the production period (circulating capital only); this means that the effect of the failure of the system to reproduce certain capital goods is more dramatic than if capital goods depreciated more slowly. We neglect the Walrasian costs of insurance and hence we do not find it necessary to introduce special prices for the services of capital. The demand for consumption goods is a n-vector $\mathbf{x} = \mathbf{x}(\mathbf{p}, \mathbf{u}, w, r)$, the supply of labor a function $L = L(\mathbf{p}, \mathbf{u}, w, r)$ and the supply of capital goods an m-vector $\mathbf{k} = \mathbf{k}(\mathbf{p}, \mathbf{u}, w, r)$. The demand for consumption goods and the supply of labor and capital goods results from utility maximization, along with a supply of savings $S = S(\mathbf{p}, \mathbf{u}, w, r)$.

Savings are negative if the rate of interest equals zero, and they are positive at some $\bar{r}$, both for any $(\mathbf{p}, \mathbf{u}, w)$. There results Walras's law, which holds identically for all prices:

$$S + \mathbf{xp} = wL + (1+r)\mathbf{ku}. \tag{1}$$

All functions are continuous, and $\mathbf{x}, \mathbf{k}, L$ are homogeneous of degree zero in $\mathbf{p}, \mathbf{u}, w$, while S is homogeneous of degree one in $\mathbf{p}, \mathbf{u}, w$. No labor is supplied if the wage is zero $(L = 0$, if $w = 0)$ for all $\mathbf{p}, \mathbf{u}, r$; the labor supply is bounded. The same holds for capital supplies $(k_i = 0$, if $u_i = 0)$. If any incomes derived from supplies of capital goods or labor are positive—hence if $(\mathbf{u}, w)$ is semipositive, written as $(\mathbf{u}, w) \geq 0$—it follows that the demand for consumption and the supply of capital goods are semipositive: $\mathbf{x} \geq 0, \mathbf{k} \geq 0$.

The supply of capital goods is elastic. For example, a woman as the owner of a house will sacrifice her own convenience and will let more rooms if a higher rent is offered. The supplies of capital goods are partly used to produce consumption goods, partly to produce new capital goods of the same kind. The vector of new capital goods produced is denoted by $\mathbf{y}$. There is a square input–output matrix $\mathbf{B} \geq 0$ for the production of capital goods, using a vector of labor $\mathbf{h} > 0$, and a rectangular matrix $\mathbf{A} \geq 0$, also using capital goods and a labor vector $\mathbf{l} > 0$. Every method of production uses an input of a capital good, and every capital good is used in one method of production in each sector of the production of capital goods and consumption goods. Morishima does not need to assume that matrix $\mathbf{B}$ is productive and that there is a positive maximum rate of profit. He asserted that his system possessed "an economically meaningful solution" (1960, 239). In fact, he proved the following theorem:

Theorem 1: there is:

$$\mathbf{p} > 0, \ \mathbf{u} > 0, \ \mathbf{x} > 0, \ r > 0, \ w > 0, \mathbf{y} \geq 0, S \gtreqless 0, \ L > 0, \ \mathbf{k} > 0$$

such that the following conditions hold:

$$(1+r)\mathbf{Bu} + w\mathbf{h} \gtreqless \mathbf{u} \tag{2}$$

$$(1+r)\mathbf{Au} + w\mathbf{l} \gtreqless \mathbf{p} \tag{3}$$

$$\mathbf{xA} + \mathbf{yB} \lesseqgtr \mathbf{k} \tag{4}$$

$$\mathbf{xl} + \mathbf{yh} \lesseqgtr L \tag{5}$$

$$\mathbf{y}\big[(1+r)\mathbf{Bu} + w\mathbf{h} - \mathbf{u}\big] = 0 \tag{6}$$

$$\mathbf{x}\big[(1+r)\mathbf{Au} + w\mathbf{l} - \mathbf{p}\big] = 0 \tag{7}$$

$$\big[\mathbf{k} - (\mathbf{xA} + \mathbf{yB})\big]\mathbf{u} = 0 \tag{8}$$

$$\big[L - (\mathbf{xl} + \mathbf{yh})\big]w = 0 \tag{9}$$

The conditions are therefore that prices are competitive, at most equal to the cost of production, equations (2) and (3); that production (demand) is limited by the supply of capital (4) and labor (5); and that unprofitable activities for the production of capital goods (6) or of consumption goods (7) are not used. Underutilized capacities are free (8), and the wage falls to zero in the case of unemployment (9). The theorem shows that the prices of consumption goods and of factors will be positive. In particular there will be no unemployment of labor, and the interest rate is positive, but saving does not necessarily take place, and it is left open whether new capital will be produced at all. The proof is based on Brouwer's fixed point theorem.

Equations (6)–(9) imply, using also (1):

$$(1+r)\mathbf{ku} + w\mathbf{l} = \mathbf{yu} + \mathbf{xp} = S + \mathbf{xp}. \tag{10}$$

Hence we find that $S = \mathbf{yu} = I$ (saving equals investment in equilibrium). The model, in its present representation, is thoroughly neoclassical: saving leads to—or one might say, creates room for—an equivalent amount of investment. In fact, equations (2)–(11) provide the image of production called forth by a demand for consumption goods based on factor incomes and a supply of savings. These are equal to investment consisting of amounts of new capital goods in such magnitudes that *the existing capital goods, to the extent that they are not used for the production of consumption goods, are used to produce new capital goods*. Their amounts are not determined by trade in futures markets—Walras, criticizing Eugen von Böhm-Bawerk, would not recognize the existence of forward markets. Nor are there expectations, represented by investment functions. The signals (in modern terminology) for the production of new capital goods are provided by prices, which reflect *present* conditions. Walras knew—and stated—that the demand for new capital goods of course emanated from entrepreneurs, but the need for them could only be signaled by the scarcities that were reflected in prices of the capital goods in use.[2]

But the analysis was in terms of long-run prices, with the rate of interest serving as the rate of profit in those processes of equations (2) and in (3), which were actually used according to equations (6)–(7). If all new capital goods were produced (equations (6) with $\mathbf{y} > 0$), the rate of profit had to be uniform for all capital goods, but how could this be if the endowments of old capital goods could in principle be given in quite arbitrary proportions in the form of vector $\mathbf{k}$? What kind of economic state could result from this construction? Eatwell (1987) showed, following hints provided by Garegnani (1960), that in general not all capital goods would be reproduced, and he made it plausible that there would be a tendency to produce only one new capital good in that line of production that was most profitable.[3]

We want to show the difficulty in more explicit form, and we shall demonstrate that not even one capital good will be produced in a wide class of cases. Although there will always be full employment of labor for reasons that will become clear at the end of this chapter, not all capital goods in the endowment will necessarily be used fully. To better understand why this is the case, it is best to start from the assumption of full employment of all resources and to analyze what this presupposes. Hence we ask how $\mathbf{y} > 0$ is possible, implying equalities in equations (2). Now we assume that matrix $\mathbf{B}$ is indecomposable and productive, with a maximum rate of profit R, and we also want the solution to be one with $0 < r < R$. Prices $\mathbf{u}$ can be interpreted as prices of a Sraffa system. Nothing prevents us from using the standard commodity pertaining to $\mathbf{B}$ as numéraire; hence, the wage rate is linearly related to the rate of profit $w = 1 - r / R$ (Sraffa, 1960). Since wage earners and owners of capital receive positive incomes, we may assume that $\mathbf{x} > 0$ (unproduced non-basics do not interest us). Because of the fixation of a numéraire, and because (2) and (3) now are equations, all prices $\mathbf{p}(r) > 0, \mathbf{u}(\mathbf{r}) > \mathbf{0}$ and the wage rate $w(r) > 0$ can be regarded as functions of the rate of profit in $(0, R)$; hence, we may write $\mathbf{k} = \mathbf{k}(r)$ and $\mathbf{x} = \mathbf{x}(r)$, where r is the rate of profit in the equilibrium, the consistency of which we are analyzing. Because of (8), the inequalities of (4) become equalities and we may write

$$\mathbf{k} - \mathbf{x}\mathbf{A} = \mathbf{y}\mathbf{B}. \tag{11}$$

We assume that our solution is such that $\mathbf{k} - \mathbf{x}\mathbf{A} > 0$, which means that positive amounts of the capital goods supplied remain for the production of new capital goods, after deducting the capital goods needed for the production of consumption goods. Such positive amounts are evidently necessary if the new capital goods are to be produced in positive amounts, $\mathbf{B}$ being indecomposable. Obviously, $\mathbf{B}^{-1} \geq 0$ is a sufficient condition for $\mathbf{y} > 0$. The necessary and sufficient condition for $\mathbf{y} > 0$ is that $\mathbf{k} - \mathbf{x}\mathbf{A} > 0$ be a convex combination of the rows of $\mathbf{B}$ with strictly positive coefficients—a condition noted by Eatwell (1987).

But how likely is $\mathbf{B}^{-1} \geq 0$? Here, the contributions by Bertram Schefold (2010) and (2013) shed new light. Essentially, the inverse of a semipositive indecomposable input–output matrix is semipositive, if it has the structure of an indecomposable permutation matrix, and the economically meaningful case is a circular matrix,[4] as discussed in Schefold (2010), where each sector uses the output of the preceding sector as its only input in terms of commodities and produces an output for the subsequent sector, and the last sector produces for the first. It is shown in the said papers that the wage curves of such systems can deviate from linearity to an arbitrary extent, that is, that they can approximate a rectangular shape. The opposite case is given by random systems, which implies tendentially linear wage curves. They are, apart from random permutations, given by matrices where the elements of each row are equal to their mean. I used such matrices for the construction of approximate surrogate production functions. Random matrices are, apart from the random perturbations, of rank 1 and hence cannot be inverted. If the matrices are perturbed, we get full rank, but, being close to a matrix of rank 1, in each case their inverse is likely to contain many negative elements.

It thus appears that the matrices most likely to lead to solutions with positive outputs of all new capital goods are matrices close to circular matrices, but these are the ones where difficulties of the type of capital reversing are most likely to show up, because the wage curves can deviate drastically from a quasi-linear shape. However, if one looks for techniques where the paradoxes of capital are largely absent, one must turn to the random systems, but then it is very unlikely that positive amounts of the new capital goods will be produced in the Walras-Morishima model. This should suffice to explain, also to readers not familiar with the analysis of Schefold (2010 and 2013), why it is not likely that the Walras-Morishima model will have solutions implying a positive production of all new capital goods unless special assumptions are added concerning the endowment of old capital goods. And we shall now show that in large classes of cases no production of new capital goods will take place at all! This possibility seems not to have been observed before. I call the solutions of the system (2)–(9) normal if the corresponding equilibrium is associated with *equations* in (2)–(5); otherwise, I speak of degenerate solutions. Perhaps I should apologize for the latter expression; however, it seems justified in the more extreme cases where the economy is incapable of reproducing the means of production.

Morishima and his followers do not assume that the matrix **B** is productive. It may be a merit if the assumptions of a model are very general, but the generality is meaningless, if it implies economically meaningless solutions. If, to begin with the extreme case, the diagonal elements of **B** are larger than 1 ($b_{ii} > 1$), it follows that all inequalities of (2) *must* be strict inequalities. One then necessarily has

$$(1+r)\mathbf{Bu} + w\mathbf{h} > \mathbf{u}, \tag{12}$$

since r is not negative. It follows that $\mathbf{y} = 0$, according to (6), and where there is no investment, net saving must be zero.

Why do such solutions arise? The special assumption made here is not ruled out by the general assumptions of the theorem. The mathematical reason is that, given our special assumption, *all* vectors $\mathbf{u} > 0$ fulfill (12), for all nonnegative r, so that the rate of interest can be so low that saving vanishes. Given $\mathbf{u} > 0$ and the rate of profit equal to some such rate of interest, the prices of consumption goods (3) are determined as equalities. The theorem guarantees that $w > 0$; hence, w may serve as numéraire; $\mathbf{x}$ now becomes a function $\mathbf{x}(\mathbf{u})$. The theorem then implies that $\mathbf{u}$ can be chosen such that $\mathbf{xA} = \mathbf{k}$, fulfilling (4), and Walras's law shows why (5) will be fulfilled as well. On the one hand, (1) reduces to $\mathbf{xp} = wL + (1+r)\mathbf{ku} = wL + (1+r)\mathbf{xAu}$. On the other hand, $\mathbf{xp} = \mathbf{x}\{w\mathbf{l} + (1+r)\mathbf{Au}\}$; hence, $w\mathbf{xl} = wL$ and (9) holds. Because of $w > 0$, (5) also holds. (8) and (9) hold. (7) holds because there are equations in (3), and so the discussion of the system is complete.

The degenerate solution so far considered may be said to be economically implausible because the input–output matrix **B** has been assumed to have diagonal elements larger than 1. However, the inequalities (12) *can* obtain also if **B** is productive. Let $\mathbf{u} > 0$ be Sraffa prices of (2), fulfilling (2) with equalities. Then, any $\tilde{\mathbf{u}}$ with $\tilde{\mathbf{u}} = \alpha\mathbf{u}, 0 < \alpha < 1$ will fulfill (12). The set of vectors $(\mathbf{u}, w) > 0$ fulfilling (12) is not of measure zero. It is not unlikely that $\mathbf{u} > 0$ and $w > 0$ will be found such that (4) and (5) will be fulfilled with no or only a few capital goods being produced. And almost the same reasoning as the one just completed can then be applied to show that such constellations are equilibria.

Before we proceed to a more detailed analysis of regular solutions in a more simplified model, some remarks are in order. Morishima himself recognized that his system exhibited structural change, if considered through a sequence of periods (Morishima 1964, 83–92). His critics (Eatwell, 1987; Petri, 2004) objected that the system was not sustainable if only one capital good was reproduced in a positive quantity. Garegnani's objection (1960) may be interpreted as the observation that arbitrary endowments are incompatible with the uniform rate of profit. Here we have found that the model may imply degeneracy such that the system suffers sudden death in that the capital is consumed entirely.

Walras himself was looking for an adaptation of a production of new capital goods to the demand of entrepreneurs. He explicitly said that "the demand of new capital goods comes from entrepreneurs who manufacture products and not from capitalists who create savings" (Jaffé's translation, as quoted by Walker, 1987, 857). A similar quote is found in Eatwell (1987, 869): "new capital goods are products; and the condition of equality between their selling price and their cost of production gives us the equations required for the determination of the quantity manufactured" (see equations (8) and (4)); however, Eatwell (ibid.) also says, "the demand price of any new good is determined solely by the demand for the stock of its services currently available." There was no other way, given that Walras neither accepted forward markets nor wished to introduce expectations based on information other than that contained in current prices. But then it is difficult to discuss investment without imposing the conditions of a steady state or, more simply, that of stationarity. This leads us to a brief discussion of a simplified model.

2. A Stationary State

The first simplification is to assume that the consumption goods are also capital goods and vice versa, which leads to a new model. It can formally be connected to the Walras-Morishima model by putting $\mathbf{B} = \mathbf{A}$, $\mathbf{h} = \mathbf{1}$ and, for normal solutions, $\mathbf{p} = \mathbf{u}$. In order to enforce normal solutions, we also assume that consumption of all goods is positive if the income is positive; hence, $(w, r) \geq 0$ implies $\mathbf{x} > 0$. The unique input matrix now is denoted by $\mathbf{A} \geq 0$; it is indecomposable and productive.

We are interested in a stationary state. We prove its existence without having further recourse to the Walras-Morishima model, except for comparison in the end. $\mathbf{k}$ is a vector of capital endowments, owned by the economic agents, and $\mathbf{y}$ the vector of capital goods to be produced; stationarity requires $\mathbf{k} - \mathbf{y}$. The vector of gross production $\mathbf{q}$ is equal to activity levels, and $\mathbf{q} = \mathbf{x} + \mathbf{y}$. In the stationary state with full employment of capital, we must have $\mathbf{k} = \mathbf{q}\mathbf{A} = (\mathbf{x} + \mathbf{y})\mathbf{A} = (\mathbf{x} + \mathbf{k})\mathbf{A}$, $\mathbf{k}(\mathbf{I} - \mathbf{A}) = \mathbf{x}\mathbf{A}$, hence:

$$\mathbf{k} = \mathbf{x}\mathbf{A}(\mathbf{I} - \mathbf{A})^{-1} > 0. \tag{13}$$

All capital goods thus are reproduced. Prices must be determined by the Sraffa equations, since all activity levels are positive, and we have, with $\mathbf{d}$ as the standard commodity,

$$(1 + r)\mathbf{A}\mathbf{p} + w\mathbf{1} = \mathbf{p}, \quad \mathbf{d}\mathbf{p} = 1, \quad w = 1 - r / R. \tag{14}$$

We therefore can write $\mathbf{x} = \mathbf{x}(r)$, $\mathbf{q} = \mathbf{x} + \mathbf{y} = \mathbf{x} + \mathbf{q}\mathbf{A}$, and positive activity levels result:

$$\mathbf{q} = \mathbf{x}(\mathbf{I} - \mathbf{A})^{-1}. \tag{15}$$

The amount of capital, expressed in standard prices, is $\mathbf{qAp} = K = \mathbf{kp}$. This amount of capital is endogenous, and the quantities of capital goods are fully employed by definition of the activity levels. But the financing of the investment is not a matter of course.

The difficulty surfaces in the formulation of Walras's law. Households formulate their supply of savings and their demand for consumer goods at alternative interest rates and prices subject to the evaluation of their incomes, to be derived from given factor endowments, at different factor prices. Here, the endowment of labor but not the endowments of the several capital goods are given. As a substitute, in what then is a hybrid model, we assume that households take the capital goods actually employed in the previous period as their endowments, as the use of those capital goods leads to the payment of the corresponding factor income. Hence Walras's law is

$$\mathbf{xp} + S = wL + (1+r)\mathbf{kp}, \tag{16}$$

where $\mathbf{k}$ is given by (13). Factor endowments and demand in (16) are therefore interdependent not only as regards the prices, but also as regards the quantities $\mathbf{k}$. The question is which decisions lead to the investment of $\mathbf{k}$ that ensures reproduction and is defined by (13).

A complementary interpretation could be based on the dual decision hypothesis. It was introduced by Clower (1965) to explain the deficiency of effective demand in an equilibrium framework. The demand emanating from workers should not be calculated on the basis of the total of labor supplied, as in (1), but according to the amount of labor actually employed, for only employed laborers have the purchasing power of the wages paid out to them, while the purchasing power of the unemployed may be zero (if they neither get unemployment benefits nor can use past savings and if they have no access to credit). In our variant of the budget constraint (16), the owners of capital command purchasing power to the extent that the capital goods are employed in the stationary state. It is conceivable and could be assumed that the endowment of capital is larger, but any excess of capital as in Walras's law (1) over capital employed as in equation (16) then does not result in additional income and therefore not in effective demand for goods. The owners of capital could thus be said to be rationed in their demand. Again the question must be posed from which decisions the quantities of capital result (13) that ensure stationary reproduction.

Mathematically, the system is consistent and leads to a solution with a given technique, whatever the endowment of labor, because capital adapts. Intuitively, if the amount of labor is increased or diminished, the amount of capital used and produced in stationary states will be higher or lower according to equation (13), and with the increase or diminution of the factor supplies, the demand for consumption goods and the supply of saving will move in parallel so that it becomes possible to find an equilibrium, using plausible additional assumptions.

An assumption regarding savings is required. We are only interested in normal solutions. Hence prices (14) can be given as functions of the rate of profit $\mathbf{p}(r)$, and similarly the wage rate $w(r)$; hence, $\mathbf{x} = \mathbf{x}(r)$, $S = S(r)$. The Walras-Morishima model assumes that

$S(0) < 0$ and that there is $\bar{r}$ such that $S(\bar{r}) > 0$, whatever the prices. Because of continuity, there must be a smallest $\tilde{r}$ such that $S(\tilde{r}) = 0$. What if $\tilde{r} > R$? A normal solution is then evidently impossible, since savings would be negative. We introduce the following assumption:

$$S(0) < 0, \quad S(R) > 0. \tag{17}$$

All variables except the rate of interest r have now been determined as functions of the rate of interest in the range for normal solutions $0 \leq r \leq R$. To close the model, we have to find the equilibrium value for the rate of interest in the capital market or in the labor market. The other market will then be in equilibrium by virtue of Walras's law. This is rewritten as follows:

$$S(r) - \mathbf{kp} = wL + r\mathbf{kp} - \mathbf{xp}, \tag{18}$$

which holds identically in r, therefore also for $r = 0$, where we get

$$S(r) - \mathbf{kp} = w(0)L - \mathbf{xp}. \tag{19}$$

The left side of this equation is certainly negative because of the assumption about S (it is easy to prove that $\mathbf{k}(0)\mathbf{p}(0) > 0$). However, we have at $r = R$:

$$S(R) - \mathbf{kp} = R\mathbf{kp} - \mathbf{xp} = \mathbf{x}\left(R\mathbf{A}(\mathbf{I} - \mathbf{A})^{-1} - \mathbf{I}\right)\mathbf{p}(R). \tag{20}$$

Since we are at the maximum rate of profit, $\mathbf{p}(R)$ is an eigenvector of $\mathbf{A}$. Using this and the commutativity of the elements of a matrix ring, for prices we can write at the maximum rate of profit:

$$(1+R)\mathbf{Ap} = \mathbf{p}$$
$$R\mathbf{Ap} = (\mathbf{I} - \mathbf{A})\mathbf{p}$$
$$\mathbf{p} = R(\mathbf{I} - \mathbf{A})^{-1}\mathbf{Ap} = R\mathbf{A}(\mathbf{I} - \mathbf{A})^{-1}\mathbf{p};$$

the right-hand side of (20) therefore is equal to zero. This implies that the capital market is in equilibrium at the maximum rate of profit, and this seems to imply an equilibrium of the labor market, insofar as the wage rate is zero. But we have not proved that the demand for labor is inferior to the supply. We need an additional assumption to enforce a normal solution at a positive wage rate with full employment. The easiest way to achieve this is to assume that consumption diminishes relative to savings as one approaches the maximum rate of profit from below so that $S(r) > \mathbf{kp} = \mathbf{xA}(\mathbf{I} - \mathbf{A})^{-1}\mathbf{p}$ for some $\bar{r} < R$. For it is plausible that the components of $\mathbf{x}(r)$ become small, as the rate of profit rises. Hence the left side of (20) now is positive at $\bar{r}$. All functions are continuous. There is therefore, by virtue of the theorem of Weierstrass, some intermediate $r^*, 0 < r^* < \bar{r} < R$, such that $S(r^*) = \mathbf{kp}$. This means that the capital market is in equilibrium at r^*, and the Walras equation reduces in r^* to a budget condition constraining the consumption out of wages and profits:

$$\mathbf{xp} = wL + r\mathbf{kp}. \tag{21}$$

This equation implies full employment equilibrium in the labor market according to

$$\mathbf{xp} = (\mathbf{q} - \mathbf{k})\mathbf{p} = w\mathbf{ql} + (1+r)\mathbf{qAp} - \mathbf{kp} = w\mathbf{ql} + r\mathbf{kp},$$

for we can divide by $w > 0$ and get, using (21), $L = \mathbf{ql}$. The same result could have been obtained more easily with a more drastic assumption that savings are equal to the profit of firms, net of interest and are retained to reproduce the capital, while wages and interest payments (rentier profits) are the source of expenditure on consumption. It would also be possible to make a direct assumption about savings and consumption of the classical kind: wages are consumed and profits are saved. But our concern here was to find meaningful conditions sufficient to generate normal solutions in a neoclassical general equilibrium of the Walras-Morishima type with inequalities. The trick has been to treat the capital goods as endogenous in (13). We can summarize the result in theorem 2 to clarify the relationship with the Walras-Morishima model:

Theorem 2: there is:

$$r > 0, w > 0, \mathbf{p} > 0, \mathbf{x} > 0, \mathbf{k} > 0, S(r) > 0$$

such that the following conditions hold:

$$(1+r)\mathbf{Ap} + w\mathbf{l} \geqq \mathbf{p} \tag{22}$$

$$(\mathbf{x} + \mathbf{k})\mathbf{A} \leqq \mathbf{k} \tag{23}$$

$$(\mathbf{x} + \mathbf{k})\mathbf{l} \leqq L \tag{24}$$

$$\mathbf{k}\big[(1+r)\mathbf{Ap} + w\mathbf{l} - \mathbf{p}\big] = 0 \tag{25}$$

$$\mathbf{x}\big[(1+r)\mathbf{Ap} + w\mathbf{l} - \mathbf{p}\big] = 0 \tag{26}$$

$$\big[\mathbf{k} - (\mathbf{x} + \mathbf{k})\mathbf{A})\big]\mathbf{p} = 0 \tag{27}$$

$$\big[L - (\mathbf{x} + \mathbf{k})\mathbf{l}\big]w = 0. \tag{28}$$

To achieve formal symmetry, (26) has been added to (25). Walras's law (1) remains, with the interpretation of the capital stock changed, however.

The hybrid character of the model results here from (23), which, in our solution with all inequalities turned into equalities, yields (13). Demand on the left and supply on the right are interdependent in (23), so that the model is not really Walrasian anymore. The stationary state must insofar be interpreted as a center of gravitation; the equations do not describe a pure neoclassical model.

Like any model with normal solutions, this one is useful for analyzing disequilibria. Starting from the equilibrium at r^*, imagine a slight change of taste. Consumers decide to save more at given $\mathbf{k}$. One expects that $\mathbf{xp}$ will fall and unemployment arises (which would have to be regarded as Keynesian).

Or assume that the rate of profit is lowered below r^* and that w rises. Savings S must fall, and consumption expenditure **xp** is expected to rise at given **k**, but this capital stock cannot be expected to be adequate for the production of the increased demand for consumption goods; hence, classical unemployment arises. Richard Kahn (1977), in the discussion surrounding Edmond Malinvaud's (1977) theory of unemployment, thought that such classical unemployment could not be sustained, because the excess demand for goods would drive up money prices and lower the real wage so that there would be a tendency to return to equilibrium (Schefold, 1997, 404). A neoclassical economist might argue that the Keynesian unemployment was unstable. Excess saving would drive down the rate of interest, savings would be reduced directly and households would be encouraged to buy more goods. This overlooks the dual decision hypothesis: the unemployed, bereft of income, could not return to the previous levels of expenditure.

The model with normal solutions thus allows a more transparent analysis of their character than is possible on the basis of a mere proof of the existence of possibly degenerate solutions to the equations of the Walras-Morishima model, but our simplified version is hybrid, because the endowment of capital goods has been determined endogenously, and yet this endowment is regarded as given (as quasi-exogenous) when the households determine their demand for consumption goods. The alternative would be to introduce capital as a value magnitude, as part of the endowment of households. Since this endowment would represent an arbitrary quantity relative to the given endowment of labor, the employment of both factors would be possible in a stationary state only if conditions for a substitution between capital and labor were introduced. This is discussed on the basis of Schefold (2013) in Schefold (2016), in order to investigate the existence of technical conditions under which production can adapt to a given capital-labor ratio (determined by factor supplies) so that full employment results. The general equilibrium models seem to be much more general than the neoclassical model based on the aggregate production function, but if one looks for the economically relevant solutions with a uniform rate of profit, if one takes the neoclassical postulate seriously that this rate of profit must be determined through supply and demand for "capital" and finally if one looks at the conditions necessary for a stable equilibrium, one is compelled to return to the surrogate production function, with its formal elegance and its logical difficulties. Garegnani (1960) sensed this more than 50 years ago and Schefold's (2016) parallel paper is an attempt to demonstrate it with more developed methods.

Notes

1 In the original: "una delle ipotesi su cui la teoria è costruita […] è incompatibile colla determinazione di un sistema di prezzi di equilibrio" (Garegnani, 1960, 119).
2 For references and for an analysis of Walras's shifting views on capital formation, see Petri (2016).
3 For details, see Petri (2004).
4 If $\mathbf{B}^{-1} \geq 0$, $\mathbf{B}$ maps the cone $/R_+^n$ onto itself, the mapping is invertible, cone is mapped onto cone, and the edges of the cone are mapped onto the edges of the image cone. Hence we have for all unit vectors $\mathbf{e}_i$, $\mathbf{e}_i \mathbf{B}^{-1} = \mu_i \mathbf{e}_j$, μ_j being some positive coefficient. $\mathbf{B}$ and $\mathbf{B}^{-1}$ must then be

permutation matrices, except in that the positive coefficients are not necessarily equal to one. This means that each process produces an input for exactly one other process. Since the system is basic, we can renumber the processes in such a way that the first process produces an input for the second, the second for the third and so on, and the last process produces the input for the first. Hence $\mathbf{B}$ and $\mathbf{B}^{-1}$ are circular matrices, as in Schefold (2010).

References

Clower, R. W. 1965. "The Keynesian Counter-Revolution: A Theoretical Appraisal." In *The Theory of Interest Rates*, edited by F. H. Hahn and F. P. R. Brechling, 103–25. London: Macmillan.

Eatwell, J. 1987. "Walras' Theory of Capital." In *The New Palgrave: A Dictionary of Economics*, vol. 4, edited by J. Eatwell, M. Milgate and P. Newman, 868–72. London: Macmillan.

Garegnani, P. 1960. *Il capitale nelle teorie della distribuzione*. Milano: Giuffrè.

———. 2011. "Savings, Investment and Capital in a System of General Intertemporal Equilibrium." In *Sraffa and Modern Economics*, vol. 1, edited by R. Ciccone, C. Gehrke and G. Mongiovi, 13–73. Abingdon: Routledge.

Han, Z., and B. Schefold. 2006. "An Empirical Investigation of Paradoxes: Reswitching and Reverse Capital Deepening in Capital Theory," *Cambridge Journal of Economics* 30, no. 5: 737–65.

Kahn, R. 1977. "Malinvaud on Keynes: Reviewing: Edmond Malinvaud, *The Theory of Unemployment Reconsidered*, Basil Blackwell, Oxford, 1977; Three Lectures Delivered for the Yrjö Jahnsson Foundation, Helsinki," *Cambridge Journal of Economics* 1, no. 4: 375–88.

Malinvaud, E. 1977. *The Theory of Unemployment Reconsidered*. Oxford: Basil Blackwell.

Morishima, M. 1960. "Existence of Solutions to the Walrasian System of Capital Formation and Credit," *Zeitschrift für Nationalökonomie* 20: 238–43.

———. 1964. "Walras' Theory of Capital Formation." In *Equilibrium, Stability and Growth*. Oxford: Clarendon.

———. 1977. *Walras' Economics: A Pure Theory of Capital and Money*. Cambridge: University Press.

Petri, F. 2004. *General Equilibrium, Capital and Macroeconomics: A Key to Recent Controversies in Equilibrium Theory*. Cheltenham: Elgar.

———. 2016. "Walras on Capital; Interpretative Insights from a Review by Bortkiewicz." Centro Sraffa Working Papers no. 17, February. Roma: Centro Sraffa.

Roncaglia, A. 2005. *The Wealth of Ideas: A History of Economic Thought*. Cambridge: University Press.

Schefold, B. 1997. *Normal Prices, Technical Change and Accumulation*. London: Macmillan.

———. 2008. "Savings, Investment and Capital in a System of General Intertemporal Equilibrium—An Extended Comment on Garegnani with a Note on Parrinello." In *Sraffa or an Alternative Economics*, edited by G. Chiodi and L. Ditta, 127–86. Basingstoke: Macmillan.

———. 2010. "Families of Strongly Curved and of Nearly Linear Wage Curves: A Contribution to the Debate about the Surrogate Production Function." In *Economic Theory and Economic Thought: Essays in Honour of Ian Steedman*, edited by J. Vint, J. S. Metcalfe, H. D. Kurz, N. Salvadori and P. A. Samuelson, 117–38. Abingdon: Routledge.

———. 2011. "Comment on Garegnani's Savings, Investment and Capital in a System of General Intertemporal Equilibrium." In *Sraffa and Modern Economics*, vol. 1, edited by R. Ciccone, C. Gehrke and G. Mongiovi, 74–87. Abingdon: Routledge.

———. 2013. "Approximate Surrogate Production Functions," *Cambridge Journal of Economics* 37, no. 5: 947–83.

———. 2016. "Marx, the Production Function and the Old Neoclassical Equilibrium: Workable under the Same Assumptions? With an Appendix on the Likelihood of Reswitching and of Wicksell Effects." Centro Sraffa Working Papers no. 18, March. Roma: Centro Sraffa.

Sraffa, P. 1960. *Production of Commodities by Means of Commodities*. Cambridge: Cambridge University Press.

Van Daal, J. 1998. "Leon Walras' General Equilibrium Models of Capital Formation. Existence of a Solution," *Revue Èconomique* 49, no. 5: 1175–98.

Walker, D. 1987. "Walras, Léon." In *The New Palgrave: A Dictionary of Economics*, vol. 4, edited by J. Eatwell, M. Milgate and P. Newman, 852–63. London: Macmillan.

Chapter Thirteen

TRADING IN THE "DEVIL'S METAL": KEYNES'S SPECULATION AND INVESTMENT IN TIN (1921–46)

Maria Cristina Marcuzzo and Annalisa Rosselli

In the Bolivian Siglo XX mine, near the mining center of Potosí, a devil figure with an enormous erection is watching over the miners risking their lives, and apparently even worse, their potency, in the dangerous work of mining tin. The Devil spirit [...] receives offerings of alcohol, cigarettes, and coca leaves, to protect the miners and help them to extract riches from the bowels of the earth.[1]

1. Introduction

In a recent paper, Alessandro Roncaglia, reconstructing the long-term developments and structure of the oil markets, noted that this "industry is complex, with production stages that are technically quite different from one another[; ...] it is characterised by strong economic and political interests intertwined in an interplay of conflicts and alliances that evolve over time, while technology, the organization of the markets and their size also dramatically change" (2015, 151).

This also applies to tin, a commodity whose characteristics made it an object of several cartels dominated by intertwined national and private interests, marked by high price volatility, control of which was pursued by various forms of international agreements, with or without the support of buffer stocks, from the 1920s to the 1980s. Tin was also the commodity that John Maynard Keynes dedicated most attention to as speculator, investor and commentator. It was probably the commodity in which he invested most, together with cotton and wheat, and where he suffered the greatest losses, alongside rubber. His trading in tin spanned from 1921, when he first bought a future contract, until his death in 1946.

In this chapter, we present a reconstruction of Keynes's dealings in tin, as economist, speculator and investor, taken as a lens through which to examine the tin market in the interwar period.[2]

2. The Tin Market in the Interwar Period: Competition and Control

The tin history of the interwar period shows five marked phases: the postwar slump and recovery (1920–24); the boom (1925–28); restriction (1929–36); high price volatility (1936–39); wartime control (1942–45).

Table 13.1 London standard tin (£ per ton), monthly average price.

	Jan	Feb	Mar	Apr	May	Jun	Jul	Aug	Sept	Oct	Nov	Dec
1921	192	167	157	164	179	170	167	155	156	156	159	170
1922	163	150	143	150	150	153	156	160	160	171	179	179
1923	182	191	220	213	203	192	181	187	198	204	221	235
1924	247	272	277	251	219	219	233	255	244	249	258	262
1925	266	262	246	237	245	252	258	259	259	278	285	285
1926	282	287	292	281	270	268	282	294	306	313	309	307
1927	298	306	313	303	295	296	289	293	280	265	263	267
1928	253	234	233	234	231	217	212	213	216	222	233	228
1929	223	223	221	207	198	200	209	210	205	191	181	179
1930	175	174	165	163	145	136	135	135	133	117	114	112
1931	116	118	122	113	104	105	111	115	118	127	133	139
1932	140	139	130	109	122	115	126	142	153	151	154	150
1933	146	149	149	158	186	220	217	215	217	223	227	228
1934	227	227	234	239	234	227	230	228	230	231	229	228
1935	231	227	216	224	228	228	232	223	224	227	226	220
1936	210	207	213	209	202	183	186	184	195	201	231	232
1937	229	234	283	267	251	250	264	265	259	224	190	190
1938	184	183	183	169	163	177	193	193	194	207	214	214
1939	215	214	215	218	226	228	230	230	229	230	230	249
1940	241	243	252	252	264	273	266	262	251	258	258	257
1941	257	265	270	270	208	263	258	257	256	256	257	258
1942*	275	275	275	275	275	275	275	275	275	275	275	275
1943*	275	275	275	275	275	275	275	275	275	275	275	275
1944*	300	300	300	300	300	300	300	300	300	300	300	300
1945*	300	300	300	300	300	300	300	300	300	300	300	300

* Prices at which the Non-Ferrous Metals Control supplied tin.
Source: Our elaboration from Knorr (1945) and *London Times, The West Australian*.

When the short-lived commodity boom after World War I was over, the price of tin dropped sharply (see table 13.1). This led the governments of Malaya and the Netherlands East Indies (NEI), which controlled more than half of the world production, to embark on the scheme—named after the location in Java (Bandoeng) where they met for a conference in 1921—designed to take tin off the market in order to raise its price (Eastham, 1936). At the time of its formation, the Bandoeng pool held as much as 34 percent of the world stocks, which it gradually released on the market until its dissolution in 1924. As from 1923, production failed to keep up with consumption, and, by 1926, the price of tin had risen more than 100 percent above the level of 1921. Prices peaked in October 1926, but in 1928 they began to fall. This was the year in which the Tin Producers Association was formed to hold tin off the market and raise its price by voluntary restriction of production. This initiative evolved into the International Tin Control Scheme (ITCS), launched in March 1931. It was an official agreement—the first of this kind that aimed at controlling price volatility—signed by the governments of Malaya, Bolivia, Nigeria and NEI, and administered by an International Tin Committee (ITC) representing the four members that produced 80 percent of the world tin output.

Table 13.2 LME tin turnovers (000 tons).

	1926	1927	1928	1929	1930	1931	1932	1933	1934	1935
Spot	24.3	24.1	21.94	20.4	16.6	19.7	15.7	13.7	12.5	10.0
Future	160	140	182	171	147	184	152	120	82	60
Production	137	150	170	187	171	142	93	85	109	139
Consumption	138	142	165	178	161	135	99	127	118	142

Source: Eastham (1936).

ITCS imposed restrictions on exports. Quotas were allotted to each participant according to the production levels of 1929 (Knorr, 1945, 108). The scheme was supported by the International Tin Pool (1931) made up of privately held stocks, the size of which was regularly published. ITCS was to last until 1933.

Before the end of that year negotiations started for a second agreement, which, like the previous one, was based on production restrictions, and began in January 1934 for a three-year period. This agreement, however, was officially supported by the Tin Buffer Stock Scheme (1934), operated by a committee appointed by the governments with representatives in the ITC, with the purpose of preventing the price from rising above £225 or falling below £215 per ton (Khan, 1982, 163). The purpose of the buffer stock was to give the industry "a working capital in metal tin, enabling it to meet immediate requirements in full when current production cannot be expanded rapidly enough to meet current consumption, or—more important—when current demand is swollen temporarily by the anticipation of an increased future consumption."[3] The buffer stock was on average successful in keeping the price within the predetermined range until 1936. According to Jack Kenneth Eastham (1936, 25), the scheme reduced speculative activity in the London Metal Exchange (LME), as measured by the turnover in 1934–35, despite the upward trend in production and consumption as from 1933 (see table 13.2).

In 1938, just before the outbreak of the war, the third agreement was launched, with the formation of another buffer stock with the price target in the range of £200–230 per ton. The agreement was intended to last until 1941.

At the outbreak of the war, nonferrous metals were put under control of a division of the Ministry of Supply. Private tin dealings on the London Metal Exchange ceased in December 1941 and the Ministry of Supply determined the price at which tin was supplied, while dealings in the other metals were suspended in 1939 (Roddy, 1995, 21). By 1940, discussions were under way to give rise to the fourth agreement, which was ratified in 1942, with a termination date set in 1946 (Hillman, 2011, 314–16). However, the agreement did not put any restriction on the production of tin, which was encouraged to build American strategic stockpiles, and the agreement eventually proved ineffective because of the Japanese occupation of Southeast Asia. The United States continued to accumulate stocks of tin, absorbing the excess of production over consumption, until 1956.

The LME was reopened in 1949, but the outbreak of the Korean War disrupted the lifting of control in the tin market. A conference was held in Geneva in 1953 and negotiations for a new agreement were initiated. Between 1956 and 1989, six other agreements were formed, making up to 70 years of control of the tin industry.

3. Betting on Derivatives: Keynes, the Speculator

Keynes's interest in tin dates to 1921, when he began his speculation in metal options and futures, together with currencies and cotton, while preparing his reports on commodities for the London and Cambridge Economic Services, the *Special Memoranda on Stocks of Staple Commodities* (henceforth *Memoranda*), which he authored between 1923 and 1930 (Keynes, 1923–30).[4]

In the tin market Keynes experimented with all the derivatives available to him at the time and held the highest number and the largest variety of contracts, experimenting with a great variety of combinations of investment strategies (see table 13.3). After 1925, he also took delivery of some of his futures and stocked tin in the London Metal Exchange warehouses, thus moving part of his operations onto the spot market (Keynes Papers, SE/11/2/38). His activity in tin derivatives ceased completely only in the years 1934–35, when the buffer-stock operation, which successfully limited the range of price variations, made speculative activity unprofitable, and again in 1937.

The pattern of high volatility that was typical of tin prices, while providing scope for speculative activity, exposed him to the risk of heavy losses when the timing of buying and selling did not match the price swings. This was particularly true in the case of option dealing, bearing in mind that only the European types (namely those which could be exercised only at maturity) were available to him.[5]

Keynes's operations always reflected expectations of an increase in the price of the metal. He was a bull in the tin market most of the time. Only very rarely did he try to take advantage of an expected decrease in the price of tin (and he failed), by buying put options (Keynes Papers, SE/11/2/35) and selling SODs (seller's option to double) (Keynes Papers, SE/11/2/33). The SOD was an option that implied the sale of a given quantity of the metal for future delivery together with the possibility of doubling the quantity to be sold at the same price. The price of a SOD was slightly lower than that of a normal future, but this loss was more than offset by the possibility of doubling the profit if the price fell below the strike price. When Keynes sold them, he expected the price to fall, but it rose and he incurred a loss. The same happened with the two puts he had bought in the expectation of a price fall, and he let them lapse (Keynes Papers, SE/11/2/38).

Most of Keynes's operations were carried out in the years 1924–27. In these years, his bull expectations led him to buy futures for considerable numbers, but also to buy call options and BODs (buyer's option to double). The latter were futures at a price higher than a normal future but with the possibility of doubling the quantity to be bought. It is not easy to understand the reasons behind Keynes's choices among these alternatives. The price of options did not follow a precise rule, and lacking information we are unable to compare the alternatives in terms of cost. We know that, given that Keynes operated on borrowed money and that the average purchase of futures cost several thousand pounds, Keynes may have preferred the far riskier (and more profitable in the case of

Table 13.3 Number of operations in tin futures and options made by Keynes.

YEAR	BOUGHT								SOLD				
	Futures	Call	Lapsed	BOD	Lapsed	Put	Lapsed	Double	SOD	Lapsed	Put	Lapsed*	Double
1921	2	0	0	0	0	0	0	0	0	0	0	0	0
1922	0	2	0	3	1	0	0	0	0	0	0	0	0
1923	4	1	0	0	0	0	0	2	0	0	0	0	0
1924	8	13	5	6	0	0	0	0	6	3	0	0	1
1925	28	6	3	0	0	0	0	3	0	0	11	11	0
1926	31	6	0	0	0	2	2	0	0	0	3	1	0
1927	31	26	13	2	2	2	0	3	1	1	0	0	0
1928	2	2	2	0	0	0	0	1	0	0	1	1	0
1929	2	0	0	0	0	0	0	0	0	0	1	1	0
1930	5	5	5	4	4	0	0	1	0	0	0	0	0
1931	6	7	2	0	0	0	0	0	0	0	0	0	0
1932	4	1	0	0	0	0	0	0	0	0	0	0	0
1933	2	1	0	0	0	0	0	1	0	0	0	0	0
1934	0	0	0	0	0	0	0	0	0	0	0	0	0
1935	0	0	0	0	0	0	0	0	0	0	0	0	0
1936	10	0	0	0	0	0	0	0	0	0	0	0	1
1937	0	0	0	0	0	0	0	0	0	0	0	0	0
1938	28	0	0	0	0	0	0	0	0	0	0	0	1
1939	5	0	0	0	0	0	0	0	0	0	0	0	0
Tot	168	70	30	15	7	4	2	11	7	4	16	14	3

* The buyer did not exercise the option.
Source: Our elaboration from Keynes's Papers.

success) call options because of lack of resources and not simply because he was indulging his gambling spirit. The price of a call option for tin varied according to market conditions, but on analyzing Keynes's ledgers we concluded that its price ranged from less than 3 percent of the future price to more than 6 percent. This means that it was never less than £6 per ton and was sometimes as high as £15 per ton. The difference between the price of a BOD and a normal future, on the contrary, was between £3 and £6 per ton, and therefore purchasing a BOD entailed the expectation of a slightly higher price in order to be profitable and a larger initial outlay for the initial quantity.

During the period May–October 1925, Keynes joined a tin pool.[6] It was in this period that he added another instrument to his speculative activities, and he dared to sell put options for substantial amounts of the metal, relying on an increase in the price of tin, over which the pool had considerable influence. The risk was high, but nearly all the put options lapsed and Keynes pocketed the premium, which was in the range of 5 or 6 percent. His sale of put options was successful 14 out of 16 times.

There are not many cases when Keynes attempted to hedge his positions. He bought put options for this reason only twice (Keynes Papers, SE/11/2/48). In a few other cases, when he had bought futures for very large amounts, he tried to minimize the cost of hedging either by selling a SOD for half the amount involved or by buying a double. The latter was an option that gave the buyer the possibility of buying or selling—whichever he preferred—a given amount at a given price at some future date. In other words, the buyer of a double bet on very high volatility of the price, at least high enough to cover the cost of the option, which was indeed high (on the contrary, the seller of a double bet on relative constancy of price). Keynes often bought and sold double options for their own sake (Keynes Papers, TC 4/3/131 and 237), but occasionally he used them for hedging purposes. In this case, he bought a future and a double for the same amount of the metal and for the same date (Keynes Papers, SE/11/2/21) so that if the price rose he could increase his profit by exercising the double as a call; otherwise, if the price fell, he could minimize the loss by exercising the double as a put.

We may wonder just how good Keynes was at predicting the price trend. A rough answer can be found first in calculating the percentage of options he exercised, and then the percentage of the put he sold and that the buyer did not exercise. In the case of call, this percentage was 57 percent; in the case of BODs it was 53 percent; in the case of the put he sold, it was 87 percent. To this we should add the percentage of the times when the price of the metal he sold at the expiration date was higher than the price of the future, and this, on the basis of our calculations, was 57 percent. Unfortunately, this undoubtedly skillful activity was not necessarily profitable, due to the high commission and transaction costs, which, in the case of futures, were 0.1 percent on the buying and selling price and 0.5 percent to the metal broker. In the case of options, commissions applied only when they were exercised as percentage of the price of the metal bought or sold.

A measure of the profitability of Keynes's operations in tin is much harder to arrive at, since investment in tin was a variable portion of his portfolio. Profits and losses are shown in table 13.4 as absolute amounts in sterling. Futures made up the greatest share

Table 13.4 Keynes's total profits and losses in tin derivatives (£).

YEAR	Futures	Put sold	Call	BOD bought	SOD sold	Double bought	Double sold	Total
1921	320	0	0	0	0	0	0	320
1922	-180	0	55	-427	0	0	0	-480
1923	1673	0	1200	0	0	0	0	2873
1924	-520	0	-1006	4152	-2221	0	350	755
1925	4793	3236	-3781	0	0	-178	0	4070
1926	8886	760	1662	0	0	-369	0	10939
1927	-4515	0	-4186	0	0	-464	0	-9165
1928	1526	-57	-538	908	-23	-343	0	1473
1929	119	175	0	0	0	0	0	294
1930	-954	5	-451	-1507	0	0	0	-2912
1931	-247	0	340	0	0	-60	0	33
1932	991	0	385	0	0	0	0	1376
1933	286	0	1	0	0	178	0	465
1934	0	0	0	0	0	0	0	0
1935	0	0	0	0	0	0	0	0
1936	2611	0	0	0	0	0	700	3311
1937	0	0	0	0	0	0	0	0
1938	4659	0	0	0	0	0	150	4809
1939	-13	0	0	0	0	0	0	-13
Total	19507	4114	-6319	3126	-2244	-1236	1200	18148

Source: Our elaboration from Keynes's Papers.

of Keynes's investment in tin (the average transaction was £6,634 compared with £258 of the average transaction in put and call options). While for futures we calculated the average return as 3.2 percent on a three-month basis, the average return for options is much less significant due to the high variance. As table 13.4 shows, Keynes made half of the total profit of the period in 1926, which he lost almost entirely in 1927. Another large loss was incurred in 1930, which might account for his reduced speculative activity in tin, which was resumed only in 1936 and 1938—years that in any case saw him extremely active in the markets.

4. From Speculation to Investment: Keynes, the Investor

Commodity speculation took the lion's share of Keynes's investments during the 1920s—a pattern that probably began to change when Keynes's second major setback came in 1927, and then in the wake of the 1929 crash. Even though Keynes went on trading commodities until the outbreak of World War II, when activity in these markets was partially suspended, early in the 1930s he shifted to equities, his main sources of income being capital gains and dividends.

In fact, Keynes's activity as an investor in shares dates back to the early 1920s, especially in his capacity as institutional investor,[7] and shares loomed large in his own portfolio in the 1930s and 1940s. There is also some indication of a change of investment strategy after the 1929 stock exchange collapse, although at the time Keynes had little exposure vis-à-vis Wall Street.

In this section, we examine his dealings in that small subset of shares that were connected to the tin industry. The reason for doing so is to compare this investment activity with his speculation activity in the metal. David Chambers, Elroy Dimson and Justin Foo (2015), investigating Keynes's investment for King's College, have shown that mine shares accounted for the major part. Keynes allocated on average four times the weighting to stocks of mining firms as compared to nonmining firms. When Keynes was convinced of the quality of an investment, besides taking it for himself, he was keen to suggest it to all the institutions he was involved in. As an example, we know that in 1936 King's College held several of the tin shares Keynes had in his own portfolio (letter from Richard Kahn to Keynes, December 24, 1936, Keynes Papers, KC/5/5/250).

The companies whose shares Keynes held in his portfolio—of which we will say more below—are listed in table 13.5. Keynes's purchases of tin-producing company shares were concentrated in two periods, which roughly coincided with the beginning of the upswings of the price of the metal: the 1924–25 and 1933–34 years. The first period of investments was over by 1929, while the price of tin was falling rapidly, as were the profits of most of the companies that produced it and the prices of their shares. Keynes avoided heavy losses by selling almost all his shares in 1928, matching the similar withdrawal from the derivative tin market. The second period of purchases of shares coincided with the years of the buffer stock, which stabilized the tin price. This period ended in 1937, as we will see below, while in 1936 and 1938 he went back to the futures market. His total investment in tin shares is shown in figure 13.1, which is based on Keynes's evaluations on January 1 of each year.[8]

Between the two periods, there was a break of almost four years, which coincided with tempestuous turmoil on the financial markets due to the Great Depression and abandonment of the gold standard by the Bank of England.

In both periods, Keynes appears to have been guided by the pursuit of rewarding dividends more than capital gains. He was not engaged in intense speculative trading. Once he had acquired the shares of a company, he kept them for months and sometimes for years. In 1924–25, he made some use of call options, but none at all in the 1930s. In total he fell back on call options 11 times in the attempt to get a lower price; however, when he failed, he bought the shares he was interested in on the market, showing that his choices were based on consideration of the company's prospects, and that he was not after quick gain.

In the first period, he invested mainly in British-owned companies in Malaya, which was then the biggest and fastest growing tin-producing country, with over one-third of the world production. His preferences were for the companies established before World War I like the Pahang Consolidated Company, established in 1906 and the largest in terms of capital in 1920, and the Kramat Pulai, established in 1906. Pahang Co. was active in lode mining, but most British companies that dominated the Malayan market had prevailed over the Chinese producers there thanks to the introduction of the new capital-intensive technique of bucket dredging. Keynes had shares of the "doyen" of these companies, the Malayan Tin Dredging Co. and of Southern Perak, another dredging company. In

Table 13.5 Keynes's holdings of tin shares (gray squares).

Company	1923	1924	1925	1926	1927	1928	1929	1930	1931	1932	1933	1934	1935	1936	1937	1938	1939	1940	1941	1942	1943	1944	1945
Arpang				■	■	■	■	■															
Arpat															■	■	■	■	■	■	■	■	■
Anglo Oriental													■	■	■								
Associated Tin of Nigeria													■	■	■								
Ayer Hitam												■			■								
British Tin												■											
Changkat																							
Kramat Pulai		■				■	■																
London Tin Corp.													■	■	■	■							
Malayan Tin Dredging					■	■					■	■	■	■	■								
Pahang		■				■																	
Petaling Tin											■					■		■					
Ropp Tin		■		■	■																		
Southern Kinta											■				■	■	■	■	■	■	■	■	
Southern Malayan Tin Dredging											■				■								
Southern Perak				■	■																		
Teja Malaya		■	■	■					■	■	■												
Tekka	■	■			■																		
Tronoh											■	■	■	■	■	■							

Source: Our elaboration from Keynes's Papers.

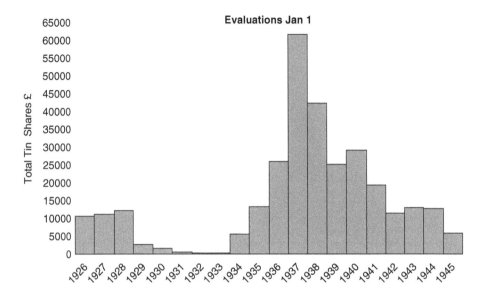

Figure 13.1 Tin shares (£) in Keynes's portfolio.
Source: Our elaborations from Keynes's Papers.

1927, Keynes added the shares of a third dredging company to his investments, the newly floated Teja Malayan Tin Dredging. This purchase was his only participation in the 1926–27 "scramble for tin mining company shares," when tin had reached £290 a ton and "a plethora of mines were floated on the London Stock Exchange and the total issued capital of British registered mining companies in Malaya shot up from £3.6 million in 1920 to £18.7 million in 1927" (Helten and Jones, 1989, 168).

However, he also tried some geographical diversification, but always within the British Empire. He invested in the Ropp Tin Company, the largest producer in Northern Nigeria, owned by South African Capital, which was particularly generous with his shareholders ("the largest dividend-payer of the field," *The Economist*, August 4, 1928). Although Keynes usually preferred companies with British and City people on their boards, he made an investment in a newcomer on the Malayan scene, the Ampang Tin, a subsidiary of the American Guggenheims' Yukon Gold, which after expensive prospecting in the 1920s, began its activity in Malaya in 1923 (Hillman, 2011, 71).

On the contrary, we found no evidence of Keynes being tempted by the 1920s activities of John Howeson, who was engaged in a rationalization of the tin industry (together with the other "tin baron" of that period, the Bolivian Antenor Patiño). He built a personal empire through acquisition and consolidation of many existing companies all over the world. As an outsider—he was born in India and his father was German—at first he was not welcomed by the London financial circle, but, step by step, thanks to an extensive network of relations and his impressive personality, he came into control of a vast financial system, responsible for investors' funds amounting to over £4 million (ibid., 64). His flagship in Malaya was the Anglo-Oriental Mining Corporation, established in

1928. In spite of the support given to Howeson by Oliver Lyttelton, probably one of the most knowledgeable men in the metal trade and a close friend of Keynes, Keynes held back from the shares of the Anglo-Oriental until 1935, when Howeson was accused of fraud and a new board was appointed without him (Howeson was jailed in 1936). Anglo-Oriental played a crucial role in the reshaping of the tin industry. At the end of the decade, three British holdings—London Tin Corporation, British Tin Investment (BTI), and General Tin Investment Ltd.—controlled 43 percent of the Malayan tin output (and 17 percent of world production) (Yacob, 2007, 77). The companies numbered nearly 80, but ownership was highly concentrated.

Keynes resumed his investments in tin shares in the spring of 1933. This was a particularly promising period for the tin industry. The International Tin Agreement of 1931 had barely succeeded in preventing the ruin of the industry, while the price of tin remained well below the threshold of £200 per ton for more than three years (1930–32) because of the depressed demand. In the spring of 1933, American demand picked up, spurred by two events: the devaluation of the dollar, which stimulated the recovery, and the end of Prohibition. Beer could again be sold freely, and the demand for cans put pressure on the available tin stocks. There were even tensions on the market, since the increased demand could not immediately be met by increased production.

By April 1934, the tin stocks that the International Tin Pool had accumulated to sustain the price of tin were entirely liquidated, world tin stocks were at what was considered a normal level and it was reasonable to assume that the price could hold firm or increase, thanks also to the buffer-stock scheme. It was then that Keynes further increased his investments in the tin industry, to peak in 1937, as did the price of tin. After 1937, Keynes began to sell most of his tin shares. By October 1937, he was writing to F. C. Scott, the Provincial Insurance Company chairman: "I feel that the time has come for reducing our holding of base metal shares without being too ambitious about prices" (quoted in Westall, 1992, 372).

In 1938, Keynes foresaw poor dividends as consequence of the fall in the tin price at the end of the previous year, although he was still optimistic about the long-term outlook of the tin shares. As he wrote to Scott in October, "In the long run Tin shares are as good as ever every way. The question is whether these long-term prospects will win over the factor of low current earnings" (Keynes Papers, PC/1/5/230).

Turning now to individual shares, we note that Keynes's largest investments were in three companies: British Tin Investments, Southern Kinta and Anglo-Oriental Mining. All of them had their main interests in Malaya. In 1934, Anglo-Oriental managed 26 mining companies in Malaya, and Keynes invested in some of them: Ampat Tin Dredging, Associated Tin of Nigeria, Changkat and London Tin Corporation.[9] The investment in Anglo-Oriental was short-lived and extremely profitable. Keynes purchased cumulative participating preferred shares, which guaranteed priority in dividend distribution. He bought them in five installments over the years 1935–36, when the company went into safer hands than those of Howeson, who had, however, given Anglo-Oriental a leading position in the Malayan industry through acquisitions and consolidations. Keynes sold his shares in 1937 at double the price he had bought them.

Anglo-Oriental also owned and managed Southern Kinta Consolidated, the largest operating company in the British Empire endowed with new dredges brought in from acquired companies so that "with direct costs of around £45 per ton of concentrate in 1939 [Southern Kinta] was capable of meeting any competition" (Hillman, 2011, 268). Southern Kinta shares were still in Keynes's portfolio in 1943—confirming Keynes's confidence in companies that were able to keep up with technological progress. Keynes held Southern Kinta throughout its most profitable period, when it paid shareholders an annual average of 23 percent. A remarkable performance, but other British tin companies in Keynes's portfolio (Ayer Hitam, Kramat Pulai, Tronoh and Pahang) yielded annual averages of 15 percent and above (Rippy, 1953, 119).

British Tin Investments was a finance house founded in 1932 by separating the production division from the equity investments of a British–American company. It specialized "in the management and technical advice of such [tin] companies and hold substantial investments in the individual companies in which they are interested"(Keynes, 1940, 14). In 1934, Lyttelton became its chairman and thenceforth was the leading figure in the tin finance. It was in 1934 that Keynes bought a first installment of BTI, to which he added a large amount one year later, when the price reached an unusually low level. His timing was not equally successful in 1937, when he bought another small lot at the highest price of the year. He kept these until the end of the war, when he sold them at a very low price.[10] However, the shares had never stopped yielding significant dividends,[11] even in time of war.

In figure 13.2, we plotted the price of tin with the price of several of the tin shares in the years in which Keynes held them in its portfolio. As a general observation, we can say that he was a momentum trader, that is, he bought on a rising market, with the exception of London Tin, in which he invested heavily when its price was falling. As expected, the share prices followed the trend in the price of tin fairly closely. With a good knowledge of the fundamentals of the metal, tin share prices could be predicted with a fair degree of certainty.

In order to understand why Keynes was so keen on investing in British-managed tin companies, an observation in his memorandum to the Treasury in October 1940 may be of some help. When advising the British government on how to increase Britain's dollar resources, Keynes declared that tin (and rubber) shares would not hold much appeal for the US private investors, mainly "for the reason that they are out of touch with the managements which are situated in London and in the East, and have no means of gauging their efficiencies" (1940, 14). Keynes clearly believed that he was able to do so.

5. Understanding Market Behavior: Keynes, the Economist

The foregoing review of Keynes's investment activity in tin, in both derivatives and shares, prompts two questions. The first is how his behavior compares with the statements he made in several speeches, memoranda and correspondence about his investment philosophy. The second is why Keynes was so fascinated by the "devil's metal," which took up such a large share in his portfolio. It is noteworthy that not a single year went by after 1921 without Keynes investing in some tin-related assets.

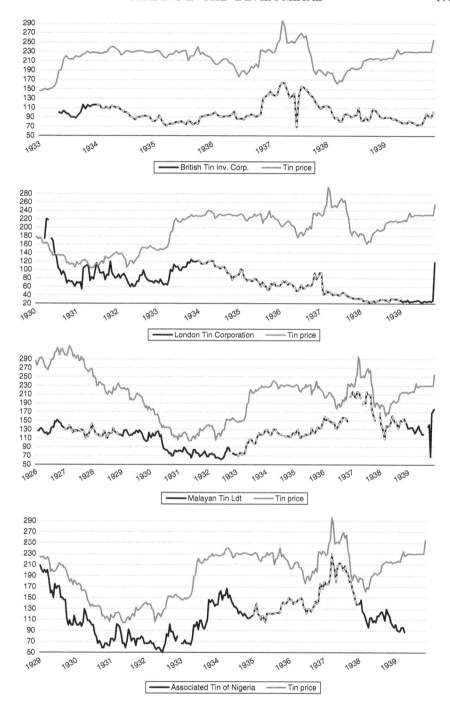

Figure 13.2 Tin prices (£ per ton) and tin shares prices (£ per unit).
Source: Our elaborations from Keynes's Papers.

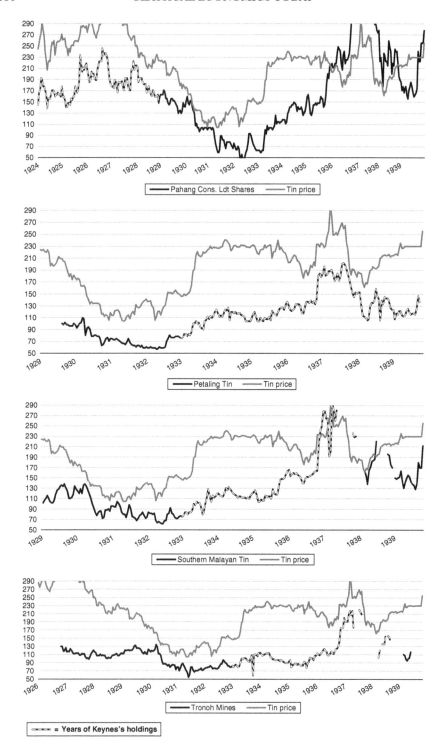

Figure 13.2 *(cont.)*

As far as trading in tin as a commodity is concerned, it was part of his general interest in commodities possibly influenced by the knowledge he was acquiring as a professional economist. In the *Memoranda* he commented on some of the commodities he traded in (cotton, copper, tin, lead, sugar, jute, rubber, wheat) as well as a few others (nitrate, coffee, tea, petroleum, wool) that he did not trade in. He provided information on the level of stocks and consumption, the flow of production and the trend of prices, always presented with assessment of the quality and reliability of the data. In fact, Keynes's approach to trading was based on evaluation of the amount of information available for each individual commodity and the degree of uncertainty about the future course of the main factors underlying it. Collection of the "relevant information" available was the premise to evaluating the "weight" of any argument that could be inferred from it, according to the conceptual framework that Keynes used in his *Treatise of Probability* to illustrate any decision-making process. As for the availability of information and the degree of uncertainty (which affects the confidence that could be accorded), information on tin, as indeed on copper and rubber, was plentiful but of variable quality, unlike cotton and wheat—the other two commodities in which Keynes invested heavily. For the latter, reliable information was plentiful but subject to considerable uncertainty due to the unpredictability of extraeconomic factors (weather, parasites).

Keynes described the characteristics of tin as follows: "Tin is a particular commodity in that both production and consumption are exceptionally insensitive to moderate changes of price, with the result that violent price fluctuations ensue whenever the difference between the two has to be absorbed into stock" (1925, 377).

It follows that with price fluctuations speculative activity is indeed potentially profitable, provided that the price swings are anticipated correctly by monitoring the level of stocks. However, this was easier said than done, since figures on tin in UK or US warehouses and afloat from or still in the producing countries could not be reckoned with precision at any given time. Even monthly figures relative to the visible stocks of tin held in warehouses in Europe and the United States "are apt […] to be extremely misleading" (Keynes, 1926a, 417). The reason is that these statistics "ignore the stocks of tin and tin ore in the Straits Settlements" and "tin which is sold direct to consumers without passing through the Metal Exchange warehouses or the export returns" (Keynes, 1928, 506).

Keynes's trading experience influenced, and in turn was influenced by, his views on speculation, which are not given systematic treatment in his work but can be sketched out in roughly chronological order, drawing on the statements he made on the subject scattered here and there in his writings.

First, there are the manuscript notes for the preparation of his *Lectures on the Stock Exchange* in preparation for the course he gave at Cambridge in 1910, where he distinguished between gambling and speculation, according as to whether risk is or is not calculable (an approach very similar to Alfred Marshall's; see Dardi and Gallegati, 1992).[12] The distinguishing criterion lies in the amount of knowledge possessed by the actor in either case: "the possession of superior knowledge [is] the vital distinction between the speculator and the gambler"). For Keynes what mattered was *not* measurement of comparative success in gambling and in speculation, which may be dependent on other factors, but evaluation of the nature of the action in the two cases. Unlike speculation, gambling is not reasonable because it is a behavior that has no basis in knowledge, although of course a gambler may at times be a winner and a speculator a loser. The next question is whether "superior knowledge" enables the speculator to predict the future course of prices. There are passages in the *Lectures* that seem to confirm this, but the view was short-lived. As Keynes became more closely acquainted with the working of the markets, he presented an analysis of speculation on different grounds (see "The Forward Market in Foreign Exchanges" (1922), incorporated into the *Tract on Monetary Reform* (1923), and his article "Some Aspects of Commodity Markets" (1923)). Here not only is the speculator not a "gambler," but his ability through superior knowledge to forecast the future is downplayed. He is not "a prophet" (ibid., 260) but rather a risk bearer: "The most important function of the speculator in the great organized 'future market' [is that of] a risk bearer" (ibid.). The point of speculator as risk bearer, and profits being the remuneration for risk bearing, not for forecasting skill, is reiterated in the *Treatise on Money*, where he presented a more refined version of his theory.

When we get to the *General Theory*, the analysis of speculation (chapter 12) marks a departure from Keynes's previous views. The nature of speculative activity is defined as that of " 'forecasting the psychology of the market' and is distinguished from enterprise, which is defined as the 'activity of forecasting the prospective yield of assets over their whole life.' " Thus "speculation" is no longer an attempt to gauge the "prospective yield," on the basis of superior knowledge of fundamentals, but a bet on a "favourable change in the conventional basis of valuation" (Keynes, 1936, 159). So that "the energies and skill of the professional investor and speculator are mainly occupied [...] not with making superior long-term forecasts of the probable yield of an investment over its whole life, but with foreseeing changes in the conventional basis of valuation a short time ahead of the general public" (ibid., 154).

Since, "as the organization of investment market improves, the risk of the predominance of speculation does [...] increase" (ibid., 158), speculation is hardly likely to constitute the bedrock for price stability in those markets.

In the case of the commodities markets, a sudden and large increase in open interest positions, unrelated to new information about fundamentals coming to the market, pushes futures prices up if the increase is in demand (an increase in long positions) and down if the increase is in supply (an increase in short positions). So accumulated net long positions in futures, constituting as they do a bet that prices will rise, actually make spot prices rise. Conversely, accumulated net short positions would make spot prices fall. In both cases a high price volatility ensues in the commodity markets.

Speculators are viewed as unable to generate a stable price environment since there is no incentive to buy surplus stocks in a falling market. Moreover, because it takes time to increase supply, speculators may act as amplifying factors in pushing up prices and stimulating uneconomic and excessive output.

The last stage in the development of Keynes's views can be located in the article on "The Policy of Government Storage of Foodstuffs and Raw Materials" (1938a), where he began to elaborate various buffer-stock schemes, as a means to stabilize prices, in a systematic way, although he had already advocated government storage of foodstuffs and raw materials in 1926 (1926b). In that article, starting from the observation that for four commodities (rubber, cotton, wheat and lead) "which are [...] fairly representative of raw materials marketed in competitive conditions, the average annual price range over the last ten years has been 67 per cent",—Keynes pointed out—"An orderly programme of output, either of raw materials themselves or of their manufactured products, is scarcely possible in such conditions" (1938a, 451). This explains the need for a buffer-stock scheme (see Fantacci et al., 2012).

As far as investing in shares is concerned, Keynes presented his golden rule in a letter to F. C. Scott on August 15, 1934: "As time goes on, I get more and more convinced that the right method in investment is to put fairly large sums into enterprises which one thinks one knows something about and in the management of which one thoroughly believes" (1934b, 57). In another letter to Scott, dated June 21, 1934, Keynes outlined the key reasons why he liked Union Corporation, the large South African mining company, one of his largest and most successful core holdings. Mainly it was the fact that "he trusted the management very highly" (1934a, 56).

And a few years later, he made clearer how many companies he knew "something about" and how many there were in whose management he "thoroughly believed": "I myself follow very closely, or think I have some knowledge, of upwards of perhaps 200 investments [...]. Now out of the 200 which one tries to follow more or less, there are probably less than 50 in all classes about which, at any given time, one feels really enthusiastic" ("Memorandum for the Provincial Insurance Company," 1938b, 98).

The tin companies fared well in this respect, as Keynes himself explained in October 1940:

> Taking only those which are quoted on the London Stock Exchange there are about 50 tin companies [...]. The nominal capital of the British owned tin shares in Malaya was (at the end of 1936) about £7 million with a present market value of between two and three times that sum. [...] There are certain finance houses, such as London Tin or British Tin [...] which specialise in the management and technical advice of such companies and hold substantial investments in the individual companies in which they are interested. (1940, 13-14)

Figure 13.3 shows how the tin companies were interconnected through an interlocking of directors and managers. There is evidence that Keynes was acquainted with several of the people involved in the management of mines-related firms. This is borne out in Chambers and Dimson (2013, 224–25), who wrote that:

> when the 7,632 potential personal contacts from Keynes's time at Eton College, Cambridge University, the Treasury during World War I and from public life are matched with the directors of the 247 firms in which he invested, Keynes was ultimately connected to 46 of those firms (Eldridge, 2012). His connections proved particularly influential in the mining sector. The existence of a connection to a director at the time of investment led Keynes to allocate on average four times the weighting to stocks of mining firms as compared to non-mining firms, and furthermore this benefited performance.

In particular, several of the tin companies whose shares Keynes's held in his portfolio in the 1930s had Lyttelton as manager or director. From 1920, Lyttelton had been

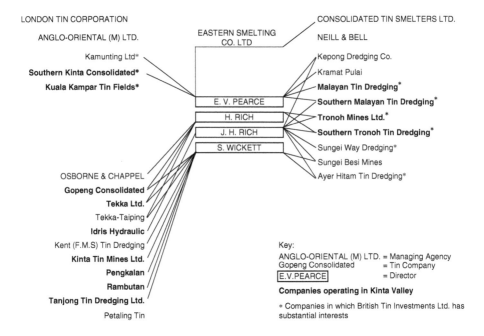

Figure 13.3 Interlocking directorships and mining agencies in tin industry. *Source*: Khoo and Lubis (2005).

employed by the British Metal Corporation (BMC), where he was managing director between 1925 and 1939. BMC was a major shareholder of Anglo-Oriental Mining and British Tin Corporation. In 1934, he was appointed as the government's primary informal adviser on zinc, lead, tin and copper. He was also chairman of the London Tin Corporation and served on the boards of a number of foreign companies engaged in the metal trade. He was one of the few people who effectively controlled the global metal trade (Ball, 2004). As Lyttelton himself recounted in his *Memoirs*, "In the international metal trade [...] no more than perhaps 25 men really counted in the industry [...]. After the retirement of Cecil Budd, I, later, was one of the 25 who could claim to have a say in this world-wide industry" (1962, 130–31). On the outbreak of World War II in September 1939, Lyttelton was appointed controller of nonferrous metals for the government.

Besides personal acquaintance with the few people who "counted in the industry", there is no doubt that Keynes knew a lot about tin from his speculation in options and futures. As early as 1926, he observed that "most of those who hold shares probably do not understand the metal market, and are constantly upset by its fluctuations" (Keynes Papers, LCE/3/114, 11 December 1926). Keynes, instead, was placed in the situation of having access to "superior knowledge" in that market and trusted tin shares to perform well. The data seem to confirm this (see table 13.6).

Table 13.6 Dividends distributed by some tin companies in Malaya from their foundation to 1951.

	No years	Initial year	Annual average%	Highest 5 years	Annual average%
Ayer Hitam	21	1930	20.4	1937–41	41.0
Kinta	48	1903	18.5	1946–50	30.5
Kramat Pulai	39	1912	39.4	1934–38	97.7
Malayan	37	1914	28.9	1936–40	60.5

Source: Rippy (1953).

6. Conclusions

Keynes was exceptionally gifted as a trader, not in terms of the gains he made in the stock exchange—which, as has now been proved, were not as large as commonly believed— but by virtue of his deep grasp of the fundamentals underlying price trends. He showed great ability in gauging the direction of prices, although he did not always get the timing right. He never ceased to gather information on the underlying forces driving prices, and remained first and foremost an economist who based his trading decisions on his professional knowledge.

As far as tin was concerned, he put his investment philosophy into practice. Having acquired a deep knowledge of that market through speculation in derivatives, he applied it to understanding the working of the tin companies, a highly concentrated industry in the hands of a few people in total control—people Keynes was acquainted with and whose ability as managers he trusted.

In the later stage of Keynes's thinking, he became more and more concerned about the role of market sentiment, conventions and herd behavior. While he granted that success of the speculator might rest on the ability to interpret market sentiment, this was never the guiding principle for Keynes's behavior as investor. Rather he trusted informed opinion on relevant data and, above all, individual judgment as opposed to the average market view.

"My central principle of investment"—he explained in 1944 to a banker who was critical of his suggestions about how to manage Eton's finances—"is to go contrary to general opinion, on the ground that, if everyone is agreed about its merits, the investment is inevitably too dear and therefore unattractive" (Keynes, 1940, 111).

Acknowledgments

We wish to thank Iolanda Sanfilippo and Giulia Zacchia for very skillful research assistance and Valeria Sebastianelli and Giancarlo De Vita for their help with data collection. We are also grateful to Pedro Duarte for his comments on an earlier version.

Notes

1 Ingulstad, Perchard and Storli (2015, 1).
2 Building on previous work (Marcuzzo and Sanfilippo, 2016; Cavalli and Cristiano, 2012), we offer here a more comprehensive and detailed analysis of Keynes's speculation in tin derivatives and tin-related shares, based on Keynes's own records as shown in his ledgers and in statements of accounts from his brokers and correspondence. Reference to the unpublished material follows the classification number given in the Catalogue of Keynes Papers, King's College, Modern Archives, Cambridge (catalogue available at https://janus.lib.cam.ac.uk/db/node.xsp?id=EAD/GBR/0272/PP/JMK).
3 Chairman's speech to the Annual General Meeting of the British Tin Investment Corporation, reported by *The Times*, January 24, 1934.
4 The relevant pages for tin are 267–506 and 512–647.
5 Bauer, Cosemans and Eichholtz (2009), using a database that comprises more than 68,000 accounts and more than eight million trades in stocks and options at a large online broker in the Netherlands, show that option trading has a detrimental impact on the performance of individual investors. Their results suggest that most option traders lose money due to excessive trading and lack of knowledge. High trading costs also contribute to the losses suffered by option investors.
6 Trading pools, i.e., temporary associations of individuals to act jointly in derivative or security operations of manipulative characters, were common in the 1920s (see Poitras, 2013, 42). Keynes's share was one-eleventh of the pool.
7 Parallel to his personal investment activities, there was an intense career as institutional investor. Keynes became director of the National Mutual Life Insurance Company in 1919, and then chairman in 1921, a post he retained until October 1938. He joined the board of the Provincial Insurance Company in 1923, limiting his involvement in the board only when he joined the Treasury in 1940. Keynes also entered the boards of a group of investment trusts founded by O. T. Falk, a former colleague of Keynes at the Treasury. He was a director of the Independent Investment Company (1923–46), the A. D. Investment Trust (1921–27) and the P. R. Finance Company (1924–36, chairman 1932–36). In 1921, Keynes became Second Bursar of King's College, Cambridge, and then First Bursar in 1924, a post he retained until the end of his life (Cristiano and Marcuzzo, 2018).
8 Data for the years 1924 and 1925 are missing. We calculated the evaluations by multiplying the number of shares by the first market price available for the year under examination.
9 The London Tin Corporation was another creature of Howeson, who had promoted the merging of two companies, the London Tin Syndicate and the Tin Selection Trust, in 1930. Anglo-Oriental owned 30 percent of their shares.
10 The only tin company whose shares were still in Keynes's portfolio at the time of his death was Ampat.
11 See the letter from F. C. Scott to Keynes, January 11, 1938: "I expect you would be as pleased to see the dividend of the British Tin as I was, and I felt grateful to you for the advice to buy" (Keynes Papers, PC/1/5/102).
12 Keynes Papers MSS, UA/6/3, Notebook, 8 Lectures on "Company Finance and Stock Exchange," Lent Term, 1910.

References

Ball, S. 2004. "The German Octopus: The British Metal Corporation and the Next War, 1914–1939," *Enterprise & Society* 5, no. 3: 451–89.
Bauer, R., M. Coseman and P. Eichholtz. 2009. "Option Trading and Individual Investor Performance," *Journal of Banking & Finance* 33, no. 4: 731–46.

Cavalli, N., and C. Cristiano. 2012. "Keynes's Speculation in the London Tin Market: 1921–1930." In *Speculation and Regulation in Commodity Markets: The Keynesian Approach in Theory and Practice*, edited by M. C. Marcuzzo, 57–78. Dipartimento di Scienze Statistiche, Rapporto Tecnico no. 21. Roma: Sapienza Università di Roma.

Chambers, D., and E. Dimson. 2013. "John Maynard Keynes, Investment Innovator," *Journal of Economic Perspectives* 27, no. 3: 213–28.

Chambers, D., E. Dimson and J. Foo. 2015. "Keynes the Stock Market Investor: A Quantitative Analysis," *Journal of Financial and Quantitative Analysis* 50, no. 4: 843–68.

Cristiano, C., and M. C. Marcuzzo. 2018. "John Maynard Keynes: The Economist as Investor." *Review of Keynesian Economics* 6, no. 2 (forthcoming).

Dardi, M., and M. Gallegati. 1992. "Alfred Marshall on Speculation," *History of Political Economy* 24, no. 3: 571–94.

Eastham, J. K. 1936. "Rationalisation in the Tin Industry," *Review of Economic Studies* 6, no. 1: 13–32.

Eldridge, R. 2012. "Keynes' Personal Investor Network." MPhil diss., Cambridge University.

Fantacci, L., M. C. Marcuzzo, A. Rosselli and E. Sanfilippo. 2012. "Speculation and Buffer Stocks: The Legacy of Keynes and Kahn," *European Journal of the History of Economic Thought* 19, no. 3: 453–73.

Helten, J-J., and G. Jones. 1989. "British Business in Malaya & Singapore since the 1870s." In *British Business in Asia Since 1860*, edited by R. Davenport-Hines and G. Jones. Cambridge: Cambridge University Press.

Hillman, J. 2011. *The International Tin Cartel*. Abingdon: Routledge.

Ingulstad, M., A. Perchard and E. Storli. 2015. "'The Path of Civilization is Paved with Tin Cans:' The Political Economy of the Global Tin Industry." In *Tin and Global Capitalism: A History of the Devil's Metal, 1850–2000*, edited by M. Ingulstad, A. Perchard and E. Storli, 1–21. Abingdon: Routledge.

Keynes, J. M. 1922. "The Forward Market in Foreign Exchanges." *The Manchester Guardian Commercial, European Reconstruction Series*, April 20. As reprinted in *A Tract on Monetary Reform*, vol. 4 of *The Collected Writings of John Maynard Keynes*, edited by E. Johnson and D. Moggridge, 94–115. London: Macmillan, 1971.

———. 1923. "Some Aspects of Commodity Markets." *The Manchester Guardian Commercial, European Reconstruction Series*, Section 13, March 29. Reprinted in *Economic Articles and Correspondence, Investment and Editorial*, vol. 12 of *The Collected Writings of John Maynard Keynes*, edited by E. Johnson and D. Moggridge, 255–66. London: Macmillan, 1983.

———. 1923–30. *Special Memoranda on "Stocks of Staple Commodities."* London and Cambridge Economic Service. Reprinted in *Economic Articles and Correspondence, Investment and Editorial*, vol. 12 of *The Collected Writings of John Maynard Keynes*, edited by E. Johnson and D. Moggridge, 267–647. London: Macmillan, 1983.

———. 1925. *Special Memorandum on "Stocks of Staple Commodities."* London and Cambridge Economic Service special memorandum no. 12, July. Reprinted in *Economic Articles and Correspondence, Investment and Editorial*, vol. 12 of *The Collected Writings of John Maynard Keynes*, edited by E. Johnson and D. Moggridge, 357–403. London: Macmillan, 1983.

———. 1926a. *Special Memorandum on "Stocks of Staple Commodities."* London and Cambridge Economic Service special memorandum no. 16, February. Reprinted in *Economic Articles and Correspondence, Investment and Editorial*, vol. 12 of *The Collected Writings of John Maynard Keynes*, edited by E. Johnson and D. Moggridge, 403–46. London: Macmillan, 1983.

———. 1926b. "The Control of Raw Materials by Governments," *The Nation and Athenaeum* 39, no. 10: 267–69. Reprinted in *Activities 1922–1929: The Return to Gold and Industrial Policy*, vol. 19 of *The Collected Writings of John Maynard Keynes*, edited by E. Johnson and D. Moggridge, 546–52. London: Macmillan, 1981.

———. 1928. "The Production and Consumption of Tin." Memorandum of 21 September. Reprinted in *Economic Articles and Correspondence, Investment and Editorial*, vol. 12 of *The Collected*

Writings of John Maynard Keynes, edited by E. Johnson and D. Moggridge, 506–12. London: Macmillan, 1983.

———. 1934a. "Letter to Francis Scott." June 21. In *Economic Articles and Correspondence, Investment and Editorial*, vol. 12 of *The Collected Writings of John Maynard Keynes*, edited by E. Johnson and D. Moggridge. London: Macmillan, 1983.

———. 1934b. "Letter to Francis Scott." August 15. In *Economic Articles and Correspondence, Investment and Editorial*, vol. 12 of *The Collected Writings of John Maynard Keynes*, edited by E. Johnson and D. Moggridge. London: Macmillan, 1983.

———. 1936. *The General Theory of Employment, Interest and Money*. London: Macmillan. Reprinted as vol. 7 of *The Collected Writings of John Maynard Keynes*, edited by E. Johnson and D. Moggridge. London: Macmillan, 1971.

———. 1938a. "The Policy of Government Storage of Foodstuffs and Raw Materials," *The Economic Journal* 48, no. 191: 449–60. Reprinted in *Activities 1931–1939. World Crises and Policies in Britain and America*, vol. 21 of *The Collected Writings of John Maynard Keynes*, edited by E. Johnson and D. Moggridge, 456–70. London: Macmillan, 1982.

———. 1938b. "Memorandum for the Provincial Insurance Company." March 7. Reprinted in *Economic Articles and Correspondence, Investment and Editorial*, vol. 12 of *The Collected Writings of John Maynard Keynes*, edited by E. Johnson and D. Moggridge, 92–99. London: Macmillan, 1983.

———. 1940. "Notes for U.S.A." October 27. Reprinted in *Activities 1940–1943. External War Finance*, vol. 23 of *The Collected Writings of John Maynard Keynes*, edited by E. Johnson and D. Moggridge, 13–26. London: Macmillan, 1979.

———. 1944. "Letter to Sir Jasper Ridley." Undated (March 1944). In *Economic Articles and Correspondence, Investment and Editorial*, vol. 12 of *The Collected Writings of John Maynard Keynes*, edited by E. Johnson and D. Moggridge, 111. London: Macmillan, 1983.

Khan, K. 1982. *The Law and Organization of International Commodity Agreements*. The Hague: Martinus Nijhoff Publishers.

Khoo, S. N., and A.R. Lubis. 2005. *Kinta Valley: Pioneering Malaysia's Modern Development*. Ipoh: Perak Academy.

Knorr, K. 1945. *Tin under Control*. Stanford: Stanford University Press.

Lyttelton, O. 1962. *The Memoirs of Lord Chandos*. London: Bodley Head.

Marcuzzo, M. C., and E. Sanfilippo. 2016. "Keynes and the Interwar Commodity Option Market," *Cambridge Journal of Economics* 40, no. 1: 327–48.

Poitras, G. 2013. *Risk Management, Speculation, and Derivative Securities*. Abingdon: Routledge.

Rippy, J. F. 1953. "Background of Point Four: Samples of Profitable British Investments in the Underdeveloped Countries," *The Journal of Business of the University of Chicago* 26, no. 2: 110–24.

Roddy, P. 1995. *The International Tin Trade*. London: Woodhead Publishing Ltd.

Roncaglia, A. 2015. "Oil and Its Markets," *PSL Quarterly Review* 68, no. 273: 151–75.

Westall, O. 1992. *The Provincial Insurance Company 1903–38*. Manchester: Manchester University Press.

Yacob, S. 2007. *The United States and the Malaysian Economy*. Abingdon: Routledge.

Chapter Fourteen

THE OIL QUESTION, THE PRICES OF PRODUCTION AND A METAPHOR

Sergio Parrinello

1. Introduction

This short chapter is inspired by a certain scientific and biographical background of Alessandro Roncaglia: his theoretical stand—close to the English and French classical economists (called the "Classics" from now onward), Piero Sraffa and post-Keynesianism—developed from both sides of the Atlantic Sea, in addition to his personal and intellectual nearness to Paolo Sylos Labini. In particular, the subject at issue is related to his claim that the theory of value and distribution and the method of the Classics need a separate analysis of an economy with exhaustible natural resources—typically the oil sector (Roncaglia, 1983 and 1985), which is characterized by specific institutional and oligopolistic features. We shall argue that Sraffa's (1960, ch. 11) equations with land can be reformulated to determine the prices of production of commodities and the rent/royalty paid for the use of oil, still preserving the level of abstraction and the method of given quantities adopted in the basic model. Instead, in the absence of additional assumptions that are alien to the classical theory of the prices of production, the same equations cannot determine the price of oil held in the ground as an asset. The present argument resumes a thesis advanced elsewhere by the author (Parrinello, 2004) and revisits the metaphor of the snapshot of an economy that Roncaglia (1975 and 2009) adopts for the interpretation of the Sraffian method of given quantities.

2. A Sketch of the "Oil Question"

Economists of different theoretical persuasions believe that the problem of the running down of oil deposits is often misplaced and misleading in most debates of economic policy and political economy as well. Such a problem of increasing scarcity—the "oil question"—can be traced back to the old "coal question" of William Jevons (1865) and to the more recent "limits to growth" (Meadows et al., 1972), which address a similar question related to the general problem of an energy shortage. Different sources and kinds of criticisms and defenses can be mentioned about this subject.

Morris Adelman (1972 and 1995) has repeatedly addressed his criticism of the claim of the increasing scarcity of oil and the empirical evidence of the so-called Hotelling's rule

(1931). The latter sets the equality—an intertemporal equilibrium condition—between the rate of interest and the rate of appreciation of the stock of a natural exhaustible resource. With important exceptions like Irma Adelman, the neoclassical literature on the oil problem has applied that rule for analyzing the interdependence between the oil sector and the rest of the economy as part of a more general energy problem for a growing economy.[1] After the oil crisis of the 1970s, a host of mixed interindustry–macro "energy models" have endeavored to formalize the interdependences between the energy sector and the rest of the economic system.[2] We limit ourselves to acknowledging that the nonscarcity argument, which I shared in my past and recent work, should avoid a too-optimistic interpretation. In fact, although it can be convincingly argued that the physical scarcity of oil is not a definite economic limit to growth, the recognition of this circumstance should take into account the related externalities that affect the environment. Furthermore, although the price of oil in a global economy, or in a large country like the United States, may not be mainly governed by the physical scarcity of known reserves of oil, the depletion of some deposits can become an oil question for a single and not-so-large country that is currently an oil producer. The scarcity and discoveries of oil reserves is unequally distributed among the oil producers, and differences in the distribution of discoveries of oil in the ground can be important. The analogy between the discoveries of oil reserves and technical progress cannot be pushed too far, considering such a distributional point of view.

Critical theoretical arguments about the oil question have been advanced by economists, who have contributed to the revival of the "reproducibility" approach adopted by the Classics and Sraffa, and advocate a theory of value and distribution that is alternative to the neoclassical "scarcity" approach.[3] Such criticisms are combined with a reappraisal of the method of long-period equilibrium (positions) in the presence of exhaustible natural resources. In the following we focus on this theoretical and methodological field of inquiry, leaving aside the institutional and policy aspects of the oil question.

It is questionable to what extent the Classics are justified for not having developed a theory of exhaustible natural resources as distinct from the theory of rent on land. However, it is just as debatable what a useful alternative to the classical "static" method of long-period positions, applied to the theory of exhaustible resources, is. It is dubious whether we should rely on a hybrid dynamic modeling, which preserves the assumption of a given distributive variable and determines a path of variable prices through a backward recursive calculation, starting from a future period when a backstop technology is supposed to be implemented.[4] This route implies the abandonment of the determination of the prices of production within a self-contained period of time and, at least in the received models, is subjected to the assumption of full knowledge of the existing oil in the ground and perfect foresight of the future technology. This is indeed a demanding requirement, compared with the original method of the Classics. In the following I wish to reinforce my claim (Parrinello, 2004) that the same price equations Sraffa uses with land can be slightly reformulated to deal with exhaustible resources, still preserving the original determination of the prices of production within a self-contained period, instead of a multiperiod time horizon. My argument departs (1) from those hybrid models mentioned above and (2) from one of my previous formulations as well.[5]

3. The Argument

After an appropriate reinterpretation, the theory of production prices (formalized by Sraffa's price equations with land) can be adopted to deal with the existence of exhaustible natural resources—oil in the case at issue—provided that the theory remains at the level of abstraction adopted in *Production of Commodities by Means of Commodities* (Sraffa, 1960), where the quantities of commodities are assumed as givens. Such reinterpretation consists of assuming that the supply of oil of each quality available for production is a given and observable flow, whereas the total stock of oil is not conceived a joint product of a production process. Only a flow of oil is technically necessary at the beginning of the period, as if it were a kind of circulating capital that disappears at the end of the same period. The residual stock of oil can be associated with a conservation process, but its price, even in the sense of accounting price, depends on conditions that do not belong to the determinants of the prices of production and can be left to a separate analysis.[6] Notice that the total stock of oil in situ cannot be assimilated to Ricardian land. This does not only derive from the fact that the former undergoes a depletion process, whereas the latter is indestructible by definition, but it depends also on the consequential circumstance that the services of all existing land are offered for cultivation in each production period, whereas only a fraction of the reserves of oil are available for a similar purpose.

Let us stress the following features of the proposed reinterpretation. First, the assumption of a given supply of oil does not rest on the assumption of perfect foresight and knowledge of the stock of oil in the ground. The total amount and the quality of oil in situ may not be known with certainty, and the knowledge of it can change as a consequence of research and development and technical innovations. Secondly, we read in J. S. Mill the following: "In some instances the owners [of the mines] limit the quantity raised, in order not too rapidly to exhaust the mine: in others there are said to be combinations of owners to keep up a monopoly price by limiting the production."[7] In this passage, Mill suggests one of the main sources of the economic, as distinct from the physical, scarcity of oil: its supply can be controlled by monopolies and oligopolies. Also, the flow of oil available in each period, which conforms to the method of given quantities, can be governed by noncompetitive practices.

4. A Formal Comparison

Let us assume an economy where n commodities are produced and used as means of production. Commodities $1, \ldots, n-1$ are produced by single-product processes (industries $1, \ldots, n-1$) that use labor and the n commodities as circulating capital. Commodity n is produced by two processes, $\mathcal{J} = 1,2$, which use not only such inputs but also a nonproduced commodity. The $n+1$ processes are described by the following notations:

Distributive variables and prices of commodities:

w is the wage rate

r is the rate of profit

$\mathbf{p} = (p_1, \ldots, p_n)$ column-vector of prices

ρ^j is rent paid for the use of the nonproduced commodity, $j = 1,2$
π^j is the price of the nonproduced commodity, $j = 1,2$;

row-vectors of commodity inputs

$\mathbf{a_i} = (a_{1i},...,a_{ni})$, $i = 1, ..., n-1$

$\mathbf{a_n^j} = (a_{1n}^j,...,a_{nn}^j)$, $j = 1,2$;

quantities of labor inputs

l_i, $i = 1, ..., n-1$,
l_n^j, $j = 1,2$.

The choice of the units of measure for quantities is such that the given absolute output of each commodity is equal to one, and the inputs coefficients denote corresponding absolute quantities.

4.1 Sraffa's Equations with Land

Let us suppose that commodity n is corn produced by two processes and that λ_n^j denotes the quantity of land used in process $n\,j$, ($j =1,2$). The price equations are the following:

$$(1+r)\mathbf{a_i}\,\mathbf{p} + w l_i = p_i \qquad i = 1,..., n-1 \tag{1}$$

$$(1+r)\mathbf{a_n^j}\,\mathbf{p} + w l_n^j + \lambda_n^j\,\rho^j = p_n, \qquad j = 1,2. \tag{2}$$

Given the rate of profit r and a standard of value (e.g. $w = 1$), the system of equations (1) and (2) can be closed assuming either extensive or intensive land cultivation. In the case of extensive cultivation, λ_n^1, λ_n^2 are quantities of land of different qualities, and one of the two is supposed to be set at the margin, with $\rho^1 \cdot \rho^2 = 0$, $\rho^1 \geq 0$, $\rho^2 \geq 0$. In the case of intensive cultivation, λ_n^1, λ_n^2 are lands of the same quality with $\rho^1 = \rho^2 = \rho$, $\rho > 0$.

Let us focus on equation (2). If we extend the condition of a uniform rate of return to all assets, land included, then the rate of profit (r), the rent (ρ^j) and the price of land (π^j) satisfy the equation:

$$\rho^j = r\pi^j \quad j = 1,2. \tag{3}$$

The price (π^j) is not a price of production. The ratio $\rho^j(t)/\pi^j(t)$ defines the rate of return to the capital invested in a type of land in period t. Equation (3) sets this rate equal to the general rate of profit, which is a given constant. If the conditions (1) and (2) are persistent, the price (π^j) derived from (1), (2) and (3) can be interpreted as a perpetual annuity capitalized at a constant rate of discount, equal to the rate of profit.

Equation (2), after substitution of ρ^j with (3), can be written[8]

$$\left(1+r\right)(\mathbf{a}_n^j\,\mathbf{p}+\lambda_n^j\,\pi^j)+w\,l_n^j = p_n + \lambda_n^j\,\pi^j \quad j=1,2, \tag{4}$$

where land appears on both sides of the equation, which means that land is an input and a joint product, respectively.

4.2 Sraffa's Equations with Oil

Now let us assume an economy where instead of land, oil is the nonproduced good and it is used for the production of commodity n, say, electric energy. In order to isolate the main problem at issue, let us suppose that oil does not require extraction costs and that the prices of the produced commodities do not change over time. Let $\lambda_n^j(t)$ denote the total quantity of oil available at time t and used in process n,j; and $\pi^j(t)$ the price of one unit (say a barrel) of oil. By analogy with equation (4), the price equation of process n, i in period t, $t+1$ would be:

$$\left(1+r\right)\left[\mathbf{a}_n^j\mathbf{p}+\lambda_n^j(t)\,\pi^j(t)\right]+w\,l_n^j = p_n+\lambda_n^j(t+1)\pi^j(t+1), \tag{5}$$

where the stock of oil appears as an input and joint product, like in the case of land.[9] Equation (5) can be rewritten:

$$\left(1+r\right)\mathbf{a}_n^j\mathbf{p}+w\,l_n^j+\left[\left(1+r\right)\lambda_n^j(t)\,\pi^j(t)-\lambda_n^j(t+1)\pi^j(t+1)\right]= p_n. \tag{5'}$$

Equations (5) and (5') represent a revaluation of a quantity of oil, and the rate of appreciation is equal to the general rate of profit (an application of the Hotelling's rule). We propose a different formulation instead of equations (5) and (5').

   Let $f_n^j(t)$ denote the flow, as distinct from the total stock, of oil used in process n, j during period t. The quantity $f_n^j(t)$ represents a flow supplied by the owners of the deposits and can be assumed equal to an observable and measurable depletion of the total stock, which instead may not be observed but possibly conjectured. The price equations for commodity n are:

$$\left(1+r\right)a_n^j\,\mathbf{p}+w\,l_n^j+f_n^j\rho^j = p_n \quad j=1,2 \tag{6}$$

where the symbols refer to the same period of time and the index t is omitted. Equation (6) has the same mathematical form of the initial equation with land (2), and the system of equations (1) and (6) can be closed in the same ways assuming either extensive and intensive "cultivation" of the given flow of oil. By analogy with the determination of the price of land through the equation $\rho^j = r\,\pi^j$, we might also write π^j (the price of a barrel of oil) equal to the capitalized value of the royalty ρ^j over one period and derive from (6) the equation:

$$\left(1+r\right)[a_n^j\,\mathbf{p}+f_n^j\,\pi^j]+w\,l_n^j = p_n \quad j=1,2 \tag{7}$$

$$\rho^j = (1+r)\pi^j. \tag{8}$$

Equation (7) looks like equation (5) at the time (T^j) of complete exhaustion of the oil deposit j, where $\lambda_n^j(t+1) = \lambda_n^j(T^j) = 0$, and (5) becomes:

$$(1+r)\left[\mathbf{a}_n^j \mathbf{p} + \lambda_n^j(t)\pi^j(t)\right] + w\, l_n^j = p_n \quad t = T^j - 1, \; j = 1, 2. \tag{9}$$

We do not propose to add the equation $\rho^j(t) = (1+r)\pi^j(t)$ to (7) in order to determine, by backward recursive calculation, a path of prices $\pi^j(t)$, $t = T^j - 1$, $t = T^j - 2,\dots$ on the basis of the Hotelling's rule and the assumption of perfect foresight. Our approach is confined to the determination of the prices $\mathbf{p}$ and $\rho^j(t)$, and leaves $\pi^j(t)$ *undetermined*. This may raise some objections, which require appropriate answers.

5. Objections and Answers

5.1 First Objection: On the Hotelling's Rule

The assumption of a given flow of oil (f_i^k) seems to be in conflict with the Hotelling's rule. In fact, if we apply the equation to two contiguous periods of time, it allows the inequality $f_n^j(t)\rho^j(t) \neq (1+r)\lambda_n^j(t)\pi^j(t) - \lambda_n^j(t)(t+1)\pi^j(t+1)$. However, the present model does not attribute the role of an explanatory condition to such a rule. The model neither prevents nor imposes that the stock left in the ground undergoes a revaluation at a rate equal to the general rate of profit in order to induce the owner of the stock to keep it in situ. Similarly, the assumption of given quantities in supply and demand includes a given demand for investment, but is compatible (not inconsistent) with a separate theory of investment based on the assumption of choices under uncertainty and long-term expectations. It should be noted that in his book Sraffa does not mention a price of land calculated as a rent capitalized at the ruling interest rate. The prices of production determined as a solution to his equations are indeed consistent with the existence of a host of real assets (land, imperfectly known deposits of exhaustible natural resources, inventories of commodities and obsolete machines) that may receive a rent or quasi rent determined by the same equations, whereas the prices of their stocks remain undetermined, without implying a violation of Jevon's law of the unique price. A simple definite relation may not exist between the price (royalty) of a flow of oil determined by Sraffa's equations and the market value of its total amount left in the ground. Furthermore, from an empirical point of view, the rate of appreciation of the resource in situ can be negligible compared with the differential rents obtained by the owner.[10]

5.2 Second Objection: On the Persistence of Given Quantities

The flow of oil supplied, besides undergoing a definite plan of extraction, can suddenly change as a result of a change in expectations and in noncompetitive practices (cartels and collusions and the like). Therefore the assumption of a given, but not constant, supply of oil seems to impinge on the persistence of the prices of production and to threaten their role as attractors of the market prices. It can be answered that such fluctuations in a quantity supplied can be of the same magnitude and frequency as the changes in the demand for investment, which is embedded in the given quantities of product in demand. The assumption of a given supply of oil does not bring about a new lack of persistence, in addition to that already implied by the assumption of given, but not constant, quantities in demand. Slow continuous changes and sudden abrupt changes *una tantum* in quantities are compatible with a method of long-period equilibrium (positions), which does not presuppose the assumption of a stationary economy.

Still—the objection may run—the nature of the deviations from a nonstationary state, due to the exogenous changes in technology and consumer tastes, is different from that attributed to the endogenous depletion of oil: the former may happen in any direction, but the latter must occur in only one direction (running down). However, one of the main sources of a nonstationary economy, in the view of the Classics, was the increase in population that leads the economy to extend the margin of cultivation of different qualities of land or to a more intensive cultivation of the same land. This is a necessary change, like the change due to the running down of certain oil deposits. Both changes can be assumed to be compatible with the method underlying the determination of production prices.

Sooner or later the prices of production *must* change under such conditions; therefore, they cannot be interpreted as constant production prices ad infinitum. Yet, we should not use a double standard by means of which we justify the method of long-period equilibrium in the presence of exogenous changes in the production conditions (in particular those depending on the dynamics of population or on technical innovations), and instead we reject the same method when an exhaustion process necessarily brings about a structural change in order to avoid a collapse of the economy. The common condition for the application of the method in both cases is that the changes admitted are to be slow or *una tantum*. Incidentally, it would not be a convincing counterargument to say that the method is obsolete because the pace of technical progress is (or looks) much faster and more abrupt nowadays compared to that prevailing when the Classics applied their method of long-period equilibrium (positions). In fact, a faster pace would affect not only the persistence of such states but also the speed of the adjustment process vis-à-vis a deviation from those states.

6. Production Prices with Oil and the Metaphor of the Snapshot

Let us distinguish the general notion of price of production from its definition within a specific model. The notion of price of production as a center of gravitation of market prices is useful, like the notion of stable equilibrium prices in a neoclassical context. However, the equilibrium prices of a Walrasian model have a meaning that is independent from the distinct property—to be demonstrated—of being stable equilibrium prices. Similarly, the prices of production in the Sraffian model have a meaning that does not imply or presuppose the notion of gravitation. They are defined by the meaning of the price equations and can be interpreted as prices of reproduction. This interpretation conforms to the following passage of Sraffa's (1960, 4; emphasis added) book: "There is a unique set of exchange-values which *if adopted by the market* restores the original distribution of the products and *makes it possible* for the process to be repeated; such values spring directly from the methods of production."

In his book, Sraffa uses only impersonal expressions and so avoids "agents" or "individuals" from being mentioned. In particular, in the passage quoted above we read "*if adopted by the market*" and "*makes it possible for the process to be repeated.*" I suggest that, if those prices adopted by the market make the reproduction of the economic process possible,[11] the given quantities, which describe the methods of production in use, should be interpreted as quantities in demand and supply at (conditional on) the prices of production determined as a solution to the same price equations. Should this condition not be satisfied, it would not make it possible for the process to be repeated. Such a correspondence between prices and quantities is consistent with the nonsymmetrical role attributed to demand and supply, granted some margin of unused capacity. The demand for produced commodities can be assumed to determine the actual quantity of products supplied; this conforms to Keynes's notion of effective demand. Instead a given supply of a nonproduced commodity (e.g., the flow of oil) can be assumed to be a quantity that sets a limit to the productive capacity and to the possibility that the effective demand becomes actual.[12]

I have argued that the given quantities should be interpreted as quantities in demand and supply, respective of produced and nonproduced commodities, and correspond— although it is not meant to be a one-to-one correspondence—to the income distribution and to the prices that satisfy the price equations. This seems to be at odds with the distinction between data and unknowns in Sraffa's price equations, where the prices are determined by given quantities, but not the other way around.[13] However, this appears as a plausible interpretation among the different meanings that might be attributed to Sraffa's clause "if adopted by the market." Note that the notion of quantities in demand and in supply do not presuppose the existence of demand and supply functions or mathematical correspondences between quantities and prices of production.

Roncaglia has used the metaphor of the snapshot of an economy to describe the approach based on given quantities[14] and to argue that the prices of production have a meaning independent of their interpretation as centers of gravitation (another metaphor) of market prices.[15] In his view the quantities, which describe the methods of production in use and are parameters in Sraffa's equations, can be conceived of as part of a picture fixed by a snapshot of an actual economy, instead of being theoretical quantities that satisfy the demand and supply.[16] It has been argued above in favor of Roncaglia's claim of the independent meaning of the production prices. Instead the metaphor is hardly sustainable for the purpose at issue, if it means a snapshot of an actual economy, arbitrarily observed.[17]

Any observation in science is theory laden. For example, the data of national accounts are typically theory laden. A camera catches what its lens sees, but the position of the lens is chosen by the cameraperson. It goes without saying that a snapshot of an economy cannot directly represent preferences, beliefs, expectations and, in particular, conjectures about the existing and future deposits of oil. More importantly, it is only by a fluke, in the case of passive observation and in the absence of a purposeful laboratory experiment, that a snapshot can represent an actual economy in a reproduction state, where the number of produced commodities is equal to the number of techniques in use. Only in principle can the quantities of Sraffa's equations be observed and fixed by a snapshot of an actual economy. Also, the exchange values determined by those equations can, in principle, be represented in the same picture. Such a comprehensive snapshot can be used only to test the consistency between the prices observed and those predicted by Sraffa's equations, given the same quantities.[18]

7. Conclusions

In the end we wonder which result our reappraisal of a repeatedly debated issue has achieved. First, we hope that the argument developed above has identified a minimal set of measurable magnitudes that are observable in principle and, for a given value of either the rate of profit or the real wage rate, are the direct determinants of the prices of production in the presence of nonproduced commodities and in a self-contained period of production. The flow of an exhaustible resource used for the production of commodities belongs to such a minimal set of measurable magnitudes; however, its total stock left in the ground does not. Secondly, the previous argument has led us to revisit the notions of price of production, which have been illustrated by means of two different metaphors: the center of gravity in Garegnani versus the snapshot in Roncaglia. The main divide between our view and the latter, and perhaps the former as well, rests on our asserted correspondence between prices of production and quantities in demand and supply. Such a correspondence neither implies nor presupposes that Sraffa's equations are a sort of slice of a Walrasian general equilibrium model that is lurking in the background.

Notes

1 See Heal and Chichilnisky (1991).
2 See Rath-Nagel and Voss (1981) for a review article.
3 See Parrinello (1982, 1983, 2001 and 2004); Roncaglia (1983, 2009 and 2016); Kurz and Salvadori (1995 and 2001); Schefold (1989).
4 Nordhaus (1973), Schefold (1989), Kurz and Salvadori (1995 and 2001), Bidard and Erreygers (2007).
5 See Parrinello (2001) and the criticism raised to it by Bidard and Erreygers (2007). My argument departs also from the sharp negative view that "no economist ever tried to explain oil prices with direct recourse to the Ricardian theory of rent" (Roncaglia, 2009, 141 fn).
6 See Schefold (1989) and Kurz and Salvadori (1995).
7 See J. S. Mill (1848, vol. 3, ch. 5). The passage quoted in the text is available at: http://www.econlib.org/library/Mill/mlP34.html, § III.5.10 and has been already reported by Kurz and Salvadori (1995, 371).
8 See Schefold (1989, ch. 19).
9 See Schefold (1989, ch. 19b).
10 See Schefold (1989, 229, ch. 19b). This remark applies, despite the fact that even an interest rate close to zero does not make the Hotelling's rule a trivial condition.
11 For simplicity the word "reproduction" is used in the text as an expression encompassing the notion of a physical self-replacing state and that of "viability," which means self-replacement in value for each industry. The distinction between the two notions has been recently resumed

and developed by Bellino (2016), who stresses the fact that both notions are not confined to a steady state or proportional growth path, but the former (physical) is more restrictive than the other (in value), which is not ruled out by all non-self-replacing states.

12 In Parrinello (2004), I used the neologism "effectual supply" to characterize the flow of an exhaustible natural resource available for production.

13 In the general model with joint production we should account for the possibility of multiple solutions.

14 See Roncaglia (1975 and 2009), According to Roncaglia, Sraffa himself has suggested this analogy in passing (cfr. Roncaglia, 2009, 50fn17).

15 This interpretation has been adopted in different writings by Piero Garegnani.

16 We read, "there is no reason to assume that the quantities produced coincide with the quantities in demand when prices of production prevail (Smith's 'effectual demand'), commodity by commodity" (Roncaglia, 2009, 133).

17 Ginzburg (2015, 72fn50) addresses his criticism to such a literal notion of snapshot, which he attributes to Roncaglia. See the reply to Ginzburg (2000) by Roncaglia (2009, 50 fn17).

18 To test the property of being (not by definition) centers of gravitation of market prices would require a whole series of snapshots (the metaphor of a sequence of frames of a film) or a cross-sectional analysis of actual states of the economy, which is a procedure beyond the scope of Sraffa's theory of prices.

References

Adelman, M. 1972. *The World Petroleum Market.* Baltimore: Johns Hopkins University Press.
———. 1995. *The Genie out of the Bottle: World Oil since 1970.* Cambridge, MA: MIT Press.
Bellino, E. 2016. "Viability, Reproducibility and Returns in Production Price System," *Mimeo.*
Bidard, C., and G. Erreygers. 2007. "The Classical Theory of Value and Exhaustible Resources." *Mimeo,* January 15. Available at: https://www.academia.edu/15071647/The_classical_theory_of_value_and_exhaustible_resources
Ginzburg, A. 2000. "Sraffa e l'analisi sociale: alcune note metodologiche." In *Piero Sraffa. Contributi per una biografia intellettuale,* edited by M. Pivetti, ch. 4. Roma: Carocci.
———. 2015. "Sraffa and Social Analysis: Some Methodological Aspects," *Situations: Project of Radical Imagination* 6, no. 1: 53–87.
Heal G., and G. Chichilnisky. 1991. *Oil and the International Economy.* Oxford: Clarendon Press.
Jevons, W. S. 1865. *The Coal Question.* London: Macmillan.
Hotelling, H. 1931. "The Economics of Exhaustible Resources," *Journal of Political Economy* 39, no. 2: 137–75.
Kurz, H. D., and N. Salvadori. 1995. *Theory of Production. A Long Period Analysis.* Cambridge: Cambridge University Press.
———. 2001. "Classical Economics and the Problem of Exhaustible Resources." *Metroeconomica* 52, no. 3: 282–96.
Meadows, D. H., D. L. Meadows, J. Randers and W. W. Behrens III. 1972. *The Limits to Growth.* New York: Universe Books.
Mill, J. S. 1848. *The Principles of Political Economy with Some of Their Applications to Social Philosophy,* vol. 3 of *The Collected Works of John Stuart Mill,* 7th ed., edited by W. J. Ashley. London: Longmans, Green & Co., 1909.
Nordhaus, W. D. 1973. "The Allocation of Energy Resources," *Brookings Papers on Economic Activity* 3: 529–76.
Parrinello, S. 1982. "Terra (Introduction and Part II)." In *Dizionario Critico di Economia Politica,* edited by G. Lunghini, 179–214. Torino: Boringhieri.

———. 1983. "Exhaustible Natural Resources and the Classical Method of Long-Period Equilibrium." In *Distribution, Effective Demand and International Economic Relations*, edited by J. A. Kregel, 186–99. London: Macmillan.

———. 2001. "The Price of Exhaustible Resources," *Metroeconomica* 52, no. 3: 301–15.

———. 2004. "The Notion of Effectual Supply and the Theory of Normal Prices with Exhaustible Natural Resources," *Economic Systems Research* 16, no. 3: 319–30.

Rath-Nagel, S., and A. Voss. 1981. "Energy Models for Planning and Policy Assessment: A Review," *European Journal of Operational Research* 8, no. 2: 99–114.

Roncaglia, A. 1975. *Sraffa e la teoria dei prezzi*. Bari: Laterza. (English edition: *Sraffa and the Theory of Prices*. Chichester: John Wiley, 1978).

———. 1983. *L'economia del petrolio*. Roma–Bari: Laterza.

———. 1985. *The International Oil Market: A Case of Trilateral Oligopoly*. London: Macmillan.

———. 2009. *Piero Sraffa*. Basingstoke: Palgrave Macmillan.

———. 2016. "How Should Prices of Production Be interpreted? The Case of Oil." In *Economic Theory and Its History*, edited by G. Freni, H. Kurz, A. Lavezzi, R. Signorino, 131–43. Abingdon: Routledge.

Schefold, B. 1989. *Mr. Sraffa on Joint Production and Other Essays*. London: Unwin Hyman.

Sraffa, P. 1960. *Production of Commodities by Means of Commodities*. Cambridge: Cambridge University Press.

Chapter Fifteen

EUROPE AND ITALY: EXPANSIONARY AUSTERITY AND EXPANSIONARY PRECARIOUSNESS

Davide Antonioli and Paolo Pini

Forgive the candour of these remarks. They come from an enthusiastic well-wisher of you and your policies. I accept the view that durable investment must come increasingly under state direction. […]. I regard the growth of collective bargaining as essential. I approve minimum wage and hours regulation. I was altogether on your side the other day, when you deprecated a policy of general wage reductions as useless in present circumstances. But I am terrified lest progressive causes in all the democratic countries should suffer injury, because you have taken too lightly the risk to their prestige which would result from a failure measured in terms of immediate prosperity. There need be no failure. But the maintenance of prosperity in the modern world is extremely difficult; and it is so easy to lose precious time.

I am, Mr. President

Yours with great respect and faithfulness,

J. M. Keynes.[1]

1. GDP Growth, Employment and Labor Income Share

1.1 Assessing the Scenario: The Trend of Selected OECD Macroindicators

The Organization for Economic Cooperation and Development (OECD) forecasts do not show a favorable trend for European Gross Domestic Product (GDP) growth.[2] The OECD countries are supposed to grow by 2.5 percent in 2014–15, while Eurozone growth is forecast to be about 1.4 percent, with Italy and Greece bringing up the rear. Even worse is the forecast employment trend, with a feeble 1 percent growth per year for OECD countries and 0.4 percent for the Eurozone, with Italy in the last group (the only country with negative growth). Thus, the OECD forecast for Europe is marked by a weak recovery without job increases. On the unemployment side, things are not better. As for the OECD countries, the unemployment rate is forecast at 7.4 percent, and the Eurozone rate is forecast to reach 11.5 percent. It is worth showing four further indicators. If we look at inflation as an indicator of the pressure of aggregate demand, we notice that in the Eurozone the PIIGS (Portugal, Ireland, Italy, Greece and Spain) show an average annual inflation rate of under 1 percent in the two year period 2014–15, with marked deflation in Greece.[3] Public debt as a ratio of gross domestic product (GDP) is increasing alarmingly in some Eurozone countries: Italy, Greece and Portugal. As for Italy, public debt in 2014–15 is expected to increase to up to 177 percent of GDP.

The gross fixed capital formation growth is expected to recover slightly above the precrisis rate. During the crisis, the Eurozone annual investment growth was negative (−3.2 percent), greater than the annual positive increase before the crisis (2.68 percent), with Germany as a low-performance country, slightly better than Portugal. The investment/GDP ratio has been declining throughout the Eurozone since 2000, and Germany had one of the lowest ratios in Europe (17.9 percent) in the period 2000–13. In terms of GDP growth/investment ratio, the Eurozone (and Germany) shows a very poor performance.

Finally, the data on the trade balance account for the Eurozone explicitly show the growth strategy developed in recent years by central and north European countries is an export-led growth strategy. The value of the trade balance for Germany is still around 7 percent of GDP for the biennium 2014–15, and the same goes for the Netherlands, Denmark, Norway and Sweden. The figures mentioned above have been calculated for the precrisis period 2000–7 and for the crisis period 2008–13.

The evidence confirms that some countries in the Eurozone—the PIIGS—seem to have suffered most from the austerity policies. In particular, the most serious scenario for these countries is the effect on the labor market, which will continue to suffer, with an unemployment rate that will worsen in the biennium 2014–15 even compared to the 2008–13 period, with the exception of Ireland. Moreover, in all these countries productivity remains low, at around a 0.5 percent increase per annum. The two-tiered Eurozone system is dramatically evident: the divergence between the two Eurozones is increasing, and there is no evidence of the miraculous effect of the "expansionary austerity" policies, indeed the opposite holds as usual: austerity lowers GDP growth and worsens other macroindicators, the public debt/GDP ratio and investment, especially that related to the labor market. This detrimental effect of austerity policies is evident in the comparison between the Eurozone and the United States, where austerity policies have been avoided since the 2008 crisis. The US GDP growth rate is expected to be more than double that of the Eurozone, employment growth four times that in the Eurozone and the unemployment rate half that in the Eurozone. At the same time, with respect to the Eurozone, inflation is expected to be higher in the United States as well as investments in capital formation, and the US economy seems to rely more on its internal demand, as the negative trade balance figure indicates. The United States is recovering better also in terms of labor productivity.

The evidence from simple descriptive data is clear. Countries in which fiscal consolidation is in effect are seeing their economies progressively worsen as well as the well-being of their population. As stated by the International Labour Organization (ILO, 2014, 32), we are in the presence of a "lackluster nature of the recovery […] caused, in part, by the continued pursuit of fiscal consolidation policy in the region." In addition, the deteriorating conditions in the labor market have increased the risk of poverty and social exclusion, particularly in the European countries most affected by the crisis, but it is the policies that have led to a deterioration of social conditions:

in the second phase of the crisis the majority of governments in the European Union countries embarked on fiscal consolidation, with significant cuts to their welfare systems and provision of public services, which disproportionately affected jobless persons and their families as well as those groups of the population that are not covered or poorly covered by social protection systems, such as first-time jobseekers, informal workers, ethnic and migrant groups, single-parent families and pensioners, with negative consequences for social cohesion and social justice. These policy choices have led to an increase in the risk of social unrest, especially in the European Union. […]. In addition, the crisis has had a negative impact on the quality of employment in most countries as the incidence of involuntary temporary and part-time employment, in-work poverty, informal work, job and wage polarization and income inequality have further increased. (ILO, 2014, 39–40)

1.2 A Close Focus on Wages and the Labor Income Share

As stated by several European leaders and institutions, one of the main policies to be implemented in order to exit the economic slowdown concerns the labor market, with particular reference to wage competitiveness. These policies have as their central pillar flexibility of labor, contracts and salaries. Also in this case, as in the case of the fallacious idea that austerity leads to growth, the labor policy has been based on an erroneous idea: an increase in employment could be achieved only if labor protection and rights were transferred from those who have them to those who have none. Where these policies were applied, the major result has been to reduce the number of protected workers without adding protection for nonprotected workers. However, not only protection and rights have been adversely affected, but also wages themselves have suffered, both for *insiders* and *outsiders*. Nominal wages have been squeezed and real wages decreased (Janssen, 2014). The latter have not even kept pace with the weak productivity growth, resulting in a further decrease in the share of labor income. The two figures 15.1a and 15.1b show the change in the labor income share distribution since the year 2000 in two distinct periods: the years before the crisis and the years during the crisis, with a projection to 2015 based on the latest OECD forecast for 2014 and 2015. As is evident, in many countries the labor income share has deteriorated substantially during the crisis and particularly in the European countries that have had to adopt the heaviest internal rulings on competitive devaluation on wages: Greece, Spain, Ireland and Portugal. Out of the PIIGS, only Italy has reduced its fall in the labor income share, which showed a slight recovery in the precrisis years (+3 percentage points), compared to the disastrous fall during the '90s (−10 percentage points of loss in one decade) (Pini, 2013a), but this precrisis recovery was more than lost with the crisis. For G20 countries, the gap between real wages and productivity has increased since 1999 and shows an upswing after 2008–9 given the stagnation of real wages.

The lesson is clear. The reduction in employment and the parallel reduction or very low increase of real wages both contribute to reducing the labor income share, and this, in turn, reduces internal consumption and internal aggregate demand, worsening, through short-sighted policies, the effect of the ongoing economic crisis.

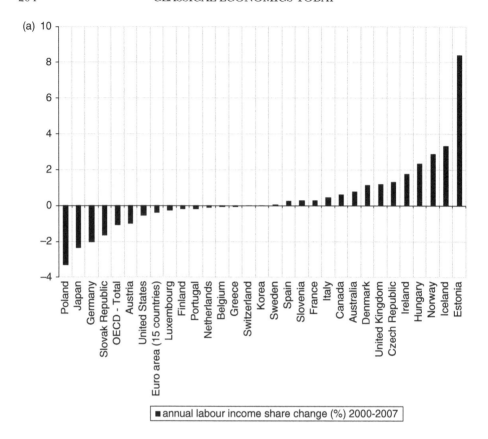

Figure 15.1a Annual change in labor income share 2000–7.
Source: Elaboration on OECD.Stat, *OECD Economic Outlook: Statistics and Projections*, May 2014.

When we look at the nominal unit labor cost as a measure of cost competitiveness, we notice that notwithstanding the compression of nominal wages in many countries, after 2005 and particularly during the crisis, competitiveness does not improve at all (figures 15.2 and 15.3a–15.3e). Only in Greece, Ireland and Spain has the dramatic decline in wages produced a strong control of unit labor cost, while in other countries, except Japan (with negative change), the index even increases during the crisis. For Portugal data are not available. In Eastern European countries, the index is expected to increase from 1 to 1.1–1.35 (except Estonia, which is a case apart). Most industrialized countries show a similar trend (from 1 to expected 1.1–1.25), with Canada and the United Kingdom faring best (over 1.25), and France, the United States and Germany (1.15) just below Italy (1.2). Japan, where a strong wage decline has been associated with productivity stagnation for a long time, is a case apart. This performance is the result of low productivity growth after 2005 and in particular during the crisis period.

This policy of wage deflation does not seem to help competitiveness or growth. Instead, it produces two effects. On the one hand, it restrains the internal demand

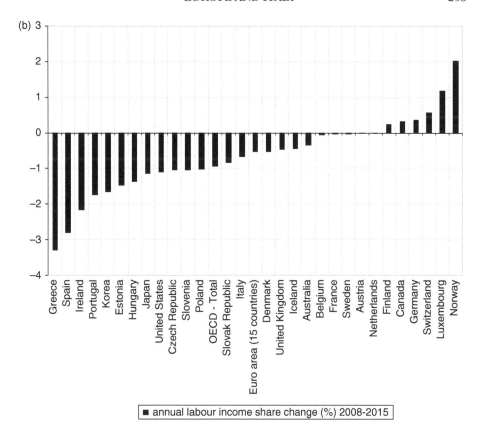

Figure 15.1b Annual change in labor income share 2008–15.
Source: Elaboration on OECD.Stat, *OECD Economic Outlook: Statistics and Projections*, May 2014; for 2014 and 2015, OECD forecasting.

originating from labor income, worsening the recessive effects of fiscal expansionary austerity. On the other, it does not encourage competitiveness given that because of scale effects (reduced production) and substitution effects (cheaper and less productive labor) productivity is stagnant throughout Europe.[4]

Despite this, the European Commission's (EC) country-specific recommendations prescribe flexibility policy on contracts and wages in the labor market to increase wage competitiveness.[5] Growth is entrusted to foreign demand, even if in Europe it counts for no more than 20 percent of total demand, whereas the remaining 80 percent is internal demand, family consumption, private and public investment and public services. In order to sustain the first, the EC demands greater coordination in symmetrical fiscal policy, even if this restrains the second, with depressive effects on income and employment, and a deterioration of the debt/GDP ratio for all European countries.

Wage competitiveness is thought to be the pillar to reach this goal, via unit labor cost reductions to support firms in global markets. Interventions are focused on reductions

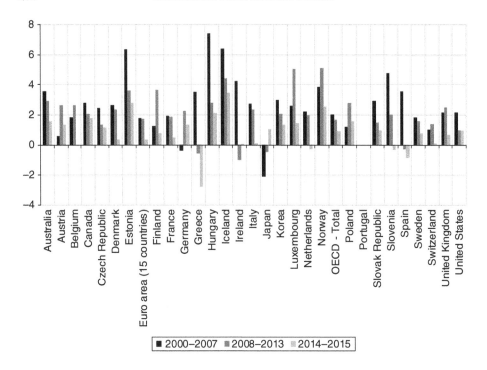

Figure 15.2 Unit labor cost (growth rates).
Source: Elaboration on OECD.Stat, *OECD Economic Outlook: Statistics and Projections*, May 2014.

in collective bargaining (national and sectorial) and on nominal wages, which instead should be aligned to firm productivity, even to single worker effort. For real wages, every mechanism such as indexation to preserve workers' purchasing power must be dismantled, because they must respond only to market conditions, where hiring and firing should accommodate the production needs of companies, without interference due to institutions and legal constraints that slow down managerial reactions to asymmetrical shocks and create barriers between protected workers, insiders, and nonstandard labor force, or outsiders. In other words, following this vision, precarious work and unemployment are the other side of the coin hampered by collective institutions: when these are dismantled, even precariousness and unemployment will magically disappear. This is very well-known storytelling, increasingly appealing to economic techniques explaining that the largest and increasing share of unemployment is structural-voluntary unemployment, with very little space left for cyclical-involuntary unemployment, in order to prove that aggregate demand is not a problem at all. Only the supply side counts, so the need for structural reforms of the labor market is the only refrain in political debate. It is an old tale renewed with new technicalities that takes us straight back to the ancien régime.[6]

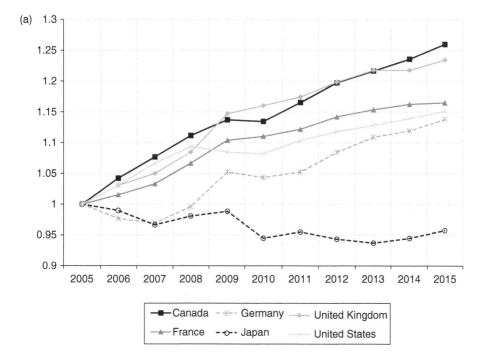

Figure 15.3a Unit labor cost index (Canada, France, Germany, Japan, United States, United Kingdom)
Source: elaboration on OECD. Stat, *OECD Economic Outlook: Statistics and Projections*, May 2014.

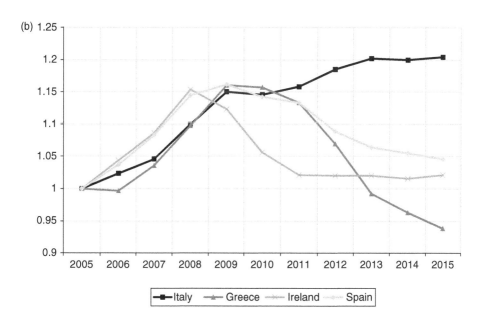

Figure 15.3b Unit labor cost index (Italy, Greece, Ireland, Spain).
Source: Elaboration on OECD.Stat, *OECD Economic Outlook: Statistics and Projections*, May 2014.

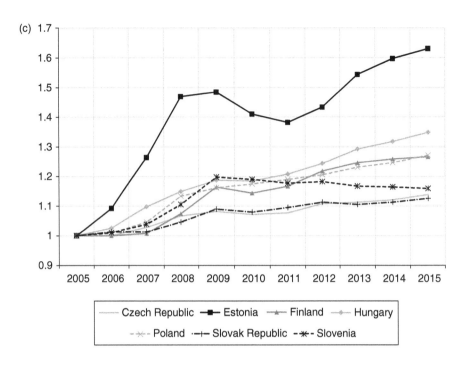

Figure 15.3c Unit labor cost index (Czech Republic, Estonia, Finland, Hungary, Poland, Slovak Republic, Slovenia).
Source: Elaboration on OECD.Stat, *OECD Economic Outlook: Statistics and Projections*, May 2014.

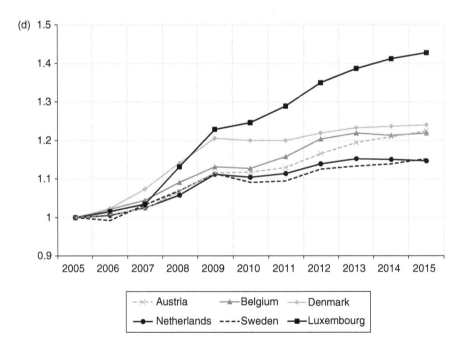

Figure 15.3d Unit labor cost index (Austria, Belgium, Denmark, Netherlands, Sweden, Luxembourg).
Source: Elaboration on OECD.Stat, *OECD Economic Outlook: Statistics and Projections*, May 2014.

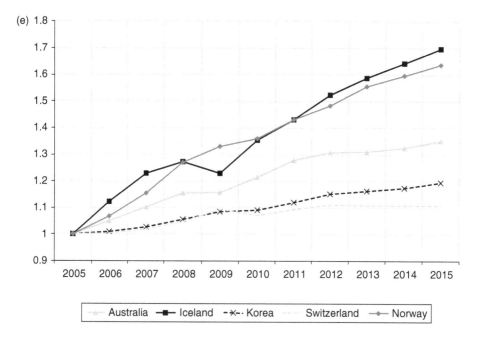

Figure 15.3e Unit labor cost index (Australia, Iceland, Korea, Switzerland, Norway).
Source: Elaboration on OECD.Stat, *OECD Economic Outlook: Statistics and Projections*, May.

2. *Errare Humanum Est, Perseverare Autem Diabolicum:*[7] Unchanging Recommendations and Plans in Europe and Italy

2.1 *Expansionary Austerity and the Work of the Last Three Italian Governments*

Although the European Union (EU) has called for fiscal consolidation since 2009, it was after the Greek crisis in 2011 that the mantra of expansionary austerity started to circulate. The Treaty on Stability, Coordination and Governance, whose fiscal part is referred to as the *Fiscal Compact*, was signed at the beginning of 2012 and came into effect on January 1, 2013. As is well known, the *Fiscal Compact* implies that stringent budgetary parameters should be met and automatic sanctions applied in case they are not. Compliance to the *Fiscal Compact* implies the implementation of recessive policies for most European countries: cuts in welfare spending, state salary freeze and pay cuts, investment project reduction and so on. The implementation of such expenditure cuts, which were preferred against tax revenue increase, started well before the *Fiscal Compact* came into effect and helped worsen the negative effects of the economic crisis.

The aberrant cycle generated by maintaining fiscal consolidation measures through expenditure cuts in a recession goes as follows: a decline in the growth rate of GDP increases the government budget deficit, which in turn puts pressure on the government to avoid an increase in the deficit (to comply with the *Fiscal Compact*), which in turn results in even stricter fiscal policies, which in turn pushes down the GDP growth rate and then the cycle starts again. The result is a permanently recessive/stagnating economy, as is apparent in several Eurozone economies: Italy is one example.

The Italian government's actions during the last three legislatures fall into this framework. All the last three Italian governments—Monti (2011–13), Letta (2013–14) and Renzi (2014)—have followed the EU recommendations (EC, 2014a) in terms of economic policy, leaving hardly any room for growth strategy but instead implementing recessive interventions in a recession period.

The Monti government followed the last Berlusconi one, not only in chronological terms but also in terms of economic policy: in 2011–12 Mario Monti endorsed the financial measures of Silvio Berlusconi's government in order to reduce the deficit of 50 billion euros, mainly through cuts to pensions, wages and public services, and he also implemented additional financial measures amounting to 24 billion euros. The government pursued rigor in public accounts but virtually no measures to sustain growth. Monti's actions closely followed the European Central Bank recommendations of the famous letter of August 2011 in which structural reforms and fiscal sustainability were demanded for Italy in order to increase potential growth and restore confidence of investors, respectively.

With Monti's government, a systematic approach for controlling and revising public finances, modeled on the British "spending review," was adopted.

After the spring 2013 political elections, during his short mandate as prime minister, Enrico Letta proceeded in the same vein: reduction of the public expenditure, regressive taxation and scanty and feeble action for growth. Soon after his assignment, his main claim was less austerity and more growth. However, his actions were limited because of the troubled political existence of the government, which took away substantial energy and attention from the economic crisis: his government of 11 months was marked by political paralysis.

And what has Matteo Renzi's government been doing since its start in February 2014? With no surprise, substantially nothing new compared to its predecessors. The line of austerity is accompanied by that of labor flexibility and precariousness. Moreover, on the labor market there is no sign of a changing policy: it is still based on nominal wage stagnation and real wage deflation.

To tell the truth, hardly anything has been done up to now, contrary to several declarations, despite the fact that Italy's economy is in long-lasting recession/stagnation, deflation is starting to be apparent, the labor market indicators perform worse year after year and a considerable part (25 percent) of the manufacturing system has been lost since the deep recession of 2009.

2.2 The Italian Jobs Act: Expansionary Precariousness

Renzi pledged to enact reforms to tackle Italy's growth and productivity crisis, but his "flexible" labor reforms—which will allow employers to fire workers on the payroll for three years without justification—will do nothing to reverse the backwardness of Italy's economy.

The decline in Italian productivity is dire. Several indicators have shown a negative dynamic, not only since 2008 but also since the late 1990s: labor productivity, the investments made by companies and the capital/labor ratio—which led to stagnation in total factor productivity (a possible measure of technological advancement)—fell from a modest 1 percent per annum in the late 1990s to close to zero in the early years of 2000 and has gone into negative territory since the crisis of 2008.[8]

What is it that happened at the turn of the 1990s and later to the present day to induce companies to stop investing in the quality of work and technology? Among the many things that happened, the two most important are wage moderation and flexibility of the labor market.

2.2.1 Deregulating Wage Bargaining

In 1993, an important agreement was signed by trade unions and the government that reformed collective bargaining—at the national and the subnational, or company, level. While the first had to ensure that wages were consistent with the reduction of inflation (inflation adjusted), the second would initiate a virtuous cycle, committing employees to increasing productivity and real wages at the same pace, while innovating in technology, the organization of work and new products. The government was to support this change with macro- and microeconomic policies, such as public investment policy, policies for innovation and industrial strategy and policies for the so-called "best work organization practices" within firms at the shop floor level.

We know how the story ended. Wages were held down, inflation was reduced, Italy achieved the Maastricht inflation criteria and this enabled them to become a part of the Eurozone, although with an "unpleasant" side effect—a loss of 10 percentage points in the labor income share, to the benefit of profits and financial returns.

As for the virtuous path and participatory approach that should have raised productivity and real wages along with technological and organizational innovation, there was no sign of this. Indeed, companies have stopped investing in the organization of work ("best practice" is unknown!) and technology.

2.2.2 Job Insecurity

Indeed, what happened in the 1990s—from the Treu Law of 1997, which kicked off the deregulation of Italy's labor market, to the Biagi Law of 2003 (infamous for its *supermarket contracts*) and most recently the contradictory Fornero Law of 2012—was a progressive deregulation to promote the flexibility of the labor market.[9] Reforms started with lowering hiring costs and facilitating hiring policy for the firm introducing a large variety of short-term labor contracts, and finished by also facilitating firing policies in the period of economic crisis, decreasing the cost and timing of individual and collective firing.

Year after year, with a two-tier reform approach, the effect was to create a dual labor market, with precarious jobs flanking steady jobs. This "drift" has prompted more companies to rely on precarious work, low pay and unproductive labor replacing steady jobs instead of innovating in the workplace and investing resources in research, training and human capital.

The state's role was, on the one hand, to deregulate labor and, on the other, to avoid any responsibility for industrial policy by adapting our productive system toward sectors with higher technological content and economic and environmental sustainability. Not only that, it has also helped close down companies that would have been able or willing to innovate, thanks to competition from companies with poorly protected workforces facilitated by the flexibility of the labor market.

The *drift of flexibility and wage moderation* has thus led us into the *trap of zero productivity growth*, which is where we are now, in the years of the euro.

2.2.3 More of the Same: A Closer Look at the Jobs Act

In this context of neoliberal restrictive policies in the EU and stagnation of Italy's economy, the Jobs Act,[10] announced by the Renzi new course of the Italian center-left in January 2014 was based on four pillars: (1) reduction of the tax wedge; (2) industrial policy to sustain Italy's manufacturing and the "Made in Italy" system; (3) restructuring of the labor market through the introduction of contracts with progressive protection; and (4) simplification/deregulation of labor law.

What is left of the pillars after 150 days of Renzi government?

The first pillar is still marked by "work in progress." The 80-euro bonus in the paycheck is nothing but a bonus: it is not a structural reform and, in addition, its financial coverage is uncertain. It should become structural with the next autumn budget law (Stability Law). Anyway, notwithstanding the summer declarations, social categories with basic needs are and will remain excluded, such as autonomous workers (who are the ones who suffer most precariousness), pensioners, the unemployed and people at risk of poverty or social exclusion. In addition, a cut of 10 percent in the Regional Tax on Productive Activities was also announced, but its financial coverage is also uncertain. Although not negligible, these steps are not going to have significant economic effects in the short term.

The second pillar seems to have been abandoned, unless we assume that *industrial policy* is synonymous with *privatization and liberalization*. Italy does not need the latter, but for sure it needs a public industrial policy for strategic sectors—mature, traditional and innovative ones—in order to realize changes in processes and products, in the organization and quality of work, in green technologies, information and communication technology and knowledge. These are all central factors that would help in combating Italy's productivity stagnation that both hampers firm competitiveness and slows down the increase in workers' wages. A strategy for industrial policy should create the opportunity to choose how and where to place Italian manufactured goods in the global market, in terms of technologies, production and products, foreign demand and value chains, and all this implies structural change of the economic systems. The reduction of the *wage wedge* should have reformed the tax system on wages and firm revenue to transfer the tax burden on finance and rent, to support firms investing in innovations, to reform fiscal deductions and marginal tax rates on labor income and to introduce a more progressive taxation system.

The third pillar has been weakened, and its application was postponed first to 2015 and after 2015 never realized. It would have been desirable that the introduction of a contract with progressive protection marked a break with the past, moving toward the elimination of the "supermarket" of contractual forms in order to encourage companies to invest in the workforce, cognitive capital and organizational innovation. On the contrary, the hypothesis is that of introducing at a first stage the new labor contract based on progressive protection alongside the multitude of other contractual forms nowadays present in Italy's labor market and in experimental form. No intervention is expected in the area of trade union representativeness, minimum wages or universal social protection systems. Instead, the wish is to reform again—after the change in 2012 (the Fornero reform)—the legislation on individual and collective firing to decrease rights and protections for workers, and to change the "chart of labor rights," which could become unenforceable for every contract in the first three years plus another three-year contract as an apprenticeship, so that for six years out of 15 (the average duration of a seniority contract for an Italian worker) the working status will be precarious.[11]

Until now the main effort of the government has been addressed toward the fourth pillar: the simplification of labor laws. In particular, some interventions, which can be considered liberalization policies instead of rule simplification, have been made on short-term contracts and apprenticeship contracts, rendering both a free-market option.

The first risk for this further deregulation is to increase the legal controversy at the national and, more specifically, the European level, because the new law revising the motivations for temporary hiring could differ from European legislation on subordinate labor contracts, interpreted as mainly permanent and not temporary. In addition, the law weakens the worker in their contractual relation with the firm, allowing even more intimidating behavior.

The second area of objections to the new law is found in economics. We stress three main objections. First, the idea that more flexibility will increase employment and decrease unemployment is not supported by consistent empirical evidence. See for example how the OECD (*Employment Outlook*, various years) has contested this thesis.[12] But even Olivier Blanchard (2006a) had in the past questioned this idea: "differences in employment protection seem, however, largely unrelated to differences in unemployment rates across countries" (2006a, 30), and in a next passage he wrote, "Many researchers, including myself, have tried to trace the differences to differences in shocks or institutions […]. I am not sure that our explanations are much more than *ex-post* rationalizations" (ibid., 44).[13] The idea is a false belief. Flexibility, instead of increasing employment, seems to support a substitution effect of standard with nonstandard work. Secondly, the contractual flexibility in temporary contracts tends to favor the repetitiveness of these contracts more than their transformation into standard contracts, without significant effects on the duration of employment status. In addition the pay tends to decrease, as has happened in Spain.[14] This is the second false belief. Thirdly, higher flexibility in hiring and firing is not positively correlated to productivity and its growth. If a relation exists, it is contrary to the common belief that reduced labor protection is associated with lower, not higher, productivity (Pini, 2013b, 2013d; Comito et al., 2014). Flexible contracts can sustain the mobility of the labor force from less dynamic firms and companies to more dynamic ones, but at the same time there is a decrease in the propensity to innovate and invest in the quality of work, whereas firms try to obtain advantages from minor labor costs instead of aiming at higher productivity. This seems to be the case for Italy, as for other countries. And here we have the third false belief.

All in all, we can sadly say that it seems that those who govern us do not learn anything. The only recipe they can think of is labor flexibility. The more recent Italian government, with the duo Matteo Renzi (prime minister) and Giuliano Poletti (labor minister for welfare), tells the tall tale of "expansive precariousness" and sells us their recipe like ticket scalpers: they believe that with just a little more flexibility and the simplification of the rules, companies will again begin to hire, will regain competitiveness and will maybe increase productivity because workers will have more certainty in finding a *permanent* job, even if the *permanent* is made by many consecutive *temporary* contracts, or so says Poletti.[15]

The risk is rather that after the decline, these gentlemen will lead us straight into the abyss. We are at the threshold of a decade of "zero" productivity growth; another step and we'll have to inaugurate the phase of "below zero" in productivity. The productivity "ice age" we'll have to call it.

3. Policy Actions for Italy

We here report three strictly connected integrated lines of policy intervention related to the labor market and to the industrial system. The three layers of intervention regard industrial policy, innovation policy and labor market policies mainly linked to wage setting. The interventions are described in consequential order, but they are complementary, and the policy actions are interrelated through the engendered effects on the specific area of application and on the related markets.

3.1 Industrial Policy

First, Italy, and Europe, need a public industrial policy for strategic sectors, both traditional and mature, both new and innovative (Pianta, 2013). This policy must be complementary to public macropolicies aimed at sustaining the aggregate internal demand whose lack is perceived by the firms (Mazzucato, 2015). However, the internal aggregate demand can now be increased only by expanding public expenditure, a strategy that seems to belong to a "dream world" given the binding rules of the *Fiscal Compact*. The problem is not public expenditure but the *Fiscal Compact*, which should be rejected (Pini, 2013e).

Setting up an industrial policy means choosing how and where to place national manufacturing in the global market in terms of technology, production and demand, and this implies structural changes in the economic system—not only quantitative growth in demand but also changes in its composition and direction. But we must not forget that since the activation of strong investment depends on the removal of budgetary constraints imposed on the Eurozone countries, the game is to play out in Europe, if the idea of industrial policy is not to remain at a purely rhetorical phase. Indeed, Europe is also where several experts call for an industrial renaissance as the new Industrial Compact, which would set the goal of bringing manufacturing to 20 percent of GDP in 2020 (EC, 2014b, 2014c). Also, the new *European Competitiveness Report 2014* states that one of the priorities is to set up the conditions to help company growth. Several key actions are singled out in the report, which also sheds light on the impact of innovation on jobs. The role of innovation is remarked on as a potential source of job creation and not only of increasing value added and productivity, which is well documented in economics literature. The report shows that product innovation has a large positive effect on employment: a 1 percent increase in the sale of innovative products leads to a 1 percent increase in employment. The same does not hold for process and organizational innovations. However, we should stress the fact that process and organizational innovations usually have a positive impact on a firm's economic performance and on product innovation as well, as also pointed out in the report (EC, 2014d, 177): "these types of innovations are very important for productivity growth, firm competitiveness and even for product innovation. In this context, our results suggest that policy support for these innovations should not be affected by fears of possible negative employment effects." As is clear, the second line of policy intervention—innovation policies—should go hand in hand with industrial policies. Configuring an industrial policy entails understanding which key sectors and key research areas the public actors should invest in, but this is closely linked to innovation policies that aim to spur innovation in the private sector.

3.2 Innovation Policy

As for innovation policies, we believe that it is time to set them up in order to foster both technological and organizational innovation, centered on labor organization changes and based also on models of direct and indirect worker participation in manufacturing and services. To this end various tools can be designed. First, reactivating the tax credit for the research and development (R&D) expenditure invested by the firms. Secondly, specific policies could be designed in order to sustain organizational innovations aimed at increasing employee participation in firms' decision-making, improving their responsibility and autonomy and reducing the hierarchical levels. Italy shows less organizational innovation than other European countries (Eurofound, 2011). So, to increase organizational innovation, Italian firms should consider adopting a shared protocol stating the minimum organizational standard to be met, with the help of economic incentives, and cut the tax wedge linked to labor organizational innovations. This intervention aims to increase productivity, setting precise targets for productivity growth (see Antonioli and Pini, (2013) and Pini, (2013e) for a detailed discussion).

In fact, it has long been recognized that organizational innovation has a positive impact on firms' economic performance, particularly when measured as labor productivity.[16] Despite vast empirical evidence showing a positive relation between organizational innovations and economic performance, especially when organizational changes are adopted in bundles exploiting their complementarities, Italian firms lag behind many European countries. To tackle this problem of insufficient innovation, we must think of implementing innovation policies that not only spur R&D or technological development but also subsidize firms introducing complementary organizational innovations. This intervention aims to increase productivity, whose growth targets are fixed at national bargaining level (see Antonioli and Pini, (2013) for a detailed discussion).

3.3 Wage Policy

In configuring this scenario of integrated industrial and innovation policy, the role of wage determination is crucial and is part of the other two actions. The rationale of wage fixing should escape the old maxim "greater effort and greater flexibility" and should point to a new dynamic to favor growth. This can be achieved by combining innovation and participation. Starting from a situation characterized by the existence of a two-layer bargaining system—central (national level) and decentralized (e.g., firm level or territorial level) levels—we recognize the importance of renewing the role of national-level bargaining: at this level, wage increases are bargained to preserve purchasing power, but at this contractual level the objective of increasing competitiveness and productivity must also be established. Higher wages should be part of national bargaining and not residually left just to the firm level. Then the social parties and the government must adopt specific measures in order to reach the targeted productivity growth: technological and organizational innovation, investment in physical and intangible capital, use of public resources to spur R&D, public and private investment to increase human capital, reduction of labor taxation (e.g., reduction of the tax wedge), reduction of tax evasion and so on. The second-level bargaining, that at a decentralized level, has the function of employing specific measures to reach the productivity goals, since the wage increases accordingly, besides the systemic and connective interventions mentioned above. At this level the adoption of a *pay for participation* model (Cainelli et al., 2002) would imply that increases in wages are linked to organizational changes and to the commitment of managers and workers (and the union representatives) to concentrate on technological innovation, product and process innovation, information and communications technology (ICT) development, the empowerment of human capital and environmental innovations among other potential interventions. A model of *pay for participation* is strictly linked to organizational changes, as noted above, and it relates to innovation policies, both because it is spurred by employee-empowering organizational innovations and because it can generate the incentives to innovate in several spheres. This proposal of linking wages and productivity, also through appropriate innovation policies, has the considerable advantage of reducing the aberrant separation between productivity and real wages that several European economies have experienced in the last decade and that contribute to reducing the labor income share, depressing the aggregate demand through the compression of consumption (Janssen, 2013, 2014). The way to follow would be that of a "golden rule for wages" in which real wages increase at the same pace of productivity. On this point we think that a part of labor policy coordination among Eurozone countries would be an agreement on the wage movement in each country in accordance to its internal and external imbalances. In particular, those countries showing large and positive surpluses in the trade balance and fast productivity growth should increase real wages at a faster pace than productivity. The joint internal consumption and unit labor cost increases both contribute to reducing the surplus in the trade balance. At the same time, countries with slow productivity growth and a trade balance with trade deficits should use the real wage dynamic as an instrument to increase productivity and to gain competitiveness in foreign markets. The latter two must be achieved through innovation rather than with a mere wage reduction, setting the real wage dynamic on the basis of productivity goals, which are in turn fixed at the national level of bargaining, with the involvement and "concertation" of the social parties and the government, as reminded above (Watt, 2007, 2010, 2012; Brancaccio, 2012; Pini, 2013e).

None of the structural reforms imposed on several European peripheral countries go in this direction, and a policy is needed to sustain growth and counterbalance the current unsustainable imbalances in the Eurozone. On the contrary, as repeatedly said by many economists, they are going in the wrong direction because fiscal consolidation does nothing more than depress aggregate demand, increase unemployment, slow down the wage dynamic and so on in a vicious circle.

4. Conclusions

Needless to say, policies in Italy are far from those here envisaged, although the public role in the deployment of the described interventions would be crucial. In fact, the measures taken to pursue fiscal consolidation have so far prevented the adoption of proper growth-enhancing policies. In the absence of these policies aimed at expanding the aggregate demand through an increase in public expenditure the three complementary policies described above are not likely to succeed. In fact, they could have an opposite effect with respect to the desired one. We could witness reduced employment instead of its expansion; firms could take advantage of the second-level bargaining against an even weaker counterpart (the unions): higher flexibility and wage squeezing could be the bargaining output, with a further depressing effect on consumption and then on aggregated demand.

The public role cannot be neglected, then, but it is fundamental. However, at the national level we are forced to act within binding rules agreed upon at the EU level. It is at the European level that we need a major change. As Paul De Grauwe (2014) recently stated in "Stop Structural Reforms and Start Public Investment in Europe,"

> In Brussels, Frankfurt and Berlin it is popular to say that this low growth performance of the Eurozone is due to structural rigidities. In other words, the low growth of the Eurozone is a supply side problem. Make the supply more flexible (e.g. lower minimum wages, less unemployment benefits, easier firing of workers) and growth will accelerate. This diagnosis of the Eurozone growth problem does not make sense. There is a better explanation for the Eurozone growth puzzle—this is that demand management in the Eurozone has been dramatically wrong since the start of the sovereign debt crisis. The latter led the Eurozone policymakers to impose severe austerity on the peripheral Eurozone countries and budgetary restrictions on all the others. This approach was based on a failure to recognize that the Eurozone was still in the grips of a deleveraging dynamic. All this leads to the question of what to do today? […] a public investment program would do two things. It would stimulate aggregate demand in the short run and help to pull the Eurozone out of its lethargic state. In the long run it would help to lift the long-term growth potential in the Eurozone.

Thus the coordination of policies at the EU level becomes as important as public intervention at a national level. We should move in a context in which the *Fiscal Compact* should not be taken for granted, because we strongly believe major revisions are needed, and we here stress the importance of coordinated labor market policies among Eurozone countries: the Eurozone countries should agree in following the "golden rule for wages," and they should also agree to developing coordinated labor market policies and institutions that are as homogeneous as possible.

Notes

1 John Maynard Keynes (1938) "Letter of 1 February to Franklin Delano Roosevelt"; emphasis added.
2 We used detailed data from the OECD *Economic Outlook* 2014. The subsequent OECD forecasts show a deterioration for the Italian scenario. Hence, the comments here presented still hold.

> The first version of this chapter dates back to winter 2014–15, the period in which the Jobs Act by the Renzi Government was discussed and then approved by the Italian Parliament (December 2014), before the Jobs Act implementation with six specific government executive decrees (March–June 2015), and before the resignation of the same government (December 2016).

> This chapter was revised in 2016 without major changes and references to the economic and political scenario of 2016–17.

3 We know that in the first half of 2014 many European countries suffered deflation. According to Eurostat (http://epp.eurostat.ec.europa.eu), in July 2014, the countries in deflation or with zero inflation were Bulgaria, Greece, Portugal, Spain, Slovakia, Estonia, Italy and Poland. Inflation decreased in 14 out of 27 European countries, and in the Eurozone inflation was 0.4 percent in July (year on year) (Eurostat 2014).
4 Keynes (1936) in the *General Theory*, bk. 5, ch. 19 on money wages, wrote,

> In the light of these considerations I am now of the opinion that the maintenance of a stable general level of money-wages is, on a balance of considerations, the most advisable policy for a closed system; whilst the same conclusion will hold good for an open system, provided that equilibrium with the rest of the world can be secured by means of fluctuating exchanges. There are advantages in some degree of flexibility in the wages of particular industries so as to expedite transfers from those which are relatively declining to those which are relatively expanding. But the money-wage level as a whole should be maintained as stable as possible, at any rate in the short period. […] In the long period, on the other hand, we are still left with the choice between a policy of allowing prices to fall slowly with the progress of technique and equipment whilst keeping wages stable, or of allowing wages to rise slowly whilst keeping prices stable. On the whole my preference is for the latter alternative, on account of the fact that it is easier with an expectation of higher wages in future to keep the actual level of employment within a given range of full employment than with an expectation of lower wages in future, and on account also of the social advantages of gradually diminishing the burden of debt, the greater ease of adjustment from decaying to growing industries, and the psychological encouragement likely to be felt from a moderate tendency for money-wages to increase.

5 On the mantra on "structural reforms" and their effects, see Zenezini (2014).
6 For a short but useful discussion on austerity policy with a critical point of view on the mainstream debate, see Roncaglia (2011 and 2013). See also Roncaglia (2010a and 2010b) on the role of the economic profession and economic thought in the crisis. In a worthy essay, D'Ippoliti and Roncaglia (2011) discuss the crisis of Italy within the general economic crisis.

7 The aphorism attributed to St. Augustine means that making mistakes is part of being human, but continuing to make the same mistakes is diabolical or evil.

8 We have to note that Roncaglia, as many others classical economists, has always been very critical of the neoclassical production function, and thus of the Total Production Function that is derived from it (see Roncaglia, 1975, ch. 5). Notwithstanding the critics, the mainstream literature continues to make use of this doubtful concept.

9 The OECD finds that Italy has the most flexible labor market among industrial countries, and has reduced job protection without any increase in productivity, with the reduction in protection for workers leading to ever-worse productivity (see Pini, 2013b and 2013c).

10 For a critical evaluation of the Jobs Act, see Pini (2015).

11 For Confindustria (2014), the main national association of employers, this new contract is no longer necessary after the changes on temporary contracts introduced in spring 2014. Confindustria rejects the introduction of a contract with progressive protections, as it prefers no protection at all.

12 Since the 1999 report until the last report in 2016, OECD questioned this thesis, showing the absence of a significant correlations among labor protection law and unemployment rate.

13 "And the history of the last 30 years is a series of love affairs with sometimes sad endings, first with Germany and German-like institutions—until unemployment started increasing there in the 1990s—then with the United Kingdom and the Thatcher–Blair reforms, then with Ireland and the Netherlands and the role of national agreements, and now with the Scandinavian countries, especially Denmark, and its concept of 'flexisecurity'" (Blanchard, 2006a, 45).

In a paper presented for a lecture hold in June 2006, Blanchard wrote on the trade-off between economic efficiency and social insurance:

> I argue that the efficiency cost of generous but well designed social insurance need not be very large, and that there is indeed a viable European model, based on three legs: competition in goods markets, insurance in labor markets, and the active use of macroeconomic policy. Europe has performed poorly since the beginning of this century. More and more observers, on both sides of the Atlantic, doubt that there is indeed a viable European social and economic model. I disagree. While I realize that definitive pronouncements on such large issues are unwise, I very much believe that the European model can work. By "European model," I mean a model that combines economic efficiency and generous social insurance. So, put more precisely, I believe, based on empirical evidence, that the efficiency cost of generous but well designed insurance need not be very large. (2006b, 1)

14 The recent debate would suggest Spain as an example, with Ireland, of the success of structural reforms applied in accordance with European recommendations. Krugman's (2014) comment on this recipe is as follows:

> One other senior Eurozone official attending the Italian forum which gathers together policy makers, business people and academics said: "Structural reforms are key." Those countries that have made these efforts are performing better: Ireland, Spain and Portugal. Italy and France should think a little bit about this.
>
> Structural reforms are key. Those countries that have made these efforts are performing better: Ireland, Spain and Portugal. Italy and France should think a little bit about this.
>
> For those of us not part of the structural reform cult, the story of Spain is this: the country experienced a full-scale depression when its housing bubble burst; this depression has led to a gradual, painful "internal devaluation" as labor costs come down, making Spain more competitive within Europe; and as a result, Spain is finally starting a slight recovery, with its growth rate in recent quarters (but only in recent quarters) higher

than France. To see this as a triumph of structural reform requires preconceptions so strong it's hard to see why you would even bother looking at data.

15 "It is clear that, if over a period of 36 months there are 6 different people who do a job in succession, I think it is better that for those 36 months the same person may have his contract extended. At the end of the 36 months it is more reasonable to assume that a person who has been there 36 months, rather than one out of those six, is hired. Anyone who argues that this increases precariousness is, in my opinion at odds with the facts" (Giuliano Poletti, *Rainews*, March 27, 2014).
16 See among others Antonietti, Antonioli and Pini (2017); Antonioli, Mancinelli and Mazzanti (2013); Antonioli, Mazzanti and Pini (2010); Addison (2005) and Arvanitis (2005).

References

Addison, J. T. 2005. "The Determinants of Firm Performance: Unions, Works Councils, and Employee Involvement/High-Performance Work Practices," *Scottish Journal of Political Economy* 52, no. 3: 406–50.
Antonioli, D., and P. Pini. 2013. "Contrattazione, dinamica salariale e produttività: ripensare obiettivi e metodi," *Quaderni di Rassegna Sindacale. Lavori* 14, no. 2: 39–93.
Antonietti R., D. Antonioli and P. Pini. 2017. "Flexible Pay Systems and Labour Productivity: Evidence from Manufacturing Firms in Emilia-Romagna," *International Journal of Manpower* 38, no. 4: 548–566.
Antonioli, D., S. Mancinelli and M. Mazzanti. 2013. "Is Environmental Innovation Embedded within High-Performance Organizational Changes? The Role of Human Resource Management and Complementarity in Green Business Strategies," *Research Policy* 42, no. 4: 975–88.
Antonioli D., M. Mazzanti and P. Pini. 2010. "Productivity, Innovation Strategies and Industrial Relations in SMEs: Empirical Evidence for a Local Production System in Northern Italy," *International Review of Applied Economics* 24, no. 4: 453–82.
Arvanitis, S. 2005. "Modes of Labor Flexibility at Firm Level: Are There any Implications for Performance and Innovation? Evidence for the Swiss Economy," *Industrial and Corporate Change* 14, no. 6: 993–1016.
Blanchard, O. 2006a. "European Unemployment: The Evolution of Facts and Ideas," *Economic Policy* 21, no. 45: 5–59.
———. 2006b. "Is There a Viable European Social and Economic Model?" Van Lanschot lecture, Tilburg University, June; MIT Department of Economics Working Paper No. 06-21. Available at SSRN: https://ssrn.com/abstract=916606 or http://dx.doi.org/10.2139/ssrn.916606.
Brancaccio, E. 2012. "Current Account Imbalances, the Eurozone Crisis and a Proposal for a European Wage Standard," *International Journal of Political Economy* 41, no. 1: 47–65.
Cainelli, G., R. Fabbri and P. Pini. 2002. "Performance-Related Pay or Pay for Participation? The Case of Emilia Romagna," *Human Systems Management* 21, no. 1: 43–61.
Comito, V., N. Paci and G. Travaglini. 2014. *Un paese in bilico*. Roma: Ediesse.
Confindustria. 2014. *Proposte per il mercato del lavoro e per la contrattazione*, May. Roma: Confindustria.
De Grauwe, P. 2014. "Stop Structural Reforms and Start Public Investment in Europe," *Social Europe Journal*, September 17. Available at: http://www.socialeurope.eu/2014/09/public-investment/.
D'Ippoliti, C., and A. Roncaglia. 2011. "L'Italia: una crisi nella crisi," *Moneta e Credito* 64, no. 255: 189–227.
European Commission (EC). 2014a. "2014 European Semester: Country-specific Recommendations. Building Growth." COM(2014) 400 final, June 2. Brussels: European Commission. Available at: http://ec.europa.eu/europe2020/making-it-happen/country-specific-recommendations/2014/index_en.htm.

———. 2014b. "Communication for a European Industrial Renaissance." EC COM(2014) 14 final, January 22. Brussels: European Commission. Available at: https://ec.europa.eu/growth/industry/policy/renaissance/actions_en.

———. 2014c. "State of the Industry, Sectoral Overview and Implementation of the EU Industrial Policy." EC SWD(2014) 14/3, Brussels, January 22. Available at: http://ec.europa.eu/DocsRoom/documents/4103?locale=en.

———. 2014d. "Helping Firms Grow. European Competitiveness Report 2014," Commission Staff Working Documents SWD(2014)277 final. Luxembourg: Publications Office of the European Union. Available at: https://ec.europa.eu/growth/industry/competitiveness/reports/eu-competitiveness-report_en.

Eurofound. 2011. "HRM Practices and Establishment Performance: An Analysis Using the European Company Survey 2009." Final Report Working Conditions. Dublin: European Foundation for the Improvement of Living and Commission. Available at: https://www.eurofound.europa.eu/publications/report/2012/labour-market-business/hrm-practices-and-establishment-performance-an-analysis-using-the-european-company-survey-2009.

Eurostat. 2014. "Euro Area Annual Inflation Stable at 0.4 Percent," *Eurostat News Release*, September 17. Available at: http://ec.europa.eu/eurostat/documents/2995521/5176990/2-17092014-AP-EN.PDF/52dd4d62-2b22-4be1-8ad4-aceeeb0e603e.

International Labour Organization. 2014. *Global Employment Trend 2014. Risk of Jobless Recovery?* Geneva: International Labour Organization. Available at: http://ilo.org/global/research/global-reports/global-employment-trends/2014/WCMS_233953/lang--en/index.htm.

Janssen, R. 2013. "The Autonomy of Collective Bargaining Matters," *Social Europe Journal*, January 25. Available at: http://www.social-europe.eu/2013/01/the-autonomy-of-collective-bargaining-matters/.

———. 2014. "European Wage Depression since 1999," *Social Europe Journal*, May 30. Available at: http://www.social-europe.eu/2014/05/wage-depression/.

Keynes, J. M. 1936. *The General Theory of Employment, Interest, and Money*. Reprinted as vol. 7 of *The Collected Writings of J. M. Keynes*, edited by E. Johnson and D. Moggridge. London: Macmillan, 1973.

———. 1938. "Letter of February 1 to Franklin Delano Roosevelt." In *Activities 1931–39: World Crises and Policies in Britain and America*. vol. 21 of *The Collected Writings of J. M. Keynes*, edited by E. Johnson and D. Moggridge. London: Macmillan, 1978.

Krugman, P. 2014. "The Structural Fetish," Krugman's *New York Times* Blog, September 9. Available at: http://krugman.blogs.nytimes.com/2014/09/09/the-structural-fetish/.

Mazzucato, M. 2015. *The Entrepreneurial State: Debunking Public vs. Private Sector Myths*. London and New York: Anthem Press.

OECD.Stat. 2014. *OECD Economic Outlook: Statistics and Projections*. Paris: Organisation for Economic Co-operation and Development. Available at: http://www.oecd-ilibrary.org/economics/data/oecd-economic-outlook-statistics-and-projections_eo-data-en.

Organization for Economic Cooperation and Development (OECD). 2014. *OECD Economic Outlook No. 95, 2014/1*. May. Paris: OECD Publishing. DOI: http://dx.doi.org/10.1787/eco_outlook-v2014-1-en.

Pianta, M. 2013. "An Industrial Policy for Europe." Paper presented at the 19th Conference on Alternative Economic Policy in Europe, London, 20–22 September. Available at: http://www.euromemo.eu/annual_workshops/2013_london/index.html.

Pini, P. 2013a. "What Europe Needs to Be European," *Economia Politica* 30, no. 1: 3–12.

———. 2013b. "Minori tutele del lavoro e contenimento salariale, favoriscono la crescita della produttività? Una critica alle ricette della Bce," *Economia e Società Regionale* 31, no. 1: 150–81.

———. 2013c. "Produttività e regimi di protezione del lavoro." *Keynes Blog*, 20 marzo. https://keynesblog.com/2013/03/20/produttivita-e-regimi-di-protezione-del-lavoro/.

———. 2013d. *Lavoro, contrattazione, Europa*. Roma: Ediesse.

———. 2013e. "Contrattazione e produttività programmata: una proposta di politica economica," *Economia & Lavoro* 47, no. 3: 33–40.

———. 2015. "Il *Jobs Act* tra surrealismo e mistificazione: una lettura critica," *Economia & Lavoro* 49, no. 2: 177–215.

Roncaglia, A. 1975. *Sraffa e la teoria dei prezzi*. Bari: Laterza. (English edition: *Sraffa and the Theory of Prices*. Chichester: John Wiley, 1978).

———. 2010a. *Economisti che sbagliano. Le radici culturali della crisi*. Roma and Bari: Laterza. (English edition: *Why the Economists Got It Wrong: The Crisis and Its Cultural Roots*. London and New York: Anthem Press, 2010).

———. 2010b "Le origini culturali della crisi," *Moneta e Credito* 63, no. 250: 107–18.

———. 2011. "Macroeconomie in crisi e macroeconomie in ripresa," *Moneta e Credito* 64, no. 254: 115–33.

———. 2013. "Le politiche di austerità sono sbagliate," *Moneta e Credito* 66, no. 262: 121–28.

Watt, A. 2007. "The Role of Wage-Setting in a Growth Strategy for Europe." In *Economic Growth: New Directions in Theory and Policy*, edited by P. Arestis, M. Baddeley and J. McCombie, 178–199. Cheltenham and Northampton, MA: Edward Elgar.

———. 2010. "From End-of-Pipe Solutions towards a Golden Wage Rule to Prevent and Cure Imbalances in the Euro Area." *Social Europe Journal*, December 23. Available at: https://www.socialeurope.eu/2010/12/from-end-of-pipe-solutions-towards-a-golden-wage-rule-to-prevent-and-cure-imbalances-in-the-euro-area/.

———. 2012. "La crisi europea e la dinamica dei salari." In *L'economia*, vol. 1 of *La rotta d'Europa*, edited by R. Rossanda and M. Pianta, 135–41. Roma: www.sbilanciamoci.info, Sbilibri. Available at: http://sbilanciamoci.info/wp-content/uploads/2012/04/Rotta_europa_1economia.pdf.

Zenezini, M. 2014. "Riforme economiche e crescita: una discussione critica." Quaderni di Dipartimento di Economia Politica e Statistica no. 696, April. Siena: University of Siena. Available at: http://www.deps.unisi.it/sites/st02/files/allegatiparagrafo/29-04-2014/696.pdf.

Chapter Sixteen

ADAM SMITH AND THE NEOPHYSIOCRATS: WAR OF IDEAS IN SPAIN (1800–4)

Alfonso Sánchez Hormigo

1. Introduction: A Lost Text in the British Library

After an unsuccessful attempt at creating a great library in his residence at Ashridge, Francis Henry Egerton, the eighth Earl of Bridgewater, in 1825 ceded to the British Museum a large number of books and manuscripts from a variety of French, Italian and Spanish authors, which he had acquired over a period of several years. Upon his death in 1829, he bequeathed a sum of 500 pounds to the library for future bibliographic acquisitions.

This made it possible for the British Library to acquire the so-called Yriarte [sic] collection in 1835, which included several manuscripts from Bernardo de Iriarte, a Spanish politician and economist exiled in 1813 for having sided with the Napoleonic government after the French invasion of Spain and the "War of Independence" (Cotarelo, 1897). Iriarte died the following year in the city of Bordeaux without leaving any direct descendants, and his niece—his only heir—sold his manuscripts, which were added to the Egerton collection under the name of the Yriarte [sic] collection.

Afterward, the erudite Spaniard Pascual Gayangos, who had established his residence in London, between 1875 and 1893 drew up a catalog containing all the Spanish manuscripts he had found in the British Museum's library (Gayangos, 1875–93), an undertaking that allowed Aragonese historiography expert Eduardo Ibarra to select from that catalog those manuscripts that came from Aragonese writers, and he included them in an appendix to a work on social economic history studies in Spain (Ibarra, 1934).

The two aforementioned works include a set of texts written by the Spanish author Juan Polo y Catalina, which contained a study on the factories and industry in Spain, written in 1804 but unpublished, together with statistics from the kingdom of Aragon and other interesting texts of an economic nature (Gayangos, 1875–93, vol. 2: 128; Ibarra, 1934, 77–78). The first of these texts, which consisted of 80 pages, was entitled "Introducción a las descripciones histórico-políticas de las Fábricas e Industria de España en la que se desentrañan los principales puntos de la Economía civil sobre esta materia y se expone el método seguido en estos trabajos" (Polo y Catalina, 1804).

If we consult this manuscript, we will discover the existence of a work by one of the leading followers of Adam Smith in Spain, which up until now has been unknown to historians of Spanish economic thought due to the simple fact that it had not been published and had not yet been located in the British Library's collections. Robert Sidney Smith, the North American Hispanicist historian, who carried out the first exhaustive study of how English economic thought was received in Spain between 1776 and 1848 (R. Smith, 1957), did not include it among the authors who were familiar with and made reference to the work of the Scottish economist in Spain. Nor was it included in some of the more recent, documented and exhaustive works carried out on the reception in Spain of the ideas of the classical economists (Lluch and Almenar Palau, 2000; Almenar Palau, 2004).

It is well known that, due to the rigors of the Inquisition and later on to the *cordón sanitario*—which Floridablanca, the minister of Spanish king Carlos IV, established in 1791 as a result of the developments taking place in France after the outbreak of the revolution—Smith's main economic work, *Wealth of Nations*, was not translated in its entirety by diplomat José Alonso Ortiz until 1794 (Smith, 1794).[1]

This was made possible in conjunction with the connivance of the powerful Minister Manuel Godoy, who collaborated in mitigating the rigors of the Inquisition (Schwartz, 2000; Fuentes Quintana and Perdices, 1996). However, two years before, the *Compendio (Esquisse)* attributed to Condorcet, had been published and it appeared in the *Bibliothèque de l'homme* and referred to Smith's work, although the author was not explicitly cited in the Spanish version.

The subsequent reception of Smith's work in Spain has been studied extensively over the last three decades by several Spanish researchers (Fuentes Quintana, 1999–2005) and has led to diverse controversies as to the real or direct influence on some of the main Spanish economists of the Enlightenment (Llombart, 2000).

For the period included between the first complete translation of the work into Spanish (Smith, 1794) and the interruption due to the War of Independence, during which the previously cited work by Polo y Catalina had appeared, several direct or indirect influences of *Wealth of Nations* were identified on writers such as the Count of Campomanes, Valentín de Foronda and G. M. de Jovellanos, among the leading Spanish economists of the period of the Enlightenment. In the decade of the 1790s, several more direct references like those appeared in other works by Alonso Ortiz, the translator of the work, together with Vicente Alcalá Galiano and Ramón Campos.

The latter wrote in 1797 what was probably the most complete Smithian text to appear up until that time in Spain—in reality it was a summary of the work—entitled *La Económica reducida a principios exactos, claros y sencillos* (Campos, 1797; Almenar Palau, 2004, 269–70).

2. Juan Polo y Catalina: From Mercantilism to Adam Smith

Juan Polo y Catalina, of Aragonese birth, studied humanities and jurisprudence and then devoted his life to the clergy. He combined his university studies with those of economics at the Cátedra de Economía Civil y Comercio of the Real Sociedad Económica

Aragonesa de Amigos del País, just founded in 1784, which followed the model of the university chair created in Naples by Bartolomé Intieri and directed by Antonio Genovesi.[2] He belonged to the third graduating class (1795–99) and studied under the first professor in this subject, Lorenzo Normante, an attorney of the Reales Consejos who taught his students cameralist ideas, and most especially those of the Baron of Bielfeld, as well as those of Richard Cantillon, Jean François Melon, David Hume, Étienne Bonhom de Condillac and Josiah Child.

Bernardo Danvila's (1779) *Lecciones de economía* was initially used as the textbook for teaching economics, and it was closely inspired by Cantillon's agrarian mercantilism.[3] Soon after these classes were initiated, Aragonese attorney Victorián de Villava translated the *Lecciones de Comercio, o bien de Economía Civil*, by Abbot Genovesi (1785–86), and from then on, it became the basic textbook of the university chair for teaching the subject. From the beginning, however, there was opposition from the more reactionary sectors of Zaragoza society, especially from the clergy, who condemned these teachings before the Court of the Inquisition.[4]

This was what Polo y Catalina was taught in the very beginning, and he proved to be an outstanding student and conducted several highly meritorious studies, among them, the elaboration of the balance of trade for the Kingdom of Aragon. As a result, when his teacher, Lorenzo Normante, was summoned to Carlos IV's court to work in the Treasury Secretariat, Polo y Catalina temporarily occupied the university chair, but for a short period of time, for two years later he himself was summoned to the court to occupy a position in the Department of Public Works of the Kingdom and of the Balance of Trade (*Oficina de Fomento*), very possibly at the request of another Aragonese, Eugenio Larruga, who had been assigned to the Trade Balance Office in 1795.

It was there that the first economic statistical studies were drawn up, among which the *Censo de frutos y manufacturas de España e islas adyacentes*, published in 1803, stands out. Larruga had an industrialist tendency (Fontana Lázaro, 1995, 15–16), which very likely, together with the studies carried out for the creation of the census, were responsible for Polo y Catalina abandoning the mercantilist ideas he had learned as a student. Little by little he began to embrace the industrialist creed that we analyze later on.[5]

At the previously mentioned Trade Balance Office, Polo y Catalina collaborated in finalizing and publishing the *Censo de frutos y manufacturas* (1803), which would later be highly criticized, and he was asked to prepare an "Interrogatorio a los pueblos de España," whose purpose was to draw up industrial statistics annually in the country. With this aim in mind, he prepared a programmatic text that established the work procedure for preparing these censuses, to which he attached an explanation based on theoretical grounds intended to justify the operations to be carried out.

The goal was none other than to determine the status of the factories and industry in Spain, for as he declared,

> If we do not know the total production of our industries, it is not possible to correctly establish the entrance and exit duties, for if we do not know the lack or excess of the different commodities, the duties would be arbitrarily established, and this arbitrary taxation could result in the prosperity or the devastation of our factories. (Polo y Catalina, 1802)

This text takes on special importance because, in the notes prepared for the elaboration of the previously cited *Interrogatorio*, Polo y Catalina evidenced a great deal of knowledge about the work of authors who had carried out similar studies in other European countries, such as Ambrose Marie Arnould, Jacques Peuchet, Jean François de Tolozan, Arthur Young, Thomas Brook Clarke and François Gerboux, and he also relied on the theoretical grounds presented by Smith, Cesare Beccaria, Germain Garnier and Jean Herrenschwand, even though, as we will see in the next section, Polo y Catalina criticized the latter two due to their anti-industrialist orientation (Sánchez, 2005, lvi–lviii). And finally, in 1804, at the request of his superiors at the Treasury Secretariat, he prepared a long text entitled "Introducción a las descripciones histórico-políticas de las fábricas e industria de España, en las que se desentrañan elementalmente los principales puntos de la economía civil sobre esta materia y se expone el método seguido en estos trabajos."

The text did not have any scientific pretensions, but it will help us analyze two relevant matters: Polo y Catalina was one of the Spanish economists who was most familiar with Smith's work, and he was also the one who conducted the most furious attack known against physiocracy and its followers in the period in which he wrote.

Polo y Catalina was especially critical of Garnier, author in 1796 of the *Abrégé élémentaire des principes de l'économie politique* (1796), and in 1802 of the most widely known translations into French—after those of l'abbé Blavet and Jean-Antoine Roucher—of *Wealth of Nations* (Smith, 1802). Polo y Catalina's text, prepared as an introduction to economic statistics of the Castilian province of Ávila, was not published for reasons of political opportunity, and it remained unpublished and somehow ended up for fortuitous reasons in the British Library.[6]

Polo y Catalina remained in the Treasury Secretariat of the Spanish government in which he was promoted as a government official until the country was invaded by Napoleonic forces in 1808. At a time when members of the government, together with the most prestigious intellectuals, were divided between the defenders of the national forces and the supporters of the emperor's brother, José Bonaparte—the so-called *afrancesados*, or pro-French supporters (Artola, 1989)—he opted for the national side and was elected as a member of the Cortes of Cádiz in 1810, of which he was temporarily appointed president. He belonged to several commissions, although we lost track of him in 1813, before the *Cortes Extraordinarias* was dissolved. When the despotic king Fernando VII returned to power in 1814, he carried out a brutal purging that did not include Polo y Catalina, for if he was alive, he would have surely been among those suffering reprisals (Villanueva, 1820).

That same year Polo y Catalina had requested a leave due to illness. In the years 1812 and 1813, there were several serious epidemics in Cádiz, one of which could have been responsible for his death. We should remember that if his papers, which included the "Informe sobre las fábricas e Industria de España," appeared in Bordeaux and from there ended up in the British Library, it is because his colleague at the Treasury Secretariat, Bernardo de Iriarte, was a pro-French supporter and found among his belongings the writings of his friend and colleague Polo y Catalina.

3. Juan Polo y Catalina: Smith against the Neophysiocrats

His "Informe sobre las fábricas e industria de España" contains—although not always in an explicit manner—one of the clearest and most intelligent versions of the Smithian doctrines in early nineteenth-century Spain. Ideas like criticism of the mercantile system, an explanation for the physiocratic attitude toward the mercantile system, application of the physics-based action-reaction principle, the importance of the division of labor principle and also production as a prior requisite for productive specialization are all expressed in a much clearer manner than the majority of the Spanish economists of that time.

Nevertheless, two clarifications should be made: Polo y Catalina made a partially industrialist interpretation of Smith that aligned him more with Jean-Baptiste Say's *Traité d'économie politique*—he was familiar with Say's French version of the book as early as 1804—and furthermore, his main goal was to use Smith's doctrines as a weapon against the ideas of neophysiocrat authors, such as Garnier, who had had a great impact in Spain.

Garnier's work was known first through the translation of his *Abregé*, which was used for teaching economics in the so-called Sociedades Económicas de Amigos del País (the predecessors of the university chairs in which economics was taught) and later on with the French translation in 1802 of *Wealth of Nations*. Its volume 5 of bibliographical notes, according to Polo y Catalina, tried to reconcile, although it really only confused, the partially modified ideas of the physiocratic economists with those of the Scottish economist.[7]

Polo y Catalina had read and was highly familiar with Garnier's translation of *Wealth of Nations*, and he recognized some merit in it, such as that of correcting Smith's doctrine through new consideration of the consumption of craftsmen as "productive." Up until then, nonagricultural activities had been considered as unproductive activities, something that proved unsustainable at this point (Polo y Catalina, 1804, 23–26).

Aside from this partial acceptance of Garnier's ideas, Polo y Catalina strongly attacked the same author for one of his arguments in which he still defended physiocratic ideas, and he did so by referring directly to chapter 9 of book 4 of Smith's work, which he quoted literally in the Spanish translation of 1794: "If the people who are engaged in activities other than the merely agricultural ones, do not deserve to be classified as sterile, nor should they be called unproductive" (1804, 24). If, in his arguments, he directly quoted Smith's text, it was because he felt that Garnier in the French translation of *Wealth of Nations* did not sufficiently clarify the idea of productivity of the theoretically idle classes for the physiocrats.

One of the most critical points directed at Garnier was his reinterpretation of Smith according to an agrarian view when he refers to one of his more sophisticated arguments, according to Polo y Catalina, taken from Swiss economist and partial physiocrat Jean Herrenschwand in defense of physiocracy: "Only by deprivation does one's own subsistence cease to enjoy part of the funds assigned to it and also by depriving oneself each year of a portion of the income and wealth which society has assigned to it, is it possible to increase it to some extent" (ibid., 13).[8]

With this criticism, he wanted to say that craftsmen and merchants also obtained profits due to surplus, not because of a deprivation of their expenses, which was

Herrenschwand's thesis and shared in part by Garnier, but as a result of the productivity of their activities. Therefore, consideration of the unproductivity of craft work had to disappear. The agrarian sectors would be relieved as they would not have to tend to the manufacture of craft work, and so the specializations derived from the principle of division of labor and the incorporation of machinery would lead to an increase in productivity.

In order to support his arguments, Polo y Catalina had to dismantle the analytical apparatus that supported the *Tableau Économique*, which justified in turn the exclusive productivity of agriculture. In order to do so, he drew up an input/output product model of a rudimentary nature for the craft sectors, which taking into account the levels of expenditure on the inputs and the different qualities in the products obtained, would serve to refute the exclusive productivity of agriculture (ibid., 28). This furnished him with new arguments for attacking the idea already mentioned that the surplus obtained by the classes of craftsmen could only originate from deprivation or abstention of consumption and not because said activities were productive in and of themselves.[9]

Such an argument was completed with the idea that thanks to the principle of division of labor and its greater applicability to manufacturing and commercial activities "the marvelous advantages, which come from the division of labor, do not show their effects in any area more than in the arts and trade; and the agricultural tasks are deprived of these benefits as they are not naturally analogous to receiving so many subdivisions" (ibid.[060,] 30). This reinforced his industrialist position.

The already mentioned criticism of Garnier's attempt to combine Smith's ideas with those of the physiocrats once again reflects Polo y Catalina's extensive familiarity with Smith's main work, from which he drew a relevant concept, that of production for change, as a prerequisite for the specialization of labor in developed societies. He thought that modern societies should not establish their guidelines for the development of personal criteria for abstract systems based on an exclusive consideration of isolated social groups, for these groups are influenced by ideas of voluntary and utopian frugality, which do not correspond to the precapitalist model of development, whose commercial and industrial nature was considered as the correct road to follow (Sánchez, 2005, cvi).

Basically, behind such severe criticism were the rejection of strategies for agrarian development and of formulas of a mixed nature in which farmers planned to also carry out manufacturing activities, a position that was supported by such traditional authors as the influential Conde de Campomanes. Even though he defended a liberalizing and modernizing process of the old and backward Spanish agricultural sector, he entirely rejected the industrialist formulas.

He was especially concerned with deauthorizing proposals that defended agrarian specialization in Spain, based on the primary products to be exchanged for manufactured goods coming from abroad (as the Marquis of Mirabeau had proposed for Spain), for in such a situation, the value added in the productive processes would be inclined in favor of foreigners:

> If we accept that foreigners bring us manufactured goods in exchange for the surplus fruits and even though this merely represents what is consumed, and thus maintains the Nation's

capital intact, the result will be that these funds leave the country, and the potential increase in our assets would be lost, while a greater capital is created for others, which even though they do not represent their fruits, they do represent those of the Nation which furnishes these excesses and assumes direct control over them. The failure to control what comes in from abroad will damage the country's own interests. (Polo y Catalina, 1804, 36).

The enemies to be defeated were not only the neophysiocrat authors but also the Spanish economists and politicians who used these ideas to prevent the application of industrialist strategies, which Polo y Catalina, from his privileged vantage point in the Office of Public Works and the Treasury Secretariat of the Spanish Government, saw as the correct road to follow.

From this point of view, what Polo y Catalina was doing was supporting the real economy, while being fully aware of the comparative economic backwardness of his country, and as a result, he abandoned the neomercantilist ideas that he himself had studied as a student of civil economy and trade in the Economics Chair of the Real Sociedad Económica Aragonesa de Amigos del País. There he was taught the ideas of Antonio Genovesi, Cantillon, Condillac, Herrenschwand and Garnier above all, and partially those of Smith, through Condorcet's *Compendio (Esquisse)*. It was not until the beginning of the nineteenth century that the writings of Smith, Say and Nicolas-François Canard began to come into play.

4. A New Setting: The Influence of Les Idéologues

The moment in which Polo y Catalina wrote his *Tratado sobre la industria de España* is highly significant, for just two years before, in 1802, a circular was published that prohibited the sale of books that came from outside Spain, in any language, even though a copy was presented before the *Consejo de la Inquisición*. That measure was made even harsher in February of 1804, when an edict was issued by the Inquisition itself, prohibiting a series of works, such as those of Gabriel Bonnot de Mably, Étienne Bonnot de Condillac and John Locke, among others.

In the month of August, other titles of works were added, because they were considered "impious, blasphemous, highly obscene, contrary to the sovereignty, calumnious or subversive," and included in this ban were several issues of the newspaper *La Décade Philosophique literaire* [sic]. All of this clearly shows the harsh attitude of the censors, especially in relation to the movement of ideas emerging from the French Revolution, which was the object of suspicion and persecution dating back to the last decade of the previous century, with a prohibitionist decree on censorship promulgated by Minister José Moñino, conde de Floridablanca (Alfaya, 1924, 21–23).

However, as historian Lucienne Domergue proved, the effectiveness of these measures was partial or null, due both to the delayed actions of the Inquisition as a result of an overly controlling system as well as to a certain tolerance on the part of the official administrators (1981). One of the best examples of the inefficiency of these measures and of the permeability in regard to French ideas during the turbulent years from 1800 to 1804 is the close relationship existing between two important publications of both countries. It is well known that in 1794, with the momentum of the *"idéologues,"* the magazine *La Décade philosophique, littéraire et politique* was created, whose editorial staff included a young Say (Régaldo, 1976).

From the beginning, the magazine showed its concern for Spain's political situation and the country's scientific backwardness, caused by, among other reasons, strong censorship. For this reason, it relied on political allies, whom the idéologues considered in possession of more advanced ideas, such as the Count of Aranda, Ministers Pedro Cevallos and Mariano Luis de Urquijo, and, in particular, Nicolás de Azara, who was the Spanish ambassador in Paris (1798–99 and 1801–3). Azara was considered a personal friend of the emperor (Sánchez, 2006, 83–84). *La Décade* also maintained contact with the group of pro-French supporters, which included Manuel José Quintana, Álvarez Cienfuegos, Leandro Fernández de Moratín and Abbot Marchena.

The strong censorship did not permit a close relationship between French and Spanish intellectuals until almost ten years after the creation of *La Décade*. The relationship between the two groups grew closer when the magazine *Variedades de Ciencias: [AS] Keep the coma Literatura y Artes* was created in Spain, which relied on the support of the aforementioned Quintana and Juan Álvarez Guerra, among other noteworthy Spanish scientists and intellectuals.

Thanks to this publication, the ideas of the *idéologues* and especially those of Jean-Louis Alibert, Condillac, Joseph Marie De Gérando and Antoine Destutt de Tracy, came to Spain (Castro, 1986, 338). The *idéologie* influenced several Spanish economists in a decisive way, such as Ramón Campos, the author of, among others, a work that covered and summarized the ideas put forth by Smith in *Wealth of Nations* (Campos, 1797). *Variedades* also published the ideas of scientists and economists, such as the Count of Rumford, Claudio Boutelou, Edward Jenner, l'abbé Rozier and Franz Joseph Gall.

Economist and politician Álvarez Guerra launched the ideas of the agrarian Arthur Young in its pages, although he criticized Young's ideas on taxation, crop specialization and most especially his ideas on the right size of agrarian properties. These criticisms, together with the fact that he had been the translator of François Rozier's *Diccionario de Agricultura*, led to a passionate debate on the historiography of the supposed influence of physiocracy on Álvarez Guerra (Sánchez, 2006, 88).[10]

The relations between the ideologues and the Spanish writers of the magazine were excellent from the very beginning, and the appearance of the Spanish magazine was received with great enthusiasm by the editors of *La Décade*, who, as soon as its first issue appeared, commented, "Les amateurs de la littérature étrangère apprendront avec plaisir que l'on publie à Madrid un journal intitulé: *Variétés dans (sic) les Sciences, la Littérature el les Arts...*" (*La Décade*, 1804, 567).

The purpose of these paragraphs is none other than to show that the *idéologie* arrived in Spain, although in a selective manner, at the end of the eighteenth century and the beginning of the nineteenth, and how some of the controversies regarding the nature of economics that had created confrontations between authors and schools in France were translated through a rather peculiar process in Spain.

5. The Translations: War of Ideas in Spain 1800–4

The supposed delay in the reception of economic thought elaborated beyond the Spanish borders was partially rejected due both to consideration of the volume of publications in other countries (after the appearance of *Wealth of Nations*) as well as to the speed with which some of the translations and reeditions of the main works of economic thought were published, especially in France and Italy, particularly after the French Revolution.

As regards the French publications before and during the Revolution, Gilbert Faccarello and Philippe Steiner proved that in the period between 1789 and 1803, there was a theoretical elaboration and that the supposed delay was similar to that occurring in other European countries (1991, 10–12). They suggested consulting Louis Auguste Blanqui's *Histoire de l'économie politique*, which distinguishes three periods: a first, "tempered," period of the Revolution, between 1789 and 1792, in which the influence of the physiocracy ceased to be felt in the Assembly and physiocratic ideas were associated with those of liberalism in general, even though they were considered terrible and containing several errors, such as the single tax (*impôt unique*).

A second period, the cruelest of the Revolution, in which the ideas of the physiocracy were abandoned, and they resorted to the formula audaciously brandished by Jean-Paul Marat: "De l'audace, encore l'audace et toujours de l'audace" (ibid., 10–12).

And finally, a third period in which Say's *Traité* would appear (1803) and later on, during the Empire, different publications such as those of Garnier, Charles Ganilh, Louis Dutens, Jacques Peuchet and François Ferrier.[11]

If the period prior to the Revolution is considered, Faccarello and Steiner show that the theoretical delay in the publications after the appearance of *Wealth of Nations* was generalized and that even Smith's work did not exercise a great deal of influence on economic policy, nor an absolute preeminence, because authors like James Steuart or the agrarian-but-not-physiocrat Young continued to be influential. The study of the influence of these authors—together with Smith's importance and later on, Say's—as well as those others theoretically inferior, such as the Benjamin Thompson, Count of Rumford, and Samuel Crumpe, help us explain the evolution of agrarian economic thought in Spain.

Whatever the case, Smith became the property of everyone in his diverse interpretations, leading to a heated controversy between the modern interpreters of Smith recovered by the preindustrialist Say and those considered neophysiocrats (like his contemporaries Garnier and Peuchet), to the more direct heirs such as Pierre Samuel du Pont de Nemours, who in turn classified the previous ones as eclectic.

Taking into account the differences in time and other particular circumstances, this last controversy was brought to Spain between 1800 and 1804 and had a special reflection, which serves as a guide for analyzing the policy of translations, beyond the aforementioned prohibitions of the Inquisition (Sánchez, 2006, 92).

In 1800, the *Principios de Economía Política,* by Swiss economist Herrenschwand (initially published in French in 1786), was translated in Spain and led to an animated controversy in the Spanish press, especially in regard to the ideal size of agricultural exploitations, between the supporters of large extensions of crops and those who defended smaller exploitations with a greater number of owners (Alfaya, 1924, 24–25).[12] A few months later, in October of the same year, a letter to the director praised Herrenschwand's work:

> Our politicians should study and meditate this book and no other, [...] and in view of these principles, all of our economic systems which our modern leaders have wanted to convince us were infallible for the achievement of Spanish happiness, are confused and damaging. That the multiplicity of owners is ruinous for agriculture; that the division of the land in small proportions is a bad idea, and recommending it would surely attract to the kingdom most promptly misery and desolation: that the maximum liberty and protection is not applicable to our state. (Martín de Campos, 1800)[13]

Just a month later, the previously cited letter was replied to in the same newspaper:

> And I say that what better study could our politicians make than traveling and examining the land and the system of the most populated nations; because the population is without a doubt the child of industry and agriculture; and if in these more numerous communities with flourishing agriculture, the rules of the referenced author continue, we would agree. To the contrary, no. II, Says: That the multiplication of owners is ruinous for agriculture: that the division of the land into small proportions is a bad idea, and that recommending it would surely attract to the kingdom most promptly misery and desolation: that the maximum liberty and protection is not applicable to our state. I have reflected on this and I have concluded quite the contrary [...]. With a few owners of all the land, the end result is that many are left without property and their subsistence has to depend on the assets of others [...]. When this number of excess individuals, which the landowner may need or want, see themselves in the country of their birth without property or possible subsistence, they will feel they have no other recourse but to emigrate. And will they return then to their country? Remedy: How can you attract these individuals back to their country? By assigning them a property. (F.M.E., 1800)[14]

The Swiss economist proposed a system that was called "relative agriculture founded on a system of manufactures," which had supposedly replaced absolute agriculture and relative agriculture, founded on a system of slavery, but it did not cease to be a neophysiocratic recreation, which in the end made all the weight of the system fall on the consumption of the farm owners who defended the large extensions of exploitations.

The controversy takes on special significance if we add that in the hectic year of 1804, Herrenschwand's *Principios de Economía Política* was imposed as an obligatory text for the teaching of economics at the Seminario de Nobles of Madrid, one of the privileged educational institutions for the training of elite leaders.

This controversy shows that at least some officials were interested in a model for agrarian development as opposed to other positions of an industrialist nature, as the one formulated by Polo y Catalina that same year. As we have already stated, it is hard to believe, even though it does not cease to be significant, that in 1804, a book whose translation was as complex as the text itself, was recommended for teaching economics at such an important institution (Sánchez, 2006, 95).

This line of defense of agrarianism would be reinforced with translations during the same period of the works of English agrarians—not physiocrats—which were read more in Spain than the physiocrats themselves, and of which Young is the clear exponent. He had a great influence in that country because his texts were reproduced extensively in the highly popular *Semanario de Agricultura y Artes* and were discussed in the economics classes given in the Economics Chairs created by the Sociedades Económicas de Amigos del País, as we have mentioned (Díez Rodríguez, 1980).

If we return to the subject of translations for the period 1800–4, we can see how the Count of Rumford's *Essay, Political, Economical and Philosophical* was translated precisely in 1800, at the request of the influential Sociedad Económica Matritense. Many extracts of this work and that of Young, among others, were published in the *Semanario de Agricultura y Artes* and in the *Diario de Madrid* (Díez Rodríguez, 1980).

In 1801, the publication of *Instituciones políticas,* by Jacob Friedrich Bielfeld (initiated in 1767), was concluded. In 1801 and 1802, works by Young, Crumpe and François de Neufchateau were also translated, and the following year, the *Lecciones de comercio, o bien de economía civil,* by Antonio Genovesi, and the *Compendio (Esquisse)* on *Wealth of Nations* (published in the *Bibliothéque de l'homme* and attributed to Condorcet), were republished.

All of this abounds in the peculiar introduction that the physiocratic ideas had in Spain, for if the thesis of the authors of the agrarian reform movement—such as Young—were widespread, this was not the case for the leading representatives of the physiocracy. Lluis Argemí and Ernest Lluch felt that some matters were shared with the physiocratic school, such as freedom of grain trade, the already mentioned discussion about the size of agrarian exploitations and the adopting of the single tax, or the combination of direct and indirect taxation. However, beyond these matters, the theoretical model of the physiocrats did not take root in a country like Spain (Argemí and Lluch, 2000).[15]

Also in 1802, in the *Semanario de Agricultura y Artes,* extracts were published of some economic texts by Jeremy Bentham, and also in the decisive year of 1804 even though, as we mentioned, there was stiff censorship and translations of Mably and Condillac were prohibited, along with several issues of the magazine *La Décade.*

The *Principes d'économie politique* by Canard was translated, a work that corroborates the introduction of mathematical economics in Spain.[16] From the end of 1804 to 1807, *Traité d'économie politique,* by Say, was translated and published, just a year after its appearance in French, and it was at that time that Polo y Catalina wrote his *Tratado sobre la Industria de España.*

It was in 1804 as well, as we have pointed out, that Herrenschwand's book, *Principios de Economía Política,* was made obligatory reading in the Seminario de Nobles de Madrid, and in 1805–6, the translation of Smith's *Wealth of Nations,* prepared in 1794 by diplomat José Alonso Ortiz, was published as a revised edition.

A year later, a text entitled *Breve exposición de la doctrina de Adan (sic) Smith comparada con la de los economistas franceses y método particular para el estudio de su obra titulada Investigación de la naturaleza y causas de la Riqueza de las Naciones* was added to that translation.

Its purpose, according to its anonymous editor (who signed with the pseudonym N. N.) was expressed as follows: "We are taking advantage now to set the record straight and at the same time forewarn those enthusiastic followers among us of that same doctrine (the physiocracy) who need to be informed of the false results and consequences which an inexact and unfair judgment might produce" (N. N., 1807).

The text that was considered for some time to correspond to Garnier's *Abregé*, was none other than the first two parts of the three making up the French translation by Garnier of *Wealth of Nations*. We have already discussed the significance of this revised edition of Smith's work through Garnier's text (Sánchez, 2006, 94–95).

6. A New Interpretation of Smith: Mathematical Economics Appear on the Scene

If the debate between physiocratic and Smithian ideas—reinterpreted by Garnier—had a strong influence in Spain, a different channel appeared, which enhanced the controversy between the defenders of the agrarian reform movement that vindicated Smith's work and tried to reconcile them with those of the French economists, andthose who supported a more industrialist approach. The maximum exponent of this line was economist and scientist Juan López de Peñalver, of whom Fabián Estapé discovered a text in 1951 (*Las reflexiones sobre las variaciones del precio del trigo*), which was analyzed afterward in depth, in 1992, by Lluch (1992).[17]

The existence of this text shows how the mathematical economics of Canard also had its defenders in Spain. The weight of Smith's work continued to be present, but now the direction approached not the reinterpretation of Garnier nor that of Say, which began with his *Traité d'économie politique*, but relied more on the principles of Canard's (1804) recently translated work, which followed along very different lines: mathematical economics.

López de Peñalver published in October of 1801, in the *Mercurio de España*—without explicitly stating the authorship of the articles—two contributions on Canard's recently published work, his *Principes d'économie politique*, which he considered the most advanced work on economic contributions of the epoch: "Because his method is analytic, clear, exact and is always guided by the spirit of observation and calculation. Without approving all of the principles which the author expresses, nor admitting all of the consequences which are deduced, we can say that his work brings the science of political economy to a point of perfection, which it had never reached before" (1801, 188).

The review of Canard's work helped him criticize the tax theories of the physiocrats: "There is no reason for saying that the tax falls entirely on the product of the land," and he quotes Canard's arguments, by stating, "Due to another very unique consequence, the author feels that every old tax is good and that every new tax is bad," for López de Peñalver thought that the new tax figures could disrupt the general economic equilibrium (Lluch, 1992, lxxviii).

From this perspective, López de Peñalver was not a follower of Say, to whom he devoted two long articles afterward in the same newspaper of which he was the director, *El Mercurio de España*, (March 15 and 31, 1804) on the occasion of the publication of Say's *Traité*. In view of Say's criterion that before Smith there was no idea of political economy, he vindicated Steuart and Condillac's works, although it is true that he considered that the first one was filled with an infinite number of errors and that Condillac's—despite Say's opinion—contained very few. The review of the *Traité* in reality served to vindicate Condillac's work and even more clearly Smith's, to which López de Peñalver was more closely related (López de Peñalver, 1804).

Furthermore, he used the critical commentary on Say's work to vindicate a more systematic analysis of economic science, and he drew from the French author the idea that the teaching of economics should not be limited to the higher classes, for it was the middle classes that served as the conveyor belt for this knowledge. More importantly still was rescuing from Say's work its new concept of the economy of "independence which is acquired with the industrial products" (Steiner, 1993).

As regards Smith's work, López de Peñalver also criticized some of its interpreters, like Garnier, who called the work of the Scottish economist dark and difficult to read: "It is true that Smith is dark and obscure in some passages, but if we ignore for the moment the confusion its translators may have created, we should say that there were very few" (1804, 373).

He was more concerned about the debate on the different methods (the analytical and the synthetic) used by both authors. Through his analysis, he tried to eliminate the criticisms of Smith for selecting the first of them, with which he defined his own methodological position: "Only in the form and general distribution of the matters can we note Say's preference for the synthetic method. Many chapters and in particular the greater part of those which discuss the products are dealt with according to the analytic method which is followed by all those who think and reason" (ibid., 370–71).[18]

Aside from López de Peñalver's notations and leaving a record of the rapid translation of the *Traité*, José Queipo's translation of Say's work was very well received and it heightened the controversy about what should be the preferred text for teaching economics. A few years had passed since Genovesi's *Lecciones,* the texts inspired by Cantillon, or those of cameralist influence, like Bielfeld's *Instituciones políticas,* which were used for this purpose. Now, from official levels—as proof of the adoption of the *Traité* in its Spanish version as an official textbook as of 1807—this last work was chosen as preferential.

The reason for the translation was stated by the translator himself in his introduction to Say's work, in which he reflects on the status of the matter regarding the controversial selection of texts: "Persuaded […] that it is a work that is absolutely lacking; for neither Garnier's *Elementary Compendium* published in 1796, nor Canard's *Economic Principles,* made public in 1801, can make up for it in any way. These two works do have their merit, especially the second one, whose translation we proposed before we received the present one by Say" (Say, 1804, xiii–xiv).[19]

7. Concluding Remarks

From the pioneer studies of Robert Sidney Smith on the reaction to classical economic thought in Spain—in which it was shown that Spanish mercantilism had been strongly resistant and long-lasting in time (hardy perennial)—progress was made in the process of reception of Smith's work and it was proven that it had undergone an unequal process, and, in many cases, the Smithian message was intermingled with mercantilism along the lines of what authors like W. Grampp had classified as the liberal elements in English mercantilism (Grampp, 1952).

Or it led to what Llombart (2000) has called, for the Spanish case, the existence of a "liberal mercantilism," a term that is apparently contradictory but that explains in a much more convincing manner the process of transition from mercantilism to liberalism in which Smith's main work—adapted to the national interests—fulfilled an important function in Spain, just as it did in other European countries.

Later studies, such as that of Cosimo Perrotta, have demonstrated the coherence of mercantilist strategies in "second-comer" countries, most especially those of southern Europe. Even though Smithian ideas were well received in the last years of the eighteenth and the beginning of the nineteenth century, they preferred to do so in a partially mercantilist way, which made it possible to support economic policies that were more coherent with their level of comparative development (Perrotta, 1993). This does not contradict Robert Sidney Smith's hypothesis but rather explains the persistence of the mercantilist message in Spain as well as the interpretations of Adam Smith in a partially mercantilist way.

However, the interest shown by Spanish researchers in the study of the Reales Sociedades Económicas de Amigos del País, the true "torches" of the Enlightenment, where the first classes in economics were taught and where important modernizing policies were launched, has relegated the study of other key institutions—such as the Balance of Trade Office and the Department of Public Works, dependent on the Secretariat of the Treasury Ministry where the first industrial statistical studies were conducted—to a second place.

Perhaps because they were created several decades after the Sociedades Económicas and due to the fact that they responded to other needs related to the country's economy, they were oriented toward adopting different ideas, leading to different interpretations of Smith's work—along a preindustrialist line—which proved to be much closer to Say's work, translated into Spanish between 1804 and 1807. This text was favored as of that moment over those of Canard and Garnier.

In a strongly agrarian society, such as the Spanish one in the second half of the eighteenth century, a decisive role was played by the physiocratic message, stripped of its theory, and even more so that of the agrarians, not physiocrats, like Young, which explains the existence of Smith's agrarian interpretations. Consequently, we see the influence of authors such as Garnier, whose *Abrégé* was not published but translated and was used for teaching in several Sociedades Económicas de Amigos del País, and in the years 1805–6, the translation of *Wealth of Nations* was even republished in Spain.

Acknowledgments

I am especially grateful to J. Conway, who sent me the manuscripts from the British Library to which I refer in the text.

Notes

1 Alonso Ortiz wrongly declared that he had used the eighth edition of Smith's work for his translation (probably he used the fifth) and confessed that he had eliminated "certain details, but very few, either because they were absolutely impertinent to our nation, or because they were not in accord with the Holy Religion which we profess. He naively claimed that what was eliminated did not in any way adulterate the essence of the work" (Schwartz, 2000, 186).

2 Professor Ernest Lluch highlighted the similarities between Naples's economic situation—whose monarch when the university chair was first created was the future king of Spain, Carlos III—and Aragon, as well as the connection between the contents put forth in the university chair with the main cameralists, who predominated in northern Italy and in the German territories. This determined that the Zaragoza chair, similar to the Neapolitan one, was oriented more toward the process of teaching the so-called state sciences, whose goal was the training of public officials capable of assuming responsibilities in the government (Lluch, 1995).

3 Professor Pablo Cervera felt that the influence of Genovesi and of the cameralist Bielfeld (Cervera, 1998, 160) was equally perceivable.

4 This episode has been extensively documented (García Pérez, 1974; Legarda, 1984; López, 1987). The main criticism centered around the declaration that celibacy encumbered the development of the useful population, the submission of the clergy to the laws of the secular government, a partially tolerant attitude of luxury and the justification of the interest on loans (Sánchez, Malo and Blanco, 2003, 139–40).

5 The Censo, which was subtitled *Censo de la riqueza territorial de España e industrial de España en el año de 1799*, was republished with an introduction, "La economía española según el censo de frutos y manufacturas de 1799," by Antonio Matilla Tascón (Polo y Catalina, 1960, iii–iv).

6 The explanation for not publishing this report was clarified when it was finally published six years later, in 1810 (without Polo y Catalina's introductory text), under the responsibility of Manuel Antonio Rodríguez, one of Say's translators, who believed that the information could be rectified and expanded. He also felt that "some of his opinions seemed too daring to publish them without risking his reputation and perhaps his life" (Rodríguez, 1810). Rodríguez's fear was justified, for in the report he attributed the agricultural decadence of the region "to the limited number of farm owners existing in the province, in regard to the many settlers or lessors [...] and the arrogance of the gentlemen and the tyranny with which they treated their people" (Alfaya, 1924, 68). This is the real reason why Polo y Catalina's *Informe sobre la Industria de España* was not published.

7 "And despite the fact that Smit [sic] doctrine and the general interest of the nations seems to have made them forget their disputes [...], the new air and novelty which the French wanted to apply to everything, also forced them to reproduce the most unique ideas of their predecessors on this matter: and even though the very same ones who reproduced them, did not adopt them in their entirety, they presented them with such force that they could prove prejudicial to a nation which was just beginning to become involved in politics" (Polo y Catalina, 1804, 6). Obviously Polo y Catalina was considering the negative influence of such ideas in Spain, for which, as we will see later on, he defended an industrialist strategy.

8 Authors such as J. J. Gislain consider Schumpeter's appraisal of Herrennschwand as a "German Physiocrat" or as one of the last rather heterodox physiocrats to be abusive: "Ce dernier qualificatif est d'autant plus problématique que les études sur les physiocrates ne donnent aucune place à Herrenschwand [...] le qualificatif de 'physiocrate hétérodoxe' est en grande partie abusif [...] à aucun moment dans son oeuvre, il ne cite les physiocrates. Il ne se réfère explicitement et fréquemment qu'a James Steuart et a Adam Smith" (Gislain, 1995, 196–97).

9 Garnier, in his *Abregé*, had clearly defended this argument: "Celui qui rend ce service, dit-il, en parlant des entrepreneurs se soumet à une privation, puisqu'il fait consommer a d'autres des choses consommables qu'il possèdent. Donc, ce sera sur l'étendue de cette privation et des risques que l'indemnité se mesurera" (Allix, 1912, 331).

10 All controversies aside, his position was explained in a comment published in *Variedades*, which is included here despite its extension because we feel it constituted one of the most relevant controversies on economic matters in a predominantly agrarian country like Spain in 1804:

"Love thy neighbour" makes us want everyone to enjoy the same fortune, and we want the surplus of the rich, to be distributed among the most needy, in order to level everything out. This is impossible; but on the other hand we would want the land to be more subdivided, so that there could be more owners and fewer day labourers or dependents upon the rich owners. Some claim that in this way, the land would be better cultivated and others, such as Young, say that the current state is the way to rouse a nation. In our newspapers, this dispute arose and for this reason, we would like a defender to emerge to confront Young and respond to his reasons, which we are ready to put forth, drawn directly from his works. (Álvarez Guerra, 1805, 96).

11 To all of the foregoing, we should add the fact that the "ideologists" did not remain unaffected by the physiocratic influence. Some writers, such as Vandermonde, suffered the simultaneous influence of physiocracy and several postulates of Steuart, while others such as Roederer preferred to rely on Turgot, who saw it as a bridge between the ideas of Gournay and Condorcet and those of Smith, beyond their physiocrat influences (Faccarello and Steiner, 1991, 27).

12 In August of 1800, the two main newspapers of the capital, the *Diario de Madrid* and the *Mercurio de España*, gave imprecise news on the translation. According to the first one, the author was Herrens Chwand [sic] and in the *Mercurio de España*, Herrens Wand.

13 The letter was published on October 29, 1800, and signed by Pedro Martín de Campos.

14 The letter, published in the *Diario de Madrid* on November 29, 1800, showed he was highly familiar with Herrenschwand's work and corrected the author of the previous one, who referred to him as Herrens Chuand, and was signed with the initials F. M. E.

15 An exception considered by Lluch was that of Argentinean Manuel Belgrano, who studied in Spain, and in 1794 he translated and published the *Máximas del Gobierno agricultor*, which was widely distributed later in Argentina in the years prior to the revolution of 1810. However, as J. C. Chiaramonte explained, Belgrano combined the ideas of the physiocrats with those of the neomercantilist Genovesi in his texts, which served as theoretical support to the model for economic change that was aimed at supporting the changes needed for Argentina's independence (Lluch, 1984).

16 The Spanish version, translated by one of the students of the *Economía Civil y Comercio* Chair of Zaragoza, Francisco Escolar, eliminated in his translation a large part of the mathematical apparatus of the work, with a supposed didactic purpose, which actually detracted to a great extent from its contents.

17 According to Professor Salvador Almenar Palau in *Las reflexiones sobre las variaciones del precio del trigo*, "There are a combination of statistics and algebra in order to establish precise relationships: 1, Between high corn prices and hospital death rates; 2, The relationship between corn prices, workers' wages and budgets; 3, Prices and shipping costs; and 4, A model showing the constant relative prices between corn and barley when the technical conditions of productions are assumed to be stable" (2004, 275).

18 However, the line followed by Peñalver adapts to the mathematical focus offered by Canard. As Lluch pointed out, Peñalver translated the work of the mathematician and a friend of Condorcet, Diannyère, in defense of freedom of trade and included in the *Mercurio*, a series of statistical studies such as the one entitled "From the mortality of the hospitals, general for men and the Passion for the women of Madrid" (López de Peñalver, 1803).

19 The translator of Say's work does not miss the opportunity to disqualify Garnier's work, which continued to be influential in Spain: "On the other hand, this author (Garnier), as Say points out, did not know how to protect himself against the main errors made by the economists" (Say, 1804, xiv).

References

Alfaya López, C. 1924. *Noticias para la Historia económica y social de España: Teorías económico-sociales (1800–1820)*. Segovia: Mauro Lozano.

Allix, E. 1912. "L'œuvre économique de Germain Garnier, traducteur d'Adam Smith et disciple de Cantillon," *Revue d'histoire des doctrines économiques et sociales* 5: 317–42.

Almenar Palau, S. 2004. "El desarrollo del pensamiento económico clásico en España." In *La economía clásica*, vol. 4 of *Economía y economistas españoles*, edited by E. Fuentes Quintana, 7–92. Barcelona: Galaxia Gutenberg–Funcas.

Almenar Palau, S., and E. Lluch. 2004. "The Itineraries of Neo-Smithian Political Economy in Spain (1800–1848)," *Économies et Sociétés* 38, no. 2: 267–97.

Álvarez Guerra, J. 1805. "Sobre una obra de Arthur Young," *Variedades de Ciencias, Literatura y Artes* 6: 96.

Argemí, L., and E. Lluch. 2000. "La fisiocracia en España." In *La Ilustración*, vol. 3 of *Economía y economistas españoles*, edited by E. Fuentes Quintana, 709–19. Barcelona: Galaxia Gutenberg–Funcas.

Arnould, A. M. 1795. *De la balance du commerce et des relations commerciales extérieures de la France dans toutes les parties du globe*. Paris: Buisson.

Artola, M. 1989. *Los afrancesados*. Madrid: Alianza.

Bielfield, J. 1767–72. *Instituciones políticas*, 6 vols. Madrid: Gabriel Ramírez.

Blanqui, A. 1837. *Histoire de l'économie politique en Europe, depuis les anciens jusqu'a nos jours, suivie d'une bibliographie raisonnée des principaux ouvrages d'économie politique*. Paris: Guillaumin.

Campos, R. 1797. *La económica reducida a principios exactos, claros y sencillos*. Madrid: Imprenta de Benito Cano.

Canard, N. F. 1804. *Principios de economía política*. Madrid: Viuda de López e Hijos.

Castro Alfín, D. 1986. "Los ideólogos en España: la recepción de Destutt de Tracy y de Volney," *Estudios de historia social* 36/37: 337–43.

Catteau, J. P. 1802. *Tableau des états danois envisagés sous les rapports du mécanisme social*. Paris: Treuttel et Wurtz.

Cervera, P. 1998. "Las lecciones de Economía Civil o de el Comercio de B. J. Danvila y Villarrasa (1779)," *Cuadernos Aragoneses de Economía* 8, no 1: 143–62.

Clarke, T. B. 1802. *Coup d'œil sur la force de l'opulence de la Grande-Bretagne, où l'on voit les progrès de son commerce, de son agriculture avant et après l'avènement de la maison de Hanovre, suivi d'une correspondance inédite du docteur Tucker et de Hume avec le lord Kaims concernant le commerce*. Paris: Levrault Frères.

Cotarelo y Mori, E. 1897. *Iriarte y su época*. Madrid: Sucesores de Rivadeneyra.

Danvila y Villarrasa, B. J. 1779. *Lecciones de Economía Civil ó de el Comercio escritas para el uso de los caballeros del Real Seminario de Nobles*. Madrid: Joachin Ibarra.

La Décade philosophique, littéraire et politique. 1794–1807.

Díez Rodríguez, F. 1980. *Prensa agraria en la España de la Ilustración: El Semanario de Agricultura y Artes dirigido a los Párrocos (1797–1808)*. Madrid: Ministerio de Agricultura.

Domergue, L. 1981. *Tres calas en la censura dieciochesca (Cadalso, Rousseau, prensa periódica)*. Toulouse: Le Mirail.

Esdaile, A. 1948. *The British Museum Library: A Short History and Survey*. London: George Allen & Unwin Ltd.

Faccarello, G., and P. Steiner. 1991. *La pensée économique pendant la Révolution Française*. Grenoble: Presses Universitaires de Grenoble.

F. M. E. (Acronym). 1800. "Letter to the Diario de Madrid," *Diario de Madrid*, November 29.

Fontana Lázaro, J. 1995. "Introduction." In E. Larruga y Boneta, *Memorias políticas y económicas sobre los frutos comercio, fábricas y minas de España*, 11–19. Zaragoza: Gobierno de Aragón, Institución Fernando el Católico e Instituto Aragonés de Fomento.

Fuentes Quintana, E., ed. 1999–2005. *Economía y economistas españoles*. Barcelona: Galaxia Gutenberg–Funcas.

Fuentes Quintana, E., and L. Perdices de Blas. 1996. "Estudio Preliminar." In A. Smith, *Investigación de la Naturaleza y Causas de la Riqueza de las Naciones*, xvi–cxiv. Salamanca: Junta de Castilla y León.

García Pérez, G. 1974. *La Economía y los reaccionarios: La Inquisición y los economistas al surgir la España contemporánea*. Madrid: Cuadernos para el Diálogo.

Garnier, G. 1796. *Abrégé des principes de l'Économie politique*. Paris: Agasse.

———, trans. 1802. *Recherches sur la nature et les causes de la Richesse des nations*, by A. Smith. Paris: Agasse.

———.1807. *Breve exposición de la doctrina de Smith comparada con los economistas franceses*. Valladolid: Viuda e Hijos de Santander.

Gayangos, P. de. 1875–93. *Catalogue of the Manuscripts in the Spanish Language in the British Library*, 4 vols. Reprint. London: British Museum, 1976.

Genovesi, A. 1785–86. *Lecciones de comercio o bien de economía civil*, 3 vols. Madrid: Ibarra.

Gerboux, F. 1803. *Discussion sur les effets de la démonétisation de l'or relativement à la France*. Paris: Le Normant.

Gislain, J. J. 1995. "Jean Herrenschwand, un physiocrate suisse hétérodoxe?" In *La diffusion internationales de la physiocratie (XVIII–XIX*)*, edited by B. Delmas, T. Demals and P. Steiner, 195–209. Grenoble: Presses Universitaires de Grenoble.

Grampp, W. 1952. "The Liberal Elements in English Mercantilism," *Quarterly Journal of Economics* 66, no. 4: 465–501.

Herrenschwand, J. 1800. *Principios de economía política*. Madrid: Imprenta de Vega y cía.

Ibarra y Rodríguez, E. 1934. "Plan para organizar los estudios de Historia de la Economía Social en Aragón." In *Primera Conferencia Económica Aragonesa*, 95–147. Zaragoza: Real Sociedad Económica Aragonesa de Amigos del País.

Larruga, E. 1787–1800. *Memorias políticas y económicas sobre los frutos, comercio, fábricas y minas de España*, 15 vols. Reprint. Zaragoza: Gobierno de Aragón-Institución Fernando el Católico–Instituto Aragonés de Fomento, 1995–97.

Legarda, A. de. 1984. "El beato Diego José de Cádiz y el caso Normante ante el Consejo de Castilla," *Collectanea Franciscana* 54: 47–100.

Llombart Rosa, V. 2000. "El pensamiento económico de la Ilustración en España (1730–1812)." In *La Ilustración*, vol. 3 of *Economía y economistas españoles*, edited by E. Fuentes Quintana, 7–89. Barcelona: Galaxia Gutenberg–Funcas.

Lluch, E. 1984. "Acaecimientos de Manuel Belgrano, fisiócrata y su traducción de las Máximas Generales del Gobierno Económico de un Reyno Agricultor de François Quesnay." In F. Quesnay, *Máximas Generales del Gobierno Económico de un Reyno Agricultor*, 11–107. Madrid: Instituto de Cultura Iberoamericana.

———. 1992. "Juan López de Peñalver en los orígenes de la economía matemática." In *Escritos de Lopez de Peñalver*, xiii–cxxiv. Madrid: Instituto de Estudios Fiscales, Instituto de Cooperación Iberoamericana.

———. 1995. "La España vencida del siglo XVIII: Cameralismo, Corona de Aragón y 'Partido Aragonés' o 'Militar,'" *Sistema* 124: 13–41.

———. 2000. "El industrialismo en la Corona de Aragón y en la Corona de Castilla (siglo XVIII)." In *La Ilustración*, vol. 3 of *Economía y economistas españoles*, edited by E. Fuentes Quintana, 577–81. Barcelona: Galaxia Gutenberg–Funcas.

Lluch, E., and S. Almenar Palau. 2000. "Difusión e influencia de los economistas clásicos en España (1776–1870)." In *La economía clásica*, vol. 4 of *Economía y economistas españoles*, edited by E. Fuentes Quintana, 93–169. Barcelona: Galaxia Gutenberg–Funcas.

López, F. 1987. "Un sociodrama bajo el Antiguo Régimen: Nuevo enfoque de un suceso zaragozano; El caso Normante." In *Actas del I Seminario sobre la Ilustración Aragonesa*, 103–15. Zaragoza: Diputación General de Aragón.

López de Peñalver, J. 1801. "Principios de economía política de N. F. Canard: Premiada por el Instituto nacional," *Mercurio de España*, October, 184–88.

————. 1803. "De la mortalidad de los hospitales, general para hombres y de la Pasión para mujeres, de Madrid." *Mercurio de España*, February: 179–83.

————. 1804. "Tratado de economía política, o exposición sencilla del modo como se forman, distribuyen y emplean las riquezas por Say, miembro del tribunado: 2 tomos en 8°," *Mercurio de España*, March 15 and 31, 355–84 and 426–39.

Martín de Campos, P. 1800. "Letter to Diario de Madrid," *Diario de Madrid*, October 29.

N. N. (Acronym). 1807. "Advertencia." In G. Garnier, *Breve exposición de la doctrina de Adan (sic) Smith comparada con la de los economistas franceses y Método para facilitar el estudio de su obra*. Valladolid: Oficina de la Viuda e Hijos de Santander.

Normante y Carcavilla, L. 1984. *Discurso sobre la utilidad de los conocimientos económico–políticos y la necesidad de su estudio metódico*. Zaragoza: Diputación General de Aragón.

Perrotta, C. 1993. "Early Spanish Mercantilism: The First Analysis of Underdevelopment." In *Mercantilism: The Shaping of an Economic Language*, edited by L. Magnusson, 17–58. London: Routledge.

Peuchet, J. 1799–1800. *Dictionnaire universel de géographie commerçante*, 5 vols. Paris: Blauchon.

Polo y Catalina, J. (s.a.) "Notas." Ms. British Library, London.

————. (s.a.) "Crítica a los Cuadernos de Cátedra de Lorenzo Normante." Ms. British Library. London.

————. 1802. "Exposición de las causas que he tenido presentes en la formación del interrogatorio y demás necesario que se me ha encargado para el desempeño del Párrafo 7 del artículo 3 sección, en todo lo concerniente a la industria." Ms. British Library. London.

————. 1803. *Censo de frutos y manufacturas de España e islas adyacentes, ordenado sobre los datos dirigidos por los Intendentes y aumentado con las principales reflexiones sobre la estadística de cada una de las provincias en la sección primera del Departamento del Fomento General del Reyno y de la Balanza de Comercio bajo la dirección de su jefe Marcos Marín*. Madrid: Imprenta Real.

————. 1804. "Introducción a las descripciones histórico-políticas de las Fábricas e Industria de España." Ms. British Library. London.

————. 1960. *Censo de la riqueza territorial e industrial de España en el año de 1799 formado de orden superior*, edited by Antonio Matilla Tascón. Madrid: Fábrica Nacional de Moneda y Timbre.

————. 2005. *Informe sobre las fábricas e industria de España (1804) y otros escritos*, edited by A. Sánchez Hormigo. Zaragoza: Prensas Universitarias de Zaragoza.

Potier, J.-P. 2007. "Les traducteurs du Traité d´économie politique de Jean Baptiste Say (1804–1854): Un premier repérage." International workshop *Influences, critiques et postérité de l'oeuvre de J.B Say au XIXe siècle*, Lyon, January 12–13.

Régaldo, M. 1976. *Un milieu intellectuel: La Décade Philosophique (1794–1807)*, 5 vols. Paris: Honoré Champion.

Rodríguez, M. A. 1810. "Estadística de la provincia de Ávila," *Gazeta de Madrid*, 7 July 7, 811–14.

Sánchez Hormigo, A. 2005. "Smithianismo e industrialismo en la España de Carlos IV." In *Informe sobre las Fábricas e Industria de España (1804) y otros escritos by Juan Polo y Catalina*, xiv–cxxiii. Zaragoza: Prensas Universitarias de Zaragoza.

————. 2006. "Los ideólogos, el pensamiento económico y los ecos de la Revolución francesa en España (1800–1808)." In *En la estela de Ernest Lluch: Ensayos sobre historia del pensamiento económico*, edited by A. Sánchez Hormigo, 83–104. Zaragoza: Gobierno de Aragón.

Sánchez Hormigo, A., J. L. Malo and L. Blanco. 2003. *La cátedra de Economía civil y Comercio de la Real Sociedad Económica Aragonesa de Amigos del País (1784–1846)*. Zaragoza: Ibercaja.

Say, J.-B. 1803. *Traité d´Économie Politique, ou simple exposition de la maniéré dont se forment, se distribuent, et se consomment les richesses*. Paris: Crappelet.

————. 1804–7. *Tratado de Economía Política, o exposición sencilla de como se forman, se distribuyen y consumen las riquezas*, 3 vols. Madrid: Oficina de Pedro María Caballero–Gómez Fuentes.

Schwartz, P. 2000. "La recepción inicial de *La Riqueza de las Naciones* en España." In *La economía clásica*, vol. 4 of *Economía y economistas españoles*, edited by E. Fuentes Quintana, 171–238. Barcelona: Galaxia Gutenberg–Funcas.

Smith, A. 1794. *La riqueza de las naciones*, 4 vols., trans. J. A. Ortiz. Valladolid: Imprenta de la Viuda e Hijos de Santander.

———. 1802. *Recherches sur la nature et les causes de la richesse des nations*, trans. G. Garnier. Paris: Agasse.

———. 1805–6. *Investigación de la naturaleza y causas de la riqueza de las naciones*. Valladolid: Viuda e Hijos de Santander.

Smith, R. S. 1957. "The Wealth of Nations in Spain and Spanish America, 1780–1830," *Journal of Political Economy* 65, no. 2: 104–25.

Steiner, P. 1993. *L'évolution de l'Économie Politique en France au XIXe siècle: Une première grille de lecture. Première partie: du Traité de J.B. Say au Dictionnaire de l'économie politique de Ch. Coquelin et G. Guillaumin (1803–1852)*. Lisboa: CISEP.

Tolozan, J. F. de. 1789. *Mémoire sur le commerce de la France et de ses colonies*. Paris: Moutard.

Villanueva, J. L. 1820. *Apuntes sobre el arresto de los vocales de Cortes, egecutado en mayo de 1814*. Madrid: Imprenta de don Diego García y Campoy y compañía.

Young, A. 1775. *Arithmétique politique: Adressée aux sociétés économiques établies en Europe*, 2 vols. Paris: Fred Gossé.

BIBLIOGRAPHY

Alessandro Roncaglia's Publications

(Up to June 2017)

Books

1975. *Sraffa e la teoria dei prezzi*. Roma–Bari: Laterza; 2nd rev. ed. 1981; Japanese trans. *Nihon Keizai Shimbun*. Tokyo, 1977; English trans. *Sraffa and the Theory of Prices*, edited by J. Kregel. London and New York: Wiley, 1978; Spanish trans. *Sraffa y la teoria de los precios*. Madrid: Piramide, 1980; French trans. of chap. 4 in *Ricardiens, Keynésiens et Marxistes*, edited by C. Berthomieu, J. Cartelier and L. Cartelier, 209–30. Grenoble: Presses Universitaires de Grenoble, 1975; French trans. of chap. 5 in *Cahiers d'économie politique*, no. 3: 103–22, 1976; and of chap. 6 in *Une nouvelle approche en économie politique? Essais sur Sraffa*, edited by G. Faccarello and P. de Lavergne, 210–21. Paris: Economica, 1977; Korean trans. (edited by M. S. Park). Seoul: National Research Foundation of Korea, 2013.

1977. *William Petty: la nascita dell'economia politica*. Milano: Etas Libri; Spanish trans. *Petty. El nacimiento de la economía política*. Madrid: Piramide, 1980; English trans. *Petty: The Origins of Political Economy*. New York: Sharpe and Cardiff: University College Cardiff Press, 1985; Japanese trans. Kyoto: Showado, 1988.

1978. (With P. Baratta, L. Izzo, A. Pedone and P. Sylos Labini). *Prospettive dell'economia italiana*. Roma–Bari: Laterza.

1983. *L'economia del petrolio*. Roma–Bari: Laterza; English trans. *The International Oil Market*. London: Macmillan and New York: Sharpe, 1985.

1984. *Keynes a un secolo dalla nascita*. Arezzo: Studi e ricerche della Banca Popolare dell'Etruria.

1985. *Manuale di economia politica*. Roma–Bari: Laterza; 2nd ed. 1989; 3rd ed. 1993. German trans. *Handbuch der modernen Wirtschaft*. Wien: Edition S, 1987.

1986. *Le politiche dei redditi. Introduzione a un dibattito*. Arezzo: Studi e ricerche della Banca Popolare dell'Etruria.

1987. *Schumpeter. È possibile una teoria dello sviluppo economico?* Arezzo: Studi e ricerche della Banca Popolare dell'Etruria.

1989a. *Lineamenti di economia politica*. Roma–Bari: Laterza; new ed. 1993; Catalan trans. *Elements fondamentals d'economia política*, Vic: EumoEditorial, 1994.

1989b. (with R. Pease, J. Darvas, R. Flowers, L. Gouni, G. Grieger and K. Koberlein). *Report on Environmental, Safety-Related and Economic Potential of Fusion Power*. Brussels: EC Commission.

1990. (With S. Biasco and M. Salvati, eds.). *Istituzioni e mercato nello sviluppo economico.Saggi in onore di Paolo Sylos Labini*. Roma–Bari: Laterza; English trans. *Market and Institutions in Economic Development*. London: Macmillan, 1993.

1995. (With P. Sylos Labini). *Il pensiero economico. Temi e protagonisti*. Roma–Bari: Laterza; German trans. *Geschichte des ökonomischen Denkens. Eine kurze Einführung*, edited by S. Falcone and P. Kalmbach. Marburg: Metropolis-Verlag, 2008.

1999. *Sraffa: la biografia, l'opera, le scuole*. Roma–Bari: Laterza, 1999; English trans. *Piero Sraffa: His Life, Thought and Cultural Heritage*. London: Routledge, 2000.

2001. *La ricchezza delle idee. Storia del pensiero economico.* Roma–Bari: Laterza; English trans. *The Wealth of Ideas: A History of Economic Thought.* Cambridge: Cambridge University Press, 2005; Spanish trans. *La riqueza de las ideas. Una historia del pensamiento económico.* Zaragoza: Prensas Universitarias de Zaragoza, 2006; Chinese trans. Shanghai: Shanghai Academy of Social Sciences Press, 2009; Russian trans. forthcoming.

2005. *Il mito della mano invisibile.* Roma–Bari: Laterza; Spanish trans. *El mito de la mano invisible.* Zaragoza: Genueve Ediciones, 2011.

2008. (with P. Rossi and M. Salvadori, eds.). *Libertà, giustizia, laicità:. In ricordo di Paolo Sylos Labini.* Roma–Bari: Laterza.

2009. *Piero Sraffa.* Houndmills: Palgrave Macmillan. Chinese trans. Beijing: Huaxia Publishing House, 2009.

2009. *Los origenes de la desigualdad social. Los castors par alas mujeres y los ciervos para los hombres.* Zaragoza: Fundación Ernest Lluch.

2010. *Economisti che sbagliano. Le radici culturali della crisi.* Roma–Bari: Laterza; English trans. *Why the Economists Got It Wrong: The Crisis and Its Cultural Roots.* London: Anthem Press, 2010. Spanish trans. *Economistas que se equivocan.* Zaragoza: Prensas Universitarias de Zaragoza, 2015.

2011. (With A. Sanchez Hormigo). *Economistas clasicos.* Madrid: Editorial Sintesis.

2016. *Breve storia del pensiero economico.* Roma–Bari: Laterza; English trans. *A Brief History of Economic Thought.* Cambridge: Cambridge University Press, 2017; Spanish trans. *Breve historia del pensamiento económico.* Zaragoza: Prensas Universitarias de Zaragoza, 2017.

2017. (With M. Corsi). *Nuovi lineamenti di economia politica.* Roma–Bari: Laterza.

Book Sections

1972. "Introduzione." In R. Torrens, *Saggio sulla produzione della ricchezza,* edited by A. Roncaglia, i–xxxii. Milano: ISEDI.

1976. "The Sraffian Revolution." In *Modern Economic Thought,* edited by S. Weintraub, 163–77. Philadelphia: University of Pennsylvania Press.

1977. "Economia classica." "Fisiocratici." "Marginalismo." "Margine." "Marshall." "Massimizzazione del profitto." "Profitto." "Rendita." "Ricardo." "Salari." "Scala mobile." "Slittamento dei salari." "Smith." "Sovraprofitto." "Sraffa." "Zona salariale." Entries in *Enciclopedia europea.* Milano: Garzanti.

1977. "Sraffa and Price Theory: An Interpretation." In J. Schwartz, *The Subtle Anatomy of Capitalism,* 371–80. Santa Monica: Goodyear; Spanish trans. in *Investigación Económica,* no. 14, 1981: 5–16.

1980. "Sraffa." In *Dieci anni di storia,* vol. 2, 353–80. Milano: Nuova CEI.

1981a. "Piero Sraffa's Contribution to Political Economy." In *Twelve Contemporary Economists,* edited by J. Shackleton and G. Locksley, 240–56. London: Macmillan.

1981b. "Le trasformazioni economiche nella società italiana." In AA.VV., *Democrazia dell'alternativa e sinistra di governo,* 35–44. Venezia: Marsilio.

1985. "Il mercato petrolifero internazionale." In *Moneta ed economia internazionale,* edited by S. Biasco and R. Panizza, 229–41. Torino: Cassa di Risparmio di Torino–Piemonte vivo ricerche.

1987. "William Petty." In *The New Palgrave Dictionary of Political Economy,* vol. 3, 853–55. London: Macmillan.

1988a. "Wage Costs and Employment: The Sraffian View." In *Barriers to Full Employment,* edited by E. Matzner, J. Kregel and A. Roncaglia, 9–23. London: Macmillan; German trans. "Lohnkosten und Beschäftigung: Sraffas Sichtweise." In *Arbeit für alle ist möglich,* edited by E. Matzner, J. Kregel and A. Roncaglia, 21–34. Berlin: Edition Sigma; Italian abridged version "Barriere al pieno impiego: l'apporto sraffiano," *Rassegna di statistiche del lavoro* 1: 22–27, 1988.

1988b. "The Neo-Ricardian Approach and the Distribution of Income." In *Theories of Income Distribution,* edited by A. Asimakopulos, 158–80. Boston: Kluwer Academic Publishers; Chinese trans. Beijing: The Commercial Press, 1995.

1988c. "William Petty and the Conceptual Framework for the Analysis of Economic Development." In *The Balance between Industry and Agriculture in Economic Development*, edited by K. Arrow, vol. 1 of Proceedings of the Eighth World Congress of the International Economic Association, 157–74. London: Macmillan.

1989. "Energia tra presente e futuro." In *Uomo, ambiente, energia: il futuro*, 21–40. Roma: ENI; English trans. "Energy: Past Trends and Future Prospects." In *Man Environment Energy: The Future*, 21–40. Rome: ENI, 1989; Abridged and rev. version in European Association for Bioeconomic Studies, *Entropy and Bioeconomics*, 501–6. Milan: Nagard, 1993.

1990a. "Some Remarks on the Relevance of Sraffa's Analysis for Economic Policy." In *Essays on Piero Sraffa*, edited by K. Bharadwaj and B. Schefold, 467–78. London: Unwin Hyman; repr. London: Routledge, 1992.

1990b. "Comment on Garegnani." In *Essays on Piero Sraffa*, edited by K. Bharadwaj and B. Schefold, 144–48. London: Unwin Hyman; repr. London: Routledge, 1992.

1990c. "Le scuole sraffiane." In *Il pensiero economico: temi, problemi e scuole*, edited by G. Becattini, 233–74. Torino: UTET; English trans. "The Sraffian Schools," *Review of Political Economy* 3, no. 2, 1991: 187–219; Spanish trans. "Las escuelas sraffianas," *Cuadernos de economia aplicada*, no. 16, 1992.

1991a. "Elementi di economia." In E. Roppo and A. Roncaglia, *Elementi di diritto e di economia*. Roma–Bari, Laterza.

1991b. (With J. Darvas, K. Steinmetz, R. Flowers, L. Gouni, G. Grieger, K. Koberlein and R. Pease). "Environmental, Safety-Related and Economic Potential of Fusion Power." In *Plasma Physics and Controlled Nuclear Fusion Research 1990*, Proceedings of the thirteenth International Conference on Plasma Physics and Controlled Nuclear Fusion Research held by the International Atomic Energy Agency, Washington, DC, October 1–6, 1990, vol. 3, 633–44.

1992. "Intervento." In *Mezzogiorno: ristagno o sviluppo?* edited by B. Moro and G. Sabattini, 222–25. Milano: Angeli.

1993. (With P. Sylos Labini). "Economia." In *Enciclopedia delle scienze sociali*, vol. 3, 300–25. Roma: Istituto della Enciclopedia Italiana.

1994a. "Lo sviluppo economico nei paesi industrializzati: le tendenze dell'ultimo decennio e le prospettive del prossimo." In *Sviluppo economico e movimenti internazionali di capitali*, edited by F. Parrillo, 79–105. Roma: ISCONA-ABI.

1994b. "Antonio Serras Theorie und ihre Rezeption." In *Antonio Serra und sein 'Breve Trattato'*, edited by A. Heertje, C. Poni, R. Ragosta Portioli, A. Roncaglia and B. Schefold, 41–64. Düsseldorf: Verlag Wirtschaft und Finanzen GmbH.

1995a. "On the Compatibility between Keynes's and Sraffa's Viewpoints on Output Levels." In *Income and Employment in Theory and Practice: Essays in Memory of Athanasios Asimakopulos*, edited by G. Harcourt, A. Roncaglia and R. Rowley, 111–25. London: Macmillan and New York: St. Martin's Press.

1995b. "Introduzione." In A. Smith, *La ricchezza delle nazioni*, 1–12. Roma: Newton Compton.

1995c. "Introduzione." In *Alle origini del pensiero economico in Italia,*vol. 1: *Moneta e sviluppo negli economisti napoletani dei secoli XVII-XVIII*, edited by A. Roncaglia, 7–14. Bologna: Il Mulino.

1996a. (With M. C. Marcuzzo and L. Pasinetti). "Introduction." In *The Economics of Joan Robinson*, edited by M.C. Marcuzzo, L. Pasinetti and A. Roncaglia, 1–18. London: Routledge; reprinted in paperback edition 2014.

1996b. "Lavoro—1. Economia." In *Enciclopedia delle scienze sociali*, vol. 5. Roma: Istituto della Enciclopedia Italiana.

1996c. "Lusso—2. Economia." In *Enciclopedia delle scienze sociali*, vol. 5. Roma: Istituto della Enciclopedia Italiana.

1996d. "Smithian Foundations of the Market Economy." In *Capital Controversy, Post-Keynesian Economics and the History of Economic Thought*, edited by P. Arestis, G. Palma and M. Sawyer, 375–85. London: Routledge.

1996e. "Russia and International Oil and Gas Markets." In *Russia in the World Economy*, special issue of *Sviluppo/Development*, edited by G. Mureddu and M. T. Salvemini, 191–99.

1997a. "Prefazione." In *Proprietà, controllo e governo delle banche*, 7–10. Roma: BNL Edizioni; English trans. *Property, Control and Corporate Governance of Banks*, 7–10. Roma: BNL Edizioni, 1997.

1997b. "Introduction," *BNL Quarterly Review: Indexes of the First Fifty Years, 1947–97*, Special Issue, September, 7–26.

1998a. "The International Oil Market: Structural Changes and Stabilization Policies." In *Method, Theory and Policy in Keynes: Essays in Honour of Paul Davidson*, edited by P. Arestis, vol. 3, 190–204. Cheltenham: Edward Elgar.

1998b. "Sraffa, Piero as an Interpreter of the Classical Economists." In *The Elgar Companion to Classical Economics*, edited by H. Kurz and N. Salvadori, vol. 2, 395–404. Cheltenham: Edward Elgar.

1998c. (With M. C. Marcuzzo, ed.). "Introduzione." In *Saggi di economia politica*, edited by M. C. Marcuzzo and A. Roncaglia, 7–10. Bologna: CLUEB.

1998d. "Introduzione." *Moneta e Credito: Indice dei primi cinquanta anni, 1948–1998*, Supplemento, September, 7–27.

1998e. "Sovrappiù, teorie del." In *Enciclopedia delle scienze sociali*, vol. 8, 277–85. Roma: Istituto della Enciclopedia Italiana.

1999a. "Comment on S. Zamagni *Social Paradoxes of Growth and Civil Economy*." In *Economic Theory and Social Justice*, edited by G. Gandolfo and F. Marzano, 242–46. Basingstoke and London: Macmillan.

1999b. "Sraffa, Piero." In *Encyclopedia of Political Economy*, edited by P. A. O'Hara, vol. 2, 1085–88. London: Routledge.

1999c. "From Utilitarianism to Marginal Utility." In *Value, Distribution and Capital: Essays in Honour of Pierangelo Garegnani*, edited by G. Mongiovi and F. Petri, 107–21. London: Routledge.

1999d. "Per una formazione meno unilaterale degli economisti." In *Trasformazioni dell'economia e della società italiana. Studi e ricerche in onore di Giorgio Fuà*, edited by Gruppo di Ancona, 457–69. Bologna: Il Mulino.

1999e. "La corsa al petrolio." In *Storia dell'economia mondiale. 4. Tra espansione e recessione*, edited by V. Castronovo, 267–81. Roma–Bari: Laterza.

2000. "*Produzione di merci a mezzo di merci* tra critica e ricostruzione: l'assunto di quantità date." In *Piero Sraffa: Contributi per una biografia intellettuale*, edited by M. Pivetti, 161–79. Roma: Carocci; English trans. "*Production of Commodities by Means of Commodities* between Criticism and Reconstruction: The Given Quantities Assumption." In *Piero Sraffa's Political Economy: A Centenary Estimate*, edited by T. Cozzi and R. Marchionatti, 207–30. London: Routledge; reprinted in *The Legacy of Piero Sraffa*, edited by H. Kurz and N. Salvadori, vol. 2, 166–82. Cheltenham: Edward Elgar, 2004; Spanish trans. "*Producción de mercancias por medio de mercancias: critica al enfoque marginalista y reconstrucción del enfoque clasico.*" In *Piero Sraffa*, edited by M. Pivetti, 269–99. Mexico City: Universidad Nacional Autonoma de Mexico, 2008.

2001. "Canons in the History of Economic Thought." In *Reflections on the Classical Canon in Economics: Essays in Honor of Samuel Hollander*, edited by E. L. Forget and S. Peart, 378–85. London and New York: Routledge.

2002. (With P. Sylos Labini). "Introduzione." In *Per la ripresa del riformismo*, edited by P. Sylos Labini and A. Roncaglia, 11–28. Milano: Nuova Iniziativa Editoriale.

2004a. "Cooperative e riformismo sociale." In *Il futuro del capitalismo*, edited by B. Jossa, 287–94. Bologna: Il Mulino.

2004b. "La macroeconomia dopo Sraffa." In *Piero Sraffa*, Atti dei Convegni Lincei no. 200, 347–72. Roma: Accademia Nazionale dei Lincei e Bardi Editore.

2004c. "Some Notes on Post-Classical Macroeconomics." In *Money, Credit and the Role of the State: Essays in Honour of Augusto Graziani*, edited by R. Arena and N. Salvadori, 271–84. Aldershot: Ashgate.

2004d. "William Petty." In *Biographical Dictionary of British Economists*, vol. 2. Bristol: Thoemmes Continuum.

2004e. "Le catene causali brevi: le variazioni di Maynard su un tema di Alfred." In *Economia senza gabbia: Studi in onore di Giacomo Becattini*, edited by N. Bellanca, M. Dardi and T. Raffaelli, 379–97. Bologna: Il Mulino.

2004f. (With R. Villetti). "Riccardo Lombardi e la strategia delle riforme." In *Per una società diversamente ricca. Scritti in onore di Riccardo Lombardi*, edited by A. Ricciardi and G. Scirocco, 215–20. Roma: Edizioni di storia e letteratura.

2005. "Le fondazioni di origine bancaria: alcuni commenti." In *Le fondazioni e le fondazioni di origine bancaria*, Atti dei Convegni Lincei no. 219, 369–76. Roma: Accademia Nazionale dei Lincei e Bardi Editore.

2006a. "Keynes and Probability: An Assessment." In *The Cambridge Approach to Economics: A Re-Invented Tradition?* edited by M. C. Marcuzzo, 3–17. Roma: Università degli Studi di Roma La Sapienza, Dipartimento di Scienze Economiche.

2006b. "Sraffa, Piero." In *Lexicon ökonomischer Werke*, 497–98. Düsseldorf: Verlag Wirtschaft und Finanzen.

2007a. (With R. Villetti). "Divisione del lavoro: capitalismo, socialismo, utopia." In *L'economia e la politica: Saggi in onore di Michele Salvati*, edited by G. Dosi and M. C. Marcuzzo, 265–83. Bologna: Il Mulino.

2007b. "L'impegno scientifico e civile di Paolo Sylos Labini." In *Atti Ufficiali dell'Accademia delle scienze di Torino, 2004–2006*, 185–97. Torino: Accademia delle scienze di Torino.

2007c. "La cultura economica del Mediterraneo: il ruolo dell'Italia." In Real Accademia de Ciencias Económicas y Financieras, *La ciencia y la cultura en la Europa Mediterránea. I Encuentro Italo-Español*, 66–71. Barcelona: Real Accademia de Ciencias Económicas y Financieras.

2008a. "Il socialismo liberale di Paolo Sylos Labini." In *Libertà, giustizia, laicità. In ricordo di Paolo Sylos Labini*, edited by A. Roncaglia, P. Rossi and M. Salvadori, 27–57. Roma–Bari: Laterza.

2008b. "Joseph Schumpeter." In *La forza dei bisogni e le ragioni della libertà*, edited by F. Sbarberi, 313–26. Reggio Emilia: Diabasis.

2008c. "Postfazione." In *La lezione sassarese di Paolo Sylos Labini (1956–1958)*, edited by D. Pireddu, 159–64. Milano: Franco Angeli.

2009a. "Premessa." In *Giacomo Matteotti. Scritti economici e finanziari*, edited by S. Caretti, vol. 1, 1–13. Pisa: Pisa University Press; reprinted as "Matteotti economist," *Mondoperaio*, no. 4 (June): 77–81.

2009b. "L'archivio digitale degli scritti di Paolo Sylos Labini." *Rendiconti* della Classe di scienze morali, storiche e filologiche dell'Accademia Nazionale dei Lincei no. 20: 437–46; reprinted in *Il Ponte* 66, no. 2, 2010: 65–74.

2009c. "Some Notes on the Notion of Production Prices." In *Economic Theory and Economic Thought: Essays in Honour of Ian Steedman*, edited by J. Vint, J. S. Metcalfe, H. D. Kurz, N. Salvadori and P. A. Samuelson, 174–88. London: Routledge.

2010a. "Il sogno infranto del libero mercato." In *Il capitalismo invecchia?* edited by C. Orsi, 71–74. Roma: Manifestolibri.

2010b. "The Origins of Social Inequality: Beavers for Women, Deer for Men." In *Production, Distribution and Trade: Alternative Perspectives: Essays in Honour of Sergio Parrinello*, edited by A. Birolo, D. Foley, H. Kurz, B. Schefold and I. Steedman, 289–303. London: Routledge.

2010c. (With P. Ciocca, R. Faucci and F. Forte). "Discussione." In *Luigi Einaudi: libertà economica e coesione sociale*, edited by A. Gigliobianco, 155–77. Roma–Bari: Laterza.

2011a. "Premessa." In G. Matteotti, *L'avvento del fascismo*, 9–16. Pisa: Pisa University Press.

2011b. "Cambridge e Italia: teorie postkeynesiane della distribuzione. Una nota." In *Gli economisti postkeynesiani di Cambridge e l'Italia*, Atti dei Convegni Lincei no. 261, 125–38. Roma: Scienze e lettere.

2012a. "A Patchwork Post-Keynesian/Evolutionary Approach to Income Distribution." In *Classical Political Economy and Modern Theory: Essays in Honour of Heinz Kurz*, edited by C. Gehrke, N. Salvadori, I. Steedman and R. Sturn, 207–18. Abingdon and New York: Routledge.

2012b. "L'economia della P2." In *Le notti della democrazia*, edited by G. Amari and A. Vinci, 97–101. Roma: Ediesse. Reprinted in *Loggia P2. Il Piano e le sue regole*, edited by G. Amari and A. Vinci, 75–80. Roma: Castelvecchi, 2014.

2012c. "Antonio Serra." In *Enciclopedia italiana. Ottava appendice. Il contributo italiano alla storia del pensiero. Economia*, 412–19. Roma: Istituto della Enciclopedia Italiana.

2012d. "Piero Sraffa." In *Enciclopedia italiana. Ottava appendice. Il contributo italiano alla storia del pensiero. Economia*, 710–17. Roma: Istituto della Enciclopedia Italiana.

2012e. "Paolo Sylos Labini." In *Enciclopedia italiana. Ottava appendice. Il contributo italiano alla storia del pensiero. Economia*, 718–24. Roma: Istituto della Enciclopedia Italiana.

2012f. "Premessa." In A. Quadrio Curzio and M. Fortis, *L'industria nei 150 anni dell'unità d'Italia*, 409–11. Bologna: Il Mulino.

2013a. "Quintino Sella: un inquadramento nella cultura economica di metà Ottocento." In *Quintino Sella: scienziato e statista per l'Unità d'Italia*, Atti dei Convegni Lincei no. 269, 459–63. Roma: Scienze e lettere.

2013b. "Introduzione." In *In ricordo di Pierangelo Garegnani*, 7–10. Roma: Università degli studi Roma Tre.

2013c. "Introduction." In A. Roncaglia, *Sraffa and the Theory of Prices*, Korean edition (edited by M. S. Park), 11–14. Seoul: The National Research Foundation of Korea.

2014a. "Introduzione." In C. Cattaneo (1861), *Del pensiero come principio d'economia pubblica*, 5–29. Roma: Edizioni di storia e letteratura.

2014b. "Il gradualismo riformatore di Riccardo Lombardi." In *Lombardi 2013. Riforme di struttura e alternativa socialista*, edited by E. Bartocci, 345–50. Roma: Fondazione Giacomo Brodolini.

2014c. "Statistics and Economics: A Complex Relationship." In *Statistical Methods and Applications from a Historical Perspective*, edited by P. Crescenzi and S. Mignani, 263–75. Cham, Switzerland: Springer International Publishing.

2014d. (With M. Tonveronachi). "Post-Keynesian, Post-Sraffian Economics: An Outline." In *Contributions to Economic Theory, Policy, Development and Finance: Essays in Honour of Jan A. Kregel*, edited by D. Papadimitriou, 40–64. Houndmills: Palgrave Macmillan.

2014e. "Institutions, Resources and the Common Weal." In *Resources, Production and Structural Dynamics*, edited by M. Baranzini, C. Rotondi and R. Scazzieri, 259–78. Cambridge: Cambridge University Press.

2015. "La storia e il presente in economia: le radici del progetto ASE." In *Gli economisti italiani: protagonisti, paradigmi, politiche*, Atti dei Convegni Lincei no. 290, 19–24. Roma: Bardi edizioni.

2016a. (With C. D'Ippoliti). "Heterodox Economics and the History of Economic Thought." In *Advancing the Frontiers of Heterodox Economics: Essays in Honor of Frederick S. Lee*, edited by T.-H. Jo and Z. Todorova, 21–38. Abingdon and New York: Routledge.

2016b. "How Should Prices of Production Be Interpreted? The Case of Oil." In *Economic Theory and Its History: Essays in Honour of Neri Salvadori*, edited by G. Freni, H. Kurz, A. Lavezzi and R. Signorino, 131–43. Abingdon and New York: Routledge.

2016c. "The Heritage of Antonio Serra." In *Antonio Serra and the Economics of Good Government*, edited by R. Patalano and S. Reinert, 299–314. New York: Palgrave Macmillan.

2017. "Piero Sraffa (1898–1983)." In *The Palgrave Companion to Cambridge Economics*, edited by R. Cord, vol. 2, 603–21. London: Palgrave Macmillan.

Journal Articles

1971. "Il capitale fisso in un modello di produzione circolare," *Studi economici* 26, no. 1–6: 232–45; reprinted in *Esperimenti intellettuali ed economia politica*, edited by N. Salvadori, 25–44. Milano: Franco Angeli, 1981; French trans. in *Une nouvelle approche en economie politique? Essays sur Sraffa*, edited by G. Faccarello and Ph. de Lavergne, 105–17. Paris: Economica, 1977; English trans. in A. Roncaglia, *Sraffa and the Theory of Prices*, 36–48. New York: Wiley, 1978.

1973. "La riduzione di lavoro complesso a lavoro semplice," *Note economiche*, no. 3: 97–112; English trans. in *Bulletin of the Conference of Socialist Economists*, no. 9, Autumn 1974: 1–12.

1974a. "Labour-Power, Subsistence Wage and the Rate of Wages," *Australian Economic Papers*, June, 133–43.

1974b. (With M. Tonveronachi). "Appunti per una teoria della distribuzione: un quadro di riferimento per il 'breve periodo'," *Note economiche* no. 3: 114–39.

1976a. "Sulle macchine utilizzate congiuntamente," *Studi economici* 31: 127–32; reprinted in *Esperimenti intellettuali ed economia politica*, edited by N. Salvadori, 147–52. Milano: Franco Angeli, 1981

1976b. "Teorie economiche e storia," *Civiltà delle macchine* 24, no. 5–6: 39–44.

1978a. (With M. Tonveronachi). "Commenti a un recente studio di Modigliani e Padoa-Schioppa," *Moneta e Credito* 31, no. 121: 3–21.

1978b. "La rivoluzione sraffiana," *Mondoperaio* 31, no. 9: 75–83. Catalan trans. In *Taula de canvi*, no. 21, 1980: 20–64.

1978c. "The 'Rediscovery' of Ricardo," *New Left Review* no. 112: 80–82.

1979a. "The Sraffian Contribution," *Challenge* 21, no. 6: 48–53; reprinted in *A Guide to Post-Keynesian Economics*, edited by A. Eichner, 87–99. New York: Sharpe.

1979b. (With M. Tonveronachi). "Monetaristi e neokeynesiani: due scuole o una?" *Quaderni dell'istituto di economia*, Università di Siena, no. 5.

1980. "Production Prices and the Theory of the Firm: A Comment," *Journal of Post Keynesian Economics* 3, no. 1: 100–4.

1982. "Hollander's Ricardo," *Journal of Post Keynesian Economics* 4, no. 4: 339–59; reprinted in *The Legacy of Ricardo*, edited by G. Caravale, 105–23. Oxford: Blackwell, 1985; also in *David Ricardo: A Critical Assessment*, edited by J.C. Wood. London: Croom Helms, 1986.

1983a. "The Price of Oil," *Journal of Post Keynesian Economics* 5, no. 4: 557–78; Spanish trans. in *Investigación Económica*, no. 175: 35–60.

1983b. "Piero Sraffa: una bibliografia ragionata," *Studi economici*, no. 21: 137–66; French trans. in *Sraffa, trente ans après*, edited by R. Arena and J. J. Ravix, 19–40. Paris: PUF, 1990.

1983c. "Piero Sraffa and the Reconstruction of Political Economy," *Banca Nazionale del Lavoro Quarterly Review* 36, no. 147: 337–50; German trans. in *Der offentliche Sektor*, no. 4, 1984: 1–16; reprinted in *Wiener Zeitung*, nos. 27, 33 and 39, 1985; Spanish trans. in *Lecturas de economia*, no. 16, 1985: 219–35; reprinted in *Piero Sraffa (1898–1983)*, edited by M. Blaug, 54–67. Aldershot: Edward Elgar, 1992; abridged version in *Nomadas*, no. 1, 2011, online journal at http://www.ucm.es.info.nomadas/MA_sraffa.

1983d. (With M. Tonveronachi). "Raices prekeynesianas de la sintesis neoclasica," *Hacienda Publica Española*, no. 83: 219–29; English abridged version "The Pre-Keynesian Roots of the Neoclassical Synthesis," *Cahiers d'économie politique*, no. 10, 1985: 51–65.

1984a. "Aktuelle Probleme der italienischen Wirtschaft," *Wirtschaft und Gesellschaft*, no. 4: 527–32; Spanish trans. in *Economia informa* no. 126, 1985: 15–18.

1984b. "Sraffa e le banche," *Rivista milanese di economia* no. 10: 104–12.

1986. "È ancora utile una politica dei redditi? Risposta a Paolo Savona," *Rivista di politica economica* 76, no. 10: 1460–61.

1989a. "Research in Fusion as Investment," *Giornale degli economisti* 48, no.7–8: 293–307.

1989b. "Italian Economic Growth: A Smithian View." *Quaderni di storia dell'economia politica* 7, nos. 2–3: 227–34.

1989c. (With P. Sylos Labini). "Economia dell'energia in Italia: due visioni alternative per l'inserimento nell'università," *Economia delle fonti di energia* 32, no. 39: 103–8.

1989d. "A Reappraisal of Classical Political Economy," *Political Economy: Studies in the Surplus Approach* 5, no. 2: 169–80.

1990a. "Is the Notion of Long-Period Positions Compatible with Classical Political Economy?" *Political Economy: Studies in the Surplus Approach* 6, nos. 1 2: 103 10.

1990b. (With P. Sylos Labini). "Riflessioni sullo sviluppo economico e l'ambiente," *Scuola e società* no. 12: 532–38; reprinted in *Il Progetto* 11, no. 65, 1990: 7–13; and in *Development*, 1990: 56–62.

1991a. "La stabilizzazione del prezzo del petrolio: alcuni commenti," *Economia delle fonti di energia* 34, no. 44: 71–78.

1991b. "Sraffa's 1925 Article and Marshall's Theory," *Quaderni di storia dell'economia politica* 9, nos. 2–3 (special issue: "Alfred Marshall's *Principles of Economics* 1890–1990," edited by M. Dardi, M. Gallegati and E. Pesciarelli, vol. 1): 373–97; reprinted in *The Legacy of Piero Sraffa*, edited by H. Kurz and N. Salvadori, vol. 1, 149–73. Cheltenham and Northampton, MA: Edward Elgar, 2004.

1992. (With M. Tonveronachi). "Disoccupazione e intervento pubblico nell'economia" *Studi economici* no. 48: 47–63; reprinted in *Il neoliberismo: teoria e politica economica*, edited by B. Jossa, 13–28. Milano: Angeli, 1994.

1993a. "Krishna Bharadwaj, 1935–1992. In Memoriam," *Metroeconomica* 44, no. 3: 187–94.

1993b. "Toward a Post-Sraffian Theory of Income Distribution," *Journal of Income Distribution* 3, no. 1: 3–27.

1993c. "L'OPEC dopo la guerra del Golfo e la disgregazione dell'URSS," *Energia* 14, no. 4: 38–46.

1994a. "The Effects of Carbon Taxes in Different Approaches to Economic Theory: A Comment on Sinclair," *The Manchester School* 62, no. 4: 438–44.

1994b. "Josef Steindl's Relations to Italian Economics," *Review of Political Economy* 6, no. 4: 450–58.

1995a. "Comment" in "Minisymposium: Locating Marx after the Fall, *History of Political Economy* 27, no. 1: 189–93.

1995b. "Multiple Discoveries: Quantitative Data and Ideological Biases: A Comment on Niehans," *European Journal of the History of Economic Thought* 2, no. 2: 289–93.

1996a. "Why Should Economists Study the History of Economic Thought?" *European Journal of the History of Economic Thought* 3, no. 2: 296–309.

1996b. "The Classical Approach and Long-Period Positions: A Comment on Cesaratto," *Review of Political Economy* 8, no. 4: 403–8.

1997. "Per un archivio storico degli economisti italiani," *Rivista di storia economica* 13, no. 2: 271–76.

1998a. "Piero Sraffa come interprete degli economisti classici," *Il pensiero economico italiano* 6, no. 1: 231–42.

1998b. "Nicholas Georgescu-Roegen, 1906–1994," *Metron* 56, no. 3–4: 5–10.

1999a. "Luigi Ceriani, 1912–1999," *Moneta e Credito* 52, no. 207: 281–90; English trans. in *Banca Nazionale del Lavoro Quarterly Review* 52, no. 210: 247–56.

1999b. "Antonio Serra," *Rivista italiana degli economisti* 4, no. 3: 421–37.

2000. (With M. C. Marcuzzo and C. Perrotta). "Il progetto Archivio storico degli economisti italiani (ASE)," *Rivista italiana degli economisti* 5, no. 1: 175–88.

2001. (With G. Roncaglia). "La 'nuova economia della conoscenza e dell'informazione' e l'"economia di Internet': un'introduzione," *Moneta e Credito* 54, no. 213: 3–15.

2002a. "Piero Sraffa: una teoria economica aperta alla storia," *Rivista di storia economica* 18, April, 111–24; reprinted in *Le vie della storia nell'economia*, edited by P. Ciocca, 155–69. Bologna: Il Mulino, 2002.

2002b. (With M. Corsi). "The Employment Issue in the European Union," *Journal of Post Keynesian Economics* 25, no. 1: 141–59.

2003a. "On the Relationship between Economic and Political Discourses: A Few Examples," *Istituzioni e sviluppo economico* 1, no. 1: 137–52.

2003b. "Energy and Market Power: An Alternative Approach to the Economics of Oil," *Journal of Post Keynesian Economics* 25, no. 4: 641–59.

2005. "Paolo Sylos Labini, economista e cittadino," *Istituzioni e sviluppo economico* 3, no. 3: 5–19; reprinted in *Paolo Sylos Labini*, edited by F. Sylos Labini, 21–35. Roma: Sapienza Università Editrice, 2015.

2006a. "I mercati internazionali degli idrocarburi," *Global Competition* 1, no. 3: 17–24.

2006b. "Paolo Sylos Labini: l'uomo e l'economista," *Economia & Lavoro* 40, no. 1: 15–20.

2006c. "Paolo Sylos Labini, 1920–2005," *Moneta e Credito* 59, no. 233: 3–21; English trans. in *Banca Nazionale del Lavoro Quarterly Review* 59, no. 235: 3–21; French expanded trans. in *Revue d'économie industrielle*, no. 118, 2007: 9–27.

2006d. "Tasa de desempleo y tasas de empleo: categorias estadisticas o construcciones teoricas?" *Investigación Económica* 65, no. 257: 45–61.

2006e. (With L. Pasinetti). "Le scienze umane in Italia: il caso dell'economia politica," *Rivista Italiana degli Economisti* 11, no. 3: 463–501.

2007a. (With M. Corsi). "A proposito di 'Salveminiani e machiavellici': un commento a Michele Salvati," *Il Mulino* 56, no. 430: 361–65; reprinted in *Economia & Lavoro* 41, no. 3: 41–45.

2007b. "Il pensiero economico di Paolo Sylos Labini," *Economia & Lavoro* 41, no. 3: 23–30.

2007c. "The History of a Journal: *Banca Nazionale del Lavoro Quarterly Review*, 1947–2007," *Banca Nazionale del Lavoro Quarterly Review* 60, no. 243: 3–26.

2007d. "Storia di una rivista: *Moneta e Credito*, 1948–2007," *Moneta e Credito* 60, no. 240: 3–29.

2007e. "*The Wealth of Ideas: A History of Economic Thought*: Response to Antony Brewer," *Adam Smith Review* 3: 234–48.

2008a. "Keynes e i Keynesiani di Cambridge," *QA: La questione agraria* nos. 3–4: 249–58.

2008b. "Moneta e credito: storia e prospettive di una rivista," *Moneta e Credito* 61, nos. 241–244: 3–36.

2008c. "From BNL-QR to PSL-QR: The History (1947–2007) and Prospects of a Journal," *PSL Quarterly Review* 61, nos. 244–247: 3–32.

2009a. "Keynes and Probability: An Assessment," *European Journal of the History of Economic Thought* 16, no. 3: 489–510.

2009b. Review of *From Political Economy to Economics*, by Dimitris Milonakis and Ben Fine. *European Journal of the History of Economic Thought* 16, no. 3: 527–29.

2009c. "Le regole del gioco, l'instabilità e le crisi," *Moneta e Credito* 62, nos. 245–248: 3–12.

2009d. "Rules, Instability and Crises," *PSL Quarterly Review* 62, nos. 248–251: 3–13.

2009e. "Gli economisti che non tacquero," *Mondoperaio*, no. 6: 41–3.

2009f. "Paura dei beni e paura delle idee," *Storia del pensiero economico* 6, no. 1: 115–20.

2009g. "Sulla storia delle misure del prodotto e sul metodo dell'economia," *Rivista di storia economica* 25, no. 3: 383–88.

2010a. "Introduzione," *Moneta e Credito* 63, no. 249: 3–5.

2010b. "Introduction," *PSL Quarterly Review* 63, no. 252: 3–5.

2010c. Review of *Paura dei beni: Da Esiodo a Adam Smith*, by C. Perrotta. *History of Political Economy* 42, no. 3: 598–600.

2010d. "Prezzi e distribuzione del reddito: una nota," *Studi economici* 65, no. 100: 261–73.

2010e. "Economia e bene comune," *Quaderni Laici*, no. 2: 53–60.

2010f. "Introduzione," *Moneta e Credito* 63, no. 249: 3–6.

2010g. "Introduzione," *Moneta e Credito* 63, no. 250: 95–98.

2010h. "Le origini culturali della crisi," *Moneta e Credito* 63, no. 250: 105–16.

2010i. "Introduzione," *Moneta e Credito* 63, no. 251: 281–83.

2010j. "Introduction," *PSL Quarterly Review* 63, no. 252: 3–4.

2010k. "Contributions on Monetary and Financial Issues: An Introduction," *PSL Quarterly Review* 63, no. 253: 97–100.

2010l. "Economic Policy Dilemmas in front of the Crisis," *PSL Quarterly Review* 63, no. 254: 179–83.

2010m. "Confronting the Financial Crisis: Surveillance and Regulation," *PSL Quarterly Review* 63, no. 255: 293–96.

2011a. "What Do We Mean by Anglo-American Capitalism?" *Adam Smith Review* 6: 283–89.

2011b. "Ancora sulla crisi," *Moneta e Credito* 64, no. 253, 2011: 9–13.

2011c. "Macroeconomie in crisi e macroeconomie in ripresa," *Moneta e Credito* 64, no. 254: 115–33; English trans. in *PSL Quarterly Review* 64, no. 257: 167–85.

2011d. "A Multi-Faceted Financial Crisis," *PSL Quarterly Review* 64, no. 256: 3–5.

2011c. "Introduction," *PSL Quarterly Review* 64, no. 258: 189–91.

2011f. (With C. D'Ippoliti). "L'Italia: una crisi nella crisi," *Moneta e Credito* 64, no. 255: 189–227.

2011g. "Profilo. Paolo Sylos Labini," *Il Mulino*, no. 6: 1052–57.

2011h. Review of *Barriers to Competition: The History of the Debate*, by Ana Rosado Cubero. *European Journal of the History of Economic Thought* 18, no. 2: 293–96.

2012a. "Commento al saggio di Giovanni Vecchi," *Rivista di storia economica* 28, no. 1: 197–201.

2012b. "Different Notions of Scarcity," *Economia politica* 29, no. 1: 3–18.

2012c. "Introduzione," *Moneta e Credito* 65, no. 258: 97–103.

2012d. "Economia politica: impostazioni a confronto, *Moneta e Credito* 65, no. 259: 229–41.

2012e. "Josef Steindl, the Trieste School and the BNL Quarterly Review," *PSL Quarterly Review* 65, no. 261: 113–16.

2012f. Review of *Theories of Value from Adam Smith to Piero Sraffa*, by Ajit Sinha. *History of Political Economy* 44, no. 4: 728–30.

2012g. "Keynesian Uncertainty and the Shaky Foundations of Statistical Risk Assessment Models," *PSL Quarterly Review* 65, no. 263: 437–54.

2012h. "Nota bibliografica: Gallino, *La lotta di classe dopo la lotta di classe*," *Moneta e credito* 65, no. 260: 335–39.

2013a. Review of *Il Tableau économique di François Quesnay*, edited by Giancarlo de Vivo. *History of Political Economy* 45, no. 3, Fall: 559–60.

2013b. "Sinistra e diseguaglianza," *MicroMega* no. 3: 201–9.

2013c. "Il ruolo delle istituzioni nell'economia: introduzione," *Moneta e Credito* 66, no. 261: 3–6.

2013d. "Le politiche di austerità sono sbagliate," *Moneta e Credito* 66, no. 262: 121–28.

2013e. "Introduction: On the Role of a Generalist Journal," *PSL Quarterly Review* 66, no. 264: 3–6.

2013f. "Hyman Minsky's Monetary Production Economy," *PSL Quarterly Review* 66, no. 265: 77–94.

2013g. "Luigi Spaventa," *Moneta e Credito* 66, no. 263: 219–47; English trans. in *PSL Quarterly Review* 66, no. 266: 171–99.

2014a. "Keynes Is Alive and Well: A Survey Article," *PSL Quarterly Review* 67, no. 268: 105–24.

2014b. "Hirschman e l'Italia," *Moneta e Credito* 67, no. 266: 153–57.

2014c. "Teorie dell'occupazione: due impostazioni a confronto," *Moneta e Credito* 67, no. 267: 243–70; English trans. "The Theory of Employment: Two Approaches Compared," *PSL Quarterly Review* 67, no. 270: 241–68.

2014d. "Should the History of Economic Thought Be Included in Undergraduate Curricula?" *Economic Thought* 3, no. 1: 1–10.

2014e. Review of *From Oikonomia to Political Economy: Constructing Economic Knowledge from the Renaissance to the Scientific Revolution*, by Germano Maifreda. *Economic History Review* 67, no. 2: 578–606.

2014f. Review of *Defending the History of Economic Thought*, by Stephen Kates. *History of Economics Review* 60, no. 1: 89–92.

2015a. (With A. Montesano). "Introduction," *Italian Economic Journal* 1, no. 1: 1–3.

2015b. "Oil and Its Markets," *PSL Quarterly Review* 68, no. 273: 151–75; Italian version "Il petrolio e i suoi mercati." In *Lectio brevis, A.A. 2013–2014*, Atti della Accademia Nazionale dei Lincei, Memorie, vol. 35, 599–611. Roma: Bardi Edizioni, 2015.

2015c. "Le barriere all'entrata e la politica delle riforme di struttura," *Moneta e Credito* 68, no. 270: 159–71.

2015d. "Sidney Weintraub e i post-keynesiani d'America," *Moneta e Credito* 68, no. 271: 273–77.

2015e. "Introduzione," *Moneta e Credito* 68, no. 272: 361–62.

2015f. "Ernesto Rossi," *Moneta e Credito* 68, no. 272: 505–13.

2015g. "Il contributo di Hyman Minsky alla teoria economica," *La Rivista delle Politiche Sociali*, no. 1: 187–92.

2016. "L'etica dell'economista," *Moneta e Credito* 69, no. 273: 7–19.

2017a. (With C. D'Ippoliti). "Un cambiamento nella continuità," *Moneta e Credito* 70, no. 277: 3–5; English trans. "Editorial: Change and Continuity," *PSL Quarterly Review* 70, no. 280: 3–5.

2017b. "La rivoluzione dello *shale oil* e i mercati finanziari," *Moneta e Credito* 70, no. 278: 173–93.

LIST OF CONTRIBUTORS

Davide Antonioli is associate professor at the University "G. d'Annunzio" of Chieti-Pescara. His research interests are about innovation and technological change, industrial relations and environmental innovation, organizational changes and firms' economic performance. His publications include articles (among others) published in *Research Policy, Papers in Regional Science, Economia Politica, Journal of Analytical and Institutional Economics, Ecological Economics, Growth and Change,* and *Economic and Industrial Democracy.*

Salvatore Biasco is retired professor from Sapienza University of Rome. His research interests are international and public economics. He has published many articles on political economy issues (such as taxation), and, among the latest, a book on *Rethinking Capitalism: Economic Crisis and the Future of the Left* (in Italian: *Ripensando il capitalismo. La crisi economica e il futuro della sinistra*).

Marcella Corsi is full professor at Sapienza University of Rome and editor of the *International Review of Sociology*. She is also associate member of the Center of European Research on Microfinance (CERMi) at Solvay Brussels School of Economics and Management. Her research interests are the history of economic thought, feminist economics and human development. Her publications include, among the latest, "Inequality and Poverty" (with G. Guarini), in *Handbook of Heterodox Economics*, edited by T. Jo, L. Chester and C. D'Ippoliti (2017); "Gender, Class and the Crisis" (with V. Cirillo and C. D'Ippoliti), in *Varieties of Economic Inequality*, edited by S. Fadda and P. Tridico (2016).

Carlo D'Ippoliti is associate professor at Sapienza University of Rome, and editor of *PSL Quarterly Review* and *Moneta e Credito*. His research interests are the history of economic thought, economics of gender and European political economy. His publications include *Economics of Diversity* (2011) and, as a coeditor, *The Handbook of Heterodox Economics* (forthcoming 2018).

Peter Groenewegen is honorary associate and emeritus professor at the University of Sydney. He is a distinguished fellow of the History of Economics Society since 2005, a distinguished fellow of the Economic Society of Australia since 2010, a distinguished fellow of the History of Economic Thought of Australia since 2010 and an Honorary Life Member of the European Society for the History of Economic Thought since 2007. His most recent book is *The Minor Marshallians and Alfred Marshall* (2012).

Geoffrey Harcourt is a graduate of Melbourne and Cambridge Universities. His research interests include post-Keynesian theory and applied work, and applications to policy; history of economic theory; intellectual biography. His publications include *Some*

Cambridge Controversies in the Theory of Capital (1972); *A "Second Edition" of The General Theory*, 2 vols., coedited with P. Riach (1997); *The Structure of Post-Keynesian Economics* (2006); *Joan Robinson*, coauthored with P. Kerr (2009); *The Oxford Handbook of Post-Keynesian Economics*, 2 vols., coedited with P. Kriesler (2013); and 13 volumes of selected essays.

Jan Kregel is director of research at the Levy Economics Institute, director of the Levy Institute master's program in economic theory and policy, and head of the Institute's Monetary Policy and Financial Structure program. He also holds the position of professor of development finance at Tallinn University of Technology. His major works include a series of books on economic theory, among them, *Rate of Profit, Distribution and Growth: Two Views* (1971); *The Theory of Economic Growth* (1972); *Theory of Capital* (1976); and *Origini e sviluppo dei mercati finanziari* (1996).

Heinz D. Kurz is emeritus professor at the University of Graz. His research interests are economic theory and history of economic thought. He has published numerous papers in journals, including *Australian Economic Papers, Cambridge Journal of Economics, Economica, European Journal of the History of Economic Thought, European Journal of Political Economy, History of Political Economy* and *Oxford Economic Papers*. He has published several books with major international publishers, including Cambridge University Press, Basil Blackwell, Polity Press, Routledge and Edward Elgar. His publications include *Theory of Production: A Long-Period Analysis*, with N. Salvadori (1995); *The Elgar Companion to David Ricardo*, edited with N. Salvadori (2015); *The Dissemination of Economic Ideas*, edited with T. Nishizawa and K. Tribe (2011); *Critical Essays on Piero Sraffa Legacy in Economics* (2008).

Maria Cristina Marcuzzo is full professor at Sapienza University of Rome. She has worked on classical monetary theory, the Cambridge school of economics, Keynesian economics and, more recently, Keynes investments in financial markets. She has published about one hundred articles in journals and books, plus authoring or editing 20 volumes.

Nerio Naldi is associate professor at Sapienza University of Rome. His research interests are focused on history of economic thought and, in particular, on biographical research on Piero Sraffa and Antonio Gramsci. His publications include "Two Notes on Piero Sraffa and Antonio Gramsci," *Cambridge Journal of Economics* (2012).

Sergio Parrinello is retired professor from Sapienza University of Rome. His research is focused on the theory of production, Keynes and Sraffa theories and developments, the theory of international trade and equilibrium and causal models. His publications include, among others, "Numeraire, Savings and the Instability of a Competitive Equilibrium," *Metroeconomica* (2010); "Causality and Normal States in Economics and Other Disciplines," *European Journal of the History of Economic Thought* (2013); "A Search for Distinctive Features of Demand-Led Growth Models," *PSL Quarterly Review* (2014).

Cosimo Perrotta is retired professor from the University of Salento. His research interests include ancient and medieval economic thought; mercantilist and Enlightenment economics; and classical and Marxist economics. His publications include many articles published in *History of Political Economy*, *European Journal for the History of Economic Thought* and many other journals and contributed volumes. Among the monographs are *Consumption as an Investment: The Fear of Goods from Hesiod to Adam Smith* (2004) and *Unproductive Labour in Political Economy: The History of an Idea* (forthcoming).

Paolo Pini is full professor at the University of Ferrara. His research activity is in the fields of technological change, innovations in firm organization and work organization, employees' participation and trade unions. Recent works have been published in various journals, both national and international, such as *Economia Politica*, *Economics of Innovation and New Technology*, *International Review of Applied Economics*, *Journal of Socio-Economics*, *Economia & Lavoro* and *International Journal of Manpower*.

Annalisa Rosselli is full professor at the University of Rome Tor Vergata. She was president of the European Society for the History of Economic Thought from 2012 to 2014. She has published (with M. C. Marcuzzo) *Ricardo and the Gold Standard* (1991); *Economists in Cambridge: A Study through Their Correspondence* (2005) and many articles on history of monetary theory, classical political economy, the Cambridge school and Keynesian policies in the 1950s.

Neri Salvadori is full professor at the University of Pisa. His research interests are economic theory and history of economic thought. He has published numerous papers in journals, including in *Cambridge Journal of Economics*, *Economic Theory*, *European Journal of the History of Economic Thought*, *European Journal of Political Economy*, *History of Political Economy*, *International Economic Review*, *Journal of Economic Behavior and Organization* and *Journal of Economic Methodology*. He has published several books with major international publishers, including Cambridge University Press, Routledge and Edward Elgar. His publications include *Theory of Production: A Long-Period Analysis*, with H. Kurz (1995); *The Elgar Companion to David Ricardo*, edited with H. Kurz (2015); and *Revisiting Classical Economics: Studies in Long-Period Analysis*, with H. Kurz (2015).

Michele Salvati is emeritus professor at the State University of Milan and editor of the journal *Il Mulino*. His present research interests are the political economy aimed at Italian and European growth and the theory of democracy. His main publications in these subjects are *Capitalismo, mercato e democrazia* (2009) and *Cinque pezzi facili sull'Italia* (2014).

Alfonso Sánchez Hormigo holds the Ernest Lluch Chair at the University of Zaragoza. He has published several articles and books on history of economic thought. His publications include *Los economistas clásicos*, with Alessandro Roncaglia (2011).

Bertram Schefold is senior professor at the Johann Wolfgang Goethe University, Frankfurt. His research interests are economic theory, history of economic thought, energy policy and general economic policy. His publications include *Essays on Piero Sraffa: Critical Perspectives on the Revival of Classical Theory*, coedited with K. Bharadwaj (1990, reprint 2017); *Business Cycles in Economic Thought: A History*, coedited with A. Alcouffe and M. Poettinger (2017); *Great Economic Thinkers from the Classicals to the Moderns: Translations from the Series Klassiker der Nationalökonomie* (2017); and *Great Economic Thinkers from Antiquity to the Historical School: Translations from the Series Klassiker der Nationalökonomie* (2016).

Mario Tonveronachi is retired professor from the University of Siena. His research interests are macroeconomic theory and policy, financial systems and financial regulation. His more recent publications include "Three Proposals for Revitalising the European Union," *PSL Quarterly Review* (2016); "Revising the European Central Bank's Operations and Euro Area Fiscal Rules to Support Growth and Employment," *Journal of Post Keynesian Economics* (2015); "Post-Crisis International Regulatory Standards and Their Inclusion in the European Framework," in *Financial Regulation in the European Union*, edited with R. Kattel and J. Kregel (2015); "Post-Keynesian, Post-Sraffian Economics: An Outline" (with A. Roncaglia), in *Contributions to Economic Theory, Policy, Development and Finance: Essays in Honor of Jan A. Kregel*, edited by D. Papadimitriou (2014).

Gianni Vaggi is full professor at the University of Pavia. His research interests are history of economic thought, economic analysis and development economics. His publications include *A Concise History of Economic Thought—From Mercantilism to Monetarism*, with P. Groenewegen (2003) and *Economic Development and Social Change: Historical Roots and Modern Perspectives*, edited with G. Stathakis (2006).

INDEX

Lightning Source UK Ltd.
Milton Keynes UK
UKHW01n0037270718
326379UK00010B/556/P